BOOK-KEEPING Made Simple

The Made Simple series
has been created
primarily for self-education
but can equally well
be used as
an aid to group study.
However complex the subject,
the reader is taken
step by step,
clearly and methodically,
through the course. Each volume
has been prepared by
experts,
using throughout the
Made Simple technique of teaching.
Consequently the gaining
of knowledge now becomes
an experience to be enjoyed.

BOOK-KEEPING Made Simple

G. M. Whitehead, B.Sc. (Econ.)

Made Simple Books
W. H. ALLEN   London
A Howard & Wyndham Company

© 1968 by Doubleday & Company, Inc., and completely reset and revised 1968 by W. H. Allen & Co., Ltd.

Made and printed in Great Britain
by Richard Clay (The Chaucer Press), Ltd., Bungay, Suffolk
for the publishers W. H. Allen & Company Ltd.,
44 Hill Street, London W1X 8LB

First edition October, 1968
Reprinted January, 1971
Reprinted April, 1972
Reprinted September, 1973
Reprinted October, 1974
Reprinted October, 1975
Reprinted with V.A.T. Appendix May, 1977
New edition February, 1978

ISBN 0 491 01512 7 Paperbound

Contents

This book covers all the basic principles of elementary book-keeping and fully provides the student with practice exercises of graded difficulty. Worked examples and test pages help the student to arrive at complete understanding of one topic before another is introduced.

Although principally designed for self-study, the book is of equal value to schools and colleges. Teachers will find that it meets their requirements for examinations up to the Ordinary Level of the University Examination Boards, and covers the syllabuses of the Certificate of Secondary Education and the Certificate of Office Studies. It also covers the first-year syllabuses of the Ordinary National Diplomas and Certificates in Business Studies.

Throughout the text the decimal system of currency has been used but monetary signs have purposely been omitted so that students may supply their own in the appropriate columns of the written work—£, U.S. $, A$, Rs., Rand, and so on.

One word of advice to the student working alone: work at your own pace. If you find you have assimilated all the important points of a chapter and have satisfactorily answered some of the questions, go on to the next chapter; don't feel you have to work laboriously through *all* the questions in a section simply because they are there. On the other hand, if you still feel a little doubtful about some aspects of a topic, continue to work at the questions, referring back where necessary, until you have a full grasp of the subject.

In preparing this book I have received much helpful assistance from a number of business firms and individuals. In particular I wish to express my grateful thanks to the following: Messrs. Olivetti Ltd. for their material on the decimal system and mechanized book-keeping; Kalamazoo Ltd. for providing material on Simultaneous Records and Wages Systems; Barclay's Bank D.C.O. Ltd. for the specimen cheques used; Mr. S. Barker of Barclay's Bank Ltd. for his personal assistance; Messrs. F. W. Woolworth & Co. Ltd. for petty cash vouchers, and Messrs. Egry Ltd. for their illustrations of 'continuous pack' invoices. The help of the University of London, the Royal Society of Arts, and the East Anglian Examination Board is especially acknowledged for their permission to publish a number of questions from their examination papers, which I have adapted and converted to the decimal system. The accuracy of all figures is, of course, my responsibility. Similarly all views expressed and statements made are my responsibility and do not represent the views of any official organization mentioned.

Teachers of book-keeping often have to invent their own questions, especially the easier ones. These introduce the student gradually to difficulties likely to be met in the final examination. In inventing such questions the names of former students fly into the brain much more easily than the names of imaginary people; if any former student of mine thinks he recognizes himself in an exercise I hope he will take it as a sign of my affectionate regard.

GEOFFREY WHITEHEAD

Foreword to 1978 Edition

The favourable response to the inclusion in the 1977 edition of a V.A.T. appendix explaining how V.A.T. becomes part of the double entry system has led me to include in the present edition a chapter on the computerisation of double entry book-keeping. The computer programmer, or computer operator, who understands double entry book-keeping has a great advantage over colleagues unable to visualise 'double entry' in the computer's activities. I am indebted to Mr. David Gooch for suggesting this addition and for his assistance in designing the charts in the new chapter.

I am also grateful to Mr. J. R. Taylor of Moore Paragon U.K. Ltd. for the invoice illustrated on page 38.

GEOFFREY WHITEHEAD

This book is jointly dedicated to my wife, Joan, and to the tutorial and administrative staff of the Commerce Degree Bureau, London University.

CHAPTER ONE

STARTING A BUSINESS—A CAPITAL IDEA

(1) Starting a Business

When a man considers setting up in business it is because he feels that he has some useful product, or service, to offer to his fellow men. We live in a world where people want things from the day they are born to the day that they die. Some of these 'wants' are physical wants, a need for goods of various sorts, food, clothing, shelter, and so on. Some of them are emotional 'wants', a need for education, entertainment, or recreation. In satisfying such wants the businessman performs a useful service to his fellow humans. In return he expects them to offer him a reward for his efforts in the form of profits on his enterprise.

Before such profits can be earned he must establish the enterprise. This involves three things: (*a*) Premises; (*b*) Furniture and Equipment; (*c*) an Organization. Having determined where and how he will conduct his affairs, the businessman may offer his goods and services to the public. The provision of these three things requires a fund of money, called the proprietor's capital. Capital is essential to the start of any enterprise, and while many businesses start off in a small way, growth is only possible if capital is accumulated as the years go by. The provision of the initial capital is the first transaction that takes place.

(2) Business Transactions

The noun 'transaction' implies a transfer of goods or services from one person to another. Any type of business deal, however simple or complicated, is a transaction. Millions of transactions take place every day. Where the transaction involves the provision of goods or services in return for immediate payment it is called a **Cash Transaction**. Where payment is delayed until a later date it is called a **Credit Transaction**. There is therefore a dual nature to all transactions:

(*a*) The good, or service, is supplied.
(*b*) Payment is made for it.

The time interval between the happening of event (*a*) and event (*b*) is termed the period of credit, and varies from no time at all in the case of a cash transaction to years in the case of Hire Purchase transactions.

(3) Keeping a Record of Transactions—The Ledger Accounts

The primary purpose of keeping a record of transactions is to record the debts of other people to the business and the debts of the business to other firms. In order to control expenses it is useful to keep a record of payments made even if they were cash transactions, and no actual debt was involved. Finally, in most countries today the government is interested in securing a share of the profits of a business, so that accurate records are required for taxation purposes. These records also enable the businessman to decide whether his profits make the business worth while, or whether the trouble is too great for the reward earned.

These records are kept in a book called a **Ledger**. It takes its name from a Saxon word meaning 'the one that lies' on a merchant's counters. The word here means 'lies down', it has nothing to do with telling lies. The shelf on which it lay became known as the ledge, and the Ledger lay on the ledge, usually under a window where the light was good. Each page in the Ledger is called an **Account**, and bears at the top the name of the person, or good, or thing which is being accounted for. Fig. 1 shows a page in the Ledger. You should note the following points:

(*a*) The page is divided down the middle.

(*b*) The left-hand side is called the **debit** side, or **debtor** side, and often has the abbreviation Dr. printed at the top.

(*c*) The right-hand side is called the **credit** side, or **creditor** side, and often has the abbreviation Cr. printed at the top.

(*d*) Columns are drawn on *each* side for the date, details, folio numbers (to be explained later), and cash.

Dr.							Cr.
Debit Side Date	Details	Folio	Cash	Credit Side Date	Details	Folio	Cash

Fig. 1. The Ledger

The student should purchase a supply of ledger paper, or a small ledger booklet, from a stationer.

(4) The First Transaction—the Contribution of the Assets by the Proprietor

When starting a business the very first transaction that takes place is the transfer to the firm of the owner's accumulated capital. These valuables may be money, stock, equipment, or vehicles which will in future be regarded as the property of the firm. Such valuables are called **Assets**, and the proprietor is called a **Sole Trader.**

(5) Classifying the Assets—Current and Fixed

The assets may be divided into two main groups. The first group consists of assets which are intended in the course of events to be changed into cash. These are called **Circulating, or Current, Assets** (French *courrant* = running). Fig. 2 illustrates this class of assets.

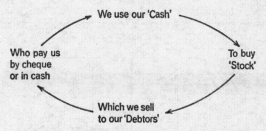

Fig. 2. Circulating Assets, or Current Assets

The commonest current assets are:

Cash in Hand
Cash at Bank
Debtors
Stock
Investments

(*Note:* If investments are held as a useful way of earning money with idle cash not at present required in the business they are current assets.)

Other assets are used to carry on the business. They are called **Fixed Assets** because they cannot be sold without seriously interfering with the conduct of the business. They will be used to manufacture, warehouse, or sell the goods offered by the proprietor, or to provide the services he makes available to the general public.

The commonest fixed assets are:

Land and Buildings
Plant and Machinery
Furniture and Fittings
Motor Vehicles

(6) Opening the Ledger

Let us imagine that a businessman, John Brown, is about to start a firm in the clothing trade. He is a qualified craftsman and has been saving up hard, that is, he has been accumulating capital. He hears of suitable premises to rent, and decides to take them. To begin his book-keeping he buys a small Ledger.

He takes the first page and records his cash on it, say 600·00. This is the amount of **Capital** he is contributing to the business. He puts the cash on the debit side of the Cash Account, as shown in Fig. 3. He enters the same amount of capital on his Capital Account, as shown in Fig. 4, on the credit side. A full explanation of the use of debit and credit columns is given on page 14.

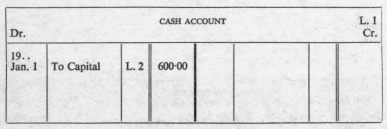

Dr.				CASH ACCOUNT			L. 1 Cr.
19.. Jan. 1	To Capital	L. 2	600·00				

Fig. 3. The Cash Account

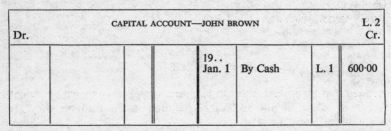

Dr.				CAPITAL ACCOUNT—JOHN BROWN			L. 2 Cr.
				19.. Jan. 1	By Cash	L. 1	600·00

Fig. 4. The Capital Account

The Ledger is now in full working order as the opening entries have been made. We shall see later that a more formal way of opening the books is used in real life, through an entry called an **Opening Journal Entry**. For the present our two accounts will illustrate the opening of the books adequately.

The proprietor has contributed 600·00 of assets, which appears on the debit side of the Cash Account. To balance this, 600·00 appears on the credit side of the Capital Account. Another name for the Capital is the **Net Worth** of the business to the owner. The sole trader's capital account will always show the net worth, that is the clear worth of the business to the owner, and this will be, in a simple case like this, equal to the assets of the business. This equality is clearly shown if we draw up a Balance Sheet.

(7) The Balance Sheet—And an Oddity of History

A Balance Sheet is a list of the accounts in the Ledger. On one side it shows the accounts that have a debit balance, and on the other side the accounts that have a credit balance.

It would be extremely sensible if these were listed in the same way that they appear in the Ledger, with the assets on the left-hand side and the liabilities on the right-hand side, as shown in Fig. 5 (*a*):

JOHN BROWN

BALANCE SHEET

(as at January 1st, 19..)

CURRENT ASSETS		CAPITAL	
Cash	600·00	At Start	600·00
	600·00		600·00

Fig. 5 (*a*). A simple Balance Sheet in logical form

But they are not listed this way at all. By a peculiar quirk of history the countries associated with Britain including South Africa, Australia, New Zealand, India, and Malaya have developed the habit of presenting the Balance Sheet the wrong way round. It is illogical that we do so. (A full explanation is given on page 224.) John Brown's Balance Sheet would therefore appear as follows (Fig. 5 (*b*)):

JOHN BROWN

BALANCE SHEET

(as at January 1st, 19..)

CAPITAL		CURRENT ASSETS	
At Start	600·00	Cash	600·00
	600·00		600·00

Fig. 5 (*b*). A simple Balance Sheet in traditional British style

We can see that a Balance Sheet is what its name says, a sheet on which we make a list of balances that already exist on the accounts. *Nothing can appear on a Balance Sheet unless it actually appears on one of the pages of the Ledger already.*

(8) Buying Assets for Use in the Business

Let us continue for a little while with Mr. Brown's affairs. He will have to pay out some rent for those premises, and buy sewing machines, work benches, and other assets.

The money spent will be recorded on the credit side of the Cash Account, and on the debit side of the Rent Account, Furniture Account, and Machinery Account. To save drawing a Ledger Account each time we will use accounts without column rulings to show quickly what these entries look like.

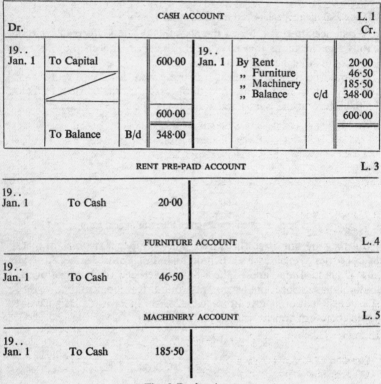

Fig. 6. Buying Assets

Brown's Balance Sheet will now have altered as shown in Fig. 7. The Capital still remains at 600·00, but the asset Cash has been partly changed into other assets, some of which are Current Assets and some are Fixed Assets.

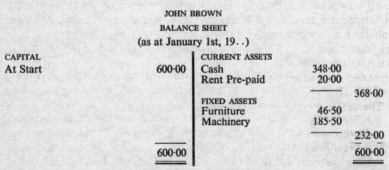

Fig. 7. A more advanced Balance Sheet

(9) Transactions Involving Liabilities

When a cash transaction takes place the goods are transferred at the same time as the payment is made, and neither party is in debt to the other. When the proprietor of a business purchases assets on credit, he incurs a liability to pay. Usually this liability will be discharged at the end of the month, when the seller renders a **Statement of Account**, which the purchaser pays. A credit transaction therefore involves a liability to pay in due course. It is the normal business procedure between businessmen who are known to one another as reliable.

The person supplying the goods becomes a **Creditor** of *the person receiving* the goods. *The person receiving* the goods becomes a **Debtor** of *the person supplying* the goods.

(10) Classification of Liabilities—Current Liabilities, Long-term Liabilities, and Capital

The type of liability referred to in the last paragraph will be settled at the end of the month, usually by cheque. It is therefore of a current nature, it will be wholly settled within the next few weeks. Such liabilities are called **Current Liabilities**. Any liability which will be settled in less than a year is called by this name, but the usual length of time will be much less, accounts being settled monthly.

The commonest types of Current Liability are:

Creditors (Accounts Payable)
Wages Due
Salaries Due
Commission Due
Bank Overdrafts (these are very short-term loans the bank can require us to repay at short notice)

A second type of liability is called a **Long-term Liability**. This is usually a formal loan of money either from a bank or a building society or some other institutional investor like a finance company. These liabilities are evidenced by a formal agreement stating the amount of the loan, the terms of repayment, the rate of interest, and the **Collateral Security** provided. Collateral means 'lying alongside' and the security provided may be a mortgage on the deeds of the proprietor's property or a life assurance policy on his life.

The commonest types of long-term liability are:

Bank Loans
Private Loans
Hire Purchase Loans
Mortgages

The third type of liability is the Capital itself. It is what the business owes back to the owner of the business. It is helpful if the student acquires early in his studies the habit of regarding the proprietor as someone separate from the business. In the final analysis he is *the last creditor* of the firm.

(11) Buying Assets on Credit and Borrowing Money

To continue our study of John Brown's affairs. He has furniture and machinery, and he has rented premises, but he still has no material to make the suits and other garments he hopes to produce. He will also need to pay wages and is therefore anxious to keep some of his capital in cash form. He sees his local bank manager who agrees to make him a loan of 1,000·00 repayable over three years, provided that Brown deposits 300·00 in his current account and also takes out a life assurance policy as collateral. This Brown does, paying a premium of 20·00 for the first year. He also buys on credit (payable at the end of January) 300·00 worth of material, cottons, etc. These assets will mean further items on the assets side of the Balance Sheet, but these are not balanced by increased capital, but by the new types of liability, Current Liabilities and Long-term Liabilities.

His Balance Sheet now reads:

JOHN BROWN

BALANCE SHEET

(as at January 21st, 19. .)

CURRENT LIABILITIES		CURRENT ASSETS		
Creditors	300·00	Cash in Hand	48·00	
		Cash in Bank	1,280·00	
		Stock	300·00	
		Rent Pre-paid	20·00	
LONG-TERM LIABILITIES		Assurance Pre-paid	20·00	
Bank Loan	1,000·00			1,668·00
CAPITAL		FIXED ASSETS		
At Start	600·00	Furniture	46·50	
		Machinery	185·50	
				232·00
	1,900·00			1,900·00

Fig. 8. A complete Balance Sheet

NOTE: (*a*) The date of the Balance Sheet has been altered to January 21st, 19. . . This is because it takes a week or two for the premium to be decided, on an assurance policy. It would be unrealistic to pretend a Life Assurance Policy could be arranged in one day.

(*b*) The separate classes of assets have been sub-totalled. This is very useful in bringing out certain statistical control figures required later.

(*c*) The separate classes of liabilities have been similarly displayed.

(*d*) The Net Worth (Capital Fund) is no longer equal to the assets, because other liabilities have entered the equation.

Throughout this book the questions are designed to give adequate practice to students, and businessmen wishing to keep their own accounts. In the answer section for each set of exercises one of the more difficult answers has been worked in full to show the student what a perfect answer should look like. For the other questions an abbreviated answer is supplied.

EXERCISES SET I

(12) Opening Balance Sheets

No. 1. Prepare a Balance Sheet from the following information, as at January 1st, 19.., of Alice Spring's affairs:

Cash	10,000·00
Stock-in-Trade	12,500·00
Land and Buildings	8,000·00
Office Equipment	6,500·00
Prepaid Rent	500·00
Capital (at Start)	37,500·00

No. 2. Prepare a Balance Sheet of A. Londoner's affairs from the following information, as at January 1st, 19..:

Cash	7,000·00
Stock	10,500·00
Office Equipment	500·00
Land and Buildings	15,000·00
Advertising Prepaid	250·00
Capital (at Start)	33,250·00

Nos. 3 and 4. Prepare Balance Sheets from the figures given. On these two you will have to find out the capital for yourself. Date, January 1st, 19..:

Sole Traders	John Smith	Peter Green
Cash in Hand	25·50	42·60
Cash at Bank	1,270·50	1,365·40
Trade Debtors	1,045·20	1,726·30
Stock	2,471·30	2,625·30
Prepaid Expenses	748·50	246·40
Motor Vehicles	1,875·00	550·00
Furniture	440·00	495·00
Plant and Machinery	2,965·00	1,875·00
Land and Buildings	7,260·00	2,640·00

Nos. 5 and 6. On the last two Balance Sheets you will have to work out the Capital, but do not forget that as there are some Current Liabilities and Long-Term Liabilities the Net Worth equation now reads:

$$Assets = Current\ Liabilities$$
$$+ Long\text{-}term\ Liabilities$$
$$+ Capital$$

Proprietor	No. 5 Jan. 1st, 19.. Mark Jones	No. 6 Jan. 1st, 19.. Peter Clemens
Cash in Hand	24·50	32·50
Cash at Bank	1,060·50	726·50
Trade Debtors	1,236·50	1,584·25
Stock	945·00	1,520·00
Prepaid Expenses	17·50	17·25
Motor Vehicles	1,750·50	1,655·50
Furniture	265·80	325·50
Plant and Machinery	1,347·20	7,240·00
Land and Buildings	3,000·00	4,000·00
Creditors	1,050·00	1,052·00
Wages Due	97·50	49·50
Mortgage	2,000·00	3,000·00
Bank Loan	1,500·00	1,000·00

(13) A Page to Test You on Capital, Assets, and Liabilities

Cover the page with a sheet of paper, then read a question at a time.

Answers	Questions
—	1. What is business?
1. Business is the conduct of commercial activities to produce goods and services in return for profit.	2. What word is used to describe each business deal?
2. Each deal is called a transaction.	3. What is the function of bookkeeping?
3. It is to record transactions.	4. What twofold process is involved in transactions?
4. (*a*) The provision of a good or a service to the customer; (*b*) the payment by the customer.	5. What is a cash transaction?
5. It is one where the goods are supplied, and the money paid at precisely the same moment.	6. What is a credit transaction?
6. It is a transaction where the goods or services are supplied, but payment is delayed until a later time.	7. What is the most usual credit period?
7. Cash 30 days.	8. What are assets?
8. They are goods bought for use in the conduct of the business.	9. What are fixed assets?
9. Assets of a durable nature for long-term use in the business.	10. Name four fixed assets.
10. Land and Buildings; Plant and Machinery; Furniture and Fittings; Motor Vehicles.	11. What are current assets?
11. Assets which change into cash as business continues.	12. Name four current assets.
12. Stock in Trade; Debtors; Cash at Bank; Cash in Hand.	13. What are liabilities?
13. They are the debts for which a business is liable.	14. What are the chief classes of liabilities?
14. Current Liabilities; Long-term Liabilities; Capital.	15. Name three current liabilities.
15. Creditors; Wages Due; Rent Due.	16. Name three Long-term Liabilities.
16. Bank Loans; Private Loans; and Mortgages.	17. What is Capital?
17. It is the sum contributed by the owner to the business, or accumulated by him out of profits ploughed back into the firm.	18. What is Collateral Security?
18. It is a security lying alongside a debt —often the deeds to a property or a life assurance policy.	19. How many did you answer correctly? Go over the list again.

CHAPTER TWO

THE LEDGER—THE MAIN BOOK OF ACCOUNT

(1) Introduction

From the earliest days of book-keeping until the last century the Ledger was a bound book which was left in the Counting House on a ledge fitted against the wall. The clerk would record all the transactions in date order in a daily record (a Day Book or Journal—which will be dealt with shortly). He then 'posted' these daily transactions into the Ledger Accounts.

Businesses are much larger today, and it is impracticable to keep the Ledger as a bound book. Loose-leaf books, card indexes, and computer records may now take the place of the bound book, but the Ledger is still the main book of account and must be posted daily with all the transactions that take place. In this chapter we attempt to develop a real understanding of Ledger Accounts.

The Ledger, then, is the main book of account. It has pages which are numbered, and each page is called 'an account'. The numbers are written in the top right-hand corner and are called folio numbers (Latin *folium*, leaf).

(2) Use of the Accounts

Transactions take place every day. Each transaction involves a change in the assets or liabilities of the business. We may spend cash and buy postage stamps, or sell stock and receive cash. To record these changes the Ledger is used. The record, or account, of each change in the value of an asset is to be found somewhere in the Ledger. An expenditure of cash will be recorded in the Cash Account. The purchase of furniture will be recorded in the Furniture Account. The loss of wealth that occurs when a debtor goes bankrupt will be recorded in the Bad Debts Account.

An account may therefore be defined as a record of the changes occurring under a particular heading.

(3) The Three Types of Account

There are three kinds of account: Personal Accounts, Real Accounts, and Nominal Accounts.

Fig. 9. Bob Cratchet at work on the Ledger in Scrooge's office
(Charles Dickens—*A Christmas Carol*)

Personal Accounts

Every Personal Account has the name of a person with whom the
business deals at the top. These may be Sole Traders (Tom Jones, for
instance) or Partnerships (Brown and Green) or Limited Companies
(R. Smith & Co., Ltd.). Whichever kind of 'person' they are the account
will keep a record of our dealings with this person. Capital Account is
a special case of a Personal Account. The value of the proprietor's
investment in the business is recorded there; the real assets he brought
in are recorded in the Real Accounts.

Real Accounts

Every Real Account has the name of an asset *the business owns* at the
top. These assets are real things; we can sit on the chairs, type with the
typewriters, spend the cash, etc. We have already seen that some assets
are Current Assets and some are Fixed Assets. All Asset Accounts are
Real Accounts.

Nominal Accounts

Every Nominal Account has the name of a loss or profit of the
business at the top of the page, e.g. Light and Heat Account, Wages
Account, Rent Received Account, etc. We keep track of these losses
and profits during the year and at the end of the year use them to work
out the final Profit and Loss Account of the business.

The word 'nominal' means 'in name only'. We may have 500·00 on
the Wages Account but it is not really there, the workers have taken the
wages home and used them to support their families.

(4) How to Keep a Ledger Account—Rules for entering in the three
     classes of accounts

A Ledger page is divided down the middle and the two sides are called
the debit side and the credit side. As there are three classes of account
it is best to learn three separate rules for making entries in the accounts,
but in fact a general rule covering all entries in accounts does apply.
The beginner in book-keeping may be puzzled to see how it fits all cases
because some experience is necessary in dealing with accounts before it
becomes really clear.

The General Rule

Debit the account that has received value (goods, services, or money);
Credit the account that has given value (goods, services, or money).

We may abbreviate this rule to read

Debit the Receiver, Credit the Giver

If we now apply this rule to the three classes of account already mentioned we have the following special applications of the general rule:

Rule for entering up the Personal Accounts

Debit the person who receives goods, services, or money from the business.

Credit the person who gives goods, services, or money to the business.

Rule for entering up the Real Accounts

Debit increases in value of the asset (the asset concerned has received a larger share of the resources of the business).

Credit decreases in value of the asset (the asset concerned has given up some of its value in the service of the business—we call this 'depreciation').

PERSONAL ACCOUNTS

TOM JONES   L. 1

Debit Jones when he receives goods, value, or money from the business.	Credit Jones when he gives goods, value, or money to the business.

REAL ACCOUNTS

LAND AND BUILDING ACCOUNT   L. 2

Debit increases in value of assets.	Credit decreases in value of assets.

NOMINAL ACCOUNTS

POSTAGE ACCOUNT   L. 3

Debit expenses in 'Loss' Accounts.	

COMMISSION RECEIVED ACCOUNT   L. 4

	Credit gains in 'Profit' accounts.

Fig. 10. Rules for keeping Ledger Accounts

Rule for entering up Nominal Accounts

Debit expenses, i.e. *losses*, in the appropriate nominal account (the expense account named has received money 'in name only' from the business).

Credit gains, i.e. *profits*, in the appropriate nominal account (the account named has given money 'in name only' to the business).

These rules are illustrated in Fig. 10.

(5) Personal Accounts—Debtors

When a merchant sells goods on credit, payable in the usual course of events at the end of the month, he is taking part in a transaction that involves a debtor. The person to whom he sells the goods will be debited with the goods received. The merchant will usually not enter into this type of transaction unless a course of business dealing has convinced him of the reliability of the customer. A new customer might be asked for a reference from his banker, or to give the names of businessmen with whom he had conducted business over a considerable time. If these references are satisfactory the transactions will be allowed to proceed.

In very large firms these accounts might be so numerous that they would be kept, not in a book, but in a card index system—we would call this card index the **Debtors' Ledger**.

As we saw in the last section, the rule for keeping Personal Accounts is to debit the person who receives goods, services, or money, and to credit him when he gives goods, services, or money.

When the rule above is used to record the transactions of our firm with a debtor, Tom Brown, an account like the one on page 17 results. The following points should be carefully noted:

(*a*) Tom Brown was a debtor on January 1st for 127·50. This was the balance on the debit side of his account, showing that he received goods of that value during December, and has not given us anything for them.

(*b*) On January 3rd Brown bought more goods from us. This time he received 25·20 worth of goods. This was our sales figure to him on that date.

(*c*) On January 4th Brown bought more goods valued at 46·30, and in addition we charged him 4·20 for transport charges, carriage on the goods to be received.

(*d*) On January 7th Brown paid us a cheque for 120·50 which was in full settlement of his debt owed at January 1st. This means that we must have allowed him discount of 7·00, which appears on the next line below.

(*c*) On January 17th Brown bought more goods valued at 75·90.

(*f*) On January 18th he returned some of the goods, which must have been unsatisfactory for some reason. 12·50 was the value of the goods given back.

(*g*) On January 20th he once again purchased goods from us for 27·25 and was charged carriage 6·25.

(*h*) The outstanding balance of 172·60 was carried down to the debit side of the account. Tom Brown is a debtor once again on February 1st for this balance. A debtor is a person who owes us money, because he has received goods or services for which he has not yet paid.

(*i*) The small column which has not yet been used is called the Folio Column. Its use will be explained later.

Dr.	Tom Brown, 27, Hill Rd., Newton, Essex.					D.L. 27 Cr.
19..			19..			
Jan. 1	To Balance	127·50	Jan. 7	By Cheque	120·50	
3	,, Sales	25·20	7	,, Discount	7·00	
4	,, ,,	46·30	18	,, Returns	12·50	
4	,, Carriage	4·20	31	,, Balance	172·60	
17	,, Sales	75·90				
20	,, ,,	27·25				
20	,, Carriage	6·25				
		312·60			312·60	
19..						
Feb. 1	To Balance	172·60				

Fig. 11. A Personal Account—A Debtor

We can see from a careful study of this Ledger Account that a complete rule for entering a Debtor's Account would be:

Rule for entering a Debtor's Account

Debit the debtor when he *receives* goods or services.

Credit him when he *gives* money or goods, *or when he is excused from payment* by being given discount.

The student should now try to record on a piece of Ledger paper each of the four accounts named below. In a real Ledger every leaf in the book is an account, and must be kept for the particular person, or thing, named at the top of the page. It would be very expensive to use a whole page for each exercise, but to make it clear that you are really keeping separate accounts it is usual to rule off right across the page when you start another account, and put a new folio number in the 'Corner' as if you really had begun a new page.

18   *Book-keeping Made Simple*

EXERCISES SET II

(6) Simple Debtors' Accounts

No. 1. R. Brown has an account with us. It is folio number D.L. 27. On April 1st, 19.., there is a debit balance of 166·13 on the account. Head the account properly, and then make the opening balance entry, followed by the entries below:

Apr. 2 R. Brown sends us a cheque for 100·00 on account. (This means he is unable to pay the full amount at present.)
3 We send Brown goods valued at 14·63.
4 We send Brown further goods valued at 175·10.
7 Brown sends us a cheque for the balance of the money that he owed us on April 1st.
9 Brown returns us goods valued at 25·50 because they are the wrong colour.
19 We send Brown goods valued at 62·50 and we also charge him carriage 1·45.
27 We send Brown goods valued at 27·35.
30 The account is balanced off and the balance brought down ready for the new month.

No. 2. J. Brown has a Ledger Account with us. Its folio number is D.L. 24. On January 1st it had a debit balance of 250·60. Open the account and make these further entries:

Jan. 2 We send Brown further goods valued at 47·26.
3 Brown pays the amount owing on January 1st by cheque and is given 5·60 discount.
4 He buys further goods valued at 27·50.
5 He returns some of the goods bought on January 2nd valued at 5·30.
26 He buys further goods valued at 44·65. We charge delivery charges 2·00.
31 Balance off the account and bring down the balance.

No. 3. One of our customers is called M. Petersen. He is a debtor with an account D.L. 95. Enter the following entries in his account:

Jan. 1 Balance owing by M. Petersen 27·16.
2 Petersen buys more goods valued at 25·50.
3 Petersen buys more goods valued at 17·25.
4 Petersen returns goods valued at 12·00.
7 Petersen pays balance owing on January 1st, less discount 1·16, by cheque.
9 Petersen buys goods valued at 180·00.
10 We charge Petersen 4·60 carriage and 1·50 insurance.
11 We sell Petersen goods valued at 14·00.
18 We sell Petersen more goods valued at 26·50.
28 Petersen returns goods valued at 4·28.
31 Balance off the account and bring down the balance.

No. 4. R. Thomas is a debtor of ours with an account D.L. 37. Enter the following items in his Ledger Account:

Jan. 1 Balance owing by R. Thomas 247·16.
     2 R. Thomas buys more goods valued at 55·00.
     3 R. Thomas sends us a cheque for 240·00 *in full settlement* of the amount outstanding on January 1st.
    14 R. Thomas buys more goods valued at 48·00. He is charged 2·50 delivery charges.
    19 He returns goods valued at 14·00.
    29 He buys further goods valued at 45·25.
    31 Balance off his Ledger Account and bring the balance down.

(7) Personal Accounts—Creditors

When a merchant buys goods on credit he undertakes to pay the supplier of the goods in due course, usually at the end of the month. The supplier's account will be credited with the goods supplied, and with any charges like carriage or insurance on the goods. The supplier will thus become a creditor—a person to whom we owe money.

Once again these accounts may be so numerous that we remove them from the Ledger and have a loose-leaf—or card index—system. This would be called the **Creditors' Ledger.**

Example:

Apr. 1 Henry Wills was a creditor of ours for goods worth 50·50 supplied during March. His account is C.L. 197.
     2 Bought goods from Wills valued at 900·50.
     3 Returned goods valued at 75·50 to Wills (not up to specification).
     5 Sent Wills a cheque for 48·50, *in full settlement* of the balance owing on April 1st.
    30 Balanced off the account.

Wills's account is seen below:

Dr.					HENRY WILLS		C.L. 197 Cr.
19..				19..			
Apr. 3	To Returns	75·50		Apr. 1	By Balance		50·50
5	„ Bank	48·50		2	„ Purchases		900·50
5	„ Discount	2·00					
30	„ Balance	825·00					
		951·00					951·00
				19..			
				May 1	By Balance		825·00

Fig. 12. A Creditor's Account

If you compare Fig. 11 and Fig. 12 you will notice that they are the opposite of each other. Instead of selling to a debtor we are purchasing from a creditor; the goods returned in Fig. 12 to Wills are received by him on the debit side. Brown was credited with the returns in Fig. 11 because he gave them back.

Rule for entries on a Creditor's Account

Debit the creditor when he *receives* payment from us, or goods that we return, or when he excuses us from payment.

Credit the creditor when he *gives* goods or services of any sort.

The student should now try to record the following matters in the Creditors' Accounts Exercises Set III.

EXERCISES SET III

(8) Simple Creditors' Accounts

No. 1. One of our suppliers is called P. Peters. His account in our Ledger is C.L. 121.

On July 1st it has a balance of 240·75 on the credit side. Open the account and then continue with these entries:

July 2 P. Peters supplies goods valued at 113·15.
      3 We pay Peters by cheque the amount owing on July 1st, less discount 3·75.
      4 Peters supplied more goods valued at 25·76. He also charges us 2·34 transport charges.
      5 We return goods valued at 12·10 (not up to specification).
     16 Peters supplies goods valued at 24·75.
     29 Peters supplies goods valued at 212·17.
     31 The account is ruled off ready for the next month's business.

No. 2. Tom Brown is a creditor of ours, with an account C.L. 28. On January 1st it had a credit balance of 365·00. Open the account and make the following further entries:

Jan. 2 We pay Brown the amount owing, 365·00, by cheque.
      3 Brown sells us more goods valued at 42·10.
    14 Brown sends us more goods valued at 247·12.
    15 We return to Brown goods valued at 7·12.
    15 Brown sends us further goods valued at 1,080·00 and charges 25·16 for delivery charges.
    29 We purchase more goods from Brown valued at 25·75.
    31 Balance off the account.

No. 3. M. Pierson is a creditor of ours with an account C.L. 129. He has a credit balance of 250·65 on June 1st. Open the account and make the following entries:

June 5 We buy goods valued at 4·65.
  6 We buy goods valued at 72·96.
 16 We return goods valued at 5·54.
 18 We pay by cheque for the goods bought during May, less 5·65 cash discount.
 19 We buy goods valued at 75·60.
 29 We buy goods valued at 75·10 and are charged insurance 2·50.
 30 Balance off the account and bring down the balance.

No. 4. Copy out this Creditor's Account. Balance it off on the last day of the month, and bring the balance down. Now answer these questions:

(*a*) What took place on October 27th?
(*b*) Who owes the balance to whom?
(*c*) Now complete this sentence. 'In this example we have a creditor who was on October 31st temporarily a . . .'

Dr.					G. M. WHITEHEAD			C.L. 59 Cr.
19. .				19. .				
Oct. 2	To Bank		705·00	Oct. 1	By Balance			720·40
2	„ Discount		15·40	11	„ Purchases			426·50
14	„ Returns		26·50	19	„ „			224·50
27	„ Motor Vehicles		750·00	20	„ Carriage			25·10

(9) Real Accounts—Accounts that Record Assets

When a proprietor sets out in business, the assets that he contributes will be recorded in separate Asset Accounts. The usual method of doing this is to draw up an opening Journal Entry, but we will deal with this a little later in our studies. For the moment let us just consider what these 'real' accounts look like. The busiest of them are the Cash Account and the Bank Account, because receipts and payments, either in cash or by cheque are extremely common. Most of the other real accounts change very little, because the assets recorded there are used over a very long time and therefore the 'account' of what happens to them has little to record. It may tell us that we depreciated the asset by a certain amount at the end of each year, and that eventually we sold it as it was obsolete or worn out. We might buy a new machine and sell off an old one, but these events will be quite rare items. Apart from the Cash Account and the Bank Account you might expect the Stock Account to be a busy one, but in fact it is the least busy of all, for the purchases of new stock are recorded in the Purchases Account—a nominal account—and the sales of stock are recorded in the Sales Account—another nominal account. The Stock Account only records the balance of stock in hand on the last day of the financial year, and therefore it only has to be entered once a year.

Here are illustrations of one or two Real Accounts; the Cash Account and Bank Account will be dealt with in more detail on page 24.

Dr.	LAND AND BUILDINGS ACCOUNT					L. 1 Cr.
19.. Jan. 1 May 31	To Capital „ Bank		1,700·00 1,850·00			

Fig. 13. A 'Real' Account

Notice that the page is headed with the name of the asset concerned.

The premises owned when business commenced were worth 1,700·00. Later we purchased other premises as well for 1,850·00.

Businessmen do not usually depreciate land and buildings; indeed land and buildings often get more valuable as the years go by. An account like this would not even be balanced off to make it look tidy— but it would be added up neatly in pencil so that we could read off the total figure of 3,550·00 if we really wanted to know it.

The student should develop the habit of picturing events from the Asset Account. What happened in Fig. 14 on June 30th? What happened on October 1st? Clearly on that date we bought a new vehicle for 900·00 and traded in the old one, removing it from the books. Its book value must have been 540·00. It does not follow that we were given an allowance of 540·00 for it. Possibly we receive more, possibly less; but we must remove the book value of the asset from the account.

Dr.	MOTOR VEHICLES ACCOUNT							L. 2 Cr.
19.. Jan. 1 June 30	To Capital „ New Vehicle		750·00 850·00	19.. Dec. 31 31	By Depreciation „ Balance	c/d	160·00 1,440·00
			1,600·00				1,600·00
19.. Jan. 1 Oct. 1	To Balance „ New Vehicle	B/d	1,440·00 900·00	19.. Oct. 1 Dec. 31 31	By Rex Garages „ Depreciation „ Balance	c/d	540·00 180·00 1,620·00
			2,340·00				2,340·00
19.. Jan. 1	To Balance	B/d	1,620·00				

Fig. 14. Another 'Real' Account

We do not want an asset that has been disposed of still recorded on our books. (Note: In this example depreciation has been deducted at 10 per cent of the book value on December 31st each year.)

Rule for entering up Asset Accounts

Debit the Asset Account whenever the asset increases in value, because the Asset Account has received the benefit of expenditure by the firm.

Credit the Asset Account whenever it decreases in value, either by depreciation or by actual sale. In these cases the asset has given service to the firm, either in use or by being turned into cash.

(10) Folio Numbers

In Fig. 14 you will notice that the letters *c/d* for 'carried down' have been inserted where the balancing figure was put on the credit side and the letters *B/d* for 'Brought down' have been inserted on the balance line below on the debit side. These are the first 'folio numbers' we have met, and they are not numbers, but letters. Every single line in the Ledger should be cross-referenced with a folio number which tells you where the other half of the double entry is. We shall learn more about double entry as we go on, but at least here you can see the double entry for the balancing items, and it is possible to fill in the folio numbers *c/d*

Dr.					CASH ACCOUNT		G.L. 25 Cr.
19.. Mar. 1	To Balance	B/d	127·50	19.. Mar. 1	By Postage	G.L. 29	2·50
1	„ Cash Sales	G.L. 37	86·10	1	„ Fares	G.L. 14	1·40
1	„ R. Jones	D.L. 36	27·55	1	„ R. Peters	C.L. 72	15·20
1	„ Staff Telephone	G.L. 40	0·10	1	„ P. Lamb	C.L. 42	16·25
				1	„ C. Avion	C.L. 1	10·25
				1	„ Cash Purchases	G.L. 73	11·25
				1	„ Sales Returned	G.L. 81	2·50
				1	„ Bank Account	G.L. 26	100·00
				1	„ Balance	c/d	81·90
			241·25				241·25
19.. Mar. 2	To Balance	B/d	81·90				

Fig. 15. A simple Cash Account

and *B*/*d*. Just why we use a small '*c*' and a capital '*B*' is shrouded in the mystery of the past.

(11) The Busiest Real Accounts—The Cash Account and the Bank Account

Later we shall see that in most businesses these accounts are treated in a special way, by being written in a special book called the **Three-column Cash Book**. Before this book was 'invented', and in small firms or clubs and societies where the number of entries is too small to justify the expense of a Three-column Cash Book, the Cash Account and Bank Account are ordinary Real Accounts on separate pages in the Ledger. They are exactly alike, but in the Cash Account it is money that is being paid and received, while in the Bank Account it is cheques that are being paid in and out.

The Cash Account shown on page 23 illustrates the keeping of these two accounts.

NOTES: *Debit Side*—

(*a*) As you would expect, because it is an asset, the 'cash 127·50' appears on the debit side at the start of the day. This is the balance received from yesterday. The folio column says *B*/*d*, brought down.

(*b*) Cash Account receives 86·10 from the sale of goods. This would be the day's takings from the tills, and some firms actually use the words **Daily Takings**. The double entry for this is in Sales Account which is in the General Ledger on page 37.

(*c*) R. Jones pays us cash, which is received in the Cash Account. Clearly he must have been a debtor, and the double entry for this would appear on the credit side of the R. Jones Account. This is D.L. 36, so that this number is shown in the folio column.

(*d*) A small sum has been received from a member of staff for a private telephone call. This will be received in the Cash Account and credited in the Telephone Account, which is G.L. 40 (account number 40 in the General Ledger).

Credit Side—

(*e*) We have expenditure on Postage, Fares, and Cash Purchases. In each case the Cash Account gave away money for these reasons and the double entry for the cash entry will be in these Nominal Accounts in the General Ledger.

(*f*) We have also paid three suppliers, Peters, Lamb, and Avion, sums of money. They must have been creditors, and the corresponding entries will appear in the Creditors' Ledger.

(*g*) The Sales Returns item is an unusual one. Shops do not usually like to return money, and will give a credit note instead which entitles the holder to spend that amount of money at a later date. They will sometimes refund cash if a customer is particularly dissatisfied and may harm their goodwill in the district. This is what has happened here. The folio number G.L. 81 is the folio number of the Sales Returns Account in the General Ledger.

(12) Double Entry Book-keeping

The student should note carefully at this stage that every transaction that takes place has a twofold nature. If we pay out cash 20·00 for a filing cabinet we shall have spent a real sum of money which we shall credit in the cash account. Cash has given 20·00. The filing cabinet will be recorded in the Furniture and Fittings Account as an increase in value, on the debit side.

We therefore have a debit entry exactly equal and opposite to a credit entry. This kind of double entry gives book-keeping its proper name **Double Entry Book-keeping**.

A full explanation of the system will be found in Chapter Three.

(13) Folio Numbers and Double Entry Book-keeping

You should, in the entries you do from now on, invent sensible folio numbers to fill in the folio column. *They are usually the numbers of the account where the double entry will be found.* Folio numbers are the signposts which tell us where to look for more information about an entry. They tell us where to find the other half of the double entry, or which subsidiary book to look at for fuller information. These subsidiary books will be dealt with later.

Rule for keeping the Cash Account

Debit the Cash Account whenever cash is received.

Credit the Cash Account whenever cash is given in exchange for goods or services.

Exercises Set IV

(14) Simple Cash Accounts

Using ordinary Ledger paper, draw up simple Cash Accounts for the following four exercises.

No. 1. Enter the following items in a simple Ledger Account—the Cash Account G.L. 27.

19..

Dec. 1 Balance of cash in hand 17·10; paid wages 12·60; drew from bank for office use 20·00; paid postage 1·15.

    2 Bought coffee 0·30; bought stationery 3·10; bought new Ledger 2·25.

    3 R. Jones sent 2·10 to us in cash; P. Brown sent cash 3·80 to us; we sent 1·15 to R. Lewis in cash.

    4 Paid sundries 2·25; tip to dustmen (Gratuities Account) 0·20; cash sales from till 24·10.

Balance off the account and bring down the Cash Balance.

No. 2. Enter the following item in a Cash Account, balance off at the end, and bring down the balance:

19..

Jan. 1 Balance of cash in hand 37·10.
     2 Paid for repairs to lock on front door 1·25.
     3 Paid garage expenses (Motor Vehicle Expenses Account) 1·72.
     4 Cash sales 14·10.
     5 Paid wages 5·10.
     6 Paid to R. Hero 2·45.
     7 Paid to P. Jacobs 14·25.
     8 Paid office expenses 1·50.
     9 Paid to R. Hero 3·15; cash sales 14·16.
   10 R. Jones paid us the sum of 24·65.
   11 Received from R. Lucas 15·26.
   12 Paid to R. Heilbrane 24·63.
   13 Paid for office expenses 0·55.
   14 Cash sales 13·75.

No. 3

19..

Jan. 1 Balance of cash in hand 32·10.
     2 Paid for postage 2·00.
     3 Paid office expenses 1·65.
     4 Cash sales 14·75.
     5 Paid wages 6·60.
     6 Paid to A. Askham 3·25.
     7 Paid to M. Bryan 12·65.
     8 Paid repairs 1·25.
     9 Cash sales 15·10.
   10 R. Jones paid us the sum of 17·16.
   11 Received from M. O'Connor 4·75.
   12 Paid to M. Haly 14·65.
   13 Paid for office expenses 0·65.
   14 Cash sales 17·75.

Enter these items in the Cash Account. Balance the account and bring down the balance at the end of the fortnight ready for next day.

No. 4. Enter the following in a simple Cash Account:

19..

Oct. 1 Balance of cash in hand 25·70.
     2 Bought stamps 0·68; bought teas for visitors 1·50.
     3 Cash sales 16·10.
     4 Paid R. Jones in cash the sum of 5·50.
     5 Paid R. Peters in cash 4·10.
     6 T. Brown paid us 5·25.
     7 M. Wilmot paid us 3·85.
     8 Paid wages 4·60.
     9 Paid M. Jones 1·60.
   10 Paid R. Brown 4·25.
   11 Cash sales 15·45.

Oct. 12 Paid into bank 5·10.
     13 R. Lomase paid us 1·15 in cash.
     14 Paid for cleaning materials 0·45; balanced off the Cash Account ready
         for the next fortnight.

(15) The Bank Account

This is kept in exactly the same way as the Cash Account. It may seem tedious to practise the same work over again, but in a later chapter we shall be dealing with the Three-column Cash Book, in which these two accounts, Cash Account and Bank Account, are combined in a rather special way. It is therefore worth while being very sure of these two accounts separately, before we learn how to combine them.

Rule for keeping the Bank Account

Debit the Bank Account whenever cheques are received, or cash takings paid in.

Credit the Bank Account whenever cheques are paid out, or are presented for the withdrawal of cash.

EXERCISES SET V

(16) Simple Bank Accounts

No. 1. Open a simple Ledger Bank Account and enter the following items:
19..
Jan. 1 Began business with a capital of 500·00 in the bank; withdrew 20·00
       for office cash box.
    2 R. Jones paid us 5·10 by cheque.
    3 T. Smith paid us 172·65 by cheque.
    4 Paid R. Miller 185·50 for goods supplied by cheque.
    5 Paid by cheque rent 40·00
    6 Paid by cheque rates 15·00.
    7 M. Blenkiron paid us 4·10 by cheque.
    8 Paid by cheque for electric fire 6·10.
    9 Balanced off Bank Account and brought down the balance.

No. 2. Enter the following items in a Bank Account, balance off at the end and bring down the balance:
19..
Jan. 1 Balance of cash at bank 32·10.
    2 Paid for repairs to lock on front door 1·25 by cheque.
    3 Paid garage expenses 1·75 by cheque.
    4 R. Brown paid us by cheque 14·10.
    5 Paid wages 5·10 by cheque.
    6 Paid to R. Hero 2·45 by cheque.
    7 Paid to M. Palmer 14·25 by cheque.
    8 Paid office expenses 6·25 by cheque.
    9 R. Silver paid us 14·16 by cheque.

 10 R. Jones paid us the sum of 24·65 by cheque.
 11 Received from Inspector of Taxes, a tax rebate of 15·25 by cheque.
 12 Paid to R. Hebron 24·65 by cheque.
 13 Paid for office expenses 6·30 by cheque.
 14 M. Thomas paid us 13·75 by cheque.

No. 3. Enter the following items in a Bank Account, L. 14, and balance off the account at the end of the week:

19..

Jan. 14 Balance in bank 1,051·17; paid R. Jones 21·45 by cheque; paid M. Thoms 42·70 by cheque.
  15 M. Chuzzlewit gave a cheque for 55·00 to our Sales Manager for goods to be delivered that day.
  16 Paid rates by cheque 42·10; paid water rate by cheque 17·50.
  18 Mrs. M. Lupin paid by cheque 24·10 for account rendered on January 1st.
  18 T. Jolly paid his Account, value 48·76, by cheque.
  19 Paid wages by cheque 42·10.
  20 Received cheque from Transportation Ltd., insurance money on goods damaged 4·75.

No. 4. Enter the following items in a simple Bank Account:

19..

Dec. 1 Balance of cash in bank 217·10; paid wages by cheque 12·65; drew from bank for office use 20·00; paid R. Johnson by cheque 1·15.
  2 Bought coffee for canteen by cheque 6·35; bought stationery 3·10 by cheque; bought new Ledger 2·25 by cheque.
  3 R. Jones sent us 2·15 cheque; P. Brown sent us a cheque for 3·85; sent 6·15 to R. Joiner by cheque.
  4 R. Howard paid us by cheque 34·10; cash sales from till 24·10 banked.

Balance off Bank Account and bring down the balance.

(17) Nominal Accounts—Accounts that Record Losses and Profits

These accounts, as mentioned earlier, are accounts which record the use of money which has been spent, not in buying assets but in buying goods or services which are necessary to the conduct of the business, but give us nothing real to show for our money. If we send a parcel to Zanzibar the postage is necessary, but its benefit is lost with the delivery of the parcel; there is no enduring asset to show for the expense. Such sums of money are expenses, or losses of the business. We keep a nominal record of them, and at the end of the year write them off the profits of the business. Here is such an account, the Rent Paid Account. The Cash Account has also been shown to bring out the double entry nature of the work.

There are many such Loss Accounts: Wages, Salaries, Postage, Telephone, Motor Vehicle Expenses, Light and Heat, Rent and Rates, etc. There are also some which are the result of the receipt of sums of

| RENT PAID ACCOUNT | | | | | | | G.L. 7 |
Dr.							Cr.
19.. Jan. 1	To Cash	G.L. 1	60·00	19.. Dec. 31	By Transfer to Profit and Loss Account	G.L. 121	240·00
Apr. 1	,, ,,	G.L. 1	60·00				
July 1	,, ,,	G.L. 1	60·00				
Oct. 1	,, ,,	G.L. 1	60·00				
			240·00				240·00

| CASH ACCOUNT | | | | | | | G.L. 1 |
Dr.							Cr.
19.. Jan. 1	To Balance	B/d	500·00	19.. Jan. 1	By Rent	G.L. 7	60·00
				Apr. 1	,, ,,	G.L. 7	60·00
				July 1	,, ,,	G.L. 7	60·00
				Oct. 1	,, ,,	G.L. 7	60·00

| PROFIT AND LOSS ACCOUNT | | | | | | | G.L. 121 |
Dr.							Cr.
19.. Dec. 31	To Rent Paid	G.L. 7	240·00				

Fig. 16. A 'Loss' Account

money. These are profits, because the money has been received and is put in the cash-box, or the bank. The double entry is recorded in a profit account, for instance the Rent Received Account, Discount Received Account, Commission Received Account, or Professional Fees Received Account.

Rule for keeping Nominal Accounts

Debit all losses in the Loss Account because that account has received the benefit of expenditure by the firm.

Credit all gains in the Profit Account because that account has given some benefit in cash to the firm.

(18) A Page to Test You on the Ledger

Cover the page with a sheet of paper, then read one question at a time.

Answers	Questions
—	1. What is the Ledger?
1. The Ledger is the main book of account.	2. What is an account?
2. An account is a page in the Ledger which records the transactions relevant to the person, asset, expense or profit named in the heading.	3. Are the accounts numbered?
3. Yes—with folio numbers.	4. What does 'folio' mean?
4. It comes from the Latin word for 'leaf'.	5. Where do we write these folio numbers?
5. In the top right-hand corner.	6. What are the three classes of accounts?
6. Personal A/cs, Nominal A/cs, and Real A/cs.	7. What are Personal accounts?
7. They are the Accounts of persons with whom we deal, i.e. our Debtors and our Creditors.	8. What is a Debtor?
8. A person who owes us money.	9. What is a Creditor?
9. A person to whom we owe money.	10. What are Real Accounts?
10. They are accounts in which we record the real things we own, i.e. the assets of the business.	11. Name five business assets recorded in Real Accounts.
11. Land and Buildings; Plant and Machinery; Furniture and Fittings; Motor Vehicles; Office Machinery.	12. What is a Nominal Account?
12. An account which records a profit or loss of the business.	13. What does 'nominal' mean?
13. 'In name only.'	14. Why is the money recorded in name only?
14. Because really it has been spent (or gained).	15. What do we use these Nominal Accounts for?
15. To work out the profits of the business at the end of the financial year.	16. What are the two sides of an account called?
16. The debit side and the credit side.	17. What is the rule for entering in the Ledger?
17. (*a*) Debit an account that has received goods, services, or money; (*b*) credit an account that has given goods, services, or money.	18. Put briefly this rule says:
18. Debit the receiver. Credit the giver.	Go over this page again until you know it all.

CHAPTER THREE

HOW DOUBLE ENTRY BOOK-KEEPING WORKS

The chart which is the chief feature of this chapter shows clearly how the double entry system of book-keeping works. This method of keeping books so that the businessman knows his exact financial position at any given time is explained in the diagram, and the student should return to it regularly to discover how each section of his studies fits into the pattern of double entry.

At this stage let us take a very quick look at the diagram on pages 32–3 to pick up the general framework of book-keeping. The numbers 1 to 5 are guideways through the diagram.

(1) The Original Documents

Every transaction that takes place, whether it is a purchase, a sale, a return, a payment, or some other type of transaction has an Original Document. These documents are called Invoices, Credit Notes, Statements, Receipts, Petty Cash Vouchers, or they may be formal agreements like a Hire Purchase Document or a Legal Contract. Even mere letters of complaint require some action to be taken.

(2) The Books of Original Entry

When you have a document you first record it in a book of Original Entry. These books may be Journals, that is Day Books, or Cash Books like the Three-column Cash Book or the Petty Cash Book. We may also have Bill Books to record Bills of Exchange, Consignment Books to record Consignments and other specialised books. These Day Books keep a record of the documents received in *chronological order*.

(3) Posting the Day Books to the Ledger

When we have entered our Original Documents in the Day Books we then post the transactions into the Ledger, which is the main book of account. Every transaction will appear twice, because one account will be receiving value and another giving it. For this reason the entries will be a debit entry in one account and a credit entry in some other account. Hundreds, even thousands, of accounts may be involved, but if we do our double entry carefully the total entries on the debit side will exactly balance the total entries on the credit side. This is the way we check the books, by taking out a Trial Balance

32

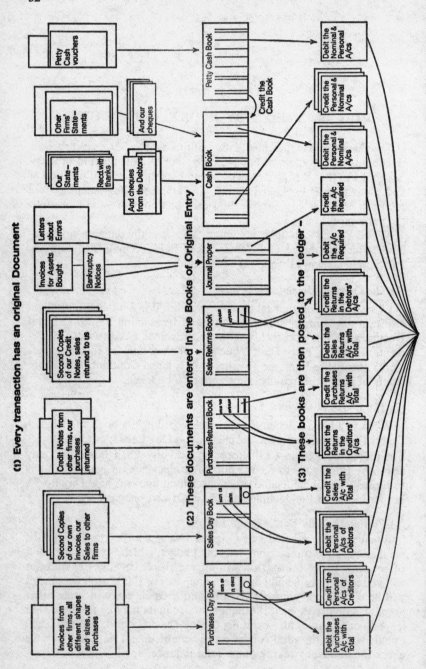

(1) Every transaction has an original Document

(2) These documents are entered in the Books of Original Entry

(3) These books are then posted to the Ledger—

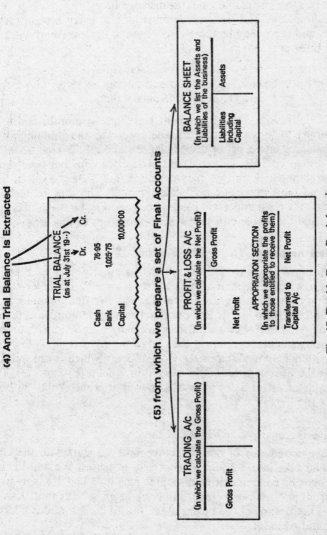

(4) And a Trial Balance Is Extracted

TRIAL BALANCE
(as at July 31st 19··)

	Dr.	Cr.
Cash	76·95	
Bank	1,025·75	
Capital		10,000·00

(5) from which we prepare a set of Final Accounts

BALANCE SHEET
(In which we list the Assets and
Liabilities of the business)

Liabilities including Capital	Assets

PROFIT & LOSS A/C
(In which we calculate the Net Profit)

Gross Profit

Net Profit

APPROPRIATION SECTION
(In which we appropriate the profits
to those entitled to receive them)

Transferred to Capital A/c	Net Profit

TRADING A/c
(In which we calculate the Gross Profit)

Gross Profit

Fig. 17. Double Entry Book-keeping

(4) The Trial Balance

This is what its name implies, an attempt to discover whether the books really do balance. If they do not we know that someone has made a mistake somewhere, and we must discover it.

To take out a Trial Balance we must look at every account in our Ledger, and there may be thousands of them. Each account will be in one of three positions:

(*a*) It may have a debit balance outstanding.
(*b*) It may be clear—having no outstanding balance.
(*c*) It may have a credit balance outstanding.

We usually do a Trial Balance at least once a month, taking the opportunity to 'tidy up' accounts where we can, and bringing all the debit balances into a list of debit balances, and all the credit balances into a list of credit balances. These two columns of balances should come exactly equal, and we may conclude that if they do, it is fairly certain we have done our book-keeping well. The idea of the Trial Balance is the most important idea in book-keeping by the double entry system, and the whole of Chapter Sixteen is given to this idea.

(5a) Final Accounts—The Trading Account

We are now ready to find out whether our business is profitable or running at a loss. To discover this we first do a simple Trading Account. This shows whether we are selling at a profit. We find our sales figure from the Sales Account; we find our purchases figure from our Purchase Account. After one or two adjustments, chiefly connected with opening and closing stocks, we discover the cost of the goods sold. A few more little matters help us discover the Cost of Sales, which is not quite the same as the Cost of Goods Sold, since it includes a few expenses. Then Sales minus Cost of Sales gives us our overall profit—called in book-keeping the **Gross Profit.**

(5b) Final Accounts—The Profit and Loss Account

In this second half of our Final Accounts we start with the Gross Profit and take into account all overhead expenses. We add items of profit, such as commission or discounts received. This leads us to the clear profit or clean profit—called in book-keeping **Net Profit.** This Net Profit is the reward of the businessman for his efforts, and is added to his Capital Account.

With partnership enterprises, and with limited companies, the Net Profit has to be shared up between the partners, or shareholders. This is done in a section of the Profit and Loss Account, called the **Appropriation Account.** We give the profit to the appropriate persons in the appropriate proportions according to the **partnership agreement,** or the resolution passed at the **annual general meeting** of the company.

(5c) The Balance Sheet

When we have prepared the Final Accounts and added the profit to the owner's Capital Account (or perhaps deducted the loss from the owner's Capital Account) we have established what degree of success the business has achieved, and all we need to do now is summarize the final position of the business by drawing up a Balance Sheet which shows the assets and liabilities of the firm.

This is the general pattern of double entry book-keeping. As the student learns about each document and how to keep each book of original entry he should study its position in the general picture by looking again at the chart on pages 32–3.

CHAPTER FOUR

SUBSIDIARY BOOKS AND ORIGINAL DOCUMENTS

(1) Introduction

We already know that the Ledger is the main book of account. The other books we use are called subsidiary books, because they give additional help to the main book. It is in these books that the original documents are recorded, so that they are the books of original entry, already referred to. The most important subsidiary book is the Journal. This is an old French word meaning 'Daily Record', and it was so called because everything that happened every day was entered into the book at once, before the businessman could forget the exact details of the transaction. It therefore gives us a **chronological record** of the transactions into which the businessman enters.

The Dividing-up of the Journal

If you have only one journal it is possible for only one book-keeper to use it at a time. In a past age it was found that when a business grew bigger one person could not do all the work himself. The journal was therefore divided into parts so that several clerks could work at once. It was also found that the work could be divided into two main sections:

(a) Transactions that happened repeatedly, because they dealt with 'goods' that the firm could call its 'normal line of business'.

(b) Transactions that happened much more rarely, say once or twice a year.

Section (a) was found to consist of the Purchase of Goods, the Sale of Goods, Returns Outwards (i.e. Purchases Returned) or Returns Inwards (Sales Returned by dissatisfied customers).

Transactions of this sort took place every day, sometimes many times a day.

Section (b) was found to consist of much rarer items, such as the purchasing of assets like furniture, which might last twenty years, or writing off bad debts which might only happen a few times a year.

Larger firms therefore began to divide the Journal, or Day Book, into five parts:

The Five Subsidiary Books

The Purchases Day Book, in which purchases were recorded.
The Sales Day Book, in which sales were recorded.

The Purchases Returns Book, in which returns outwards were recorded.

The Sales Returns Book, in which returns inwards were recorded.

The Journal Proper, containing all the items not to do with 'goods' that are the firm's 'Normal line of Business', i.e. the rarer items of section (*b*).

(2) The Pattern of Business in an Established Trading Firm

Once a trading business has been successfully launched the profit-yielding activities are repeated endlessly. The businessman buys goods, which he calls **Purchases** and records in his Purchases Day Book. Eventually he sells them, recording the **Sales** in his Sales Day Book. Now and then an unsatisfactory purchase will be returned and its return will be recorded in the Purchases Returns Book, while occasionally the customer who bought goods will be dissatisfied and return them as Sales Returns. The endless succession of these activities is called **Turnover.** The turnover of any business is a very important figure.

Each of these transactions begins with an original document. Purchases and Sales begin with **Invoices.** Purchases Returns and Sales Returns are acknowledged by a **Credit Note.** In every case it is the seller who makes out the document, sending one copy to the other party in the transaction. You should study carefully the documents shown in this chapter and follow the copies as they move to the departments where they are required, and where they will be recorded in the Day Books.

(3) Documents for Sales and Purchases—The Invoice

Definition: An invoice is a business document which is made out whenever one person sells goods to another. It can be used in the courts of law as evidence of a contract for the Sale of Goods. It is made out by the person selling the goods, and in large businesses it may have as many as five copies, of different colours.

Fig. 18 (*a*) on page 38 shows the usual form of invoice in use in large firms. It must have the following information:

(*a*) Names and addresses of both the interested parties to the sale.

(*b*) The date of the sale.

(*c*) An exact description of the goods, with quantity and unit price, and details of the trade discount (if any) given.

(*d*) In the United Kingdom it must give details of the V.A.T. charged as it becomes a tax invoice for V.A.T. purposes.

(*e*) It may give the terms on which goods are sold, i.e. discount and credit period. The words 'Terms Net' mean no discount is allowed. The words 'Prompt Settlement' mean no credit period is allowed.

Lastly, many firms write 'E. & O.E.' on the bottom of the invoice.

These letters mean 'Errors and Omissions Excepted'. If an error or omission has been made, the firm selling the goods may put it right. In English law written evidence may not be varied by oral evidence so that if an invoice were presented in the courts it could not be said orally, 'But my Lord, that was a mistake.' But the words 'E. & O.E.' written on the invoice would permit this to be done. In fact this has been tested in the Courts. In the case of Webster *versus* Cecil (1861) it was held that a genuine slip of the pen could be corrected so that the phrase 'E. & O.E.' is not really necessary.

What Happens to the Four Copies?

Top Copy: This is sent by post or by hand to the person buying the goods, and he uses it to enter in his Purchases Day Book. He then keeps the invoice as his copy of the contract of sale.

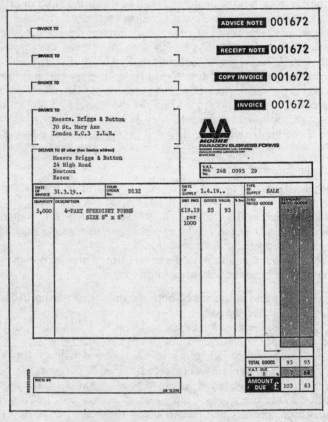

Fig. 18 (*a*). A four-copy invoice system . . .

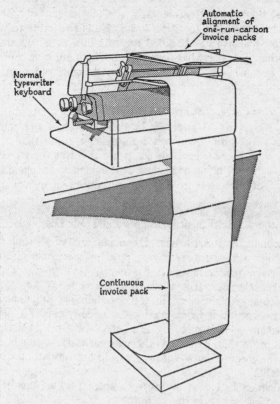

Fig. 18 (*b*). . . . and the machine on which they were typed

Second Copy: This is usually the Sales Day Book copy, which is kept by the seller, entered in his Sales Day Book, and then filed to be kept as his copy of the contract of sale.

Third and Fourth Copies: These are sent together to the Stores Department of the seller, where the storekeeper takes the goods out of store. The third copy, often called the **Delivery Note**, is given to the carman to take with him to the buyer's warehouse, where he presents it with the parcel of goods and gets a signature on it to prove that the goods arrived safely. This copy is then taken back by the carman to the storekeeper and is filed in the store after being entered in the Stores Record Book. The fourth copy is wrapped up in the parcel before it is given to the carman. It is often called the **Advice Note** and it enables the buyer's storekeeper to check the contents of the parcel and record the stores that have just arrived in his Stores Record Book.

Sometimes there is a **Representative's Copy** which is sent to the commercial traveller who took the order. He is then able to prove to the buyer that his firm has handled the sale in a proper manner and can remind the customer what he ordered. This may save a great deal of his time because the buyer may say 'All right, old man; repeat that order will you?'

How Long Do We Keep an Invoice?

Usually for six years. Under the Limitation Act of 1939 an action in the courts on a simple contract cannot begin more than six years after the contract was made. If we keep our invoices for six years the chance of the invoice being needed as legal evidence disappears. Many firms get rid of their old invoices by shredding them into packing material.

(4) Cash Discounts, Settlement Discounts and Trade Discounts

Cash Discounts and **Settlement Discounts** are very similar. Cash Discount *is given to customers who pay 'prompt cash'*. Settlement Discount *is given to debtors who pay promptly for their goods when the time for payment arrives*. It is a great inconvenience to a businessman to have debtors who are slow in settling their accounts, because it means that his capital is being used by somebody else. To encourage prompt payment a cash discount is offered. Naturally this means a smaller total profit than he would otherwise earn, but it may be cheaper to give this discount than to allow debts to accumulate and perhaps suffer bad debts.

In the specimen Ledger Account in Chapter Two we saw how these types of discount appear in the account.

Trade Discount is quite different. *It is a reduction in the catalogue price of an article, given by the wholesaler or manufacturer to the retailer, to enable him to make a profit.*

Take the example of a manufacturer of bicycles. He will produce leaflets about his particular brand of bicycle explaining the merits of the machine. The price will either be printed on this literature or on a separate price list supplied on request, but the important point is that he, and everyone else, will think of this particular machine as the 28·50 model. When invoicing a supply of machines the simple way to invoice them is to list them at the catalogue price. The invoice might therefore read:

6 'Mercury' bicycles, 26-inch frame at 28·50 = 171·00

Clearly the retailer cannot sell these at the catalogue price if he has bought them at the catalogue price. The manufacturer therefore deducts Trade Discount at an agreed rate, usually somewhere between 10 per cent and 45 per cent of the catalogue price. If these figures seem high the student must remember that durable goods of this sort may remain in stock for some considerable time before being sold, and the profit margin must be fairly large on such slow-moving items.

$$6 \text{ 'Mercury' bicycles 26-inch frame at } 28 \cdot 50 = 171 \cdot 00$$
$$\textit{Less } \text{Trade Discount } 25\% = 42 \cdot 75$$
$$\overline{128 \cdot 25}$$

IMPORTANT NOTE

Trade Discount never enters an account of any sort at any time. It is deducted on the Purchases Day Book or Sales Day Book when the Invoice is recorded but it is not part of the debtor's debt; he owes only the net figure of 128·25 and there is *no such thing as a Trade Discount Account*.

(5) The Debit Note—A Document Very Like an Invoice

Definition: A Debit Note is a document which is made out by the seller whenever the purchaser has been undercharged on an invoice, or when he wishes to make some charge on a debtor which increases the debtor's debt. It may also be made out whenever a purchaser returns goods. It then advises the creditor what goods are being returned, and invites him to send a credit note (see page 56).

Suppose that an invoice has been sent to a purchaser of a typewriter value 100·00, but by mistake the typist had typed 10·00 as the purchase price. Clearly the seller will want to correct this undercharge, but another invoice would not be appropriate since no 'goods' are being delivered. A debit note for 90·00 treated exactly like an invoice and put through the Day Books in exactly the same way as an invoice will put this matter right. In the same way charges for carriage, or insurance, which were not known at the time the invoice was made out, could be charged to the debtor by means of a Debit Note.

(6) The Purchases Day Book

When a businessman places an order for goods that he needs, the seller of the goods makes out an invoice. The top copy of this invoice is received by the purchaser and is recorded in the Purchases Day Book. There may be several of these invoices arriving every day, possibly as many as a hundred. They will all be the top copies of other firm's invoices, and since they may have come from a hundred different firms the bundle of invoices will look like that shown in Fig. 19.

These invoices would now be recorded in the Purchases Day Book. The ruling of the Purchases Day Book is basically as shown in Fig. 20, but many firms use larger paper with additional columns for collecting statistical data. These rulings will be discussed later under 'Analytical Purchases and Sales Day Books'.

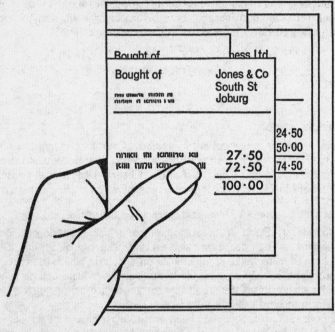

Fig. 19. This morning's collection of Purchases Invoices
(*Note:* They are of assorted shapes, sizes, and colours—can you say why?)

19..					P.D.B. 1
Jan. 1	R. Brown & Co.				
	2 dozen sheets at 1·50 each	C.L. 1			36·00
17	Peter Young Ltd.				
	4 dozen counterpanes at 3·50		168·00		
	2 dozen pillowcases at 0·10		2·40		
21	Ambrose Smith Ltd.	C.L. 2			170·40
	6 dozen ounces wool at 0·20		14·40		
	3 dozen ounces wool at 0·15		5·40		
31	Major & Co. Ltd.	C.L. 3			19·80
	12 'Bettawear' machines at 27·10		325·20		
	Less Trade Discount at 33⅓%		108·40		
		C.L. 4			216·80
					443·00
					G.L. 27

Fig. 20. The Purchases Day Book

Explanation: In fact there will be many invoices each day, filling several pages of the book by the end of the month. The four invoices shown are supposed to represent the hundreds of invoices dealt with in a month. The following points should be noted:

(*a*) The name of the supplier is written, or typed, on to the next clean line of the paper, next to the date. It is underlined.

(*b*) The details of the transaction are recorded on the next line down, giving a separate line to each item of goods supplied.

(*c*) Where the invoice is for a single item the first money column is ignored and the final column is used to record the cash value.

(*d*) Where the invoice is for more than one item the first money column is used to record the separate items, which are then totalled and carried into the final money column.

(*e*) If Trade Discount is given, the first column is used to record

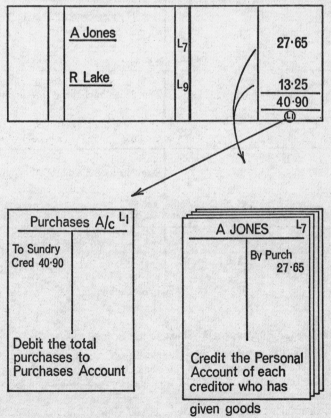

Fig. 21. Posting the Purchases Day Book

the catalogue price; the Trade Discount is then deducted and the net figure only goes into the end column. (*N.B. Trade Discount is never entered in the books apart from the Day Books. It does not (like Cash Discount) appear on the Ledger Accounts.*)

(*f*) The folio numbers of the Ledger Accounts are recorded in the folio column as we do the postings to the Ledger.

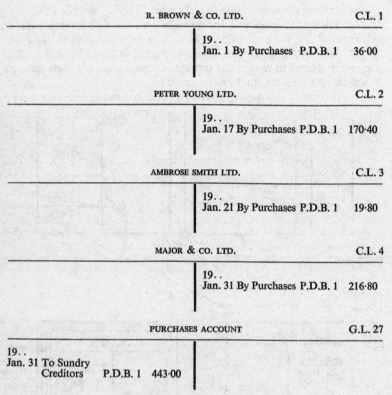

R. BROWN & CO. LTD.	C.L. 1
	19..
	Jan. 1 By Purchases P.D.B. 1 36·00

PETER YOUNG LTD.	C.L. 2
	19..
	Jan. 17 By Purchases P.D.B. 1 170·40

AMBROSE SMITH LTD.	C.L. 3
	19..
	Jan. 21 By Purchases P.D.B. 1 19·80

MAJOR & CO. LTD.	C.L. 4
	19..
	Jan. 31 By Purchases P.D.B. 1 216·80

PURCHASES ACCOUNT	G.L. 27
19..	
Jan. 31 To Sundry	
Creditors P.D.B. 1 443·00	

Fig. 22. Ledger Accounts to Fig. 20

(7) Posting the Purchases Day Book to the Ledger

Posting is the name given to the action of entering into the Ledger accounts the figures recorded in the books of original entry. It is at this time that the transactions come into the Ledger—the main book of account.

Each supplier has given us goods as stated on the invoice. Probably these have been supplied on monthly credit terms, so that at present we have not paid for them. Since the suppliers have given value their accounts will be credited, and since we have received goods our account will be debited. Our account in this case will be the Purchases Account, a nominal account in which we record the goods received.

It is at this point that we can achieve a great saving of labour in the posting of these entries into the Ledger. Each of the *Creditors*, the people to whom we owe money because they have given us goods, must be credited on his account with the value of the goods supplied. The double entry for these items will be a debit to Purchases Account, but we need not debit them individually. It will be enough if the *Total of the Purchases Day Book* only is debited to Purchases Account. The entire month's credit entries in hundreds of accounts will be balanced by a single entry in the Purchases Account. Fig. 21 and Fig. 22 illustrate these postings. To save space, a ledger account without ruled columns is shown instead of ruling up proper Ledger pages.

Rule for Posting the Purchases Day Book

Credit each creditor's personal account because he has given goods to us.

Debit the Purchases Account with the total purchases for the month since this is our account and we have received the goods.

EXERCISES SET VI

(8) The Purchases Day Book

No. 1. You are the book-keeper who keeps the Purchases Day Book. Enter the following invoices in the Purchases Day Book and then post them to the Ledger:

19.

Apr	1 Bought of G. Emerson 2 dozen books at 0·35 each	= 8·40
	3 R. Longfellow sold us stationery as follows:	
	200 boxes envelopes at 0·25 box	= 50·00
	100 writing pads at 0·05	= 5·00
	14 M. Twain supplies goods:	
	4 dozen books at 0·20 each	= 9·60
	3 dozen books at 0·10 each	= 3·60
	25 S. Clemens sells us goods—boxes of paints and paint brushes	= 10·50
	30 H. Melville sends us goods:	
	20 dozen boxes sticky tape at 0·05	= 12·00
	5 dozen boxes paper clips at 0·02	= 1·20

No. 2. Enter the following invoices in the Purchases Day Book and then post them to the Ledger. Do not forget to post the total of the book to the Purchases Account.

19..
May   2 Bought from M. A. Jorca the following goods:
                2 dozen boxes grapes at 2·20   = 52·80
                6 dozen cases oranges at 1·00   = 72·00
      13 Received goods from C. Del Sol as follows:
                30 Spanish Leather handbags at 2·50   = 75·00
      14 Bought of M. Lorenza:
                20 cases grapefruit at 1·10 per case   = 22·00
                5 cases mandarin oranges at 0·90 per case   = 4·50
      25 Bought from C. Del Sol 24 pairs 'Estancia' boots at 2·20
                per pair   = 52·80
      26 Bought of R. Mendoza 7 cases grapes at 1·25 per case   = 8·75
      31 Bought of M. A. Jorca a repeat order of goods supplied on May
                2nd.

No. 3. Enter the following items in the Purchases Day Book of C. Allen, and
then post to the appropriate Ledger Accounts:

19..
May   1 S. Allen sold us 2 white damask table cloths at 1·75 each   = 3·50
      12 H. Bartlett sold us goods as follows:
                2 dozen linen tablecloths at 0·80 each   = 19·20
                2 dozen tea towels at 0·15 each   = 3·60
      23 J. Broomfield sold to us as follows—4 only pale blue
                counterpanes at 1·10 each   = 4·40
      31 S. Burch sold to us as follows:
                20 yards roller towelling at 3·50 the 20-yard length   = 3·50
                40 yards roller towelling at 2·15 the 20-yard length   = 4·30

No. 4. Enter the following items in the Purchases Day Book of Janet
Butcher, milliner, and post to the Ledger:

19..
Aug. 1 Bought of R. Carr floral decorations assorted types at 5·50 the
                collection.
      12 Bought of M. Darwood felt for trimmings—24 sheets 30 × 20
                inches at 5·00 the dozen sheets.
      23 J. Fielding sold us the following items:
                2 dozen flowered hats at 0·50 each   = 12·00
                3 dozen straw boaters at 0·15 each   = 5·40
                2 dozen berets at 0·15 each   = 3·60
      31 F. Ford sold us the following items:
                1 dozen riding hats at 0·65 each   = 7·80
                1 dozen reinforced 'Military Style' peaked hats at 0·85
                each   = 10·20

No. 5. Enter the following items in the Purchases Day Book of S. Pretty,
a stationer and office equipment dealer:

19..
Jan.   1 Received from O. Spinoza 3 Letra typewriters at 56·00 *Less* 25%
           Trade Discount.
       12 Received from R. Ingram:
           12 Bruch teletypers at 340·00
           6 long carriage Bruch manual typers at 40·00
           24 Portable Bruch typewriters at 30·00
           All less 33⅓% Trade Discount.
       23 W. Owndell sells us 200 reams white duplicating paper at 0·55 a ream
           Less 10% Trade Discount.
       31 M. Tobler sends goods as follows:
           300 dozen scribbling pads at 0·05 each   = 180·00
           50 dozen scribbling pads at 0·03 each   = 18·00
           Both subject to 33⅓% Trade Discount.
       Post to the Ledger on January 31st.

No. 6. Enter the following items in the Purchases Day Book of John
Fisher, a dealer in chemists' sundries.

19..
Oct.   1 Received from R. Jones:
           2 dozen toothbrushes at 0·10 each   =   2·40
           1 dozen toothbrushes at 0·07 each   =   0·84
       12 M. Brown sent us 1 gross 1000's Aspirin at 0·55 per 1000 = 79·20
       23 R. Jones sent us 1 gross feeding bottles at 0·15 each   = 21·60
       31 M. Litham sold us goods as follows:
           24 dozen Cutie soap tablets at 0·02   =   5·76
           30 dozen Snappie dog biscuits at 0·08   = 28·80
           10 dozen packets toilet tissues at 0·03   =   3·60

(9) Invoices for Services—The Expenses Journal or Expenses Day Book

Very similar to the invoices described in the last section which are
issued whenever one person sells goods to another are invoices for
services supplied, sometimes called **Expense Invoices**. These are sent
out by Gas Companies, Water Boards, Electric Power Authorities,
Local Councils, and Government Departments of various sorts.
Garages send invoices for fuel supplied and repairs carried out to
vehicles. All such invoices must be recorded in a Day Book very similar
to the Purchases Day Book. The personal account of the suppliers
will be credited since that person is now a creditor to whom our
firm owes money for services rendered. The other half of this double
entry will be in the nominal account, i.e. loss account, for instance
Light and Heat Account, Motor Vehicle Expenses Account, and so
on.

Where a firm is only in business in a small way and the volume of
work would not merit the trouble of having a separate Expenses Day

Book such invoices would be dealt with through the Journal Proper, which is discussed later, in Chapter Six.

(10) The Sales Day Book

When a businessman supplies goods he makes out an invoice of the type described earlier and sends the top copy to the purchaser who records it in his Purchases Day Book. The delivery of the goods will now take place, but meanwhile the supplier who made out the invoice has to record the transaction in his books. The book of original entry is now the *Sales Day Book* and the second copy of the invoice, which is retained by the supplier, will be entered into this book by his Sales Day Book clerk.

Imagine you are going down the corridor at your office and you meet Charlie, the office boy, carrying the bunch of invoice second copies to the young lady who keeps the Sales Day Book. He is holding this bunch of invoices tightly because he doesn't want to lose any. Scattering sales invoices like confetti is a great nuisance; they have to be picked up and

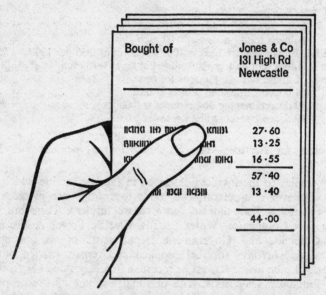

Fig. 23. This morning's collection of Sales Invoices

put in order, and there is always the chance that one will fly down the back of a radiator and be lost. Compare this illustration with the one in the Purchases Day Book section (page 42).

You will notice at once that this time we have a collection of invoices that look alike; they are the same size, shape, and colour. This is clearly because they have all come from the same firm, our firm, and if we were to look through them we would find they were all about the same type of goods, the goods that we sell to our customers. Every day the bundle of Day Book copies of the invoices typed yesterday by the invoice department, whose top copies have already been sent through the post to the purchasers, will be taken to the Sales Day Book clerk, who will enter them in the Sales Day Book.

The ruling of the Sales Day Book is exactly the same as the Purchases Day Book, and is illustrated below.

19..				S.D.B. 1
July 1	R. Smith & Co. Ltd.			
	1 set Roll-over Doors	L. 27		17·50
4	M. Brown			
	6 sets Roll-over Doors		105·00	
	6 sets Keys		1·50	
			106·50	
	Less 20% Trade Discount		21·30	
		L. 3		85·20
11	R. Jones			
	1 set Lift Doors 10′ wide	L. 15		86·50
19	M. Luce			
	3 sets Roll-over Doors	L. 17		52·50
				241·70
				L. 46

Fig. 24. The Sales Day Book

Explanation: There is no real difference between the layout of this book and the layout of the Purchases Day Book shown earlier.

The student may like to note the following points:

(*a*) A common mistake made by book-keepers is to write the folio numbers on the wrong line. The correct line is opposite the final money figure going to the personal account of the debtor. This is 85·20 on July 4th. Do NOT write it on the line that says M. Brown, nor against any of the inset figures.

(*b*) The folio number for the total of the book is written under the ruling-off lines. This gives us a monthly total figure which is clear and has obviously been posted into L. 46, the 46th page in the Ledger.

(*c*) Not all invoices would have Trade Discounts, since many goods are not supplied direct to the trade. In this case, garage doors may be supplied in quantities to builders developing a site, or in single items to private persons. The latter would be charged the full catalogue price.

(11) Posting the Sales Day Book into the Ledger

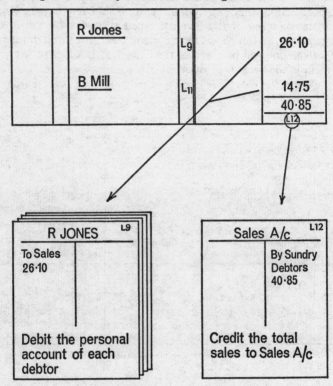

Fig. 25. Posting the Sales Day Book

If Fig. 24 was posted into the Ledger Accounts the entries would appear as in Fig. 26.

Once again the student should note that the double entry is perfect. We have on the debit side, scattered through four accounts, amounts which total 241·70; the exact amount credited in the Sales Account. The Debit Entries therefore equal the Credit Entries.

(12) How to 'Carry Forward' from One Page to the Next

Whichever book we use in book-keeping, we are bound to come sooner or later to the bottom of the page. If we are to keep the book tidy and arithmetically correct we have to 'carry forward' from one page to the next. This is illustrated in Fig. 27 (note *c/f* means 'carried forward' and *B/f* means 'Brought forward'):

R. SMITH & CO. LTD.   L. 27

19..			
July 1 To Sales	S.D.B. 1	17·50	

M. BROWN   L. 3

19..			
July 4 To Sales	S.D.B. 1	85·20	

R. JONES   L. 15

19..			
July 11 To Sales	S.D.B. 1	86·50	

M. LUCE   L. 17

19..			
July 19 To Sales	S.D.B. 1	52·50	

SALES ACCOUNT   L. 46

	19..	
	July 31 By Sundry Debtors	
	S.D.B. 1	241·70

Fig. 26. How Sales appear in the Ledger Accounts

		L. 12		171·50
R. T. Smith				
1 set passe-pictures			50·25	
2 gross hinges			3·75	
1 gross packets			19·25	
		L. 7		73·25
		c/f		1,786·95

				S.D.B. 56
		B/f		1,786·95
M. Jones				
2 dozen plastic frames		L. 11		12·75
P. Loiter				
1 dozen passe-pictures			50·25	
1 gross hinges			1·88	
		L. 29		52·13

Fig. 27. Carrying forward from one page to the next page

Notice that the page that is nearly filled is ruled off with a single line and added up, but the adding up is not closed off with two ruled lines as it would be in an ordinary addition sum. This total of 1,786·95 is left open, and the letters *c/f* are written in the folio column. This open figure is then carried forward to the start of the next page, where it is labelled *B/f* in the folio column.

EXERCISES SET VII

(13) The Sales Day Book

The student should now try the following Sales Day Book exercises. In each case you have to enter the invoices in the Sales Day Book, total the book at the end of the month and post it to the Ledger Accounts not forgetting the:

Rule for Posting the Sales Day Book

Debit the personal accounts of the debtors.
Credit the total sales for the month in the Sales Account.
To help him carry forward the student should particularly try No. 5.

No. 1

19..
Mar. 1 R. Goalie purchases from us a Snifter 51 pencil case at 2·30.
    2 D. Shooter purchases a pen and pencil set at 2·50 and six cigarette lighters at 4·40 each.
    3 R. Goalie purchases 6 Snifter 51 pencil cases at 2·30 each.
    4 W. Attack purchases from us 2 cigarette lighters at 4·40 each, a silver pencil at 0·85, and 2 dozen ball-point pens at 0·10 each.
    5 R. Defence purchases 24 silver pencils at a special price of 0·60 each.
    6 D. Shooter purchases 3 cigarette lighters at 4·40 each.

No. 2

19..
May 1 R. Pianola purchases goods as follows:

2 dozen boxes dominoes at 0·15 each	= 3·60
3 dozen boxes draughts at 0·20 each	= 7·20
2 dozen boxes ludo at 0·25 each	= 6·00

   2 A. Guitar purchased goods as follows:

3 dozen dartboards at 0·45 each	= 16·20

  23 M. Percussion bought goods as follows:

1 grand piano (model size)	= 7·60

No. 3

19..

July 3 J. Rover bought from us 3 refrigerators 'Nanook' type at
65·00 each   = 195·00

    7 M. Humber bought from us 4 typewriters 'Tapitout
Standard' type at 54·25 each   = 217·00

  19 R. Grover purchased from us goods as follows:
3 standard 'Tapitout' typewriters at 54·25   = 162·75
2 portable 'Tapitout' typewriters at 28·50   = 57·00

  27 M. Grudge purchased from us goods as follows:
3 'Nanook' type refrigerators (wall model) at 38·75   = 116·25

No. 4

19..

June 1 R. Brown brought from us coloured silk worth 27·60.

    3 M. Smith brought from us coloured silk valued at 13·45 and best
linen piece goods at 7·65.

  11 Sold to R. Farmer cottons at 4·10, needles at 3·80, and pins at
2·25.

  17 Sold to M. Lucas cotton sheeting 27 yards at 0·15 per yard = 4·05
and linen goods = 2·55.

  24 Sold to R. White cotton goods 42·50 and linen goods at 17·75.

  30 Sold to M. Thomas goods: white fabric value 13·60 and blue fabric
value 7·65.

No. 5

19..

Jan. 1 S. Marner buys goods as follows:
2 dozen articles of clothing at 0·45 each   = 10·80
3 dozen pairs shoes at 2·25 per pair   = 81·00
4 dozen pairs socks at 0·14 per pair   = 6·72

    2 Sold to G. Eliot goods as follows:
1 dozen suits at 4·55 each   = 54·60
2 dozen pairs of socks at 0·14 per pair   = 3·36
3 dozen pairs of shoes at 2·25 per pair   = 81·00

    3 G. Cass purchases as follows:
3 dozen pairs shoes at 2·25 per pair   = 81·00
2 dozen pairs shoes at 2·95 per pair   = 70·80

    4 D. Calthorpe purchased goods below
7 dozen pairs of socks at 0·15 per pair   = 12·60
3 dozen pairs stockings at 0·28 per pair   = 10·08

    8 Sold goods to D. Varden as follows:
4 dozen sets nylon underwear at 1·35 per set   = 64·80
2 dozen sets night negligée at 2·65 per set   = 63·60

  11 Sold to M. Archer goods as follows:
3 dozen pairs of stockings at 0·28 per pair   = 10·08
4 dozen sets nylon underwear at 1·35 per set   = 64·80

17 M. Brown buys goods as follows:
2 dozen pairs stockings at 0·28 per pair   =   6·72
2 dozen pairs shoes at 2·95 per pair   =   70·80
3 dozen pairs shoes at 2·25 per pair   =   81·00
18 R. Ebenezer buys goods as follows:
3 dozen pairs shoes at 2·95 per pair   = 106·20
23 Sold to G. Eliot goods as follows:
2 dozen suits at 4·55 each   = 109·20
27 G. Cass purchased goods as follows:
3 dozen pairs shoes at 2·25 per pair   =   81·00

No. 6. This exercise has Trade Discount in it. You will find some information about Trade Discount in Chapter Four (4), page 40. Read it before you do this exercise.

Enter the following items in your Sales Day Book. As your goods are nationally known articles like 'Scrumptious—the biscuits your dog will really enjoy' you quote the price to the public on your invoices and give the retailer Trade Discount.

19..
Jan. 1 R. Harper buys goods as follows:
24 dozen tins of Scrumptious Biscuit Meal at 0·15 per tin = 43·20
12 dozen packets Scrumptious Dog Biscuits at 0·10 per
packet   =   14·40
Trade Discount of 25% given on the total value of the invoice.
    3 We sell T. Birchin goods as follows:
30 dozen tins of Scrumptious Biscuit Meal (family size)
at 0·50 per tin   = 180·00
Less 25% Trade Discount.
   14 We sell R. Harper goods as follows:
24 dozen tins of Scrumptious Biscuit Meal at 0·15 per
tin   =   43·20
6 dozen packets Scrumptious Dog Biscuits at 0·10 per
packet   =   7·20
Trade Discount of 25% given on total value.
   25 We sell M. Jones goods as follows:
3 dozen tins Scrumptious Biscuit Meal (family size) at
0·50 per tin   =   18·00
6 dozen packets Scrumptious Biscuit Meal at 0·15 per
packet   =   10·80
Trade Discount of 25% on total value of invoice.

(14) Documents for Returns—The Credit Note

Introduction

We must expect in the course of business that some of our customers will return goods for valid reasons. A purchaser is not entitled to return something just because he has changed his mind about having it; but occasionally we may oblige a client by accepting this type of return. The usual reasons for returning goods are:

(*a*) The purchaser holds that the goods are unsatisfactory for some reason, e.g. wrong colour; wrong size; not up to sample; not up to specification; imperfectly finished; damaged in transit, etc.

(*b*) The purchaser returns goods which he is entitled to return, for instance goods sent on approval.

In these circumstances the document used is the Credit Note.

Definition

A credit note is a business document made out whenever one person returns goods to another. It is usually printed in red, to distinguish it from an invoice, and like an invoice, is made out by the seller of the goods, who is now receiving them back again. Usually there are only two copies.

The credit note should show:

(*a*) The names and addresses of both parties to the transaction.

(*b*) An exact description of the goods being returned.

(*c*) The unit price, the number and the total value of the goods returned.

Other Reasons for Sending a Credit Note

(*a*) Sometimes goods that are unsatisfactory for some reason are not returned because of the inconvenience and cost. A piece of furniture that has been damaged by rain in transport may only need repolishing. The purchaser may be perfectly prepared to have this repolishing carried out by one of his own employees, provided the seller will make him an allowance to cover the cost. This will be done by sending a credit note for the agreed amount. This is called an **Allowance**.

(*b*) We saw in Chapter Four, page 41, that when an undercharge is made on an invoice a document called a debit note was sent to increase the original invoice to the proper figure. Invoice typists can make errors which result in overcharges instead of undercharges. Supposing the typewriter valued at 100·00 was invoiced at 1,000·00. Clearly a credit note for 900·00 will be required to correct the overcharge.

Credit notes may therefore be sent for three reasons:

(*a*) To credit a debtor with returns.

(*b*) To credit a debtor with an allowance.

(*c*) To credit a debtor to correct an overcharge.

CREDIT NOTE

Messrs Brewis and Jeffrey,

Cherrydown,

Newtown,

Essex.

No. 7864

RIDER & Co. Ltd.
High Street
London, W.C.2.

DATE	20th May	19..	REP.	M. TYLER.

No.	Description	Code	Pub. Price	Trade Discount	
3	Dining Chairs (damaged in transit)		1·50	—	4·50

Fig. 28. A Credit Note; the Original Document for Returns
(N.B. Credit notes are always printed in red.)

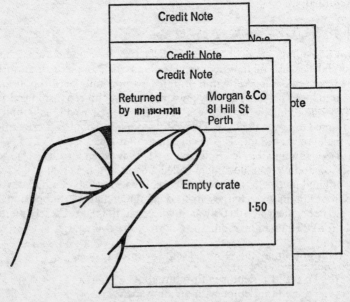

Fig. 29. This morning's postbag of Credit Notes for purchases we have returned

A Pitfall for Students—'Catalogue Price'

Students using this book to prepare for examinations should beware of a common pitfall set for them in written papers: there may be an entry which reads as follows:

> July 10th Jones returns goods sent to him on July 3rd, Catalogue price 10·00.

If the student refers to July 3rd he will almost certainly find that these goods were sold at a Trade Discount in the original order. It would be quite wrong to give the customer a credit note for the full catalogue price when he was only charged the trade discount price on the original invoice. This would be as good as giving him his profit. For instance, if the Trade Discount were 25 per cent he would have been invoiced for the goods at 7·50. If we made him a refund of 10·00 he would finish up 2·50 better off. Clearly this is wrong.

The credit note will only be made out for 7·50, to cancel out the original invoice.

What Happens to the Two Copies?

Usually credit notes are made out in duplicate. The top copy is sent to the purchaser who has returned the goods, and is recorded in his Purchases Returns Book. The duplicate is kept by the seller and is recorded in his Sales Returns Book.

(15) The Purchases Returns Book

This is the third subsidiary book. An examination of Fig. 30 will reveal the following points:

PURCHASES RETURNS BOOK			P.R.B. 1
19..			
Jan. 7 R. Miles			
1 packing crate	L. 5		0·50
11 M. Joynson			
2 boxes address cards (incorrectly displayed)	L. 7		2·50
29 R. Brown			
1 dozen boxes invitation cards (on approval—not required)	L. 11		4·25
			7·25
			L. 3

Fig. 30. The Purchases Returns Book

(*a*) The book is kept in exactly the same way as the other day books.

(*b*) The first money column does not carry many entries as it is rare to have more than one item returned as unsatisfactory. If it did happen that an order of several items was returned the first column could have been used to add up the items, so that the total figure only would appear in the end column.

(16) Posting the Purchases Returns Book into the Ledger

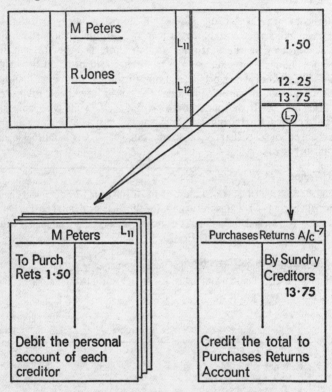

Fig. 31. Posting the Purchases Returns Book

If Fig. 30 was posted into the Ledger accounts the entries would be as in Fig. 32.

The balances on the credit side were put in to make the accounts look more realistic. Clearly if we are returning goods to a creditor we must have had some goods to return. It would be possible to have no balance on the accounts and still return goods, if they were goods for which we had already paid in full. In that case our creditor would owe us money for the goods returned, and would temporarily turn into a debtor. At present it is best to disregard this type of complication. Notice that the creditor has been debited with the return since he has received the goods back again. Our account, the Purchases Returns Account, has been credited because we have given the goods back again.

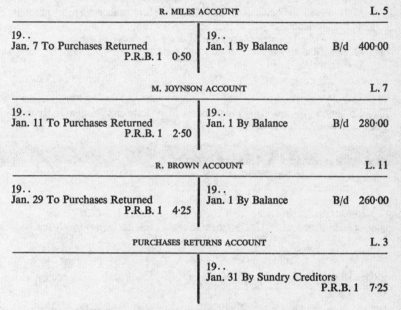

R. MILES ACCOUNT			L. 5
19..	19..		
Jan. 7 To Purchases Returned	Jan. 1 By Balance	B/d	400·00
P.R.B. 1 0·50			

M. JOYNSON ACCOUNT			L. 7
19..	19..		
Jan. 11 To Purchases Returned	Jan. 1 By Balance	B/d	280·00
P.R.B. 1 2·50			

R. BROWN ACCOUNT			L. 11
19..	19..		
Jan. 29 To Purchases Returned	Jan. 1 By Balance	B/d	260·00
P.R.B. 1 4·25			

PURCHASES RETURNS ACCOUNT			L. 3
	19..		
	Jan. 31 By Sundry Creditors		
	P.R.B. 1		7·25

Fig. 32. How Purchases Returns appear in the Ledger Accounts

Rules for Posting the Purchases Returns Book

Debit the personal account of the creditor who is receiving the goods we have returned.

Credit the Purchases Returns Account with the total returns for the month, since we have given them back.

(17) The Purchases Returns Book

No. 1. Enter the following items in Thomas Brown's Purchases Returns Book and post to the Ledger:

19..

Apr. 5 Returned to H. White & Co. containers valued at 0·50.

12 Returned to R. Robertson containers valued at 1·25.

17 Returned to M. Smith 2 dozen copies of Dickens' 'Old Curiosity Shop' (sections sewn in upside down) at 0·25 per copy = 6·00.

24 Returned to R. Jones 1 picture (definition poor) at 2·10.

No. 2. Enter the following items in Roger Freedom's Purchases Returns Book and post to the Ledger.

19..
July   3 Returned to H. Jones & Co. crates valued at 0·65.
      15 Received a credit note from M. Lomax for goods returned to him as follows:
          1 white leather-covered dining suite and table at 40·25.
      17 Returned to M. Norrish goods valued at 40·00:
          1 whitewood kitchen set at 12·00
          1 rosewood suite at 28·00.

No. 3. Enter the following credit notes in P. Palmer's Purchases Returns Book and post to the Ledger.

19..
Sept. 4 Returned to M. Haddock:
          1 white bedspread at 1·25
          1 set sheets and pillowcases at 1·75
          Damaged in transit (rainwater).
      14 Returned to R. Plaice 1 packing case charged at 0·50.
      27 Returned to B. Harlow 2 mattresses 14·00 each (not up to sample).

No. 4. Enter the following credit notes in T. Harman's Purchases Returns Book. Total the book and post to the Ledger.

19..
Oct.   3 Returned to M. Venables 1 woollen jumper (seams not sewn properly) at 1·25.
      14 Returned to M. Spurgeon 2 tablecloths, best linen (faded) at 1·35 each.
      17 Received a credit note from H. Morton as follows:
          2 white woollen scarves (marked) at 0·55 each
          1 'Orlon' jumper (wrong colour) at 1·35.

No. 5. Enter the following credit notes in R. Eldridge's Purchases Returns Book. Total the book and post to the Ledger.

19..
Oct.   4 Received a credit note from Middel & Legge Ltd., 1 dining chair (broken in transit) at 5·25.
      12 Received a credit note from D. L. Horne & Co. Ltd., 1 piano stool returned (polish imperfect) at 4·35.
      13 Returned to M. Lindsay a group of assorted furnishing items (not up to sample) total value 48·50.

No. 6. Enter the following credit notes in B. March's Purchases Returns Book. Total the book and post to the Ledger.

19..

Oct. 13 Returned to B. Harwich 1 roll wire netting (imperfectly welded) at
1·50.

17 Returned to S. Sorensen 2 pairs wire cutters (rivets loose) at 0·38
each.

18 Returned to Major Oil Co. 2 drums (paraffin) at 0·50 per drum and
15 cylinders Calor Gas at 0·50 per cylinder.

29 Returned to B. Harwich 1 chain link fence (rusty) at 6·50.

(18) The Sales Returns Book

When the seller makes out a credit note in duplicate, he sends the
top copy to the purchaser who has returned the goods. The second copy
is taken to the clerks in the Accounts Department, who proceed to

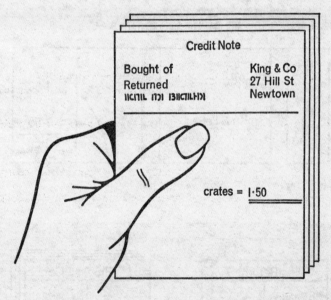

Fig. 33. This morning's collection of Credit Notes for Sales Returned to us;
the second copies go from the typist to the Accounts Department

enter it into the Sales Returns Book. This is the last of the four subsidiary
books which deal with the movement of goods into and out of our
business.

Once again it is interesting to visualize this morning's collection of
credit notes on its way to the Accounts Department. This time it is a
bundle of second copies of our own credit notes, the top copies having
been sent off yesterday to the creditors who returned the goods. Unlike
the untidy collection in Fig. 29 (page 56), they form a neat bundle.

When entered in the Sales Returns Book these credit notes will appear as shown in Fig. 34. Again the ruling of this book is exactly the same as the other day books.

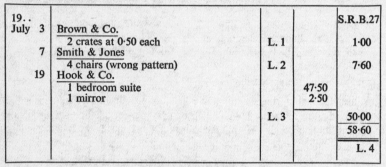

19.. July	3	Brown & Co.			S.R.B.27
		2 crates at 0·50 each	L. 1		1·00
	7	Smith & Jones			
		4 chairs (wrong pattern)	L. 2		7·60
	19	Hook & Co.			
		1 bedroom suite		47·50	
		1 mirror		2·50	
			L. 3		50·00
					58·60
					L. 4

Fig. 34. The Sales Returns Book

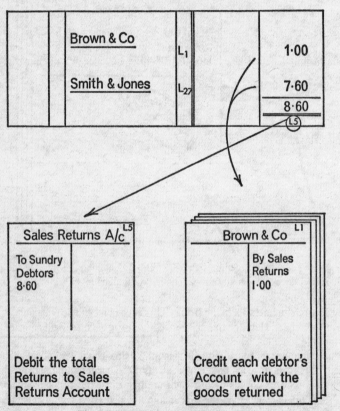

Fig. 35. Posting the Sales Returns Book

(19) Posting the Sales Returns Book into the Ledger

Once again when we post the Sales Returns Book into the Ledger we have to ask ourselves the question 'Who is the receiver in this case, and who is the giver?' Since we are dealing with Sales that have been returned the 'person' receiving the goods is our own firm, the persons giving the goods are the debtors who are dissatisfied with them. The rule for posting Sales Returns is therefore:

Debit the Sales Returns Account with the total returns for the month.
Credit the individual amounts in the debtors' accounts to reduce their debts to us.

When posted into the Ledger Accounts Fig. 34 now appears as follows:

BROWN & CO.   L. 1

19..			19..		
July 1 To Balance	B/d	120·00	July 3 By Sales Returns S.R.B. 27		1·00

SMITH & JONES   L. 2

19..			19..		
July 1 To Balance	B/d	65·50	July 7 By Sales Returns S.R.B. 27		7·60

HOOK & CO.   L. 3

19..			19..		
July 1 To Balance	B/d	72·80	July 19 By Sales Returns S.R.B. 27		50·00

SALES RETURNS ACCOUNT   L. 4

19..				
July 31 To Sundry Debtors				
	S.R.B. 27	58·60		

Fig. 36. How Sales Returns appear in the Ledger Accounts

NOTES: Once again it makes the accounts more realistic if we invent some balances of goods unpaid for on the Ledger Accounts of our debtors. They will be most likely to return goods in the first few days after delivery, before they have actually paid for them. In this respect the period of credit given before payment is needed. It acts as a safe-guard to the debtor. He has the chance of rejecting the goods before he has paid for them.

(20) The Sales Returns Book

No. 1. Enter the following credit notes in R. Jones's Sales Returns Book and post to the Ledger:

19..

Jan.   4 Sent M. Smith a credit note for 2 steam irons at 2·85 each (heating element faulty).
   15 Sent R. Thompson a credit note for 3 electric fires at 3·30 each (switches faulty).
   17 Sent R. Leighton a credit note for a 'Washette' dishwasher (faulty motor) at 37·50.
   18 Sent M. Kehu a credit note for an overcharge on an invoice (typing error), 10·00.

No. 2. Enter the following credit notes in R. Johnson's Sales Returns Book and post to the Ledger:

19..

July 12 Sent R. Day a credit note for goods returned as follows:
       1 table (leg broken) at 12·75
       2 containers for Zahl polish valued at 0·50 each.
   17 Sent M. Grossmith credit note for goods returned as follows:
       2 dozen tiles (broken) valued at 1·20 altogether.
       1 chair (not glued in manufacture) at 4·75.
   29 Sent R. Thorpe credit note for goods as follows:
       1 imitation Chesterfield suite (not up to quality of sample) at 48·50.

No. 3. Enter the following credit notes in R. Larkin's Sales Returns Book and post to the Ledger:

19..

Aug.   4 M. Seager returned to us goods valued at 4·50 (picnic outfit crushed in transit).
   11 R. Loiter returned to us goods as follows:
       1 camp bed (joints insecurely riveted) at 5·50
       2 camp tables (painting inferior) at 3·25 each.
   17 M. Shoreditch returns goods valued at 7·25 (tent damaged in proofing process).
   29 M. Leman sent back goods as follows:
       1 kit bag (eyelets torn) at 1·25
       2 sleeping bags (mildewed due to bad storage) at 2·50 each.

No. 4. Enter the following credit notes in R. Lowry's Sales Returns Book:
19..
Aug. 7 Sent M. Team a credit note value 0·45 for containers returned
         empty.
     13 Sent R. Jorgensen a credit note value 17·75 (for 2 tile fireplaces—
         concrete frame not at right angles to base).
     27 Sent M. Stevens a credit note as follows:
           1 wrought-iron gate (hinges defective) at 7·55
           1 wrought-iron lampholder (insecure welding) at 2·65.

No. 5. Enter the following credit notes in M. Kosker's Sales Returns Book:
19..
May 9 Sent M. Lipton a credit note for 4·35 (1 case eggs damaged in
         transit).
     17 Sent M. Schumann a credit note for 3·75 (1 sack raisins contami-
         nated with paraffin oil).
     24 Sent D. Quichot a credit note (barrels returned empty) 2·25.
     30 Sent M. Sanders a credit note for 4·50 (1 case tinned salmon—tins
         rusty).

No. 6. Enter the following credit notes in R. Loyola's Sales Returns Book:
19..
Jan. 2 Sent K. Champagne a credit note as follows:
           1 pipe 12-inch diameter 'S' bend = 1·55
           2 corner pieces 6-inch radius at 0·65 each.
     13 Sent Q. Iroquois a credit note as follows:
           2 rain gutters at 0·95 each
           1 end stop at 0·15.
     17 Sent M. Antoine a credit note for 3 water-main covers (imperfect
         casting) at 0·85 each.
     29 Sent R. Liebermann credit note for 36·00 for overcharge on 1 lorry
         load of sand at 4·00—charged as 40·00 in error.

(21) Recapitulation

We have now considered in this chapter the four subsidiary books
that deal with the movement of goods into and out of our business.
Remember 'goods' are the items that we normally buy and sell in our
type of business. Flour is 'goods' to a baker, and so are cakes and bread,
but a filing cabinet is not 'goods' to a baker even though it is a useful
commodity and most large-scale bakeries would buy many of them. A
filing cabinet is an asset, and would be recorded in the Journal Proper,
which is dealt with in Chapter Six.

A really sound knowledge of these four Day Books, and of the
postings to the ledger from them, is vital to any book-keeper. Any
businessman who wants to keep his own accounts, and any student, is
strongly advised to work through at least some of the exercises in order
to acquire real experience in the handling of these entries.

(22) A Page to Test You on the Journals

Cover the page with a sheet of paper, then read one question at a time.

Answer	Question
—	1. What is the main book of account?
1. The Ledger.	2. What do we call all other books?
2. Subsidiary Books.	3. What does 'subsidiary' mean?
3. 'Giving additional help to.'	4. Which is the most important subsidiary book?
4. The Journal.	5. What does 'journal' mean?
5. Daily Record.	6. Is the Journal still in existence in its original form as a day book in which everything that happens every day is written down?
6. No. It is split up into five parts.	7. What are the names of five 'Day Books' or Journals now?
7. The Purchases Day Book; The Sales Day Book; The Purchases Returns Book; The Sales Returns Book; and the Journal Proper.	8. What are the first four of these books concerned with?
8. The Purchase, Sales, and Returns of goods.	9. What are 'goods'?
9. They are the commodities that form our normal line of business.	10. Is bread 'goods' to a baker?
10. Yes.	11. Is a delivery van 'goods' to a baker?
11. No. He doesn't buy and sell delivery vans.	12. Would a garage call 'delivery vans' goods?
12. Yes, because garages buy and sell vans.	13. Where do we enter it when we buy something that is not our normal line of business, i.e. typewriters for use in the office?
13. We enter it in the Journal Proper.	14. Where would we put a Bad Debt entry?
15. In the Journal Proper.	15. How many questions did you get right out of 14?

Do the test again and again until you get *all* the answers right.

(23) A Page to Test You on Invoices and Debit Notes

Answer	Question
—	1. What is an invoice?
1. An invoice is a business document which is made out whenever one person sells goods to another.	2. Is it a legal document?
2. No, but it may be used as evidence of a contract of sale.	3. How many copies are there?
3. Usually three, four, or five.	4. Name the five possible copies, and the places they go to.
4. Top Copy, sent to purchaser, who puts it in his Purchases Day Book; Day Book Copy, goes to Accounts Dept. to go in Sales Day Book; Delivery Note, goes to stores and is taken by carman for signature on delivery; Advice Note, goes to stores to be wrapped with goods so that purchaser can check them; Representative's Copy, goes to commercial traveller who took the order.	5. How long do we keep invoices?
5. Six years.	6. Why six years?
6. Because the Statute of Limitations says if six years expire from the time an ordinary contract is made, then legal action cannot be taken.	7. What must an invoice have on it?
7. (a) Names & Addresses of both parties; (b) exact description of goods; (c) value of goods; (d) terms and conditions of sale; (e) it often has E. & O.E. (f) VAT details	8. What does E. & O.E. mean?
8. Errors and Omissions Excepted.	9. Why is this put on the invoice?
9. Because otherwise a genuine mistake or omission would perhaps not be able to be corrected.	10. What is a debit note?
10. It is a business document which is made out whenever an invoice has an undercharge on it, to correct the undercharge.	11. What else could it be used for?
11. To charge carriage or insurance.	

(24) A Page to Test You on Credit Notes

Answer	Question
—	1. What is a Credit Note?
1. It is a business document made out whenever a buyer returns goods to a seller.	2. Who makes it out, and when?
2. The seller makes it out when the goods return to his premises.	3. What safety device prevents anyone mistaking a Credit Note for an invoice?
3. A Credit Note is always made out in red and may be printed with the red ribbon on the typewriter.	4. How many copies are made out?
4. Two copies.	5. Where do they go?
5. One copy is sent to the debtor who returned the goods; he enters it in his Purchases Returns Book. The other copy is kept by the seller and entered in his Sales Returns Book.	6. Why might a debtor return goods?
6. (*a*) Because they were damaged on arrival; (*b*) because they were the wrong size, colour, or type; (*c*) not up to sample; (*d*) not up to specification; (*e*) goods sent 'on approval' and not required.	7. Can the buyer return the goods because he has decided after all he doesn't want them?
7. No. This would be a breach of contract.	8. Why else do we send someone a Credit Note (two reasons)?
8. (*a*) If an invoice is incorrect, having been overstated, a Credit Note will put it right; (*b*) if goods are not satisfactory, the buyer may agree to have them at a cheaper price instead of returning them. This is called 'an allowance' and it is made by sending him a Credit Note.	9. How many questions did you get right out of 8? Go over the page several times till you get it all correct.

CHAPTER FIVE

THE THREE-COLUMN CASH BOOK

(1) Introduction

In Chapter Two we learned how to keep the Ledger, with its collection of personal, nominal, and real accounts. As a business grows bigger two problems present themselves to the businessman. Firstly, the ledger grows thicker and thicker as more and more customers and creditors enter into business relationships with the firm. Secondly, some sub-division of the work becomes necessary as it is impossible for two clerks to work with only one book.

A natural subdivision of the work occurs if we remove from the ledger the two busiest accounts of all, the Cash Account and the Bank Account. These two accounts are extremely active accounts; hardly a day goes by without twenty or thirty items being paid or received by the normal small business, and large businesses may handle hundreds of items daily. It therefore seems sensible to move these two accounts from the ledger and put them into a separate book in the special charge of one person, called the **Cashier**.

(2) Cashiers, Bound Books, and Fidelity Bonds

Of all the valuable items in which a business deals, cash is the most easily misappropriated. Many small businessmen try to keep control of the cash themselves, or ask their wives to handle the cash side of the business. If this is not possible the cashier may be a trusted employee whose reliability is beyond doubt, and who will be paid a salary commensurate with the responsibilities of the post. Even then it is usual to take precautions against defalcations.

One such precaution is to have a bound book for a Cash Book. A loose-leaf book is most unsuitable, because it is possible to rewrite pages and insert them without the owner's knowledge. Loose-leaf books are unsafe even for ordinary Ledger Accounts; for the Cash Book they are particularly unwise. If a cashier keeps his records in a bound book it makes it extremely difficult for him to rewrite a page.

A second precaution is to take out a Fidelity Bond on the Cashier. This is an insurance policy to cover any defalcations up to a limit of, say, 5,000·00, that may occur while he is keeping the Cash Book. A firm employing less reliable personnel as cashiers safeguards itself in this way. It is usual for the employee to be asked to agree to take out the policy, the premium for which is deducted from his salary. Naturally a cashier is paid a salary commensurate with his responsibilities so that the premium deductions are hardly noticed as the new cashier is being paid on a higher scale than formerly. There is one important feature of these policies that students should know about: compensation is only paid to the employer when the employee has been convicted in the courts. The employer cannot say: 'You have been dishonest but I will forgive you this time, and collect my compensation from the insurance company.' It is against public policy, that is to say crime would only be encouraged, to allow the criminal to escape the rigour of the law at the expense of the insurance company.

(3) Why have a Three-column Cash Book?

We shall understand this most easily if we consider a two-column Cash Book first. We have decided to remove the Cash Account and the Bank Account from the Ledger, and put them into a special bound book, called the Cash Book, kept by a responsible employee, the cashier. We are doing this firstly because they are very busy accounts, and the cashier can be fully employed entering up the cash and cheques; secondly because they are very vulnerable accounts and we want to protect them. We may even build our cashier a small office to himself where the safe, the cash till, and the cash book can all be locked up securely.

What will be the point of having these two accounts on separate pages? The cashier will have to keep turning the pages from one account to the other, blotting them as he does so, and if the book is a big one, with about 300 pages, he will suffer considerable physical strain turning to the page he wants if we have the Cash Account at the beginning and the bank account half-way through.

The genius who decided to put the two accounts side by side has been lost in history, like the man who invented the wheel, but he certainly had a very happy idea. He had invented the Two-column Cash Book. No doubt a few years went by before some other genius added a discount column to either side and changed the Two-column Cash Book into the Three-column Cash Book, but we shall see that this book is most appropriate to our needs.

Explanation

(*a*) The Three-column Cash Book is really two ledger accounts, the Cash Account and the Bank Account set out side by side. They are completely unconnected; each is a separate account with a debit side and a credit side.

(*b*) The Discount Column is not an account. The Discount Allowed Account and Discount Received Account are both in the ordinary

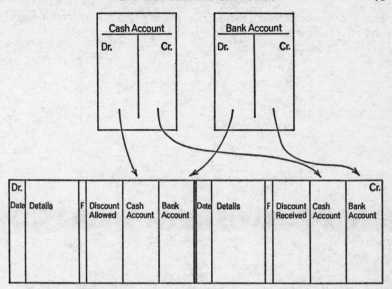

Fig. 37. The layout of the Three-column Cash Book

Ledger—two Nominal Accounts. These columns are **Memorandum Columns** only; they help us remember how much discount has been allowed or received.

(*c*) In order to give plenty of room in the column for details a Three-column Cash Book is spread out across the whole double page of a book. It follows that when you first open a new Three-column Cash Book the first page you come to just inside the cover is only half a page; you have to ignore it and turn over to the first full width double page.

(4) Original Documents for the Three-column Cash Book

Just as purchases, sales, and returns all begin with the preparation of original documents so the entries made in the Cash Book start with an originating document.

These documents are the **Statement,** the **Cheque,** the **Receipt,** and the **Cheque Book Counterfoil.** Small items may be vouched for by a Petty Cash Voucher, but as these are usually dealt with in the Petty Cash Book a discussion of them is postponed until later.

The Statement

Overleaf is a picture of a simple statement. It is a business document which is sent out at the end of the month to all the debtors of our firm, reminding them what they owe us for the purchases they have made during the past month. The phrase 'To account rendered' is used to save the trouble of listing the various invoices, debit notes, credit notes, and receipts which have been sent to them during the month.

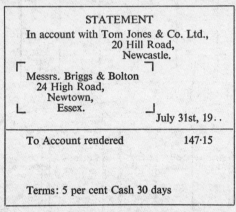

STATEMENT
In account with Tom Jones & Co. Ltd.,
20 Hill Road,
Newcastle.

Messrs. Briggs & Bolton
24 High Road,
Newtown,
Essex.

July 31st, 19. .

To Account rendered	147·15

Terms: 5 per cent Cash 30 days

Fig. 38. A simple Statement

Mechanized Statements

Many firms today are using mechanized forms of book-keeping. There are several mechanized systems. The statement shown opposite is printed by kind permission of Olivetti Limited. You will notice that it does not just contain the words 'To account rendered' but instead contains details of all payments by the debtor and of goods sent to him and items returned by him. This is because under mechanized book-keeping the statement is typed automatically as the other entries are made during the month. It therefore is ready to be sent out as soon as the end of the month comes, and no extra labour is involved.

What Happens to the Statements We Send Out?

The debtor who receives our statement first checks it against his book-keeping records. If it is correct he then uses it as a covering document for his cheque, which he draws up and sends with the covering statement to our accounts department. If he is entitled to deduct 5 per cent cash discount he will write on the statement 'Less 5 per cent Cash Discount', deduct it, and send us the cheque to cover the net amount.

What Happens to the Statement We Receive?

The same process as above, because we are now the debtor and it is up to us to pay our debt after deducting Cash Discount if we are entitled to do so.

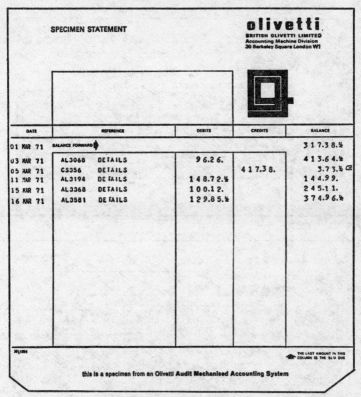

Fig. 39. A mechanized statement

Cheques

A cheque is an order to a banker to pay money to someone at once. It may be written on any piece of paper or indeed on anything. One wag wrote a cheque out on his cricket bat. These days bankers prefer cheques to be of a certain size because they are dealt with by machines. Odd bits of paper do not fit the machines. This is also true of cricket bats.

The Advantages of Paying Money by Cheque

(*a*) It is just as easy to pay 1,000·00 as it is to pay 1·00. You do not need 1000 pieces of paper as you do with 1·00 notes.

(*b*) A cheque can be safeguarded by crossing it so that even if it is stolen it is useless to the thief.

(*c*) The money never leaves the bank so it is perfectly safe.

(*a*)

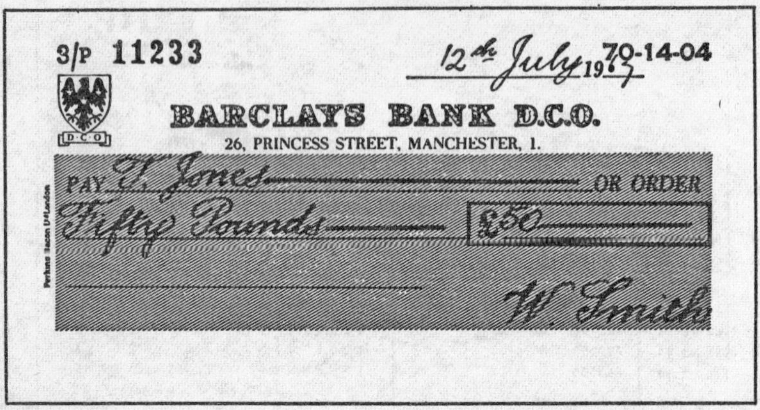
3/P 11233
12th July 1967
70-14-04
BARCLAYS BANK D.C.O.
26, PRINCESS STREET, MANCHESTER, 1.
PAY T. Jones OR ORDER
Fifty Pounds
£50
W. Smith

(*b*)

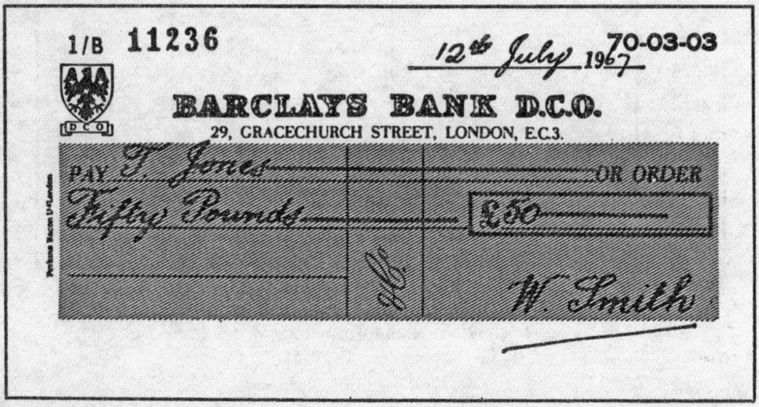
1/B 11236
12th July 1967
70-03-03
BARCLAYS BANK D.C.O.
29, GRACECHURCH STREET, LONDON, E.C.3.
PAY T. Jones OR ORDER
Fifty Pounds
£50
W. Smith

(*c*)

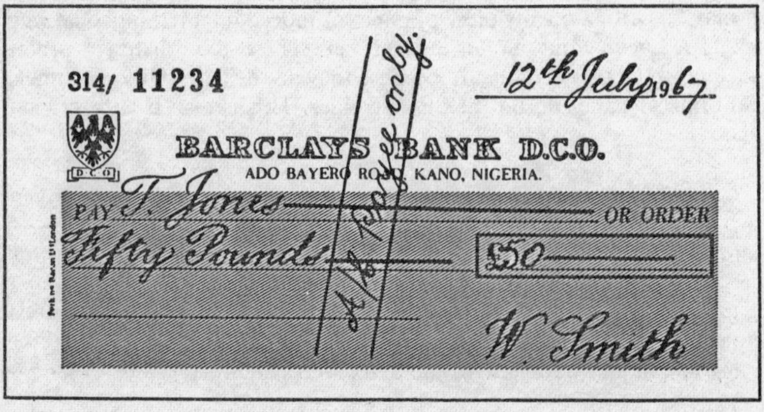
314/ 11234
12th July 1967
BARCLAYS BANK D.C.O.
ADO BAYERO ROAD, KANO, NIGERIA.
A/c Payee only.
PAY T. Jones OR ORDER
Fifty Pounds
£50
W. Smith

(*d*)

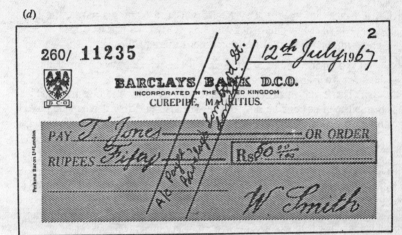

Fig. 40. Safeguarding a cheque

(*d*) In some countries, for instance in the United Kingdom (by the Cheques Act of 1957), the cheque is a receipt. It is proof, once it has been cleared, that you did pay the money.

Explanation of the four cheques in Fig. 40

(*a*) This is an open cheque; it can be cashed at the bank by anyone who presents it and says he is T. Jones. He will have to endorse it. This means he must sign his name on the back when he cashes the cheque. Although this is not much of a safeguard it does have a deterrent effect on thieves, because signing the name T. Jones on the cheque when you are not Mr. Jones means you have committed the crime of forgery, which is more severely punished than mere theft. There is an even more unsafe cheque, called a 'Bearer' cheque, which is made out 'Pay Bearer'. This is very unsafe indeed and does not require endorsement, because the name of the Bearer is not important. Anyone who presents it is entitled to payment on it. Generally speaking it is safer to cross a cheque, and banks issue books of cheques that are already crossed for those who prefer to play safe.

(*b*) This is a general crossing—two lines with or without '& Co.'. It will not be cashed across the counter of the bank but must be cleared into a bank account. It is therefore much safer than (*a*), but it can be cleared by anyone so long as T. Jones has endorsed it (written his name on the back). Notice that it is possible to pay this cheque into *any* account. It does not have to go into the account of the man named on the cheque, T. Jones. This is possible because it is an Order Cheque. At the end of the line it says 'Pay T. Jones...............or Order'. This means that if Jones endorses it 'Pay R. Brown' and signs his name, the bank concerned will obey the order and pay R. Brown not T. Jones.

The simpler rules about endorsement are as follows:

(i) No endorsement is necessary if the payee pays an order cheque into his own account.

(ii) If the payee orders the bank to pay someone else he must endorse the cheque. The new payee will also endorse it when he pays it into his account.

(c) Crossed A/c Payee. Another general crossing! The payer safeguards himself by suggesting that it should be paid only into the account of the payee. If the cheque is paid into any other account the bank is 'put upon inquiry' over the circumstances; that is, they will be liable to the payer if an unauthorized person should collect the money. The bank must inquire whether the payee has given authority for the cheque to be cleared through the account of the person who has paid it in.

(d) This is a special crossing. Not only is it A/c Payee, but the bank into which it is to be paid is clearly stated.

What Happens to the Cheques We Receive?

Cheques that arrive from debtors are taken to the cashier who enters them on the debit side of the Bank Account. If a receipt is required he writes a receipt, acknowledging that the debt has been settled by this payment, and returns it to the debtor. In the United Kingdom cheques are accepted as receipts under the Cheques Act 1957, but a debtor who wishes to do so may still demand a receipt. After entering the cheques in the Cash Book they are paid into the bank, the same day usually, and the bank collects payment from the debtors' banks through the clearing system.

What Happens to the Cheques We Make Out to Pay Our Creditors?

They are entered on the Cheque Book Counterfoil and are then posted off to the creditors so that they can collect payment. The Cheque Book Counterfoils are then used as the entry media for the Cash Book. The entries are made in the Bank Account on the credit side.

What Is a Receipt?

A receipt is a business document which is given to a debtor when he pays a debt; as proof of payment. It should be made out at once on receiving the payment and be either given to, or sent through the post to the debtor.

As explained in the section on cheques, the law has been changed in the United Kingdom by the Cheques Act 1957 so that receipts are not necessary now when payments are made by cheque.

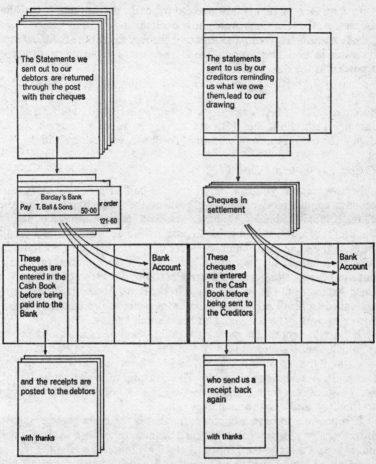

Fig. 41. Original Documents and the Cash Book

(5) Explanation of the Three-column Cash Book—Including Contra Entries

Like any other real account the Cash Account and the Bank Account are debited with increases in value and credited with decreases in value. Looking more closely at the entries (see page 80) we notice the following points:

Debit Side

January 1st—The opening balances are those that the Cash Account and Bank Account have received from the owner of the business. The folio number says J. 1 because this is coming from a Journal Entry, which is dealt with in Chapter Six.

January 2nd—When goods are sold for cash, the amount of cash increases, so that the Cash Account is debited.

January 3rd—H. Kemp has sent us a cheque, so that the bank balance increases in size. The discount we allowed him for paying promptly is recorded in the discount column.

January 4th—Robot has also sent us a cheque, which is debited in the Bank Account.

January 7th—More cash sales, as on January 2nd. The entries on January 11th, 13th, and 15th are similar to those already discussed except for the very important entry 'To Bank', on January 15th.

Contra Entries in the Cash Book

In any account you can only have one-half of a double entry. An account cannot receive and give both at the same time; but in the Three-column Cash Book we have two accounts, the Cash Account and the Bank Account. It is possible to have both a debit entry and a credit entry at the same time. The two halves of the double entry on January 15th both appear on opposite sides of the Three-column Cash Book, but not on opposite sides of the same account. The debit entry is in the Cash Account but the credit entry is in the Bank Account. Such entries are called Contra Entries, from the Latin prefix *contra* meaning 'opposite or against'. The folio column has a small 'c' in it.

The kind of contra entry we have in this specimen Cash Book is one in which cash has been taken out of the Bank Account on the credit side (the Bank Account has given) and has been put into the Cash Box (the Cash Account has received). This drawing of cash from the bank is a frequent occurrence; whenever we run short of cash we have to go to the bank and draw some money out.

It is possible to have a contra entry that is the exact reverse of this. If we sell a great many goods for cash the amount of cash in the till will increase and must be banked for safety. This involves a credit entry for the Cash Account, which is *giving*, and a debit entry for the Bank Account, which is *receiving* an increase of deposits.

Contra Entries are a very important part of the Three-column Cash Book; they can only occur because there are two accounts side by side, and it is quite untrue to say, as thoughtless students often do, that the Cash Book is the only account that can have a debit entry and a credit entry on it at the same time. *The Cash Book is not an account; it is two accounts, laid side by side for the greater convenience of the Cashier.*

Credit Side

Whenever payment is made, either in cash or by cheque, the account concerned suffers a reduction in value.

January 2nd—The Cash Account is credited with 5·00 which has been spent on postage stamps. Similar cash expenditure on wages, rates, and wages again takes place on January 7th and 15th respectively.

January 4th—R. Leverhulme, a creditor, is paid by cheque the sum of 128·75, in full settlement of a debt of 130·00. In other words he allows us discount, which is recorded in the Discount Received column. The same kind of entry occurs on January 5th, 13th, and 14th.

January 12th—On this date the proprietor withdrew 12·50 from the bank for his own use. This is rather like wages; it is money for him to support his family during the coming week. As the proprietor of a business is not entitled to wages it is called **Drawings**. It implies that he has drawn out some of the capital invested in the business. Even this is not quite a fair picture, for what he has really drawn out is some of the profit he hopes that he has made during the period in which he has been operating. If the student likes to regard Drawings as 'Drawings in expectation of profits made', then he probably has the best picture of what Drawings really is.

January 14th—F. Fish is paid a small account, not by cheque but in cash. The Cash Account has to be credited with this decrease in value.

January 15th—Here we see the other half of the Contra Entry already described.

On the same date the two accounts are balanced off and the balances are brought down. In many businesses it would be necessary to do this daily and 'cash up'—check the cash in the till and see that it agreed with the cash balances as shown on the books.

What is the Best Wording for the Details Column?

It is often a problem to a book-keeper to know what words to use in the Details Column. There is a very simple rule which solves the problem for him. Whenever a debit entry is made on an account we begin with the word 'To' and follow with **the name of the account where the other half of the double entry is to be found**. The only exception is where we write 'To Opening Balance'. All other entries show the account where the other half of the double entry may be seen, and the folio column tells us on which page to find it in the ledger. This rule even applies for the Contra Entry, since the phrase 'To Bank' tells us that the other half of the double entry is in the Bank Account and the folio number 'C' tells us it is 'contra' or 'opposite'.

Similarly, when a credit entry is made in an account we begin with the word 'By' **and the name of the account where the double entry is to be found**. On January 2nd it will be found in the Postage Account, etc.

What Happens to the Discount Columns?

The Discount columns are added up as shown in Fig. 42. They are then posted into the Discount Allowed Account and Discount Received Account. The student must pay particular attention to the posting of

Dr. (Receipts side)

Date 19.. Jan.		Details	F	Discount Allowed	Cash	Bank
Jan.	1	To Opening Balances	J.1		24·50	17,035·35
	2	" Cash Sales	L.7		42·25	
	3	" H. Kemp	L.3	1·35		52·65
	4	" R. Robot	L.11			1·63
	7	" Cash Sales	L.7		34·40	
	11	" M. Starr	L.14	0·65		17·35
	13	" North London Rail (Refund)	L.29			0·65
	15	" M. Jordan	L.42	0·75	20·00	15·35
	15	" Bank	C			
	15	" R. Peters	L.15	1·20		17·80
	15	" H. Kemp	L.11			12·24
				3·95 L.9	121·15	17,153·02
Jan.	16	To Balances	B/d		6·32	16,953·57

Cr. (Payments side)

Date 19.. Jan.		Details	F	Discount Received	Cash	Bank
	2	By Postage	L.49		5·00	
	4	" R. Leverhulme	L.27	1·25		128·75
	5	" R. Morgenthal	L.28	0·35		7·35
	7	" Wages	L.50		50·65	
	12	" Drawings	L.38			12·50
	13	" L. Amaranth	L.5	0·15		5·65
	14	" J. Jarvis	L.12	0·35		7·95
	14	" P. Heron	L.26	0·85		17·25
	14	" F. Fish	L.23		0·65	
	15	" Cash	C		17·63	
	15	" Rates	L.55		40·90	20·00
	15	" Wages	L.50		6·32	
	15	" Balances	C/d			16,953·57
				2·95 L.80	121·15	17,153·02

Fig. 42. Specimen Three-column Cash Book

these two accounts, which is dealt with in the next section. The posting of these entries is the only difficult thing in the Cash Book, and a cause of very common errors in book-keeping. The folio numbers of these accounts are written just below the totals, as shown in Fig. 42.

(6) Posting the Three-column Cash Book to the Ledger

When we removed the Cash Account and the Bank Account from the Ledger and put them into the Cash Book they did not cease to be accounts. We now have two accounts which are not in the Ledger. Only one-half of the double entries in these accounts has already been done. The other half is done when we post the Cash Book to the Ledger. Every item on the debit side of the Three-column Cash Book requires a credit entry on the credit side of some other account. Similarly every item on the credit side of the Cash Book requires a debit entry on the debit side of some other account. There is also a rather difficult little matter of the Discounts to deal with. These are the **only entries that do not change sides**, as shown in Fig. 43.

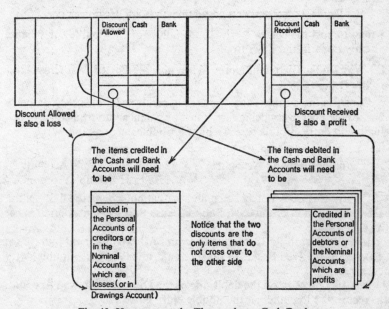

Fig. 43. How to post the Three-column Cash Book

The Ledger Accounts connected with the Three-column Cash Book shown in Fig. 38 will therefore appear as in Figs. 44 and 45. To save space only the first personal account on each side has been shown; the others will be exactly the same. Notice that it would be **absolutely**

SALES ACCOUNT   L. 7
_____
                           | 19. .
                           | Jan. 2 By Cash   C.B. 1 42·25
                           | 7   „   „   C.B. 1 34·40

H. KEMP ACCOUNT   L. 11
_____
19. . | 19. .
Jan. 2 To Balance   B/d   54·00 | Jan. 3 By Bank   C.B. 1 52·65
     12   „ Goods   S.D.B. 112·24 | 3   „ Discount   C.B. 1   1·35
(These are invented to make sense— | 15   „ Bank   12·24
a debtor must owe money before he | (Notice that both the cheque and the
pays it.) | discount are entered.)

All the other debtors' accounts will look the same as H. Kemp's Account.

DISCOUNT ALLOWED ACCOUNT   L. 79
_____
19. . |
Jan. 15 To Sundry Discounts 3·95 |
   Notice that discount is the only|
entry that does not cross over to the|
credit side. |

Fig. 44. Ledger Accounts posted from the Cash Book: debit side

wrong to post the contra entries, both halves of the double entry being
already done in the Cash Book.

(7) Why Do the Discount Figures, When they are Posted, Not Cross Over to the Other Side?

Consider the double entry for the payment by H. Kemp on January
3rd. Remember every debit entry must be balanced up by a corresponding credit entry. In this case we have a double entry as follows:

DEBIT SIDE	CREDIT SIDE
52·65 in the Bank Account	52·65 in H. Kemp's Account
(see Fig. 42)	1·35 in H. Kemp's Account

Clearly this does not balance and we cannot count the 1·35 in the
Discount column of the Cash Book because the Discount column is **not
an account.**

If we do post this 1·35 into the Discount Allowed Account it must not
go over to the credit side; to do so would unbalance the double entry
even more.

The 1·35 must go on the debit side of the Discount Allowed Account,
to record the loss and get the double entry correct.

The student should now develop a similar line of argument to explain
why the Discount Received Account does not change over sides.

(8) Bank Overdrafts

Sometimes the local bank manager will permit us to draw cheques
to a greater value than the money that we have in the bank. Such

POSTAGE ACCOUNT   L. 49

19..			
Jan. 2 To Cash	C.B. 1	5·00	

R. LEVERHULME ACCOUNT   L. 27

19..			19..		
Jan. 4 To Bank	C.B. 1	128·75	Jan. 1 By Balance	S.D.B. 1	130·00
4 ,, Discount	C.B. 1	1·25			

All the other personal accounts of creditors will appear exactly like the one above.

WAGES ACCOUNT   L. 50

19..		
Jan. 7 To Cash	C.B. 1	50·65
15 ,, ,,	C.B. 1	40·90

DRAWINGS ACCOUNT   L. 38

19..		
Jan. 12 To Bank	C.B. 1	12·50

RATES ACCOUNT   L. 55

19..		
Jan. 15 To Cash	C.B. 1	17·63

DISCOUNT RECEIVED ACCOUNT   L. 80

	19..		
	Jan. 15 By Sundry		
	Discounts	C.B. 1	2·95

(Notice that this account is the only one that does not cross over to the debit side.)

Fig. 45. Ledger Accounts posted from the Cash Book: credit side

overdrafts represent a loan to us of the outstanding balance. Of course, the bank will charge interest on the sum borrowed in this way, and if it exceeds a purely nominal amount the bank may even ask for **Collateral Security**. This is a security lying alongside the debt, which gives the bank a chance to recover its money should we not repay it when asked. Collateral Security is dealt with more fully in Chapter Six.

When a Bank Account is overdrawn in this way the account ceases to be an asset and becomes a liability. It cannot have a debit balance, like an asset account; the balance will be a credit balance.

In these circumstances our Three-column Cash Book has a debit balance on the Cash Account, but a credit balance on the Bank Account: By Bank Overdraft. It is impossible to have a credit balance on the Cash Account, since, unlike a Bank, you cannot get more out of a cash box than you put into it.

The student is now ready to try some entries in the Three-column Cash Book. The first four exercises in Set X merely ask him to record the entries in the Three-column Cash Book. The remainder ask him to post the Cash Book to the Ledger when he has finished making the entries, putting in the folio numbers as he does so.

Exercises Set X

(9) The Three-column Cash Book

No. 1. Enter the following items in the Three-column Cash Book, and balance off the book on January 5th:

19..
Jan. 1 T. Brophy commences business with cash 1,000·00; he pays 950·00 into the Bank Account from the cash box (Contra Entry); he buys goods (cash purchases) for cheque 230·00.
    2 He pays rent 45·00; pays legal costs 7·35, both by cheque.
    3 He settles a debt of 25·00 due to H. Jones by cheque, deducting discount at 5%.
    4 P. Brown pays Brophy a debt of 10·60 by cheque, less 5% discount.
    5 Pays wages 7·50 in cash; draws 12·00 for personal use (Drawings) from the cash box.

No. 2. Enter the following items in B. Jorgensen's Three-column Cash Book, and balance off at October 26th:

19..
Oct. 1 Balances in hand, cash 7·10 and bank 795·50.
    2 Paid to R. Jones by cheque 212·50, discount 10·50.
    4 Received from B. Meths cheque for 41·00. Allowed him discount 1·00.
    5 Paid water rate 3·18; paid for repairs to office safe 0·65; paid office cleaner 0·35; all these payments made in cash.
    6 Drew 10·00 from bank for office cash (Contra Entry).
    7 Paid R. Tompkins cash 2·68, received discount 0·14.
    9 Received from E. Lyne cash 15·95; gave him discount 0·55.
    10 Paid to F. Acomb cheque 360·10, discount 7·95.
    17 Received cheque from Dockerty & Sons 21·00; they were allowed discount 1·10.
    25 Paid cheque to F. Handsome 11·19.
    26 Drew cheque for wages 16·10; paid into bank from office cash 15·00; drew cheque for personal use 25·00 (Drawings).

No. 3. Enter the following in T. Charles' Cash Book:

19..

Feb. 1 T. Charles had a balance of cash in hand of 46·10 and a balance at the bank of 376·55.

2 Paid E. Cremer in cash 34·25, being allowed discount 2·95 by him.

3 Received from T. Horwell cheque for 52·10; gave him discount 3·10.

4 Paid for carriage on goods sold 1·55 in cash.

5 Drew from bank for office cash 25·00.

6 Received from J. Farmer cash 19·85; allowed him discount 1·67.

8 Paid by cheque 31·75 to Horton & Co., being allowed discount 1·75.

10 Bought goods at sale of bankrupt stock for cash 25·36 (Cash Purchases).

11 Paid M. Jenner by cheque 30·10 being allowed discount 2·10.

14 Received from M. Waters cheque 15·00.

15 Balanced off Cash Book and brought down balances.

No. 4. Enter the following in R. Jollyboy's Cash Book and balance off on May 7th:

19..

May 1 Balances: Cash Box 27·25; Bank 1,300·26; paid R. Brown (by cheque) 5·10, discount 0·50.

2 M. Slow paid by cheque 24·56; allowed him discount 0·74.

3 Paid postage in cash 1·26; rent 12·00 in cash; paid T. Brownjohn by cheque 42·10, receiving discount 2·10.

4 Drew cash from bank for office use 20·50.

5 R. Little sent us a cheque for 130·00 in full settlement of his account of 135·50.

6 Cash sales for week 125·10.

7 Bought machinery at auction for cash 95·10; paid wages in cash 12·50; paid for stamps in cash 0·95.

No. 5. L. Lewis's cash book is a Three-column Cash Book. Make the following entries in it for the first week of July:

19..

July 1 Balances in hand: cash 57·69, bank 1650·15.

2 Bought goods for re-sale for cash 42·60.

3 Drew cash from bank for office use 40·00; R. Long paid cash 5·26, allowed him discount 0·74.

4 Paid J. Roberson cheque 37·76.

5 Paid telephone account 7·25; sundry expenses 0·85; postage 0·64, all in cash.

6 Paid R. Matthias 37·10 by cheque; received discount 2·90.

7 Received from T. Jonah 3·55 cash.

8 Paid salaries 16·50 in cash; paid office cleaner 1·50 cash; paid for goods to be re-sold, by cheque 14·10; entered cash sales from till 39·17.

Balance off the Cash Book and post it to the Ledger.

No. 6. On May 1st, 19.., R. Jolson set up in business by putting 1,500·00 in his Bank Account. He then paid rent 100·00, by cheque, bought goods

22·50 by cheque, and paid electricity connexion charges 3·10 by cheque. He also drew out 20·00 for the office cash. Enter these items and also the following in his Cash Book, and post them to the Ledger:

19..

May 2 Cash sales 14·28; paid postage 0·64 cash; R. Brownjohn paid by cheque 7·10, gave him discount 0·90.

3 Paid for repairs to window 4·65 in cash; paid signwriter 2·87 in cash.

4 Johnson & Co. paid 4·47 by cheque; gave them discount 0·53.

5 R. Thomas sent a bill for 43·60; paid it by cheque; paid wages 3·15 in cash.

The following two questions, Nos. 7 and 8, require special care. They have bank overdrafts to begin with.

No. 7. On May 1st R. Lunnis has the following balances on his Cash Book: cash 27·60, bank overdraft 175·45. Enter these balances and record the following in his Cash Book. Post to the Ledger.

19..

May 1 R. Brown paid 127·56 by cheque; Lunnis allowed him discount of 1·44; bought stamps for 2·40 cash.

2 M. Jones sent a cheque for 112·56; no discount given as it was overdue.

Sent P. Robinson a cheque for 42·10; discount received 2·90; paid wages 4·50 in cash; paid for repairs 1·65 in cash.

3 R. Thompson paid 32·00 in cash; cash sales 114·50.

5 Paid carriage on parcel 0·64 in cash; paid 130·00 into the bank from the cash box.

No. 8. On May 1st John Brown had 27·50 in his cash box and was overdrawn at the bank by 270·65. Enter these opening balances in his Cash Book, enter the following items, balance off the Cash Book and post it to Ledger:

19..

May 2 Paid for postage stamps 2·60 in cash; paid for repairs 1·47 in cash; paid to R. Jones a cheque for 27·10. Jones gave discount 1·90.

3 R. Wich paid in cash 5·00 to Brown; paid travelling expenses 0·35 in cash.

4 Cash sales 87·70; paid 50·00 out of the cash box into the bank.

5 Bought goods by cheque at an auction 17·50; paid rent for month 29·50 by cheque; paid wages 10·00 in cash.

6 R. Libbey paid by cheque 97·10 in full settlement of 100·00 which he owed us.

7 Rates paid by cheque 22·65; drew for personal use from cash box 15·00.

No. 9

19..

Jan.1 C. French began business with 500·00 which he paid into his Bank Account except for 20·00 which he kept in the office cash. Open up his Three-column Cash Book, enter the starting capital and then the following entries. Balance the book off on January 5th.

2 Paid rates 5·00 cash; bought office stationery 2·64 cash; paid S. Green Ltd. 37·25 by cheque, receiving discount 1·75; paid J. Holland's Sweet Co. Ltd. 184·55 cheque, receiving discount 3·45; cash sales 10·40.

3 Paid for window cleaner 0·15 in cash; cash sales 31·16.

4 Cash sales 34·12; paid B. Irving cheque for 18·75; paid for scales at auction 2·25 cash.

5 Cash sales 62·17; wages 5·12 in cash; banked 100·00 from the cash box.

No. 10. M. Jotman starts business on April 1st putting 750·00 in the Bank Account. Open his Three-column Cash Book and record the following further entries:

19..

Apr. 1 Paid R. Spiller by cheque for lease on property 80·00; paid local County Council cheque 5·50 for licence; drew 25·00 from bank for office cash.

2 Cash purchases 4·15; cash sales 12·66.

3 Paid R. Horace 40·60 by cheque; cash sales 17·10.

4 Paid for hire of telephone equipment 2·65 by cheque.

5 Received from M. Smythe cheque 4·75, discount 0·25.

6 R. Loman paid Jotman by cheque 14·75, discount 0·75.

7 Sent Eastern Electricity Board by cheque 5·00.

8 Paid wages 14·26 cash; repairs 18·50 cash.

9 Balance off the Cash Book and bring down the balances.

(10) A Page to Test You on the Three-column Cash Book

Cover the page with a sheet of paper, then read one question at a time.

Answer	Question
—	1. Why do we take the Cash Account and the Bank Account out of the Ledger?
1. (*a*) Because they are busy accounts; (*b*) because they are vulnerable.	2. What do we call the theft of money by a trusted employee?
2. Embezzlement.	3. What is the missing money called?
3. A Defalcation.	4. What insurance policies cover this risk?
4. Fidelity Bonds.	5. Why are there three columns on each side of the Three-column Cash Book?
5. (*a*) One for the Cash Account; (*b*) one for the Bank Account; (*c*) one for the Discount column.	6. Do the Discount columns form an account?
6. No. They are only Memorandum columns.	7. What type of accounts are the Cash Account and Bank Account?
7. They are both real accounts.	8. What is the rule for these accounts?
8. (*a*) Debit increases in value; (*b*) credit decreases in value.	9. What is a Contra Entry in the Cash Book?
9. A Contra Entry is one where both the debit and credit entries appear on the page at once, one in the Cash Account and one in the Bank Account.	10. Can a Contra Entry like this appear anywhere else in the ledger?
10. No—because this is the only place where two accounts are written side by side.	11. How do we post the Cash Book to the Ledger?
11. (*a*) Everything on the debit side of the Cash Account and Bank Account is posted to the credit side of an account in the Ledger; (*b*) everything on the credit side of the Cash Account and Bank Account is posted over to the debit side of the Ledger.	12. Is there anything that does not change sides?
12. Yes. The totals of the Discount Allowed column and Discount Received column do not change sides.	

(11) A Page to Test You on Statements and Receipts

Answer	Question
—	1. What is a Statement?
1. A business document which is sent out at the end of the month to all our debtors.	2. What does it tell them?
2. How much they owe us altogether on the last day of the month.	3. What words are used on it?
3. 'To A/c Rendered.'	4. What does the debtor do when he receives the statement?
4. (1) He checks it; (2) he deducts Cash Discount if he is paying it promptly, and if the terms of sale allow it; (3) he pays it, usually by cheque returning the statement with the cheque.	5. How does a Mechanized Statement differ from an Ordinary Statement written out by the Ledger Clerk at the end of the month?
5. The Mechanized Statement is made out at the same time as the Ledger Account so that it is an exact copy of the Ledger Account and shows all the debits and credits on the Account, giving the final balance owing to the debtor.	6. What happens when the cheque and the statement are returned to the creditor?
6. (1) The cheque is entered in his Cash Book; (2) the statement is receipted, if a receipt is required, and posted back to the debtor.	7. Why may a receipt not be needed?
7. Because under the Cheques Act, 1957, a cheque itself is a receipt.	8. What is a receipt?
8. A legal proof of payment.	9. What form does it take?
9. A document on which is written 'received with thanks', followed by the amount, and the signature of the creditor.	

(12) A Page to Test You on Discounts

Answer	Question
—	1. What are the three kinds of Discount?
1. Cash Discount, Settlement Discount and Trade Discount.	2. What are Cash Discount and Settlement Discount.
2. Amounts deducted from a purchase or a statement paid promptly.	3. When should a debtor pay his debts?
3. When the period of credit expires, which is usually at the end of the month.	4. What do we call it if a debtor does not pay when he should?
4. A breach of 'Good Faith'.	5. What are the usual rates of discount?
5. 2½% and 5%.	6. Suppose you owe 50·00 and receive a statement that allows 5% discount. What do you do?
6. Write on the statement below the total figure = 50·00 Less 5% Cash Discount = 2·50 Cheque enclosed 47·50 and send a cheque for 47·50.	7. What do 'Terms Cash Net' or 'Terms Strictly Nett' mean?
7. They mean that no Cash Discount is allowed.	8. What is Trade Discount?
8. It is a reduction in the catalogue price of a branded good to enable the retailer to make a profit when he sells at this catalogue price.	9. What are the usual rates of Trade Discount?
9. 10–45% are quite common.	10. When is the rate of Trade Discount small?
10. When the turnover is rapid, i.e. chocolates, cigarettes.	11. When is it large?
11. When the items are slow-moving, i.e. furniture.	12. Why is it large with these items?
12. To enable the retailer to cover overhead expenses of a longer period.	13. Who writes the Trade Discount on the invoice?
13. The supplier before he sends it out.	14. Does cash discount go in the books?
14. Yes. It is entered in the Cash Book and posted to the Ledger.	15. Does Trade Discount go in the books?
15. It is entered in the Day Book but is *never* posted to the Ledger.	16. Is there a Trade Discount Account?
16. No. It never goes in the Ledger.	

CHAPTER SIX

THE JOURNAL PROPER

(1) Introduction

We have now dealt with most of the really common transactions in business: the purchases, sales and return of goods, and the payment and receipt of cash. We now turn to a consideration of some of the less common items which occur, not every day, but a few times a year only. These items are usually dealt with through the **Journal Proper**, a Day Book which has been in use since the Middle Ages.

The ruling of this Day Book is exactly the same as the rulings we have already seen in the four subsidiary books discussed in Chapter Four, but the columns are used in a different way.

There are about nine chief types of entry that are made through the Journal Proper, but as this is the *residual* Day Book, that is, the only Day Book left to accommodate all other items, the range of entries made through the Journal is very great indeed. The nine commonest items are:

(*a*) Opening entries.
(*b*) Closing entries.
(*c*) Purchase of assets.
(*d*) Depreciation of assets.
(*e*) Sale of worn-out or obsolete assets.
(*f*) Bad Debts entries.
(*g*) Correction of errors.
(*h*) Dishonoured cheques.
(*i*) Bank loans, interest and charges.

Some other entries that would be passed through the Journal Proper are the issue of shares and debentures, goodwill valuations, dissolution of partnership entries, and some adjustments for Final Accounts.

(2) Journal Proper Paper

19.. Date	Account to be Debited 　　　To account to be Credited Being, etc.	Dr.	F F	20·55	20·55

Fig. 46. Paper for Journal Entries

Explanation

(*a*) The paper for the Journal Proper is exactly the same as the paper used for the specialized Day Books (see Chapter Four, page 42), but it is now used in a different way. Instead of the first column being just an adding-up column for use where there are several items on an invoice or credit note, the *two columns are equally important. The first column is the **debit** column and the second column is the **credit** column.*

(*b*) The date is put in once on each Journal Entry.

(*c*) The account that is to be debited is named at the beginning of the line; the letters 'Dr.' come at the end of the line, and the money value is inserted in the first column.

(*d*) On the next line we indent a little way, write the word 'To' followed by the name of the account to be credited, and enter the money value in the second money column. You may think it is really rather silly to put 'To' when it would be more sensible to put 'By', but this is another ancient custom which has been handed down from the Middle Ages. Students who want to put 'By' may do so, but some examiners might not like it.

(*e*) Lastly we write a short **narration**—an explanation of the entry. A narration accompanies every Journal Entry because they are all so different from one another. Usually the narration begins with the word 'Being . . .' and explains exactly what has been done.

(*f*) Finally we post the Journal Entry to the Ledger, debiting the account that has to be debited and crediting the account that has to be credited. We put the folio numbers in and rule off across the wording column.

(*g*) Except for Opening Journal Entries, which are rather special, Journal Entries are *not* added up, though usually each page is totted up in the Journal just to see that the debits and credits do balance.

Here is a typical Journal Entry:

19.. Jan. 7	Motor Vehicles Account Dr. To Rex Garages Ltd. Being a Morris Mini XYZ127 pur- chased on this date on credit	L. 7 L. 19	500·50	500·50

Fig. 47. A Typical Journal Entry

It so happens that this is the purchase of an asset, a motor vehicle. We will now look at the nine common types of Journal Entry.

(3) Journal Entries No. 1—The Opening Journal Entry

When business first begins, the owner of the business puts some money into the firm. This is his capital and usually it is in the form of a current account balance in the bank.

Supposing Tom Brown sets up in business on July 1st with a capital of 50·00 in the cash box and 950·00 in the bank. The Cash and Bank Accounts will receive value and must be debited. The Capital Account must be credited since it is the capitalist (or owner of the capital) who has given value. The cash and bank moneys are assets of the business; things the business owns. The capital is a liability of the business, since the business owes it to the owner of the business. Many students think that capital is an asset, but it is *not*; it is a *liability* of the business.

Here is the opening Journal Entry for Tom Brown. Notice that as this is an Opening Journal Entry, and marks a special point in the existence of the business, we do add it up and put a clear currency sign. I have put the £ sign but readers in other countries will use their own signs of course.

The usual narration for an opening Journal Entry is the one shown here.

| 19.. July 1 | Cash
Bank
To Capital | Dr.
,, | C.B. 1
C.B. 1 | 50·00
950·00 | 1,000·00 |
| | Being assets and liabilities at this date | £ | 1,000·00 | 1,000·00 |

Fig. 48. A simple Opening Journal Entry

We also may record an opening entry on the first day of every year if we wish, to bring the record of the owner's assets up to date. In the rather artificial world of a book-keeping textbook, where we are asking students to pretend that an exercise represents a real-life business, we may have to open up each exercise as if a new business was beginning. You will be expected to do this in Chapter Eight, which is about book-keeping to the Trial Balance.

This kind of opening entry has rather more accounts to be opened because we usually assume that the business has been in existence for some time. The example given below, and illustrated in Fig. 49, has nine accounts to be opened.

Example: John Brown is a master carpenter, and on January 1st his assets and liabilities are as follows: Cash 50·00; Bank balance 1,320·00; Tools and equipment 400·00; Premises 1,200·00; Debtors, A. Pearce 45·00, B. Lebon 27·55; he owes 36·50 to Wood Suppliers Ltd., and

1,000·00 to the Master Builders' Building Society. Do the opening Journal Entry.

Rough Work: Make a list of all the assets and liabilities:

Assets		Liabilities	
Cash	50·00	Wood Suppliers Ltd.	36·50
Bank	1,320·00	Mortgage	1,000·00
Tools, etc.	400·00	Capital	?
Premises	1,200·00		
A. Pearce	45·00		
B. Lebon	27·55		

The assets and liabilities are the Dr. items and the Cr. items for the Journal Entry. They must be equal, but clearly they are not. This is because we have been left to work out the capital. The capital is practically always a liability; if you ever get a debit balance on capital account it is called a 'deficiency' and means that the trader concerned is insolvent, and will soon be out of business. In this case the capital works out as 2,006·05.

The Journal Entry looks like this:

19.. Jan. 1					
	Cash Account	Dr.	C.B. 1	50·00	
	Bank Account	„	C.B. 1	1,320·00	
	Tools and Equipment Account	„	L. 2	400·00	
	Premises Account	„	L. 2	1,200·00	
	A. Pearce	„	L. 3	45·00	
	B. Lebon	„	L. 4	27·55	
	To Wood Suppliers Ltd.		L. 5		36·50
	„ Mortgage		L. 6		1,000·00
	„ Capital		L. 7		2,006·05
	Being assets and liabilities at this date			3,042·55	3,042·55

Fig. 49. A more difficult Opening Journal Entry

In the exercises which follow, you are asked to draw up the opening Journal Entries and then to post them to the Cash Book and the Ledger. Remember that the accounts are the really important records, and in order to open the accounts in a formal way we need the opening Journal Entry.

(4) Opening Journal Entries

No. 1. Tom Cortes starts up in business as a jobbing carpenter on January 1st. He has 50·00 which he puts into a Bank Account, his kit of tools worth 85·00, and general equipment valued at 25·00. Work out the capital he has invested in his business; do the opening Journal Entry and post it to the Cash Book and the Ledger.

No. 2. Elmer Ridge sets up in business as a music dealer, with the following assets: Cash 100·00; Cash at bank 2,500·00; Stocks of instruments 480·00; Records 185·00; Musical manuscripts 65·00; Furniture and fittings 80·00. Work out the total capital he has invested in the business and do the opening Journal Entry on May 1st. Post it to the Cash Book and the Ledger.

No. 3. Arthur Bryants opens up in business as a Turf Accountant with the following assets and liabilities: Cash 400·00; Bank moneys 5,000·00; Furniture and fittings 280·00; Premises 1,400·00. He has two debtors, T. Train and B. Bridges, for 5·00 and 40·00 respectively, and he also owes M. Tanner 180·00 for equipment supplied. Calculate the total capital he has invested in the venture, do the opening Journal Entry, and post to the Ledger and Three-column Cash Book. The date is August 1st.

No. 4. M. Price is in business as a retail tobacconist. On January 1st he has assets and liabilities as follows: Cash 50·00; Cash at bank 180·00; Stocks 760·00; Premises 1,400·00; Debtors, R. Hood 27·10 and L. John 14·60; Creditors, Universal Tobacco Co. Ltd. 294·10. Richmond Tobacco Co. Ltd. 180·00; Bank loan 150·00. Work out his total capital and do the opening Journal Entry. Post it to the Cash Book and the Ledger.

No. 5. M. Longshore is in business as a fish merchant, with the following assets and liabilities: Herring Drifter 27,000·00; Nets 1,000·00; Premises 6,800·00; Refrigerators 4,300·00; Stores of spare parts for ship and machinery 840·00; Furniture and fittings 280·00; he has Cash 24·10; Bank moneys 13,288·50; and debtors as follows: L. Jones 5·00, Ice Packers Ltd. 486·10, and R. Billingsgate 84·12. He has creditors, M. Ramsey 248·00 and L. Liverpool 496·66. Work out the total capital invested; do the opening Journal Entries and post to the Cash Book and the Ledger.

No. 6. M. Morgan is in business as Scrap Partners Co. in association with his partner A. Sleepy. The assets are: Premises 2,000·00; Land 4,600·00; Cash 30·00; Bank balance 1,650·00; Furniture 384·00; Stocks 2,960·00; he has debtors, A. Woollenworker 496·00 and R. Ironclad 792·00. There is one liability, M. Mortgagor to whom they owe 4,000·00. A. Sleepy's capital is 3,000·00. Calculate M. Morgan's capital and do the opening Journal Entry and the postings to the Cash Book and Ledger.

No. 7. R. Lummer is in business as a wholesale grocer, and on January 1st he has assets and liabilities as follows: Cash 40·00; Cash at bank 2,760·00; Stock 27,500·00; Furniture and fittings 4,500·00; Bank loan 5,000·00; Creditors, R. Jorgen 26·00, M. Lowe 550·00, and R. Shave 775·26; Debtors, M. Smith 19·25, R. Lowery 49·70, and M. Tinkel 276·50. Work out the capital and do the opening Journal Entry.

No. 8. B. Irving is in business as a ladies' dressmaker and on March 1st has the following assets and liabilities: Cash 270·00; Cash at bank 4,300·00; Stock 5,800·00; Machines and equipment 2,106·00; Furniture and fittings 840·00; Debtors, B. Morgan 36·70, T. Slow 72·60, and M. Jordan 50·68; Creditors, T. Young 505·70 and M. Smith 65·00; Mortgage on property 600·00. Work out the capital and do the opening Journal Entry.

No. 9. A. Jordan and C. French are in partnership equally as booksellers. They have the following assets and liabilities on April 1st: Cash 270·00; Cash at bank 4,300·00; Stock 4,700·00; Materials 230·00; Office equipment 280·00; Furniture and fittings 756·00; Premises 3,400·00; Investments 450·00; Creditors, 270·00 owing to R. Keen, and 380·00 owing to B. Bunyan; Debtors 405·00 owing by B. Trotman, and 660·00 owing by M. Wrenn. Work out the capital and do the opening Journal Entries.

No. 10. Abel Patterson was in business on his own account, and his financial position on August 1st was as follows: Cash in hand 60·00; Cash at bank 580·00; Stock 500·00; Sundry debtors, M. Larkin 50·00 and P. Holm 80·00; Furniture 400·00; Sundry Creditors, R. Romer 140·00 and F. Cruncher 140·00. Work out his capital and do the opening Journal Entry.

(5) Journal Entries No. 2—Closing Entries

Opening Entries are made when a business is started, and are repeated once a year on the first day of the year. Closing Entries are made at the end of a financial year, when the losses and profits of a business are set against one another, and the success or otherwise of the year's activities is determined. Closing Entries are dealt with in Chapter Seventeen, page 205.

(6) Journal Entries No. 3—Purchases of Assets

When we purchase anything we receive an invoice from the seller. Invoices can be divided into three types:

(*a*) Invoices dealing with 'goods' for resale—these are entered in the Purchases Day Book.

(*b*) Invoices dealing with expense items, like stationery, advertising, materials, motor vehicle repairs, etc. These are entered in the Expenses Day Book (see Chapter Four, page 47).

(*c*) Invoices dealing with the purchase of assets. These are the subject of Journal Entries.

Example 1. On January 15th we bought from Typebetta Ltd.:

1 new electric book-keeping machine value 520.00, on credit, Ref. No. of machine 12708/5/CD.

The rules for purchasing an asset are:

(*a*) **Always debit the Asset Account.**

(*b*) **Always credit** (i) *the Cash Account* if you paid cash, (ii) *the Bank Account* if you paid by cheque, (iii) *the Creditor* if you bought on credit.

In our example we bought on credit. The Journal Entry therefore looks like this:

19..
 Jan. 15
	Office Machinery Account Dr.
	     To Typebetta Ltd.
	 Being the purchase of electric book-
	     keeping machine.
	 Ref. 12708/5/CD at this date
		L. 27
		 L. 38
			520·00	J. 5
				 520·00

Fig. 50. The Purchase of an Asset

Notice that this Journal Entry has not been added up. Also notice that the recording of reference numbers is very desirable on all office equipment, which is easily stolen and finds a ready market. Type-writers, for instance, should always be recorded officially on the books where the reference numbers are available for police purposes in the event of a burglary.

When posted to the Ledger Accounts these will appear as follows:

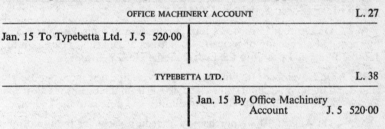

OFFICE MACHINERY ACCOUNT   L. 27

Jan. 15 To Typebetta Ltd.   J. 5   520·00

TYPEBETTA LTD.   L. 38

Jan. 15 By Office Machinery
             Account   J. 5   520·00

Fig. 51. Ledger Accounts for the purchase of an asset

Example 2. On January 16th we attended a sale of bankrupt's effects and purchased the following, paying by cheque:

2 Filing Cabinets (Ref. Nos. 1786/5 and 1786/6), 12·00 the pair; 1 Motor Vehicle (XZ 1274), 135·50; goods for resale 45·50.

Clearly the Journal Entry here will involve a number of accounts. Some of the items purchased are assets and some are our normal goods for resale. As we have paid by cheque there is no creditor, but the credit entry will be in the Cash Book, a credit to Bank Account.

The Journal Entry will now appear like this:

19..
 Jan. 16
	Office Equipment Account Dr.
	 Motor Vehicle Account ,,
	 Purchases Account ,,
	     To Bank Account
	 Being assets and goods for resale
	    purchased at bankrupt's sale. Fil-
	    ing Cabinets Ref. Nos. 1786/5 and
	    1786/6. Motor Vehicle XZ 1274.
		L. 1
		 L. 2
		 L. 3
		 C.B. 1
			12·00
			 135·50
			 45·50
				193·00

Fig. 52. Assets bought for Cash

Some book-keepers consider there is no real need to journalize entries which are cash transactions since the Cash Book is the appropriate book of original entry. It is true that many firms 'cut corners' and leave out the occasional journal entry, but in doing so, useful details may be left out. For instance, in Fig. 52 we have recorded the reference numbers of the filing cabinets; these may prove useful one day. In book-keeping you may cut as many corners as you like when you are really confident you know what you are doing, but when studying at an elementary level it is best to keep to the rules.

EXERCISES SET XII

(7) Purchases of Assets

No. 1. On July 14th Thomas & Co. Ltd. purchased a new typewriter for cash from Reditype Ltd. for 75·00, paid in notes. Do the Journal Entry and post it to the Ledger. Serial No. 17065/2.

No. 2. On October 15th Mears Ltd. purchased a new machine for 165·00 by cheque at an auction of property involved in a bankruptcy case. Do the Journal Entry and post it to the Ledger. Serial No. 2599/4a/65.

No. 3. On November 11th your firm buys on credit a new piece of property (Land and Building Account) valued at 2,800·00 from the Loamshire Property Development Trust Ltd. Do the Journal Entry and post it to the Ledger.

No. 4. On August 1st we purchased on credit a yacht for the use of our sports club members for 280·00 from Seaway Ltd. Do the Journal Entry and post it to the Ledger. You will have to decide on a suitable name for the Asset Account.

No. 5. On February 24th we purchased camping equipment for the Staff Recreational Club. The equipment, value 220·50, was purchased on credit from Tuff Hessian Supplies Ltd. Do the Journal Entry and post to the Ledger.

No. 6. On July 5th we purchased a new showcase, Serial No. 516c, from Shopfitters Ltd. for 60·00 on credit. Do the Journal Entry and post to the Ledger.

No. 7. On August 24th at a bankruptcy sale, we purchased for cash goods value as follows: Weighing machine 40·00; Shelving and cupboards 25·00; goods for resale (purchases) 220·00; Motor vehicle 120·00. Do the Journal Entry and post to the Ledger. (Clearly there will be several Accounts to be debited in this exercise.)

No. 8. On August 1st K. Khamis sets up in business. Next day he purchases on credit the following from Business Supplies Ltd.: 1 office desk 28·50; 2 filing cabinets at 19·80 each; 1 electric typewriter, Serial No. 72/69310, 97·50; and a letter-folding machine 64·25.

These items are to be kept on his books in two Asset Accounts only. Do the Journal Entry for the purchases.

No. 9. Dry Gulch Rural District Council purchases equipment as follows: Irrigation pipe layer 1,000·00; Trench cutter 1,850·00; Water bulk transport truck 1,450·00; 2 electric pumps at 850·00 each. The Council's rule is that equipment whose initial cost is 1,000·00 or more will be recorded in a separate Asset Account of its own. Equipment costing less than this will be recorded in the General Equipment Account. The whole of these purchases were paid for by cheque on the day of delivery, August 11th, when the Journal Entry was made. Make this Journal Entry.

No. 10. John Lowsan recently started in business with capital of 10,000·00 bequeathed to him by a rich aunt. On February 1st he purchased the following, paying by cheque: Plant and machinery 2,200·00; Motor vehicle 450·00; Stock for resale 800·00; Furniture 280·00. Make the Journal Entry.

(8) Journal Entries No. 4—Depreciation of Assets

A full account of the different methods of Depreciation is dealt with in Chapter Fourteen, but we will here take a preliminary look at Depreciation.

What is Depreciation?

Depreciation is a reduction in the book value of an asset due to fair wear and tear. For instance, a new motor-car bought this year may be worth 1,000·00. By next year it will be worth less than this, about 800·00, and in ten years' time it will be ready for the scrap heap. We cannot keep the motor-car on our books valued at 1,000·00 down the years. Every year we depreciate it by a fair amount. Just how much we deduct from its value depends on our estimate of its fall in value, but at best it can only be a guess. Here is such an account, showing the reduction for depreciation over the years:

MOTOR VEHICLE ACCOUNT   L. 25

19..			19..		
Jan. 1	To New Vehicle	1,000·00	Dec. 31	By Depreciation	200·00
			31	„ Balance	800·00
		1,000·00			1,000·00
19..			19..		
Jan. 1	To Balance	800·00	Dec. 31	By Depreciation	200·00
			31	„ Balance	600·00
		800·00			800·00
19..			19..		
Jan. 1	To Balance	600·00	Dec. 31	By Depreciation	200·00
				„ Balance	400·00
		600·00			600·00
19..					
Jan. 1	To balance	400·00			

Fig 53. The depreciation of an Asset over the years

Below is the type of Journal Entry which would authorize the reduction in value.

19.. Dec. 31	Depreciation Account Dr. To Motor Vehicles Being the writing off of fair wear and tear at this date.	L. 73 L. 25	200·00	200·00

Fig. 54. A Depreciation Journal Entry

The amount transferred to Depreciation Account would be written off the profits at the end of the year. The Depreciation Account is one of those Nominal Accounts where losses are collected together preparatory to being written off.

DEPRECIATION ACCOUNT   L. 73

Dec. 31 To Motor Vehicles J.17 200·00	19.. Dec. 31 By transfer to Profit
31 „ Furniture and Fittings J.18 50·00	and Loss J.24 650·00
31 „ Plant and Machinery J.21 400·00	
650·00	650·00

Fig. 55. Collecting Losses together before writing them off

EXERCISES SET XIII

(9) Depreciation of Assets

No. 1. Show the Journal Entry required when the Motor Vehicles Account is depreciated by 200·00. Show also the Ledger Accounts, assuming that the motor vehicle was new on January 1st, cost 1,000·00, and today's date is December 31st, the same year.

No. 2. My furniture and fittings are valued at 880·00, of which 600·00 is furniture. Do the Journal Entry for depreciation at 20 per cent on furniture and 10 per cent on fittings. Post to the Ledger.

No. 3. Plant and Machinery for Cross Ltd. is valued at 3,800·00 at June 30th. At December 31st they depreciate it by 10 per cent per annum. (Careful, it's only a half-year.) Show the Journal Entry and both Ledger Accounts.

No. 4. Michael Saunders is a bookmaker, and his electronic computer was valued at 30,000·00 on January 1st. On December 31st of that year he depreciates it by 10 per cent, and on December 31st of the next year he depreciates it by a further 10 per cent on the original valuation. Show the Computer Account on the three dates named, bringing down the balance at the end of each year.

No. 5. A farmer depreciates his equipment as follows: Tractors 20 per cent; Ploughs, harrows, and other tools 10 per cent; Fencing and gates 25 per cent; Barns 10 per cent; Buildings 5 per cent. Show the Journal Entry for a year's depreciation on Tractors 1,500·00; Ploughs, etc. 390·00; Fencing, etc. 500·00; Barns 2,800·00; Buildings 15,000·00.

No. 6. Mixitwell Cement Co. depreciates its huge mixing machines as follows: for the first two years at 25 per cent of cost; for the next two years at 10 per cent of cost; for all further years 5 per cent of cost. Show the Journal Entry for depreciation on their machines for the present year. They are as follows:

Machine No. 7	Cost 7,000·00 this year.
„ No. 6	„ 5,000·00 last year.
„ No. 5	„ 8,000·00 bought three years ago.
„ Nos. 1, 2, 3, 4	„ 4,000·00 each—all eight years old.

More advanced questions on Depreciation appear at the end of Chapter Fourteen.

(10) Journal Entries No. 5—The Sale of Worn-out Assets

When most fixed assets get old they lose their value, for two reasons:

(*a*) Repairs get more frequent, so that both the cost of the repairs, and the loss of production and convenience while the machine is idle, increase.

(*b*) The machine becomes obsolete, that is, newer ideas which are an improvement on the machine we are using make it uneconomical to continue with the old one.

When this happens we usually sell the old machine and buy an up-to-date model. Very often we get a 'trade-in' allowance for the old model from the supplier of the new one.

What this means in terms of book-keeping depends upon the value of the old asset on the books, and its value when we actually sell it. There are three possibilities:

(*a*) The book value may be exactly the same as the real value on the market.

(*b*) The book value may be excessive, the market value is less than the book value.

(*c*) The book value may be too small—the real value on the market is greater than we expected.

Let us consider these cases, but remember that all three can only result from our *guesses* about depreciation. If we guess accurately, situation (*a*) will face us; if we guess poorly, either situation (*b*) or (*c*) will apply.

Example 1. The sale of a worn-out asset at its book value.

We have on our books a machine valued at 100·00. We sell it on May 31st for exactly 100·00 in cash. Clearly the asset will disappear from our books and be replaced by an exactly equal asset, cash.

The Journal Entry will be as follows:

19.. May 31	Cash Account Dr. To Machinery Account Being sale of machine 7/71656/d at this date.	C.B. 9 L. 17	100·00	100·00

Fig. 56. Selling Machinery at Book Value

When posted to the credit side of the Machinery Account this entry
will remove the 100·00 machine from the books, replacing it with the
cash debited to Cash Account.

Example 2. The sale of a worn-out asset for less than its book value.

Imagine that we are disposing of the same machine but find we can
only get 60·00 for it. This means we have guessed the depreciation
wrongly over the years, which is hardly surprising. Remember that
depreciation is, at best, an informed guess.

Clearly we shall only have 60·00 cash to replace 100·00-worth of
machine, but we must write off the total book value of the machine.
We cannot leave 40·00 of a non-existent machine on the books. Whatever we get for our worn-out machine the rule is:

Always credit the Asset Account with the book value of the old asset

The Journal Entry will therefore appear as follows:

19.. May 31	Cash Account Dr Depreciation Account „ To Machinery Account Being sale of machine 7/71656/d at a loss on its book value.	C.B. 9 L. 21 L. 17	60·00 40·00	100·00

Fig. 57. Selling Machinery at less than its Book Value

Notice that the balance of 40·00 is simply treated as further depreciation that needs to be written off as a loss to Depreciation Account.

Example 3. The sale of a worn-out asset at more than its book value.

The third possibility is that the asset realizes more than its book value.
When this happens we have clearly been guessing too great a figure for
depreciation. The machine has not depreciated as much as we expected.
In real life scrap values vary so much with the world political situation
that no one can be blamed for guessing inaccurately. A machine
containing valuable metal may fetch a top price, or a rock-bottom price,
according to what is happening in the economic world.

Imagine that the machine in Example 1 fetches 170·00 when sold for scrap. Clearly this time a new asset Cash, value 170·00, will replace the old asset, value 100·00. We cannot take more than 100·00 off the machinery account; to do so would be to remove part of some other machine's value as well. The rule is the same: deduct the book value of the old machine from the Machinery Account. The rest will have to be taken to Depreciation Account as a **profit**. You might almost be tempted to call it an *appreciation*, but it is not really an appreciation (increase in value); it is simply a correction of an over-depreciation in years gone by. It will reduce the amount of total depreciation that needs to be written off at the end of the year.

The Journal Entry will look like this:

19..					
May 31	Cash Account Dr.	C.B. 9	170·00		
	To Machinery Account	L. 17		100·00	
	,, Depreciation Account	L. 21		70·00	
	Being sale of machine 7/71656/d at a figure in excess of its book value.				

Fig. 58. Selling a machine at more than Book Value

While Depreciation Account will perhaps look like this:

DEPRECIATION ACCOUNT   L. 21

19..				19..			
Dec. 31	To Motor Vehicles	J. 4	600·00	May 31	By Cash Account	J. 7	70·00
31	,, Furniture and Fittings	J. 5	42·50	Dec. 31	,, Transfer to Profit and Loss Account	J. 7	738·00
31	,, Machinery	J. 6	165·50				
			808·00				808·00

Fig. 59. Taking back into Depreciation Account the Profit on an old Machine.

The student should now try the following exercises on the sale of worn-out assets.

EXERCISES SET XIV

(11) The Sale of Worn-out Assets

No. 1. On May 20th we sell a typewriter valued on the books at 10·00 for exactly that sum in cash. Do the Journal Entry.

No. 2. On May 21st we sell a machine valued on the books at 100·00 to R. Dealer, who will pay for it at the end of the month. Do the Journal Entry. Price to R. Dealer is 100·00.

No. 3. On May 22nd we sell a motor vehicle valued on the books at 250·00 for exactly that sum to A. Garagerunner. A. Garagerunner pays by cheque. Do the Journal Entry.

No. 4. On May 23rd we sell a typewriter valued on the books at 4·00 for 2·50 to Anne Employee, who pays in cash. The rest is treated as Depreciation. Do the Journal Entry.

No. 5. On July 27th we sell a combine harvester valued on the books at 810·00 for 800·00 to A. Farmer. He pays later. Do the Journal Entry.

No. 6. On July 30th we sell a chicken brooder valued at 12·50 for 10·50 to R. Birdraiser, who pays by cheque. Do the Journal Entry.

No. 7. On August 4th R. Smith purchases on credit from us a machine valued on our books at 660·00 for 750·00. Do the Journal Entry.

No. 8. On August 31st L. Lebon purchases from us a tool shed, valued on our books at 8·00, for 12·00 cash. Do the Journal Entry.

No. 9. On May 7th R. Cooper buys from us on credit a motor vehicle, valued at 50·00, for 90·00. Do the Journal Entry.

No. 10. On December 12th we sell T. Thomas a pile-driver valued at 380·00, for cash 300·00, and 2 office machines valued at 100·00 each. Do the Journal Entry, treating the profit as regained depreciation.

No. 11. R. Lowson asks us to exchange a motor vehicle valued at 50·00 on our books for a supply of spare tyres valued at 60·00 and 15·00 in cash. Show the Journal Entry on December 12th.

(12) Journal Entries No. 6—Simple Bad Debts

When a debtor owes us money and is unable to pay there is very little point in keeping the debt on our books as if he will be paying us very soon. We must either take steps to force him to pay, or recognize the fact that we have lost our money.

If we decide to take legal action through the Courts to force payment of the debt, the result will eventually be a Receiving Order by the Court, which puts the debtor in the hands of the Official Receiver. This government official will then seize the debtor's assets and sell them to pay the debts. If the sale of the debtor's assets realizes sufficient to pay the debts the debtor will not be made a **bankrupt**, but usually the proceeds are insufficient and bankruptcy follows. The whole affair is conducted under carefully devised rules, the aim of which is to set the debtor free from his burden of debts so that he may start life anew, but with certain safeguards that will prevent him from getting into the same muddle again.

A visit to the Bankruptcy Court in your own area is the best way of gaining experience of the law's attitude to the bankrupt. Overseas readers should check the law of their own countries on these matters.

Sometimes we do not bother to have a debtor bankrupted, either out of pity, or because it would be 'throwing good money after bad', or because adverse criticism in Court may affect our own goodwill with the public. In such cases we will merely write off the money owing as a **Bad Debt**.

Three possible situations arise:

(*a*) A debt that is wholly bad.
(*b*) A debt that is partially bad.
(*c*) A bad debt recovered, with interest.

Example 1. A debt that is wholly bad.

On March 13th we hear that A. Debtor who owes 25·00 has died in tragic circumstances, leaving a widow and five children. We decide to write off the debt as a loss, to Bad Debts Account.

The Journal Entry would appear as follows:

| 19..
Mar. 13 | Bad Debts Account   Dr.
   To A. Debtor
Being bad debt written off at this
   date—debtor killed in bank raid | L. 12
L. 15 | 25·00 | 25·00 |

Fig. 60 (*a*). A Debt that is Wholly Bad

A. DEBTOR (before death)   L. 15

| 19..
Mar. 18 To Balance | B/d | 25·00 | | |

A. DEBTOR (after writing off debt)   L. 15

| 19..
Mar. 1 To Balance | B/d | 25·00 | 19..
Mar. 13 By Bad Debt | J. 1 | 25·00 |

BAD DEBTS ACCOUNT   L. 12

| 19..
Mar. 13 To A. Debtor | J. 1 | 25·00 | | |

Fig. 60 (*b*). Clearing a Debtor's Account

Note that the debit item on the Debtor's Account—when it is cleared —is replaced by a debit item on a Loss Account, the Bad Debts Account.

Usually we also take the precaution of writing clearly in *red ink* across the Debtor's Account

Fig. 61. A Warning Sign on a Bad Debtor's Account

This warns any member of staff who may receive inquiries about the debtor, or even requests for further supplies, that we no longer wish to deal with him.

Example 2. A bad debt that is partially bad.

Imagine the same debt as before, but this time A. Debtor has not died in tragic circumstances, he is simply a bad payer. We do not feel any sympathy at all for this type of debtor, and after doing our best to collect the money we take action through the Courts. The action eventually results in the Official Receiver taking over the debtor's assets. We are not being vindictive in taking this action; if a debtor cannot live by the normal standards of honourable business, then he has no right to be in business at all. For the good of the community we should take such action as will prevent him buying on credit in future. If he is not a rogue but just a fool, then for his own good we should put him out of business before he gets even deeper in debt.

The result of the Official Receiver's activities will be that such sums of money as can be collected by the sale of the debtor's effects are collected, and made available to the creditors. The amount available after paying the Receiver's expenses is shared among the creditors as a certain fraction in the 1·00. Suppose that the Receiver is able to pay 30 pence in the £1, or cents in the Dollar or Rand, we have a debt of 25·00. We shall therefore receive

$$25 \times 0.30 = 7.50$$

the rest of the debt having to be written off as bad.

The Journal Entry will appear as follows:

19.. July 15					
	Bank Account	Dr.	C.B. 7	7·50	
	Bad Debts Account	„	L. 12	17·50	
	To A. Debtor		L. 15		25·00
	Being the writing off of a bad debt on receiving cheque from Official Receiver 0·30 in the 1·00				

Fig. 62. A Debt that is Partially Bad

Note that the date is much later than the actual debt; legal processes always take a considerable time. In this case we would certainly write 'Bad Debtor' clearly across the face of the account.

Example 3. A bad debt recovered.

The Bankruptcy Laws set a man free from debt so that he can begin life again, but he may not enter business life again (except as an employee) without permission from the Court. It is an offence to obtain goods, etc., on credit while an undischarged bankrupt, and this is one reason why many bankrupts do their best to pay up their debts, with interest. Cases are recorded every month of people doing this many years after their bankruptcies, and thus re-establishing their good names.

Imagine that A. Debtor pays up his outstanding debt of 17·50, with interest at 5 per cent, which we will imagine adds a further 3·50 to the debt. One morning our postbag will include an unexpected 21·00. We shall, of course, be agreeably surprised by this, and the cheque will be banked in our Bank Account on the debit side. Which account shall we credit? We have already cleared the Debtor's Account and probably, if we have a loose-leaf system, the 'dead' page will have been removed after a while from the book.

The part which represents interest on the original debt is pure profit; it is a payment for the use of our capital in the months that have passed by, and it should be credited to Interest Received Account. The other part, which represents the actual debt itself is best treated as a credit (profit) item in the Bad Debts Recovered Account; it will reduce this year's bad debts by 17·50 when transferred to Profit and Loss Account.

The Journal Entry will therefore look like this:

19..
Oct. 31
	Bank Account Dr.
	    To Interest Received Account
	    ,, Bad Debts Recovered Account
	Being bad debt recovered with interest from A. Debtor at this date.
		C.B. 19
		L. 77
		
		L. 12
			21·00	3·50
				
				17·50

Fig. 63. A Bad Debt Recovered

and the Ledger Accounts like this:

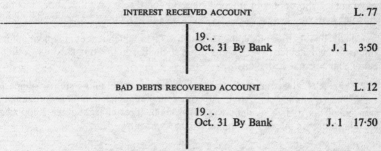

INTEREST RECEIVED ACCOUNT   L. 77

	19.. Oct. 31 By Bank	J. 1 3·50

BAD DEBTS RECOVERED ACCOUNT   L. 12

	19.. Oct. 31 By Bank	J. 1 17·50

Fig. 64. Two Nominal Accounts with Profits on them

EXERCISES SET XV

(13) Simple Bad Debts

No. 1. On July 9th we hear that A. Debtor who owes us 3·12 has disappeared without trace. Do the Journal Entry to clear the debt.

No. 2. On August 14th we hear that A. Borrower who owes us 50·00 has been killed in a railway disaster. As a gesture of goodwill to his bereaved relatives the debt is written off. Show the Journal Entry.

No. 3. On July 19th a debtor, Anne Alien, who owes 100·00 informs us that in view of difficult economic circumstances the government of her country will only sanction the payment of half the money. It is decided to clear the whole debt in view of the political situation in the country concerned. Do the Journal Entry.

No. 4. A debtor, B. Henriques, who owes us 240·00 is declared a bankrupt. He pays 0·05 in the 1·00, and the debt is written off. Do the Journal Entry, and post it to Henriques' Account, the Bank Account, and the Bad Debts Account.

No. 5. On June 17th X sold goods on credit to Y valued at 400·00. In November he learned that Y had become bankrupt, and on November 30th he received a cheque for a final settlement of 0·70 in the 1·00. Show the Account of Y in X's Ledger and the Journal Entry for November 30th.

No. 6. A Jorgenson becomes bankrupt, owing us 130·00. We prove the debt in his bankruptcy and in due course receive a settlement of 0·55 in the 1·00. Show the Journal Entry and A. Jorgenson's Account after it is written off.

No. 7. P. Dallas was written off as a debtor some time ago for the sum of 60·00. On August 8th he sends you a cheque for the full amount and asks for your receipt. Show the Journal Entry necessary.

No. 8. R. Losalamos was written off as a debtor some time ago for 280·00. On July 12th he sends us a cheque for 295·00 in full settlement. Show the Journal Entry, the Bank Account, and any other accounts.

No. 9. J. Houston was written off as a debtor some time ago for 300·00. On November 5th he sends us a cheque for 315·00 representing the complete payment of the debt and interest thereon for the intervening time. Do the Journal Entry.

No. 10. F. Worth sends you a cheque for 73·15 which represents payment in full of a bad debt of 60·00, and interest on it for the outstanding period. Show the Journal Entry on May 8th.

No. 11. R. Galveston sends you a cheque for 100·00, and a supply of spare tyres valued at 80·00. This is in complete payment of a debt previously written off as bad. This debt was for 155·00, legal charges were 13·00 and 12·00 represents interest on the debt. Do the Journal Entry.

(14) Journal Entries No. 7—The Correction of Errors

Countless errors can occur in a set of books if they are kept by inefficient book-keepers, and it would be impossible to describe them all and show how they should be corrected. The great thing is to learn one's book-keeping as fully as possible, paying real attention to detail.

The basic rule is this: examine the error that has been made and do what you must to put it right. This will usually involve a double entry of some sort; very rarely do we get a matter that only requires a single-sided entry.

Here are some typical errors:

Example 1. Item debited to the wrong debtor.

On January 14th it is discovered that Mr. H. Smith has been debited with 15·00 which is actually owing from Mr. H. B. Smith. Mr. H. Smith's Account looks like this:

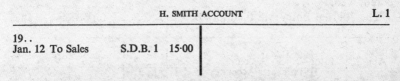

H. SMITH ACCOUNT   L. 1

19..			
Jan. 12 To Sales	S.D.B. 1	15·00	

The Journal Entry will look like this:

19..				
Jan. 14	H. B. Smith Account Dr. To H. Smith Account Being correction of error in posting.	L. 2 L. 1	15·00	15·00

And after posting the two accounts will look like this:

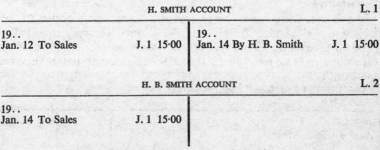

H. SMITH ACCOUNT   L. 1

19..			19..		
Jan. 12 To Sales	J. 1	15·00	Jan. 14 By H. B. Smith	J. 1	15·00

H. B. SMITH ACCOUNT   L. 2

19..		
Jan. 14 To Sales	J. 1	15·00

Fig. 65. Correcting an error in Posting

Example 2. Purchase of an asset entered in the Purchases Day Book.

If an invoice for an asset is mistakenly entered in the Purchases Day Book with invoices for goods, the Asset Account will not be debited. Instead the Purchases Account will be debited and as this account is used for working out the profits or losses at the end of the year, this mistake will make our calculations wrong.

It is an error of principle to treat assets as if they were goods, and if such an error is made, a Journal Entry is required to correct it. Consider the following case:

T. Hansard, a bookseller, bought a delivery van for 400·00 on August 4th. On August 31st it was noticed that the invoice had been treated not as the purchase of an asset but as an ordinary purchase in the Purchases Day Book.

It is clear here that the 400·00 will have been posted to the Purchases Account on the debit side, instead of being debited in the Motor Vehicles Account. To get the matter right we must debit the Motor Vehicles Account and credit the Purchases Account, so that the 400·00 is removed.

The Journal Entry will therefore be:

19.. Aug. 31	Motor Vehicles Account Dr.
	      To Purchases Account
	Being an error of principle in which
	   an asset was treated as goods.
		L. 27
		L. 32
			400·00	400·00

Fig. 66. Assets mistaken for 'goods'

Example 3. A single-sided error.

When adding up the Sales Day Book on July 31st an error of 10·00 was made in the addition, so that the total posted to the Sales Account was 10·00 more than it should have been. How is the error corrected on August 4th?

In this case there is nothing wrong with the amounts posted to the debit side of the Ledger Accounts of the debtors. The only error is the 10·00 mistake on the Credit side of the Sales Account.

To put it right we simply debit the Sales Account with 10·00. This is a one-sided entry.

The Journal Entry will look like this:

19.. Aug. 4	Sales Account Dr.
	      To ....
	Being a single-sided entry required
	   to correct an over-addition in the
	   Sales Day Book.
		10·00	—

Fig. 67. An unusual entry

An alternative way of dealing with this is actually to cross out the Sales Account figure and rewrite it correctly, initialling the alteration.

If a **Suspense Account** had been open at the end of July this would change the treatment again, but this will be dealt with in the section on Suspense Accounts, Chapter Nine, page 148.

(15) The Correction of Errors

No. 1. Prepare Journal Entries for the following, showing the narrative used:

(*a*) The purchase of a typewriter, value 75·50, has been wrongly included in purchases.

(*b*) A credit note issued to R. Morgan for goods returned to the value of 60·00, less 5 per cent trade discount, has been posted to the account of R. Morton.

No. 2. Show by means of Journal Entries how the following errors would be corrected in the books of C. Careless:

(*a*) Machinery valued at 500·00 purchased on credit from Excel Engineering Company had been debited to the Purchases Account.

(*b*) When paying J. Johnson, a creditor, Careless had deducted 5·00 discount. Johnson had disallowed this discount.

(*c*) Depreciation of 200·00 on motor vehicles had been credited to the Fixtures and Fittings Account.

(*R.S.A.—Adapted*)

No. 3. A Sales Invoice made out to Alan Gee for goods supplied to him valued at 230·00 was posted by mistake to G. Allen's account in the Ledger. Correct this error on December 5th.

(*East Anglian Examination Board—Adapted*)

No. 4. Show by means of Journal Entries how the following errors would be corrected in the books of V. Slack:

(*a*) Depreciation of 100·00 on motor vehicles had been credited to the Machinery Account.

(*b*) When paying S. Jones, a creditor, Slack had deducted 7·50 as cash discount. Jones had disallowed this discount.

(*c*) Machinery valued at 1,000·00, purchased on credit from Steel Engineering Company, had been debited to the Purchases Account.

(*d*) A sale to Derby & Co. amounting to 275·50 had been entered in the Sales Day Book as 257·50 and this latter figure had been posted to the respective Ledger Accounts.

(*R.S.A.—Adapted*)

No. 5. Correct by means of Journal Entries the following mistakes in the books of E. Nartey, a retail draper:

(*a*) Sale of a suit on credit to M. Haji for 20·00 was wrongly entered in G. Haji's account.

(*b*) The total of the Purchases Day Book was wrongly brought forward as 1,050·00 instead of 1,500·00.

(*c*) An office typewriter costing 65·50 was wrongly entered in the Purchases Day Book instead of Typewriter Account.

(*d*) The total of the Discount Allowed Column, 27·15, was wrongly posted to the Credit side of Discount Allowed Account. (Be careful with this entry.)

No. 6. Correct the following errors by Journal Entries:

(*a*) An allowance of 1·40 made to a debtor R. Cornish had been entered in the Sales Returns Book as 14·00 and posted to Cornish's Account at that figure.

(*b*) Stators (the stationary part of electric motors), purchased for electric motor assemblies, value 150·00, which should have been recorded in the Purchases Account, were incorrectly debited in the Stationery Account.

(*c*) Sales to P. Robson of 45·00 were posted in error to P. Robison's Account.

(*d*) The purchase of an oil-fired boiler for 1,000·00 had been entered in the Purchases Day Book instead of the Fixed Machinery Account.

No. 7. Give Journal Entries to correct the following items:

(*a*) A credit entry of 60·00 was made in the books of E. Kemp instead of E. Kempster.

(*b*) A lorry was recorded in the books of C. Phillips at 190·00. It was bought by Garage Ltd. at an agreed value of 150·00, but the book-keeper did not remove the 40·00 extra from the Motor Lorry Account.

(*c*) Goods sold to L. Bates valued at 88·40 were entered in the Sales Day Book as 48·80 and posted at that figure to the accounts.

(*R.S.A.—Adapted*)

No. 8. Correct the following items by means of Journal Entries (a Suspense Account has *not* been opened up):

(*a*) The total of the Discount Received Column in the Cash Book was posted on May 31st to the wrong side of the Discount Account. The figure was 31·78.

(*b*) A final dividend of 36·00 from a bankrupt, R. J., was received from the Official Receiver and posted to the credit side of R. J.'s Account. R. J.'s Account had already been cleared to Bad Debts Account the previous December 31st.

(*c*) The sale of an obsolete machine for 42·50 on credit to Sun Garage Ltd. was entered in the Sales Day Book in error and posted to the accounts. The machine had been sold at book value.

No. 9. Correct the following item by means of Journal Entries:

(*a*) On March 31st the purchase of an asset, furniture, value 180·00, had been completely overlooked and omitted from the books. Following an indignant letter from the vendors it was agreed to pay this account at the end of the current month, with interest at 5 per cent *per annum*. On September 30th you are asked to journalize the total amount payable at the end of the month.

(*b*) 40·00 debited to H. R. Brown's Account should have gone into H. R. Browne's Account.

(*c*) Two Cash Book entries had been muddled when posted to the Ledger. 30·00 wages and 25·00 repairs had been posted as 25·00 wages and 30·00 repairs.

No. 10. Correct the following items by Journal Entries:

(*a*) A machine, value 120·00, was debited to Mackay & Co. Ltd. instead of to the Machinery Account.

(*b*) An entry for 37·25 in the Account of R. Hughes should have been 37·52. The other half of the double entry had been done correctly.

(*c*) A sale of equipment to R. Honey had been agreed at 25 per cent discount. In fact the sale had been invoiced at the full catalogue value, 200·00.

(16) Journal Entries No. 8—Dishonoured Cheques

When a cheque is received from a debtor there is no guarantee that he has funds in his account to cover the cheque. When we enter the cheque on the debit side of the Cash Book and post it to the credit side of his account there is always the possibility that we shall have to reverse the process later.

If a cheque is dishonoured in this way it is returned to us marked **Refer to Drawer.** Such a cheque should immediately be referred to the person who drew it.

It is an offence to pass a cheque in this way. Often the explanation will be acceptable to us; the drawer will phone his bank and arrange for the cheque to be honoured. We shall present it again and this time all will be well. If the explanation is unsatisfactory we shall refer the matter to the police. In the meantime we have to put through a Journal Entry which cancels the original entry for the cheque.

The rule for dishonoured cheques is:

Restore the debt to the debtor

Remove the bad cheque from the Cash Book (i.e. **Debit** the debtor, **Credit** the Bank Account)

Example 1. A. Brown sends us a cheque for 56·50 which is banked and credited to his account. Subsequently it is returned 'refer to drawer' and we find that A. Brown is temporarily in difficulties.

The Journal Entry will appear like this:

19..
July 12
	A. Brown Dr.
	    To Bank Account
	Being a dishonoured Cheque—debt
	    restored to debtor
		L. 17
		C.B. 9
			56·50	56·50

Fig. 68. Clearing a Dishonoured Cheque

A further complication arises where a debtor whose cheque subsequently 'bounces' has been given discount for prompt payment. Since he has not now paid promptly we must clearly restore the full debt, not

Book-keeping Made Simple

just the amount of the cheque. The following example illustrates this point:

Example 2. On April 4th A. Morton pays a debt of 150·00 by sending a cheque for 147·00, the rest being discount. This cheque is returned 'refer to drawer' on April 6th. Restore the debt to the debtor.

The Journal Entry now becomes:

19. .
Apr. 6
	A. Morton Dr.
	    To Bank Account
	    .. Discount Allowed Account
	Being debt restored in full to A.
	Morton's Account on dishonour of
	cheque.
		150·00	147·00
			3·00

Fig. 69. A Dishonoured cheque where Discount has been given

The discount debited in the Discount Allowed Account as a loss must be credited to remove the loss—we are not suffering this loss any more. Of course we may suffer a much bigger loss if Morton does not pay, but that remains to be seen in the future.

EXERCISES SET XVII

(17) Dishonoured Cheques

No. 1. On May 19th a cheque for 52·50 received two days earlier from R. Thomas was returned marked 'refer to drawer'. Restore the debt to the debtor.

No. 2. On July 11th two cheques are returned marked 'refer to drawer'. One was for 50·95 from L. Jones and the other 26·45 from T. Peterson. Do the Journal Entry restoring these debts to the Debtors' Accounts.

No. 3. M. Lucas paid us 42·20 on May 5th. On May 8th the cheque was returned marked 'refer to drawer'. Restore the debt to Lucas.

No. 4. R. Jowett, who paid us 56·55 in full settlement of a debt of 59·50 on May 8th, dishonours his cheque. It is returned 'refer to drawer', on May 11th. Restore the debt to the debtor with a Journal Entry.

No. 5. M. Cole's cheque for 364·50, which was in full settlement of a debt of 370·00, is returned dishonoured. Restore the debt to the debtor with a Journal Entry dated June 11th.

No. 6. T. Cruiser dishonours a cheque for 180·80 which was in full settlement of a debt of 184·00. Do a Journal Entry to restore the debt to his account.

(18) Journal Entries No. 9—Bank Loans, Interest, and Charges

Where a bank lends money other than by means of an overdraft an agreement will be drawn up and signed covering the terms of the loan. This agreement will usually specify the amount of the loan, the rate of interest payable, the period over which it is to be repaid, the amount of the monthly repayment, and the collateral security to be provided.

Once this agreement is signed the bank puts the amount of the loan into our ordinary Current Account, but also opens up a **Loan Account**, which records the amount loaned, and to which our monthly repayments will be credited. We shall do the same in our books, as shown by the following example:

Example 1. Briggs Bank Ltd. agree to lend us the sum of 1,000·00 against the security of a life assurance policy on the proprietor. The Loan Agreement is signed on April 1st.

The Journal Entry will be as follows:

19.. Apr. 1	Bank Account Dr.
	  To Briggs Bank Loan Account
	Being loan received on this date
	  against life assurance policy
		C.B. 1
		L. 29
			1,000·00	1,000·00

Fig. 70. A Loan Entry

The Loan Account is credited with 1,000·00, but as the repayments are made, the sums credited in the Bank Account are debited to the Loan Account, as shown in Fig. 72.

Bank Interest Payable

Interest charged by the bank is a loss to the person paying it, and a profit to the bank.

The periodic amounts of interest charged will be credited to the Loan Account, since the bank becomes a creditor for the amount of the interest, and will be debited to **Loan Interest Account** as one of the losses of the business. The Journal Entry for this will be as follows, taking 30·00 as the interest due:

19.. Oct. 1	Loan Interest Account Dr. To Loan Account, Briggs Bank Being interest due for half year.	L. 28 L. 27	30·00	30·00

Fig. 71. Recording Interest Due

The Loan Account now looks like this, assuming a 40·00 a month repayment:

LOAN ACCOUNT   L. 27

19..				19..			
Apr. 30	By Bank	C.B. 7	40·00	Apr. 1	By Bank	C.B. 5	1,000·00
May 31	,, ,,	C.B. 9	40·00	Oct. 1	,, Interest	C.B. 22	30·00
June 30	,, ,,	C.B. 13	40·00				
July 31	,, ,,	C.B. 15	40·00				
Aug. 31	,, ,,	C.B. 18	40·00				
Sept. 30	,, ,,	C.B. 21	40·00				

Fig. 72. Repaying a Loan

Bank Interest Receivable

Bank interest is paid on loans, but it may also be received if we have a Deposit Account. There are two kinds of Bank Account used by traders: the Current Account and the Deposit Account.

Current Accounts do not earn interest, because the bank cannot rely upon the use of money in a Current Account. We make use of the bank's services, the Cheque System and the Credit Transfer System, and we must expect to pay for them. With a Current Account, therefore, it is usual for the bank to make Bank Charges. Sometimes, if a fairly substantial sum is left unused in the Current Account the bank will not charge 'Bank Charges', but will carry out these services free in return for the use of the stable portion of our funds.

With Deposit Accounts the depositor agrees to give the bank seven days' notice before withdrawing the deposit. The bank is then able to use the funds we have deposited to lend to borrowers at a rate of interest which is usually 2 per cent above Minimum Lending Rate. The bank, in return for this use of our money shares its earnings with us, by giving us some of the interest it is receiving from the borrower; usually 2 per cent less than the Minimum Lending Rate. In this way we could receive **Bank Interest**—this time as a profit of our business.

Such interest is added by the bank to the Deposit Account. To record this profit in our books we need a Journal Entry that looks like this:

19..
Oct. 1
	Bank Deposit Account Dr.
	    To Bank Interest Received
	Being interest from the bank at this
	    date.
		7·50	7·50

Fig. 73. Bank Interest Received

Bank Charges

Like Bank Interest Payable, Bank Charges are a loss to the business. If the bank charges us sums of money for using its services it will deduct these sums from our Bank Account. When we find that this has been done we have clearly to deduct the Bank Charges from our Cash Book, or we shall find that our Cash Book differs from the Bank Account. Strictly speaking a Journal Entry is not absolutely neccessary for this, but if we do decide to journalize, the Journal Entry will appear as follows:

19..
Aug. 4
	Bank Charges Account Dr.
	  To Bank Account
	Being Bank Charges deducted at this
	  date.
		L. 17
		C.B. 24
			5·50	5·50

Fig. 74. Journalizing Bank Charges

EXERCISES SET XVIII

(19) Bank Loans, Interest, and Charges

No. 1. On May 14th the General Bank agreed to lend us 500·00 against the security of the deeds to our shop. Record this loan in a Journal Entry.

No. 2. On December 31st R. Pace borrows 1,000·00 privately from A. Friend, giving his life assurance policy as collateral. Record this loan in R. Pace's books, through a Journal Entry. This 1,000·00 is banked.

No. 3. Steady Bank Ltd. lend Overdrawn Ltd. 10,000·00 secured on the plant and machinery of the firm. Record the Journal Entry as it would appear in the books of Overdrawn Ltd. on March 31st.

No. 4. On September 30th Steady Bank Ltd. charge Overdrawn Ltd. 325·00 interest on the loan described in question 3. Record this interest charge in the Journal of Overdrawn Ltd.

No. 5. On October 1st R. Smith is notified by his bank that interest on his gilt-edged securities has been received from the Bank of Australia and credited to his account. The payment is 30·00. Record this interest received in his Journal.

No. 6. On December 31st T. Jones asks his bankers for a Bank Statement and finds that on December 15th they charged him Bank Charges of 2·75. Record this in his Journal and post to the Ledger and Cash Book.

No. 7. On December 31st R. Moy is notified by his Building Society that business deposits in his Savings Account have earned interest of 27·65 for the half year. Do the Journal Entry for this profit and post to the Ledger. (Debit Building Society Savings Account.)

CHAPTER SEVEN

THE COLUMNAR PETTY CASH BOOK—IMPREST SYSTEM

(1) Introduction

There are many items of quite small importance in business which nevertheless must be accurately recorded, especially if a code of honesty is to be established in the business. For instance, postage stamps must be accurately recorded or they may be used by staff for their own purposes. Telephone calls are very cheap but if staff use the telephone for private calls they will increase the bills payable by the business. All such items are called **Petty Cash** items.

The word 'petty' comes from the French word 'petit' meaning small, and the Petty Cash Book is a book where small items are recorded by the 'Petty Cashier'. We have already seen that the cashier is an important and trusted servant, paid a salary commensurate with his responsibilities. The petty cashier is usually a young and inexperienced person, whose honesty has not been entirely proved yet, although we have every reason to believe him trustworthy. Many cashiers begin life as petty cashiers, and this is one of the useful functions of the Petty Cash System; it develops inexperienced staff and makes them responsible. It has certain safeguards built into it, one of which gives the system its name—**Imprest System**.

(2) The Imprest System

An Imprest is a certain sum of money which has been set aside for a particular purpose. It is an advance of cash, with an implied promise that there is more to come later whenever it is needed, and when the present Imprest has been accounted for by the petty cashier. The main cashier starts the petty cashier off with a sum deemed to be sufficient for his needs for a limited time, say one week. Since postage is the commonest use for this system, the post girl is often the petty cashier. Given an imprest of 20·00 she will buy the stamps, pay for the telegrams, etc., and she will also pay out petty cash to anyone who needs it. The office boy may need petty cash for bus fares, or for him to buy odd items required in a hurry, like string, cellulose tape or similar office sundries.

When the petty cashier begins to run short of money, he makes up his book in the way shown on page 122, and goes with it, and the Petty Cash Box, to the cashier. The cashier then checks the books, agrees that the record has been properly kept, counts what is left in the till, and **restores the Imprest**. This means he gives the petty cashier the amount of money spent, **so that he finishes up with the original Imprest again, ready to start the next week.**

This is the really important point about the Imprest System; the petty cashier is not given a further sum of 20·00 because with what he has left over he would have more than the agreed Imprest. He is simply given enough money to bring the total to 20·00 again, thus **restoring the Imprest position.**

Advantages of the Imprest System

(*a*) It saves the main cashier being endlessly bothered for trifling sums of money, and enables him to get on with his work.

(*b*) It trains young and inexperienced staff and develops their sense of responsibility.

(*c*) The sum of money chosen for the Imprest is not large enough to present much of a temptation either to the petty cashier or to the other employees. This does not mean that care should not be taken with petty cash. In most cities the majority of crimes connected with offices involves thefts of petty cash, usually at lunch-time. The petty cashier should always lock the till before he leaves his desk, and should lock it away in a safe as well when he goes to lunch.

(*d*) Even if it is stolen the loss does not represent a serious one to the firm.

(*e*) There is a very great saving **in the posting of expenses to the Nominal Accounts, because of the analysis system.** This is dealt with on page 124.

(*f*) At any time the till can quickly be checked, for the cash left + the value of the **payment vouchers** = the original imprest.

(3) Original Documents—The Petty Cash Voucher

Every transaction in business starts off with its original document and in the case of petty cash items the document concerned is the Petty Cash Voucher. 'To vouch' is to certify the honesty of something, and the Petty Cash Voucher certifies the honesty of the petty cash disbursement made. Petty Cash Vouchers may be receipts obtained from someone outside the business or may be an internal voucher. The former are preferable since they give less opportunity for dishonesty to the employee. Even then one cannot always be certain. If the office boy is sent to buy a ball of string he is expected to produce a bill for it. Any shopkeeper will provide one on request when a purchase is made. In this way a check can be kept of the money actually spent. Even so, fraudulent conspiracies are not uncommon, as any newspaper will show. Every week one reads in the police reports about such minor cases. A van driver who has been told to buy petrol and to ask for a receipt

S.75 Y/SY

**Customer's
Receipt for
Cash Purchase**

14th July ____19

STORE NAME AND ADDRESS STAMP

6–40 Watt Electric Light Bulbs @ 0·12	0·72
1 – Candle Lampshade	0·35
1 – 13 Amp Plug	0·18
For F. W. Woolworth and Co. Limited	1·25

RECEIVED
WITH THANKS_____

AMOUNT

Fig. 75. An 'External' Petty Cash Voucher

Petty Cash Voucher   Folio *PCV27*
Date *May 15th* ___19

For what required	AMOUNT
Methylated spirit	0·20
Sealing Wax	0·15
	0·35

Signature____*G. M. Jones*_____
Passed by____*A. A. Kenningham*____
Manager

Fig. 76. An 'Internal' Petty Cash Voucher

when he buys it, may give the garage employee a fat tip and ask him for a receipt showing a quantity greater than that really issued and paid for. When he shows the false receipt and is reimbursed from the petty cash, the driver is cheating his employer. This sort of practice can easily be detected if regular checks are made of the mileage per gallon. The low-mileage-per-gallon vehicle which is as new as other vehicles but unaccountably uses more petrol may have a dishonest driver.

Petty Cash Vouchers may be very small—bus tickets are an example. Such tickets may be stuck in books, or on larger sheets of paper, but they are proof of money spent and are therefore valid as vouchers. Where it is impossible to produce a voucher from outside the business— for instance when letters are posted—it is usual to provide an internal voucher, signed by the manager or some person in authority, to vouch for the expense.

These vouchers are numbered, and the numbers are recorded in the P.C.V. column in the Petty Cash Book. They are then filed away in numerical order, so that if required the auditors may inspect them.

(4) The Columnar Petty Cash Book—Explanation (see pages 122–3)

(*a*) Notice that the centre of the book is misplaced to the left, so that the debit side has only a cash column. This is done to save paper, which would otherwise be wasted, since the receipt of cash is quite a rare item. The petty cashier usually receives cash only from the cashier when he collects the Imprest at the beginning of the week. About the only other cash he receives is when staff pay for private telephone calls, as may be seen in Fig. 77 on March 28th.

(*b*) Since there is no Details column on the left-hand side, the petty cashier writes all the details on the right-hand side, using the word 'To' for the debit entries going on the debit side and the word 'By' for the credit entries.

(*c*) These credit entries are not only entered in the Total column but are analysed into columns farther over; this enables us to collect the total expenses, under the various headings, into one sub-total. This is one of the great advantages of the columnar Petty Cash Book; it saves a great deal of posting. Instead of posting each item of expenditure to the various accounts we need only post the totals once a week.

(*d*) As the expenses are paid they are entered into the total and the analysis columns. There is one special column at the end, the Ledger Account column. Notice that it has a folio column next to it. This Ledger Account column is used to collect any items for Personal or Real Accounts. The expenses (losses) will be going into Nominal Accounts and can be collected from the sub-total columns. While it is sensible to post all the postage to the Postage Account it would not be sensible to post Mr. Jones's 1·34 with Office Equipment 1·65. These are posted to their own accounts and the folio number is put in the folio column.

(*e*) At the end of the week the book is totalled, then cross-totalled to double check the entries; the balance of cash in hand is calculated and carried down to the credit side. Clearly this balance must agree with the cash in hand, and before going to the cashier, the petty cashier will obviously check that the book agrees with the Cash Box. He will also post the sub-totals to the debit side of the Loss Accounts concerned,

Dr.   **Cr.**

Receipts	Date	Details	P.C.V.	Total	Postage	Fares	Cleaning	Sundry Expenses	Stationery	Folio	Ledger A/cs
20·00	19.. Mar. 25	To Imprest	C.B. 9								
	25	By Stamps	1	1·50	1·50						
	26	,, Postage	2	0·65	0·65						
	26	,, Cleaning	3	0·45			0·45				
	27	,, Sundries	4	0·32				0·32			
	27	,, Fares	5	1·45		1·45					
0·30	28	To Telephone Call	L. 3								
	28	By R. Jones	7	1·34						L. 19	1·34
	29	,, Cleaning	8	0·65			0·65				
	29	,, Sundries	9	0·40				0·40			
	29	,, Travelling	10	1·65		1·65					
	30	,, Envelopes	11	0·45					0·45		
	30	,, Office Equipment	12	1·65						L. 15	1·65
	30	,, Sundries	13	0·15				0·15			
	31	,, Totals	—	10·66	2·15	3·10	1·10	0·87	0·45		2·99
	31	,, Balance	c/d	9·64							
20·30				20·30	L. 5	L. 11	L. 27	L. 36	L. 49		
9·64	Apr. 1	To Balance	B/d								
10·36	1	,, Restored Imprest	C.B. 11								

Fig. 77. The Petty Cash Book

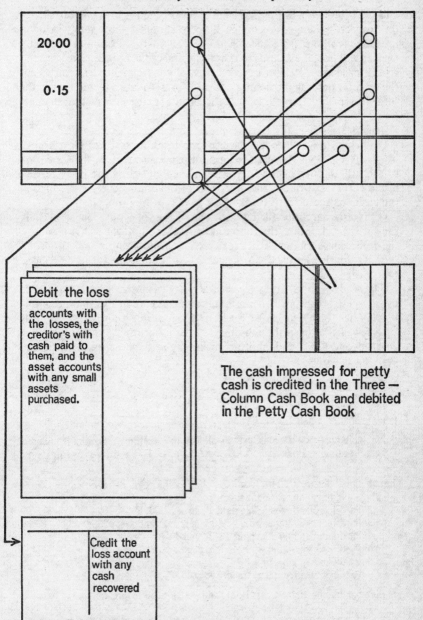

20·00

0·15

Debit the loss

accounts with the losses, the creditor's with cash paid to them, and the asset accounts with any small assets purchased.

The cash impressed for petty cash is credited in the Three — Column Cash Book and debited in the Petty Cash Book

Credit the loss account with any cash recovered

Fig. 78. Posting the Petty Cash Book

and post the items in the Ledger Accounts column to the debit side of the respective Ledger Accounts. If there should be any debit items in the debit column (like the telephone call in this example) the petty cashier will post these sums to the credit side of the appropriate account. In this case the Telephone Account is, of course, a Loss Account, but the amount paid by the member of staff for a private call will reduce the total loss to be charged against the profits at the end of the financial year.

This posting is really fairly complex, but Fig. 78 explains it.

(*f*) When the cashier has checked the book he restores the Imprest, by giving the petty cashier the amount needed to restore the Cash Box to the full amount of the Imprest. This is debited by the petty cashier in the Petty Cash Book; the other half of the double entry is credited in the cashier's main Cash Book as he pays out the money.

(*g*) Notice carefully all the positions of the folio numbers, especially the Cash Book folios, the folio numbers at the bottom of the columns, the folio numbers in the Ledger Account folio column, and the folio number in the Petty Cash Voucher column against the telephone entry.

The student should now try several petty cash exercises. It is possible to buy petty cash paper from a stationer, but as in examinations one usually has to rule up paper for Petty Cash exercises, it is better to rule up a few sheets, even though this is rather laborious. Another way is to rule up one sheet and photo-copy it if you have access to a photo-copying machine.

EXERCISES SET XIX

(5) The Petty Cash Book

No. 1. Rule up a Petty Cash Book for five columns: Sundry Expenses, Fares, Stationery, Postage and Ledger Accounts. Enter the following items: 19..

Jan. 1 Drew Imprest 30·00 from the chief cashier; paid for office teas 0·35; postage stamps 1·35; fares 0·55.
    2 Paid for envelopes 2·28; paid P. Jones 2·73.
    3 Paid fares 0·32; cleaning materials 0·63.
    4 Paid stationery 1·33; paid P. Brown 1·16.
    5 Paid for cleaning materials 1·25; paid fares 0·53.
    6 Paid for ball of string 0·14.
    7 Paid for sundry items for office use 0·86.

Balance off the Petty Cash Book and restore the Imprest.

No. 2. Enter the following items in a Petty Cash Book which is kept on the Imprest System. At the end, balance off the book and restore the original Imprest. Use analysis columns for Fares, Postage, Sundry Expenses,

Stationery, and Ledger Accounts, and invent appropriate folio numbers and Petty Cash Voucher numbers.

19..

Oct. 1 Drew Imprest from cashier 10·00.

2 Paid fares 0·53; bought postage stamps 0·38.

3 Paid for office teas 0·45; paid for stationery 0·66; paid for ball of string 0·15.

4 Paid fares 1·15; paid for gum for office 0·23.

5 Postage stamps 0·28; paid General Insurance Co. Ltd. 0·85; paid J. Thomas 1·08.

6 Paid fares 0·33; paid cleaner 0·25; paid dustman 0·10.

No. 3. Tom Brown runs his office petty cash on the Imprest System. He has five columns: Postage, Travelling Expenses, Cleaning, Sundry Expenses, and a column for Ledger Accounts. Enter the following items, balancing the book at the end of the week, and restoring the Imprest:

19..

Mar. 25 Drew Petty Cash Imprest 20·00; bought stamps 1·10.

26 Paid postage 0·36; paid cleaner's wages 1·50.

27 Paid for string 0·15; fares 1·45; postage 0·35.

28 Paid sum of 1·75 to R. Jones.

29 Paid for cleaning materials 0·45; sundry expenses 0·25; postage 1·45.

30 Paid 1·25 to L. Robbins; bought scales for office use (Furniture and Fittings Account) 1·38; paid travelling expenses 0·63.

NOTE: The scales are clearly the purchase of an asset and should be the subject of a Journal Entry. This does not affect the Petty Cash Book which will still credit the sum paid and record the analysis in the Ledger Accounts column.

No. 4. Enter the following in a Petty Cash Book with six columns, for Postage, Fares, Office Sundries, Cleaning, Repairs, and Ledger Accounts. Invent appropriate folio numbers and Petty Cash Voucher numbers.

19..

Oct. 15 Drew petty cash Imprest 50·00; paid postage 3·50.

16 Paid fares 0·48; bought ball of string 0·15; paid window-cleaner 0·25 and a creditor, T. Brown, 5·65.

17 Paid postage 1·55; bought envelopes 2·50; bought cleaning materials 0·65.

18 Paid R. Johnson 1·65; member of staff paid 0·45 for private telephone call; paid fares 0·33.

19 Paid fares 2·75; paid cleaner's wages 6·35; paid for repairs to window catch 0·85; paid M. Smith 4·15; paid postage 0·50.

Balance the book and restore the Imprest.

No. 5. Make out the Petty Cash Book for a firm which gives its petty cashier an Imprest of 25·00 and requires her to analyse expenses under the headings: Postage, Travelling Expenses, Sundry Expenses, Wages and Ledger Accounts.

19..

Jan. 1 Received Imprest from cashier 25·00; paid for postage stamps 2·50.

2 Repairs to lock, after burglary, 2·45; paid dustman 0·10; paid for postage 4·25; paid R. Morgan 1·75.

3 Paid sundry expenses 0·62; cleaner's wages 2·50.

4 Paid postage on parcel 0·36; travelling expenses 0·25.

5 Sundry expenses paid 0·55; stamps 1·45.

6 Postage 1·43; wages to part-time workers 3·65.

Balance off the book and restore the Imprest, inventing appropriate folio numbers and Petty Cash Voucher numbers.

No. 6.

(*a*) J. Peach keeps his Petty Cash Book on the Imprest System. What does this mean?

(*b*) What are the advantages of the Imprest System?

(*c*) Peach's book has the following matters recorded in the first week of the year. Draw up the book, balance it off, and restore the Imprest, inventing suitable folio numbers and Petty Cash Voucher numbers. Use columns for Postage, Fares, Sundry Expenses, and Ledger Accounts.

19..

Jan. 1 Drew Imprest of 10·00 from cashier; paid postage 1·65.

2 Paid fares 0·45; postage 0·23; collected private telephone call money from staff 1·42.

3 Paid for paper and string 0·22; paid L. French 2·76.

4 R. Peters paid J. Peach 1·65 which was put into the Petty Cash till; paid postage 1·45.

5 Paid fares 0·15; taxi for visitor 0·45.

No. 7. Rule a Petty Cash Book that will record the total expenditure under the headings: Postage, Stationery, Travelling, General Expenses, and Bought Ledger Accounts paid.

Enter the following transactions and balance at the end of the week showing the amounts to be posted to the Ledger:

19..

June 21 Cash in hand 20·00.

22 Paid office tea bill 1·95.

23 Paid for typewriter ribbons 1·15; paid railway fares 1·34.

24 Paid for 1,000 envelopes 1·25; paid Marlow & Co. 0·55.

25 Paid for postage stamps 2·50; paid bus fares 0·65.

26 Paid for cleaning office windows 1·05; paid for postage on registered letters 0·50; cashed a cheque for the total spent in the week, to restore the Imprest.

(*R.S.A.—Adapted*)

No. 8. Draft a Petty Cash Book showing twelve items of expenditure in the week beginning March 7th in accordance with instructions that the total amounts spent on Travelling, Postage, Printing and Stationery, Carriage and General Expenses will be required, as well as one Personal Account item.

Balance the book and show the amount received to bring the cash in hand to the original balance of 20·00.

No. 9. Enter the following items in a Petty Cash Book which is kept on the Imprest System. At the end restore the original Imprest. Use analysis columns for Fares, Postage, Sundries, Stationery, and Ledger Accounts.

19..

Oct. 1 Drew Imprest from cashier 10·00.

    2 Paid fares 0·50; paid for stamps 0·35.

    3 Paid for office teas 0·42; paid for envelopes 0·65; paid for string 0·10.

    4 Paid fares 1·15; paid for glue for office use 0·15.

    5 Gave proprietor 1·00 from till for his personal use.

    6 Paid J. Thomas 1·15; paid cleaner 0·25.

No. 10. K. Jarndyce employs a cashier who keeps a Petty Cash Book on the Imprest System. It has six analysis columns for Postage, Travelling, Stationery, Cleaning, General Expenses and Ledger Accounts. Rule special Petty Cash paper and record the following week's transactions, inserting appropriate folio numbers and Petty Cash Voucher numbers:

19..

Jan. 1 Drew Imprest of 20·00 from cashier; paid postage 2·50; paid R. Jones' account 2·25.

    2 Paid fares for office boy 0·26; paid for envelopes 0·55; collected from staff for private telephone calls 1·68.

    3 Paid for cleaning materials 0·28; paid for tea and cakes for typist's birthday 0·42.

    4 Paid postage 1·22; paid L. Smith's account 2·28.

    5 Paid cleaner's wages 5·00; paid fares (chauffeur) 0·12; gratuity to dustman 0·10.

Rule off the book, bring down the balance in hand, and restore the Imprest to 20·00.

(East Anglian Examination Board—Adapted)

No. 11. A Petty Cash Book is kept on the Imprest System, the amount of the Imprest being 10·00. It has four analysis columns: Postage and Stationery, Travelling Expenses, Carriage, Office Expenses. Give the ruling for the book and enter the following transactions:

19..

Jan. 4 Petty Cash in hand 1·50; received cash to make up the Imprest; bought stamps 2·00.

    7 Paid railway fares 0·25; bus fares 0·13; telegrams 0·36.

    8 Paid carriage on small parcels 0·42; paid railway fares 0·32; bought envelopes 0·89.

    10 Paid for repairs to typewriters 0·75; paid carrier's account for December 2·21.

    11 Paid office tea lady 1·50.

Balance the Petty Cash Book as on January 11th and bring down the balance.

(R.S.A.—Adapted)

No. 12. On June 30th the debit (or receipts) side of a trader's Petty Cash Book showed a total of 50·00 this being the amount of the fixed Imprest; on the same date the Total Payments column showed a total of 47·17, and the analysis columns showed individual totals as follows: Carriage Inwards 18·10; General Expenses 2·15; Postage and Telegrams 2·10; Stationery 0·15; Travelling Expenses 21·13, and Ledger Accounts 3·54. There was only one item in the Ledger Accounts column, and it was written up in the Particulars column as follows: 'A/c Clerys Ltd. for air-freight charges to Dublin'.

Answer the following questions:

(*a*) On June 30th how much would the petty cashier collect from the principal cashier in order to restore his balance in hand to the Imprest figure?

(*b*) Which Ledger Accounts would be debited, and with what amounts, in order to complete the double entry?

(*c*) Which Ledger Account would have its page number written in the Ledger folio column against the item of 3·54?

(*R.S.A.—Adapted*)

(6) A Page to Test You on the Petty Cash Book
Cover the page with a sheet of paper, then read one question at a time.

Answer	Question
—	1. What does 'petty' mean?
1. Small or unimportant.	2. What system is used for Petty Cash?
2. The Imprest System.	3. What is an Imprest?
3. A sum of money set aside for a particular purpose.	4. What are the advantages of the Imprest System?
4. (a) It saves bothering the main cashier; (b) little risk, and little temptation; (c) trains young staff; (d) saves time on posting to the Ledger because of the analysis columns (e) is easily checked.	5. Where is the 'middle' of a page in a Petty Cash Book?
5. Set towards the left-hand side of the page.	6. Why is this done?
6. Because the petty cashier doesn't often receive money.	7. When does he receive money?
7. (a) When he draws the Imprest from the cashier; (b) when members of staff pay for telephone calls, etc.	8. Why does the credit side need more room than in an ordinary Cash Book?
8. Because there are extra analysis columns.	9. What is the point of these analysis columns?
9. To collect together similar minor expenses and to make it possible to post the total each week in only one posting per column.	10. Why is the end column different?
10. Because where postings are to either Personal or Real Accounts they must be kept separate. Only expenses for the Nominal Accounts can be added together.	11. How do you finish off a Petty Cash Book?
11. (a) Add the columns, then add across to check the work; (b) find the balance, check that the till is right, balance the books and bring down the balance; (c) ask the cashier to restore the Imprest.	12. What is the document for which the Petty Cash Book is the Book of Original Entry?
12. The Petty Cash Voucher.	13. Where should a Petty Cash Voucher come from ideally?
13. From outside the business.	14. As we post the Petty Cash Book what must we write on it?
14. The folio numbers of the Ledger pages.	—

CHAPTER EIGHT

BOOK-KEEPING TO THE TRIAL BALANCE

(1) Introduction

Advertisements will often be seen in the Press offering employment to persons who can keep books to the Trial Balance level. This is the first stage of book-keeping work, and the student who approaches this chapter with a good sense of achievement on the work of earlier chapters is about to make a breakthrough to the point where he can call himself a 'Book-keeper to the Trial Balance'. Such a student should not feel too disappointed if his Trial Balances do not come out first time. It is a lucky book-keeper who does not make some slip in his month's work, and it takes a good level of experience to get even a text-book exercise right first time. The important thing is to persevere; by the time you have done six or seven of these major exercises you will begin to know what you are doing.

(2) What is Involved in Book-keeping to the Trial Balance?

Trial Balances in small offices are usually done once a month, on the last day of the month. They cannot be done more frequently because the work involved is too great, nor should they be done less frequently. The purpose of the Trial Balance is to discover any mistake; if there is one, it may be a long task finding it, even if there is only one month's work to look through. To delay making a Trial Balance for five or six months would mean Herculean labour if a mistake were discovered.

During one month we have been recording a wide range of transactions:

(*a*) Opening the books, with an Opening Journal Entry, unless of course they were already open from last month, in which case we start with last month's balances already on the books.

(*b*) Recording a great many Purchases, Sales, Purchases Returns, and Sales Returns in the Day Books, and posting them to the Ledger.

(*c*) Recording in the Cash Book cash received and paid, and posting it to the Ledger Accounts.

(*d*) Recording Petty Cash received and paid, and posting it to the Ledger Accounts.

(*e*) Recording several less common items like the Purchase of Assets and the Correction of Errors in the Journal Proper and posting them to the Ledger.

The final result of all these activities is a set of Ledger Accounts which have been entered accurately on the double entry method, so that every debit entry has a corresponding credit entry. If everything has been done correctly, a list of the debit balances will exactly equal a list of the credit balances. This is what a Trial Balance is: *a list of all the debit balances and of all the credit balances, each totalled to see whether the two totals agree*. If they do agree we may conclude that our book-keeping has been correct. (In fact this may not be true because there are five classes of error which do not show up on the Trial Balance. These will be discussed in Chapter Nine, page 146.)

(3) Tidying Up the Ledger Accounts and Extracting a Trial Balance

A Trial Balance is a list of the balances on the accounts. As we draw up the Trial Balance we usually 'tidy up' the accounts. This means balancing them off and bringing down the balances but there is no point in doing this if it looks exactly the same afterwards as before. Consider this account:

Example 1.

R. JONES   L. 27

19..			
Jan. 14 To Goods	S.D.B. 1	427·50	

Fig. 79. A 'tidy' Personal Account

This account is as clear as it can possibly be. R. Jones is a debtor for 427·50, and even if we balance it off and bring down the balance the account will be no clearer than it is already. This is shown below:

R. JONES   L. 27

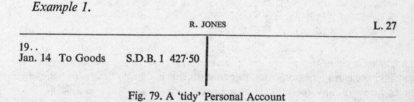

19..				19..			
Jan. 14 To Goods	S.D.B. 1	427·50		Jan. 31 By Balance	c/d		427·50
		427·50					427·50
19..							
Feb. 1 To Balance	B/d	427·50					

Fig. 80. No 'tidier' than Fig. 79

As there is no point in balancing off in this way, we simply take the balance as shown in Fig. 79, direct to the Trial Balance like this:

M. BROWN AND T. JOHNSON

TRIAL BALANCE

(as at January 31st, 19..)

	Dr.	Cr.
R. Jones	427·50	

Fig. 81. Starting a Trial Balance

Notice the following points:

(*a*) The Firm's Name is written at the top.

(*b*) The heading 'Trial Balance' always has a date on it; in this case 'as at January 31st' because a Trial Balance is only the same for one moment of time. As soon as February 1st comes a new set of transactions will alter the balances we have listed. For instance, Jones may pay his debt and his account will then be cleared. An account that is clear need not be brought into the Trial Balance at all.

(*c*) The debit balance is put in the debit row; a credit balance is put in the credit row.

Example 2. Now consider the following account:

M. LICHMAN   L. 33

19..			
Jan. 15	To Goods	S.D.B. 1	36·25
17	,, ,,	S.D.B. 1	49·50
27	,, ,,	S.D.B. 1	160·50
27	,, Carriage	S.D.B. 1	5·25

Fig. 82. An account with entries on one side only

There is no real point in balancing off this account either. All we want to know on any account is: how big is the balance, and is it a debit or a credit balance? In this case it is clearly a debit balance and all we do is add it up and pencil in the total using small figures. This account adds up to 251·50.

M. LICHMAN   L. 33

19..			
Jan. 15	To Goods	S.D.B. 1	36·25
17	,, ,,	S.D.B. 1	49·50
27	,, ,,	S.D.B. 1	160·50
27	,, Carriage	S.D.B. 1	5·25
			251·50

← Pencil figures—the Balance owing— to be taken into the Trial Balance.

Fig. 83. Totalling in pencil for Trial Balance purposes

M. Lichman's balance is now ready to be taken to the Trial Balance as shown in Fig. 86.

Example 3. The last of our three examples of Personal Accounts shows an account that does need 'tidying up'. We cannot see clearly what the balance is at present.

J. OUTRED   L. 52

19..				19..			
Jan. 4	To Cash	C.B. 7	125·00	Jan. 1	To Balance	B/d	127·50
4	,, Discount	C.B. 7	2·50	12	,, Purchases	P.D.B. 5	140·45
14	,, Returns	P.R.B. 4	5·50	18	,, ,,	P.D.B. 7	136·25
				18	,, Carriage	P.D.B. 7	5·50
				27	,, Purchases	P.D.B. 15	185·25
				27	,, Insurance	P.D.B. 15	4·75

Fig. 84. A busy account that needs balancing off

If we balance this account off and bring down the balance we shall find the figure we need for the Trial Balance, and at the same time clarify the account. Imagine that the phone rings. J. Outred is on the other end, inquiring if we can oblige him by settling our account by tomorrow Before he agrees the manager will probably ask the ledger clerk to tell him what the balance is on the Ledger Account. At the moment the picture is confused. The ledger clerk will need a pencil and paper to sort it out. Imagine what a muddle it would be if it had not been tidied up for five or six months. If the account is tidied up at the end of each month it will be easy to see the present state of affairs.

J. OUTRED   L. 52

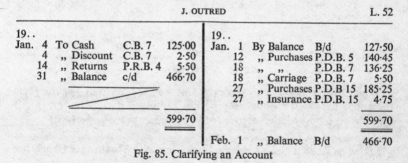

19..				19..			
Jan. 4	To Cash	C.B. 7	125·00	Jan. 1	By Balance	B/d	127·50
4	,, Discount	C.B. 7	2·50	12	,, Purchases	P.D.B. 5	140·45
14	,, Returns	P.R.B. 4	5·50	18	,, ,,	P.D.B. 7	136·25
31	,, Balance	c/d	466·70	18	,, Carriage	P.D.B. 7	5·50
				27	,, Purchases	P.D.B 15	185·25
				27	,, Insurance	P.D.B. 15	4·75
			599·70				599·70
				Feb. 1	,, Balance	B/d	466·70

Fig. 85. Clarifying an Account

It is now quite clear that the balance on this account is 466·70 and that this is a credit balance. Our Trial Balance now looks like this:

M. BROWN AND T. JOHNSON

TRIAL BALANCE

(as at January 31st, 19..)

	Dr.	Cr.
R. Jones	427·50	
M. Lichman	251·50	
J. Outred		466·70

Fig. 86. Building up a Trial Balance

If we continue to go through the accounts, tidying them up if necessary, we shall eventually produce a complete Trial Balance, like the one shown below:

D. GOOCH AND SON

TRIAL BALANCE

(as at December 31st, 19. .)

	Dr.	Cr.
Cash	70·00	
Bank	2,085·25	
Motor Vehicles	2,385·00	
Plant and Machinery	1,785·35	
Land and Buildings	4,035·95	
Debtors and Creditors	1,619·05	2,409·00
Sales Returns and Purchases Returns	145·40	200·00
Purchases and Sales	4,595·50	12,770·00
Carriage In	83·50	
Wages	1,281·40	
Salaries	615·60	
Opening Stock	1,185·20	
Rent and Rates	155·80	
Light and Heat	215·75	
Sundry Expenses	69·25	
Loan from Bank		4,000·00
Postage	66·00	
Discount Allowed and Received	59·60	86·50
Investments	4,535·40	
Capital		5,523·50
	24,989·00	24,989·00

Fig. 87. A Trial Balance

When the Trial Balance agrees in this way we say that—*prima facie* (at a first look)—the book-keeping has been well done. However, it is still possible that hidden errors could be present (see page 146).

(4) How to Keep a Sole Trader's Books for One Month and Check for Accuracy

Before a book-keeper can call himself a 'book-keeper to the Trial Balance' he must be able to keep the books of a small business for one month, and then prove by means of a Trial Balance that he has done the work accurately. The procedure is as follows:

(*a*) Do the Opening Journal Entry, and post it to the Ledger and the Cash Book. This will open up the Cash Book with a cash and bank balance on these two accounts, and open up the Ledger with any other assets or liabilities, including the Proprietor's Capital Account.

(*b*) Now begin the month's transactions. This means that the documents for any sales or returns are made out and sent off, the duplicates being recorded in the Sales Day Book and Sales Returns Book. Any purchases invoices or purchases returns credit notes are recorded in the Purchases Day Book and Purchases Returns Book and all these four books are posted to the Ledger. Any of the rarer items that require Journal entries are journalized, and then posted to the Ledger. All cash and cheques received are debited in the Cash Book, and all cash and cheques paid are credited in the Cash Book. The Cash Book is then posted to the Ledger. Lastly, if a Petty Cash Book is kept the petty cash payments and receipts are recorded and posted to the Ledger.

This sounds rather involved but the student should console himself with the thought that once he masters the procedure he will really understand the mystery of book-keeping, and the many advantages of the double entry system. Whatever the problems, they will already have been dealt with in the earlier chapters.

(*c*) At the end of the month the totals of the Day Books must be posted to the respective accounts—the Purchases Account, the Sales Account, the Purchases Returns Account, and the Sales Returns Account. This is a vital process that many students forget. The final thing on these books is the posting of the totals to the Ledger Accounts. It is this that **completes the double entry** for the hundreds of invoices and credit notes recorded.

(*d*) Lastly draw up the Trial Balance. After heading the paper properly and putting the date, the Ledger Accounts must be inspected, tidied up if necessary, and the balances brought into the debit and credit columns. Do *not* forget the balances on the Cash Account (including the Petty Cash) and the Bank Account. These are the only two accounts that are not in the Ledger and are often forgotten. Do not forget the Discount Allowed and Discount Received columns of the Cash Book, which have to be posted to the Discount Accounts. Remember they do not change sides.

Do not forget that every account that has a balance on it must appear on the Trial Balance. If an account is clear there is no need to bring it into the Trial Balance, since there is no debit or credit balance to record.

(5) What to Do if a Trial Balance Does Not Agree

If a Trial Balance does not agree there is a systematic procedure for discovering the error. Some of the steps in this procedure are rather complex and the reader will not yet fully understand them; they are discussed in detail later. The stages of the work in tracing errors are as follows:

(*a*) Add up the Debit and Credit columns again. It is easy to make a slip in addition, and a recheck is advisable.

(b) If the Trial Balance still does not agree take the total of one side from the other and find the difference. Imagine it is 27·56. Someone in the office may now have a bright idea like, '27·56—that's what we paid for the second-hand duplicator we bought at the auction.' This kind of happy thought may save hours of work. When we check the item we find that it has been left off the Office Machinery Account.

(c) If no one has a happy thought like that, the next thing is to halve the difference and look for something on the wrong side of the Trial Balance. Half of 27·56 is 13·78. If a figure of 13·78 appears on the Trial Balance check to see if it is on the proper side. 13·78, for example, put on the debit side when it should be on the credit side will make the debit side 13·78 too large and the credit side 13·78 too small—making a difference of 27·56.

(d) If we can't correct the Trial Balance this way then our problem is more serious, but before we go on to other possibilities let us notice two more simple things. Firstly, if an error is 1, or 10, or 100, or 1,000, or 0·10, or 0·01 it is probably due to a slip in addition. Somewhere we may have made a mistake in arithmetic that has put a balance out. For mistakes of this type a systematic check-up on all additions and subtractions is desirable.

Secondly, if an error divides by 9 it may be due to the transposition of figures. For instance, if a book-keeper writes 72 instead of 27 the error will be 45, which divides by 9. If an error divides by 9, then this is a possible cause of the trouble. Some people are very prone to make this kind of error because they are 'crossed laterals'—people whose dominant eye is not the same as their dominant hand. They may be right-handed and left-eyed, or left-handed and right-eyed. If you find that one book-keeper repeatedly makes this kind of mistake warn him to be especially careful about it.

(e) The next step is to check the extractions from the accounts into the Trial Balance. It is easy to make a slip here, and a quick 'calling over' of the Ledger Accounts to see if they have been extracted correctly will discover the error.

(f) If this has been done properly and the Trial Balance still does not agree, then we may be able to isolate certain sections of the work and prove that they are right by taking out **Control Accounts**. This is an important process which requires a whole chapter to itself, and the student is advised to disregard it for the present. It is dealt with in Chapter Thirty, page 378.

(g) We must now check the entire month's activities, going over every single item and checking that a perfect double entry has been made in every case. This means checking all the additions, carrying forward, etc. It is a great labour, but to find the mistake it may be necessary.

(h) Finally, if we cannot find our mistake, we can open a Suspense Account. This means we take a new page in the Ledger and open up an

These ledger accounts to Exercise 88 have been printed here to enable the reader to see pages 138 and 139 without turning a page.

The Ledger Accounts

A. Smith L.2

To Op. Bal. 85·50	By Sales
" Sales 170·00	" Rct. 25·50
	" Bank and
	B. Debt 230·00
BAD DEBT	
255·50	255·50

P. Rose L.3

To Bank 34·00	By Op. Bal. 35·00
" Dis 1·00	
35·00	35·00

Stock A/c L.1

To Op. Bal. 400·00

M. Jordan L.4

To Rct. 5·50	By Op. Bal. 165·50
" Bal. 208·50	" Purchases 48·50
214·00	214·00
	By Balance 208·50

Capital A/c L.5

By Op. Bal. 643·00

M. Nicholay L.6

To R. Williams 20·00	By Purch. 125·75
" Bal. 105·75	
125·75	125·75
	By Bal. 105·75

Purchases A/c L.7

To Sund. Cred. 174·25

Purchases Rct A/c L.8

By Sund. Cred. 25·50

Bank Loan A/c L.9

By Bank 100·00

Bad Debts A/c L.10

To A. Smith 130·00

R. Toyne L.11

To Sales 28·50

Sales A/c L.12

	By Sund. Cred. 198·50
	" Bank 68·00
	" " 70·65

Sales Rct A/c L.13

To Sund. Debt 25·50
" Cash 7·55

Antonios L.14

To Bank 70·00

Wages L.15

To Cash 15·00
" " 15·00

Drawings L.16

To Bank 25·00

Repairs L.17

To Cash 2·65

Disc. Recd L.18

By Cash 1·00

Fig. 88. Ledger Accounts to the specimen exercise

account with the difference on the books. In the case we imagined earlier we would put 27·56 on the Suspense Account on the side where it was needed to make the books balance. The books will now agree, for the debits balance the credits; but, of course, sooner or later the mistakes are going to be discovered. The Suspense Account is a last resort solution to the problem.

The student should now work through the following specimen exercise.

(6) A Specimen Exercise to the Trial Balance

Robert Morgan started business with these assets and liabilities on July 1st:

Cash in hand 28·00, Cash at Bank 330·00, Stock 400·00, Debtor: A. Smith 85·50, Creditors: P. Rose 35·00, M. Jordan 165·50.

Open the accounts by means of an Opening Journal Entry, posted to the Ledger and the Cash Book. Then enter the following transactions in the appropriate Book of Original Entry, post them to the Ledger, and extract a Trial Balance to prove the accuracy of your work.

19..
July 1 Sold goods for cash 68·00.
    3 Received a loan from the bank 100·00.
    4 Sold goods on credit to A. Smith for 200·00 less 15% Trade Discount.
    5 Paid salaries by cheque 70·00.
  10 A. Smith returns goods, catalogue price 30·00.
  11 Paid wages in cash 15·00.
  13 Settled P. Rose's account in full, by cheque 34·00.
  15 Purchased goods on credit from M. Jordan 48·50.
  18 Cash Sales 70·65.
  20 Banked 100·00 from cash box.
  21 Drew from bank for private use 25·00.
  22 Refunded cash to a customer for goods returned 7·55.
  23 Sold goods on credit to R. Toyne 28·50.
  24 Purchased goods on credit from M. Nickolay 125·75.
  25 Paid for minor repairs 2·65 cash.
  26 Returned goods to M. Nickolay 20·00.
  27 A. Smith is in difficulties; agreed to accept 100·00 cheque in full settlement—rest treated as a bad debt.
  28 Paid wages in cash 15·00.
  31 Received a credit note from M. Jordan (allowance) 5·50.

The solution is shown on the next few pages. After careful study the student should try *several* exercises from Set XX.

Notes on specimen exercises opposite. First we must do the Opening Journal Entry, and post it to the Ledger and the Cash Book. We are then ready to begin the July transactions. Here are a few hints:

19..

July 1 This is Cash Sales; debit the Cash Book.
   3 We have to do a Journal Entry for a Bank Loan.
   4 Sold goods on credit is a Sales Day Book item.
   5 Credit the Cash Book for salaries paid.
  10 Goods returned go in the Sales Returns Book (beware Trade Discount).
  11 Cash Book—credit side of Cash Account—money is going out.
  13 Credit the Cash Book—Bank Account—cheque is going out.
  15 Purchases on credit go in the Purchases Day Book.
  18 Cash Book—debit side of Cash Account.
  20 This is a Contra Entry—Cash Book, both sides.
  21 Drawings—credit Cash Book—Bank Account.
  22 Sales Returns, but cash not credit; money going out of Cash Book. Credit side of Cash Account.
  23 Sales Day Book item.
  24 Purchases Day Book item.
  25 Credit Cash Book—Cash Account.
  26 Purchases Return Book item.
  27 Journal entry—Bad Debt.
  28 Cash Book item—Cash Account.
  31 Purchases Returns Book item.

If the student treats each line as a separate problem and asks himself in which book of original entry he should enter the transaction, and then thinks carefully how to post the transaction to the Ledger, he should have little difficulty in doing this type of exercise. In an office the same problems arise; the book-keeper decides what to do and then makes the necessary entries.

19.. July 1					J. 1
Cash Account	Dr.	C.B. 1	28·00	
Bank Account	„	C.B. 1	330·00	
Stock Account	„	L. 1	400·00	
A. Smith Account	„	L. 2	85·50	
To P. Rose Account		L. 3		35·00
„ M. Jordan Account		L. 4		165·50
„ Capital Account		L. 5		643·00
Being assets and liabilities at this date			843·50	843·50

The Opening Journal Entry

Fig. 88. A Merchant's Books to the Trial Balance

OTHER ENTRIES IN THE JOURNAL PROPER

19..				

July 3	Bank Account Dr.
	    To Bank Loan Account
	Being loan granted by bank at this
	    date
		C.B. 1
		L. 9
			100·00	100·00

27	Bank Account Dr. Bad Debts Account „ To A. Smith Being Bad Debt written off	C.B. 1 L. 10 L. 2	100·00 130·00	230·00

SALES DAY BOOK

19..				

July 4	A. Smith
	   Goods
	     Less 15% Trade Discount
			200·00
			30·00	

	R. Toyne	L. 2		170·00
23	Goods	L. 11		28·50
				198·50
				L. 12

SALES RETURNS BOOK

19..				

July	A. Smith
	   Returns
	     Less 15% Trade Discount
			30·00
			4·50	

		L. 2		25·50
				25·50
				L. 13

PURCHASES DAY BOOK

19..				
July 15	M. Jordan Goods	L. 4		48·50
24	M. Nicholay Goods	L. 5		125·75
				174·25
				L. 7

PURCHASES RETURNS BOOK

19..				
July 26	M. Nicholay Goods	L. 6		20·00
31	M. Jordan Allowance	L. 4		5·50
				25·50
				L. 8

Fig. 88 (Continued)

THE THREE-COLUMN CASH BOOK

19.. July					19.. July						
1	To Opening Balances	J.1	—	28·00	330·00	5	By Salaries	L.14			70·00
1	" Cash Sales	L.12		68·00		11	" Wages	L.15		15·00	
3	" Bank Loan account	J.1			100·00	13	" P. Rose	L.3	1·00		34·00
18	" Cash Sales	L.12		70·65	100·00	20	" Bank	C		100·00	
20	" Cash	C			100·00	21	" Drawings	L.16			25·00
27	" A. Smith	J.1				22	" Cash Sales Returns	L.13		7·55	
						25	" Repairs	L.17		2·65	
						28	" Wages	L.15		15·00	
						31	" Balances	c/d		26·45	501·00
			—	166·65	630·00				1·00	166·65	630·00
Aug. 1	To Balances	B/D		26·45	501·00			L.18			

ROBERT MORGAN

TRIAL BALANCE AS AT JULY 31ST., 19..

	Dr.	Cr.
Cash	26·45	
Bank	501·00	
Stock	400·00	
M. Jordan		208·50
Capital		643·00
M. Nicholay		105·75
Purchases	174·25	
Purchases Returns		25·50
Bank Loan		100·00
Bad Debts	130·00	
R. Toyne	28·50	
Sales		337·15
Sales Returns	33·05	
Salaries	70·00	
Wages	30·00	
Drawings	25·00	
Repairs	2·65	
Discount Received		1·00
	1,420·90	1,420·90

Fig. 88 (Continued)

(7) Book-keeping to the Trial Balance

No. 1. Peter Newman had the following balances on his books on 1st October: Cash in hand 66·00; Cash in bank 800·00; Premises 2,800·00; Debtors: A. New 400·00, B. Castle 90·00, Stock 600·00; Creditors: J. Horne 850·00, J. Harper 180·00. Make the opening Journal Entry and post it to the Ledger and to the Cash Book.

The following transactions then took place:

19..
Oct. 1 Cash sales 90·00.
3 Paid office expenses in cash 5·00.
5 Purchased furniture for office use by cheque 180·00.
8 Paid wages in cash 19·50.
10 Sold goods to B. Castle 40·00 on credit.
12 A. New settled his account by cheque, less 2½% cash discount.
14 Received a loan from the bank, 250·00 secured on a Life Assurance Policy. (Interest on this loan will not be paid until December.)
16 Paid J. Horne on account 500·00 by cheque.
19 Sent B. Castle a credit note for goods returned 8·00.
21 Bought goods on credit from J. Harper 40·00.
24 Paid rates by cheque 24·75.
26 Withdrew from bank for private use 20·00.
28 Cash sales 120·00.
29 Bought goods on credit from J. Horne 85·55.
30 Paid office-cleaning expenses 6·25 in cash.
31 Paid into bank from office cash 100·00; paid salaries by cheque 124·00.

Enter them in the appropriate books of Original Entry, post to the Ledger, and extract a Trial Balance.

No. 2. Alan Dawlish has the following balance on his books on June 1st: Cash in hand 50·00; Cash at bank 380·00; Premises 1,000·00; Furniture and fittings 600·00; Debtors: R. Sind 100·00, P. Quilter 150·00, Stock 500·00; Creditors: A. Jolson 70·00, L. Toft 180·00. Show the opening Journal Entry and post to the Ledger.

These are his transactions for the month of June. Enter them in the appropriate subsidiary books, post to the Ledger, and extract a Trial Balance.

19..
June 1 Cash sales 40·50.
4 Purchased machinery by cheque 180·00.
5 Paid wages in cash 19·75.
9 Paid office expenses by cash 7·35.
10 R. Sind settled his account by cheque less 2½% cash discount.
13 Sold goods to P. Quilter 150·00 on credit.
14 Sent a credit note for goods returned to P. Quilter 40·00.
16 Received a loan from the bank 500·00.
19 Paid A. Jolson cheque in full settlement less 5% cash discount.
22 Withdrew from bank for private use 30·00.

24 Bought goods on credit from L. Toft 65·50.
27 Paid rates by cheque 24·00.
28 Bought goods on credit from L. Toft 70·00.
29 Cash sales 130·65.
30 Paid into bank from cash box 100·00; paid salaries by cheque 60·00.

No. 3. Derek Webster was in business as a retail furniture dealer and his financial position on July 1st was as follows: Cash in hand 56·10; Cash at bank 1,036·50; Stock 1,384·00; Furniture and fittings 270·10; Debtors: A. Evans 27·19, B. Turner 38·15; Creditors: A. Presley 290·17. Make the opening Journal Entry, and post it to the Ledger and Cash Book.

His transactions for the month of July were as follows:

19..
July 1 Sold goods on credit to A. Evans 160·00 less 10% trade discount.
2 Received from B. Turner a cheque for 37·00 in full settlement.
4 Paid rent by cheque 30·00.
5 Bought on credit from Redditype Ltd. typewriter for office use 75·00.
6 Paid cash for stationery 14 00.
7 Paid postage in cash 3·00.
8 Drew cash for personal use from bank 30·00.
9 Sent A. Presley cheque for 280·00 in full settlement.
12 Bought goods at auction for cheque 30·00; sent A. Evans credit note for 10·70 for goods returned (not up to specification).
19 Cash sales 100·00 of which 75·00 was banked.
20 Paid cash for stationery 3·10.
23 Sold to A. Jorgensen goods 40·00 on credit.
25 A. Jorgensen sent cheque on account 20·00.
26 Paid wages in cash 15·00.
28 A. Jorgensen's cheque returned dishonoured.
31 Cash returned to a customer 4·12 for goods returned.

Record the transactions, post to the Ledger, and extract a Trial Balance.

No. 4. R. Palmer is a young man who enters the building trade with a capital of 3,500·00, which he puts in the bank on January 1st, 19... The same day he purchases for 80·00 on credit furniture and fittings from Shop-fitters Ltd. and for 380·00 tools and equipment from Builders' Materials Ltd. Here are his first month's transactions. Enter them in the appropriate books of original entry, post to the Ledger, and take out a Trial Balance.

19..
Jan. 1 Drew 25·00 for cash from bank; bought typewriter 40·00 by cheque; Lea Builders Supply sent goods 240·00 on credit.
2 Received from R. Brown 50·00 in cash—deposit on house; paid rent 15·00 in cash.
3 Sold goods to R. Ellis 24·25 on credit; paid Shopfitters Ltd. the amount owed, less 2½% cash discount by cheque.
14 Bought goods, 25·00 on credit, from Builders' Materials Ltd.; paid wages 7·50 cash; bought stationery for cash 1·65.
15 Sold goods to R. Ellis 14·50 on credit; cash sales 20·30.
18 Paid rent 15·00 cash.
19 Lea Builders Supply Ltd. sent goods, value 80·00, on credit.

20 R. Ellis returned goods valued at 3·10 (wrong colour).

21 Paid Builders' Materials Ltd. the amount owed on January 1st, less 5% cash discount by cheque.

28 Paid wages 10·00 cash; paid rent 15·00 cash; personal drawings 40·00 by cheque.

31 Received cash from R. Brown 100·00 further payment on house being erected.

No. 5. On June 1st the following balances were extracted from George Dickens's books: Machinery 2,000·00; Stock 750·00; Cash in hand 100·00; Sundry Debtors: M. Mysore 82·00, S. Hyderabad 66·00, Bank overdraft 40·00; Sundry Creditors: R. Robot 60·00, S. Electra 220·00.

Make the opening Journal Entry, enter the transactions, post to the Ledger, and extract a Trial Balance.

19..

June 1 Paid wages in cash 25·00.

2 Cash sales 120·00 of which 100·00 was banked.

3 M. Mysore pays his account by cheque less 5% cash discount.

4 Sold goods on credit to S. Hyderabad 150·00.

10 Purchased goods on credit from S. Electra 100·00.

12 Cash purchases 25·00.

13 Bought office equipment on credit from Comfichairs Ltd., 550·00.

14 Sold machinery for 500·00 (its proper value on the books). The buyer paid by cheque.

15 Cash sales 85·00.

18 Paid wages in cash 24·00.

19 Refunded cash to a customer 10·50 for goods returned.

20 Paid rent by cheque 35·50.

22 Paid for repairs to premises 35·00 by cheque.

23 S. Hyderabad returns goods valued at 37·75 (poor quality).

24 Paid carriage charges 5·00 in cash.

25 S. Hyderabad settles the account owing at June 1st with 5% discount deducted, by cheque.

29 Paid S. Electra a cheque on account 160·00.

30 Paid salaries by cheque 40·00; banked 80·00 from cash box.

No. 6. On January 1st Thomas Pecksniff's financial position was as follows: Cash in hand 25·00; Cash at bank 1,034·10; Land and buildings 5,000·00; Furniture and fittings 750·00; Plant and machinery 3,400·00; Debtors: T. Pinch 25·10, R. Chuzzlewit 125·65. He had a creditor, Jonas Finance Co., 2,500·00 and the only other account was his Capital Account. Open the books of Thomas Pecksniff and enter the following January transactions:

19..

Jan. 1 Paid cash for the following items: Stationery 4·65; postage stamps 1·10; repairs 0·60; goods for resale 7·60.

2 J. Westlock & Co. sent us goods, value 24·10, on credit.

3 Sent Jonas Finance Co. cheque for 100·00 on account.

4 T. Pinch paid account owing on January 1st, less 1·10 discount; he paid in cash; paid postage 0·65 cash.

5 Bought a new showcase on credit from Showcases Ltd., 35·00; cash sales 50·12.

11 Bought goods at auction 37·50 paid for by cheque.

13 R. Chuzzlewit returned goods valued at 5·12 (wrong colour).

17 Bought goods from M. Tapley 100·50 on credit.

19 Sold goods to T. Pinch 140·50 on credit.

20 Cash sales 75·12.

21 Paid into bank 75·00 from cash till.

22 R. Chuzzlewit paid amount owing less 4·18 discount by cheque.

24 R. Chuzzlewit's cheque returned marked R.D.

29 Paid wages cash 30·00.

31 Paid salaries by cheque 85·10.

Post all the books of original entry to the ledger, balance off such accounts as need to be balanced, and extract a Trial Balance.

CHAPTER NINE

LIMITATIONS OF THE TRIAL BALANCE: SUSPENSE ACCOUNTS AND THE CORRECTION OF ERRORS

(1) Introduction

We have already seen that the chief use of the Trial Balance is to check the accuracy of the book-keeping. The agreement of the debit and credit totals is reasonably good evidence that the book-keepers have done their work well, but it is not conclusive.

Sometimes we are unable to find the cause of a disagreement between the sides, and are reduced to inventing a Suspense Account which will hold the balance until the true reason for the difference is discovered. Indeed, some firms make it a matter of policy not to look for the mistakes on their books, since this is time-consuming and expensive. Such firms simply open a Suspense Account at once, and allow the problems to solve themselves in the course of time. Sooner or later someone will complain that his account has been underpaid, for instance.

(2) Errors that the Trial Balance Does Not Disclose

There are five classes of error which the Trial Balance does not disclose. They are:

(a) Original Errors.
(b) Errors of Omission.
(c) Errors of Commission.
(d) Errors of Principle.
(e) Compensating Errors.

(a) *Original Errors*

These are errors in the original entries—errors made in copying from the documents from which all book-keeping entries are made. If we take an invoice for 500·00 and enter it as 550·00 in the Purchases Day Book, posting it correctly to the creditor's account, and posting the total correctly to the Purchases Account, our Trial Balance will come out correctly, and the mistake will not be discovered. Our books are *prima facie* correct—but in fact there is an error in them.

(b) *Errors of Omission*

If something is omitted completely from the books it will neither appear on the debit nor credit side of the Trial Balance. A book-keeper was once given thirty invoices to enter in the Purchases Day Book. As he dropped the heavy Day Book on to his desk, the top invoice blew away unnoticed down the back of a filing cabinet. The Trial Balance was correct at the end of the month, and the staff congratulated one another on an excellent month's work, until the irate creditor wrote in demanding payment.

One way to avoid such errors today is to use an adding-listing machine to add up the total of the invoices received every day. This 'list' and the invoices can be clipped together and when the Day Book has been entered, the day's entries can be checked with the 'list'.

Some firms do not bother to keep a Purchases Day Book at all, but use the file of invoices as a Day Book. This saves work, but gives a less permanent and reliable record. In such cases the adding-listing machine 'list' gives the total figure for the day to be entered in the Purchases Account. Instead of a monthly total to be debited in the Purchases Account, we have a daily total. Some of our gain in not having to keep a Purchases Day Book is lost on more frequent entries into the Purchases Account.

(c) *Errors of Commission*

These are errors in the actual performance of an operation like posting. The word 'commission' here means 'doing'. If we do something wrongly—for instance enter a debt in the wrong debtor's account—the Trial Balance will balance but there will be a hidden error in the books. If J. Smith is debited instead of T. Smith the Trial Balance will not be affected, but J. Smith will resent receiving a statement at the end of the month, while T. Smith will be delighted not to receive one.

(d) *Errors of Principle*

An error of principle is an error which offends against the basic ideas of book-keeping. One of these basic ideas (dealt with fully in Chapter Twenty, page 232) is the distinction between capital and revenue expenditure. This has already been referred to briefly in the section on the correction of errors in Chapter Six.

If we buy goods for resale the invoice is recorded in the Purchases Day Book. If we buy assets, the invoice is recorded in the Journal Proper as the purchase of assets. To record the purchase of assets as the purchase of goods for resale offends against the basic principles of book-keeping.

Such an error would not show up in the Trial Balance. Our debit in the Purchases Account would enable the Trial Balance to balance, even though it should really be a debit in the Asset Account.

(e) *Compensating Errors*

These are errors which make up for one another. They usually arise from two pieces of bad arithmetic. Imagine that in adding up the Purchases Day Book we make a slip, and the total is 10·00 out. Clearly this should show in the Trial Balance, but if it is compensated for by another 10·00 error in the addition of the Sales Day Book the debit and credit sides will appear to balance, although each has a 10·00 error.

Routine checking of additions by comptometer operators will prevent this kind of error from slipping through.

(3) Suspense Accounts and the Correction of Errors

If a Trial Balance has been put right by the invention of a Suspense Account, this account will only stay on the books as long as is necessary. As soon as the mistake is discovered the Suspense Account can be cleared off.

Consider the following examples:

Example 1. A Trial Balance will not agree; the debit side is 40·50 greater than the credit side. A Suspense Account is therefore opened. Here it is:

SUSPENSE ACCOUNT   L. 171

	Aug. 31 By Difference on books 40·50

Fig. 89. A simple Suspense Account

Notice that the 40·50 has been put on the credit side so that both sides agree; the debit side is no longer 40·50 greater than the credit side.

Subsequently it was discovered that the mistake was due to the duplication of an invoice to R. Jones. R. Jones's premises had caught fire and our invoice for 40·50 had been burnt. Jones had asked for a duplicate invoice, which, before dispatch, had been debited in Jones's Account. It had not been passed through the Day Book, otherwise it would have been credited in the Sales Account too, and would have been an Error of Commission, one not discovered by the Trial Balance.

The real error in the Trial Balance therefore was that the debit side was 40·50 too much. We could remove this error by crediting R. Jones with 40·50. This would now leave the credit side 40·50 too much because of the balance in the Suspense Account. If we debit the Suspense Account as we credit Jones, we should put the books right.

This obviously requires a Journal Entry like the one below, posted into the two accounts. The books would then be correct.

19.. Sept. 9	Suspense Account Dr. To R. Jones Being correction of error due to double posting of an invoice	L. 171 L. 39	40·50	40·50

R. JONES ACCOUNT   L. 39

| 19.. Aug. 4 To Sales 17 ,, ,, | S.D.B. 1 ,, | 40·50 40·50 | 19.. Sept. 3 By Cash 3 ,, Discount 7 ,, Suspense Account | C.B. 1 ,, J. 1 | 39·00 1·50 40·50 |

SUSPENSE ACCOUNT   L. 171

| 19.. Sept. 9 To R. Jones J. 1 | 40·50 | 19.. Aug. 31 By Difference on books | 40·50 |

Fig. 90. Writing off the Suspense Account

Example 2. A Trial Balance will not agree; the debit side is 30·65 less than the credit side. A Suspense Account for this amount is accordingly opened.

SUSPENSE ACCOUNT   L. 161

| 19.. Aug. 31 To Difference on books 30·65 | |

Fig. 91. Another Suspense Account

Afterwards the following mistakes are discovered:

(*a*) A sum of cash received from a debtor was debited correctly in the Cash Book, but credited twice to the debtor's account. The amount was 12·25 from R. Jordan.

(*b*) Instead of the Discount Account being debited with 111·75 discount allowed, and credited with 134·25 discount received, these items had been crossed over. The 134·25 had been debited and the 111·75 had been credited.

(*c*) Purchases Returns of 63·40 to a creditor J. Miles had not been posted at all to his account, but the credit note had been properly entered in the Purchases Returns Book.

It is clear that the Suspense Account balance is not caused by a single error, but by a series of errors. Each of these errors now has to be put right and this involves careful, logical thought. Taking the errors in turn, we find:

(*a*) The debtor's account will look like this:

R. JORDAN   L. 12

19..				19..			
July 15	To Sales	S.D.B. 5	12·25	Aug. 14	By Cash	C.B. 12	12·25
				14	„ „	C.B. 12	12·25

Fig. 92. A Debtor's Account which has been posted twice

The book-keeper who made the second entry was not thinking what he was doing, and it is obvious that this entry will give trouble later on. To put it right we shall need to debit R. Jordan, and credit the Suspense Account.

(*b*) The Discount Account mistake is a more difficult one. This firm puts both Discount Allowed and Discount Received in the one Discount Account, but the mistake has resulted in a debit balance of 22·50 instead of a credit balance of 22·50.

DISCOUNT ACCOUNT   L. 94

19..				19..			
Aug. 31	To Discount Received		134·25	Aug. 31	By Discount Allowed		111·75
				31	„ Balance	C/d	22·50
			134·25				134·25
Sept. 1	By Balance	B/d	22·50				

(*a*) The Account as it looks at present.

DISCOUNT ACCOUNT   L. 94

19..				19..		
Aug. 31	To Discount Allowed	111·75		Aug. 31	By Discount Received	134·25
31	„ Balance	C/d	22·50			
			134·25			134·25
				Sept. 1	By Balance	B/d 22·50

(*b*) The Account as it should be.

Fig. 93. Mistakes on the Discount Account

To correct this error we have to change the present debit balance of 22·50 into a credit balance of 22·50, which means we must credit the account with 45·00. This means debiting the Suspense Account with 45·00 too.

(*c*) The third error is straightforward enough. J. Miles, the creditor to whom we have returned goods worth 63·40, should have been debited with 63·40. If we debit his account, the Suspense Account will have to be credited. The Journal Entries for these corrections are like this:

19.. Sept. 4	R. Jordan Dr. To Suspense Account Being correction of posting error	L. 12 L. 161	12·25	12·25
11	Suspense Account Dr. To Discount Account Being correction of mis-posting	L. 161 L. 94	45·00	45·00
13	J. Miles Dr. To Suspense Account Being correction of mis-posting	L. 48 L. 161	63·40	63·40

Fig. 94. Journal Entries to clear the Suspense Account

R. JORDAN   L. 12

19.. July 15	To Sales	S.D.B. 5	12·25	19.. Aug. 14	By Cash	C.B. 12	12·25
Sept. 4	„ Suspense Account	J. 1	12·25	14	„ „	C.B. 12	12·25
			24·50				24 50

DISCOUNT ACCOUNT   L. 94

19.. Aug. 31	To Discount Received	134·25	19.. Aug. 31	By Discount Allowed		111·75
			31	„ Balance	C/d	22·50
		134·25				134·25
Sept. 1	To Balance B/d	22·50	Sept. 11	By Suspense Account	J. 1	45·00

J. MILES   L. 48

19.. Sept. 13	To Suspense Account	J. 1	63·40	19.. Aug. 14	By Purchases	P.D.B. 5	85·60

SUSPENSE ACCOUNT   L. 161

19.. Aug. 31	To Difference on books		30·65	19.. Sept. 4	By R. Jordan	J. 1	12·25
Sept. 11	„ Discount Account	J. 1	45·00	13	„ J. Miles	J. 1	63·40
			75·65				75·65

Fig. 95. Clearing the Suspense Account

(4) Trial Balances and Suspense Accounts

No. 1. What is a Trial Balance? What steps would you take if a Trial Balance failed to agree? Describe these steps in the order in which you would take them.

No. 2. 'An agreed Trial Balance is only proof of arithmetical accuracy. It does not mean that the book-keeping is correct.' Do you agree or disagree with these statements?

No. 3. Certain types of book-keeping error do not affect the agreement of the Trial Balance. One such error is called an 'Error of Principle'. What is an 'Error of Principle', and why does it not affect the Trial Balance?

No. 4. Explain 'Error of Omission' and 'Error of Commission'. In what way are these errors similar?

No. 5. What are: (*a*) an 'Error in the Original Entry' and (*b*) a 'Compensating Error'? What is their significance with regard to a Trial Balance that agrees?

No. 6. On March 31st A. Lauderdale's Trial Balance failed to agree and he opened a Suspense Account. The error subsequently proved to be a miscasting in the Bank Account which caused his favourable Bank Balance of 656·60 to be carried down as 756·60. Show (*a*) the Journal Entry correcting this error on April 6th, and (*b*) the Suspense Account after the Journal Entry had been posted.

No. 7. On August 31st R. Meson's Trial Balance failed to agree, the debit side being 27·60 greater than the credit side. He opened a Suspense Account. The errors proved to be as follows:

(*a*) A debtor R. Lang had paid his account, 21·50, in full but this had not been credited to his account.

(*b*) The total of discount received for one week, 6·10, had not been posted to the appropriate account. Show (i) the Journal entries to correct these errors, and (ii) the Suspense Account after the corrections had been completed.

No. 8. During the half year ending June 30th a book-keeper of the Y-Z Company made the following errors (the rest of his work was accurate):

(*a*) Goods valued at 10·00 sold to E. Bates were debited to E. Bateson.

(*b*) Expenditure of 0·85 for telegrams was charged to the nominal account as 0·58.

(*c*) The Purchases Book was undercast by 9·00.

(*d*) An item of 9·27 discount allowed was not transferred to the Discount Account.

(i) Considering each error separately, state which column—debit or credit—of the Trial Balance, dated June 30th, would be the greater and by how much.

(ii) What entry would you make in a Suspense Account prior to the correction of the above errors?

(R.S.A.—*Adapted*)

No. 9. A book-keeper finds his Trial Balance to be 13·75 in excess on the Debit Side. A Suspense Account is opened to get the Trial Balance right, but later is cleared by the following discoveries:

(*a*) A balance due to R. Haggerty had been omitted from the Trial Balance although Haggerty's account was correct at 11·55.

(*b*) A motor lorry purchased for 165·00 cash was entered correctly in the Cash Book but posted to the Motor Lorry Account as 156·00.

(*c*) Bank interest received of 11·20 had been entered in the Cash Book but not posted to the Nominal Account.

Make the Journal Entries and show the Suspense Account as it will finally appear. (Be careful with Journal Entry (*a*).)

No. 10. A book-keeper failed to balance his Trial Balance, the debits exceeding the credits by 46·65. This amount was entered in a Suspense Account. Later these errors were discovered:

(*a*) The Sales Day Book had been undercast by 10·00.

(*b*) 10·15 received from a Debtor whose debt was already written off as bad had been debited correctly in the Cash Book but credited both to the Debtor and to the Bad Debts Recovered Account.

(*c*) A credit balance on Rent Received Account of 60·45 had been entered in the Trial Balance as 64·50.

(*d*) A cash payment of 50·85 made by a debtor had been entered properly in the Cash Book but had not been posted to the Debtor's Account.

Make the Journal Entries and show the Suspense Account as it would finally appear.

No. 11. On April 30th R. Jones extracted a Trial Balance from his Ledgers. The Trial Balance did not agree and a Suspense Account was opened for the difference. The Suspense Account was debited with 86·60. A further check revealed the following errors:

(*a*) The Discount Account had been debited 156·00 with discounts received and credited 180·30 with discounts allowed.

(*b*) A cheque was paid to R. Lee in payment of his account: 200·00 less 5 per cent cash discount. This was correctly entered in the Cash Book. No entry for the discount had been made in Lee's account.

(*c*) A cheque for 24·58 paid for heating had been correctly entered in the Cash Book, but had been debited to the Heating Account as 42·58.

(*d*) A credit note for 16·60 received from F. Brown had been correctly entered in the appropriate subsidiary book, but had been posted to Brown's Account as 61·60.

(*e*) A sale of goods, value 91·00, to J. Place had been correctly entered in the Sales Book but had not been posted to Place's account.

Show by means of Journal entries how the above errors would be corrected and show the Suspense Account as it should appear after the correction of errors.

No. 12. R. T. Ingram finds at December 31st that his Trial Balance will not come right, and he opens a Suspense Account with a credit Balance of 24·00.

The following errors which accounted for the difference in the Trial Balance were subsequently discovered:

(*a*) The loss on the sale of a machine, 24·00, had been correctly entered in the Motor Vehicle Account but had been charged to the Depreciation Account as 42·00.

(*b*) Bank Charges 14·00 had been entered in the Cash Book, but the double entry had not been completed.

(*c*) Two payments of 40·00 to R. Jones on succeeding days had been correctly entered in the Cash Book, but only one had been entered in Jones's Account.

(*d*) A sale of goods to T. Morgan for 48·00 was correctly entered in the Sales Day Book but posted to Morgan's Account as 84·00.

(*e*) The Purchases Day Book has been overcast by 20·00 and posted to Purchases Account.

(*f*) A credit note for 4·00 had been entered twice on R. Mellish's account. Mellish was a creditor.

Make the Journal Entries needed to correct these errors, and show the Suspense Account after it has been cleared.

(5) A Page to Test You on the Trial Balance

Answer	Question
—	1. What is a Trial Balance?
1. It is a list of all the accounts that have balances on them.	2. When is it taken out?
2. At least once a month.	3. What do we take it out for?
3. To discover whether the book-keeping has been carefully done.	4. What will happen if we have done our book-keeping properly?
4. The Trial Balance will balance—that is the debit balances will exactly equal the credit balances.	5. Is the agreement of the Trial Balance conclusive evidence that the books are correct?
5. No—only *prima facie* evidence.	6. Why is it not quite conclusive?
6. Because five types of errors do not show up on the Trial Balance.	7. What are these five types of errors?
7. (a) Original Errors; (b) Errors of Omission; (c) Errors of Commission; (d) Errors of Principle; (e) Compensating Errors.	8. Explain each of these in turn.
8. Original Errors are errors in the original documents to be recorded; Errors of Omission occur when we leave something out altogether; Errors of Commission are errors where we make a slip in doing the work, i.e. enter an item for D. Brown in G. Brown's books; Errors of Principle are errors where we do not understand our basic principles of book-keeping, i.e. Purchase of Assets treated as Purchases of Goods. Compensating Errors are Errors that compensate for one another, i.e. a 10·00 adding up mistake on each side.	9. What do you do if a Trial Balance does not agree?
9. (a) Add it up again in case we've made a slip; (b) see if anyone remembers an amount for the difference, say 48·00; (c) if this doesn't help, divide by 2 and see if 24·00 is on the wrong side; (d) if this doesn't help, check the extractions to the Trial Balance from the Ledger; (e) if this doesn't help, take out Control Accounts on the Sales and Purchases Ledgers; (f) if this doesn't help, check everything; (g) If we still haven't found the mistake, open up a Suspense Account.	10. Go over this again until you are perfectly sure of it all.

CHAPTER TEN

MECHANIZED LEDGER SYSTEMS AND SIMULTANEOUS ENTRIES

(1) Introduction

In Chapter Two the student was introduced to Ledger Accounts in their traditional form, with the page divided down the middle into debit and credit sides. This is not the only form of Ledger Account; there are positive advantages in adopting a 'continuous balance' type of Ledger Account.

Business efficiency experts have been devising better methods of doing book-keeping for about fifty years, and this systematic analysis of the quickest and best ways to keep business records has progressed with staggering speed over the last twenty years. Probably half the students who read this book will proceed to use their knowledge in more advanced techniques which take short cuts, use mechanical aids, and probably rely in the end on balances stored in the data banks of a computer. Book-keeping never fundamentally changes but it obviously differs in technique between the giant business firm which is fully mechanized and the small firm employing the minimum of staff. Whatever the circumstances it is essential to have a clear understanding of the basic principles.

(2) 'Continuous Balance' Ledger Accounts

The ledger card opposite shows a very useful type of Ledger Account called the 'continuous balance' or 'running balance' type of account. This is most useful in a simple mechanized system where the machine can do the calculations automatically. If a book-keeper kept his accounts in this way he would waste a great deal of time doing the calculations involved. The accounting machine is very quick and cannot make mistakes.

The advantage of this type of account is that it never needs balancing off. It is balanced off after every entry, the machine either adding on or subtracting the entry, according to the programme laid down.

Such ledger cards have to be repeatedly inserted into the machine and must therefore be fairly durable. They are not made of paper, but of thin Manilla card, and are fed into the machine from the front. The picture shown on page 158 is of an Olivetti machine. The ledger card and statement are fed into the front feed guides side by side, but not until

```
 O                              LEDGER

 NAME        PEARSON & CO                        ACCOUNT No.   5416
 ADDRESS     HIGH STREET S.W.26.                 SHEET No.     1
```

DATE	PARTICULARS		DEBIT	CREDIT	BALANCE	PROOF CODE
FEB 71	AK1702	DETAILS	1 2 1.1 8.9		1 2 1.1 8.9	2 4 3.1 7.6
FEB 71	AK1943	DETAILS	5 6. 6.7		1 7 8. 5.4	3 5 6.1 0.8
FEB 71	AK2196	DETAILS	5 3.1 9.4		2 3 2. 4.8	4 6 4. 9.4
FEB 71	RT287	DETAILS		5 6. 6.7	1 7 5.1 8.1	3 5 1.1 6.2
FEB 71	AK2501	DETAILS	1 4 1. 9.7		3 1 7. 7.8	6 3 4.1 5.4
D-DAY71	BALANCE FORWARD				3 1 7.38.½	6 3 4.7 7.
MAR 71	AL3068	DETAILS	9 6.2 6.		4 1 3.6 4.½	8 2 7.2 9.
MAR 71	CS356	DETAILS		4 1 7.3 8.	3.7 3.½CR	1 1.2 0.½
MAR 71	AL3194	DETAILS	1 4 8.7 2.½		1 4 4.9 9.	2 8 9.9 8.
MAR 71	AL3368	DETAILS	1 0 0.1 2.		2 4 5.1 1.	4 9 0.2 2.
MAR 71	AL3581	DETAILS	1 2 9.8 5.½		3 7 4.9 6.½	7 4 9.9 3.

```
 3811005
```
this is a specimen from an Olivetti Audit Mechanised Accounting System

Fig. 96. A 'Continuous Balance' Ledger Card

these guides are opened. This will not happen until the operator has picked up the old balance and the proof code from the ledger card. The machine is programmed to decide automatically whether the old balance and the proof code have been picked up correctly. An error by the operator on either pick-up will lock the front feed guides and clear the machine, returning it to the starting-place again. The operator is thus invited to try again. A further safety device can also be programmed to ensure that if the operator picks up the wrong ledger card the machine will refuse to operate. Notice that these safety devices operate *before* the entry is made, so that the correction of errors is unnecessary, for none can be made at this stage.

Having picked up the balance and the proof code properly, the operator is able to insert the ledger card and statement into the open front feed guides, and makes the entry required. She waits while the machine prints the entries on both ledger card and statement, adjusts the balance to a new figure, invents a suitable proof code and prints it

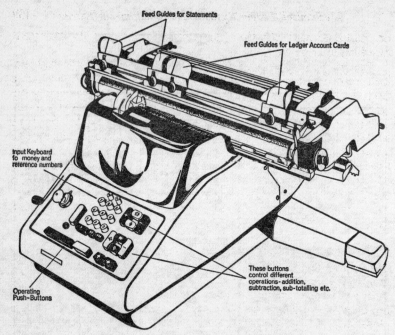

Fig. 97(*a*). An Audit class Accounting Machine

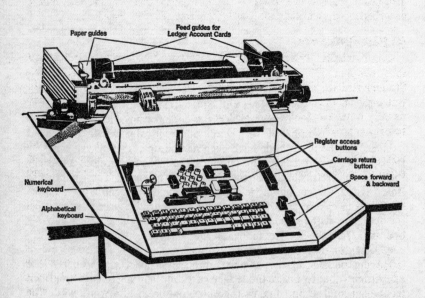

FIG. 97 (*b*). A similar machine with an alphabetical keyboard as well

on the ledger card. She then removes the ledger card and statement returning them to the tray.

There is one possibility of error in this work. The operator may mis-read the entry from the media she is posting. The check on this comes from the pre-list. If the operator has to post thirty-seven invoices she works out a pre-list on an adding-listing machine before she starts. This may even be done by someone else who is preparing the operator's work for her. At the end of the thirty-seven entries the machine prints a total of entries for the day. If this total does not agree with the pre-list total the operator must check to see where the error occurred, and make any necessary correction. The final agreed figure is then entered on the Control Account to give a complete check of the Ledger tray.

It is difficult to imagine a more ingenious or fool-proof book-keeping system than these mechanized ledger systems.

(3) Book-keeping Machines and Statements

As illustrated in Chapter Five (4), the monthly statements which remind debtors how much they are due to pay are easily prepared on these accounting machines at the same time as the ledger card is made up. Each time a ledger card is placed in the machine the statement is placed with it. By typing them simultaneously mistakes are avoided in the preparation of statements. Whatever goes on the ledger card will also go on the statement and a 'running balance' of the amount due is recorded ready for dispatch on the last day of the month.

(4) Bank Statements

One particular type of statement that is very important, and which most people see fairly regularly if they have a Bank Account, is a Bank Statement. Banks do not send these out to private persons every month, but only on request. Since banks have many accounts to keep they usually have a sophisticated accounting system, and the statement we receive is nearly always in 'continuous balance' form these days.

One interesting feature used to be that these Bank Statements changed from a black print to a red print when the balance on the account fell past zero and became an overdraft. The customer who received this type of Bank statement was said to be 'in the red'. This is no longer true of some computerized accounts.

(5) The Preparation of Simultaneous Records

One of the most time-saving and ingenious ways of keeping records is the 'simultaneous record' system. Many firms now produce this type of system, which is particularly useful for the smaller business, but the most celebrated name in this field is probably 'Kalamazoo'. The system described and illustrated overleaf by kind permission of Kalamazoo Ltd. is called the 'Compact System'.

The basic idea of the system is the simultaneous entry of invoices in the Day Book, the Ledger, and also on the statement. The Day Book takes the form of loose-leaf sheets housed in a binder. The same binder can hold both the Purchases and Sales Journals, and the Returns Journals.

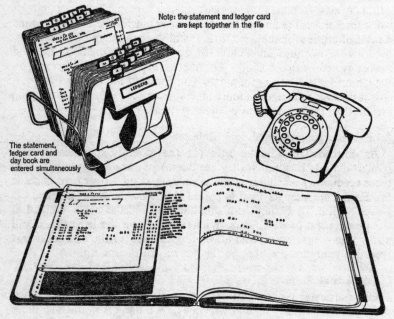

Fig. 98. Records made simultaneously

The interesting feature of the system is the line of holes punched down the edge of the Day Book pages, which enable a flat board called a Collator to be secured under the Day Book page by the studs which stick up through the holes down the edge. The page is raised a little, the collator slipped underneath so that its studs stick up through the holes, and a sheet of carbon paper is placed on top.

The ledger card and the statement, which are always kept together in a Mini-Tray are now positioned over the Day Book page so that what is written will occupy the next clean line on all three records. The invoice details are then written, and simultaneously bring the statement, the ledger card, and the Day Book up to date. The ledger card and statement are replaced in the tray, the next account due to be entered is selected and positioned, and a further entry is made from the next invoice. Checks are built into the system to ensure that the total value of invoices received or dispatched that day equals the total value entered in the Day Books. Our Day Book then provides the figures for posting to the nominal accounts, and also any analysis figures required about particular departments.

The ledger cards, or accounts, have already been posted, and no errors in posting can have occurred, while the statements are kept up to date and are ready for dispatch on the last day of the month.

It is difficult to imagine a more simple or efficient system.

A further example of these methods is given in Chapter Fifteen, page 188, which deals with Wages Books.

Exercises Set XXII

(6) Continuous Balance Accounts

Prepare the following Ledger Accounts in 'continuous balance' style. Rule up paper similar to Fig. 96, but ignore the proof code.

No. 1. From the following information prepare R. Bird's account as it would appear in your mechanized ledger:

19..

Jan. 1 Balances due from Bird 160·00.

    14 Bird paid 30·00 by cheque and was allowed 1·50 discount.

    16 Sold Bird goods for 120·00 less 10% trade discount.

    18 Purchased furniture from Bird for 200·00.

    21 Bird returns goods sold to him on the 16th instant, the catalogue price being 20·00.

    29 Received a credit note from Bird in respect of defective furniture 30·00.

From your running balance state whether you owe Bird, or Bird owes you, money.

No. 2. From the particulars given below show the account of M. Bagret in the Ledger of George & Co. for the month of March.

19..

Mar. 1 Balance due from Bagret 150·00.

    10 Sold to Bagret 5 dozen table lamps at 2·00 each, less 20% trade discount.

    11 Bagret paid the balance due from him on March 1st, deducting 5% for cash discount.

    18 Bagret reported that six of the table lamps sold to him on March 10th were badly finished, and an allowance of one-half of their price was agreed.

    19 Sold to Bagret two tables at 37·50 each.

    20 Paid carriage on tables 4·00, to be charged to Bagret.

    29 Bought from Bagret a second-hand lorry for 250·00.

State whether the balance should be inserted in the debit or credit column of a Trial Balance extracted on that date, and whether Bagret or George & Co. should pay the amount of the balance.

(R.S.A.—Adapted)

No. 3. From the following information prepare the account of B. Grey, a credit customer, as it would appear in the Sales Ledger of a trader. The account should be kept on the running balance method.

19..

Feb. 1 Grey owed 190·00.
6 Grey's cheque received for $\overline{120}$·00.
10 Charged Grey 80·00 in respect of goods supplied.
13 Cheque—less 5% cash discount—received from Grey for the goods supplied on the 10th.
18 Grey purchased goods catalogued at 210·00, subject to trade discount of 10%.
20 Cheque for 70·00 received from Grey.
22 Sent Grey a credit note in respect of goods purchased on the 18th, catalogued at 40·00, returned as unsuitable.

(*R.S.A.—Adapted*)

No. 4. (*a*) From the information given below prepare the account of J. Mace as it would appear in the Purchases Ledger of B. Barnes; balance the account and bring down the balance on January 1st.

19..

Dec. 1 Balance owed to Mace 200·95.
4 Barnes bought goods from Mace, value 90·00; Mace charged Barnes carriage 2·00.
6 Barnes sent Mace a cheque for 85·00.
7 Barnes returned goods to Mace, 9·00.
11 Barnes sent Mace a cheque for 65·85.
30 Mace accepted a van from Barnes in part payment, 100·00.

(*b*) Give the source of the information from which the entries on December 4th, 7th, 11th, and 30th would be made.

(*R.S.A.—Adapted*)

No. 5. John Billings is a credit customer of George Hurst, and on June 1st he owed Hurst 320·00. During June the following transactions took place between the two parties:

19..

June 8 Billings sent Hurst a cheque for 300·00 on account.
9 Hurst sold to Billings goods charged at 200·00.
10 Billings settled by cheque for the goods purchased the previous day and was allowed 2½% cash discount.
15 Hurst sold goods to Billings, charged at catalogue price 400·00, less 10% trade discount.
17 Billings returned as unsuitable goods purchased by him on June 15th, worth 30·00 at catalogue price.
26 Hurst bought from Billings a second-hand motor van for 425·00, and gave him credit for that amount.

You are required:

(*a*) to write up Billings's account in the Sales (or Debtors') Ledger of George Hurst, using the running balance method;
(*b*) to state who owes whom the outstanding balance.

No. 6. Clark is in business as a wholesaler, and the following are his transactions with Johnson for the month of August:

19..

Aug. 1 Balance due to Clark 75·80.

     4 Sales to Johnson 85·10, less 20% trade discount; Clark charged Johnson 1·12 for containers.

     8 Clark received goods returned by Johnson valued at 17·00 (catalogue price) and the containers, the latter for credit in full; purchases by Johnson valued at 95·00 net.

   31 Johnson sent cheque for the amount due on August 1st, less 5% cash discount; Clark purchased from Johnson fixtures and fittings valued at 100·00.

You are asked:

(*a*) to prepare from the above information Johnson's account as it would appear in Clark's ledger; in running-balance style.

(*b*) to state how the double entry would be completed in respect of the purchase on August 31st.

CHAPTER ELEVEN

BANK RECONCILIATION STATEMENTS

(1) Introduction—The Meaning of Reconciliation

If two friends quarrel, or fail to agree about some matter, the disagreement may temporarily end the friendship between them. When they become friends again we say they have been reconciled with one another. Reconciliation is therefore the resuming of friendly relations as a result, very often, of reasonable explanations. In business we often have sets of figures which are apparently in disagreement with one another, but reasonable explanations for the difference will reconcile the two sets of figures and show that, in fact, **both are right**.

The Two Figures for 'Bank' Moneys

In business we keep our Bank Account in the Cash Book, as part of the Three-column Cash Book. It is made up every day, and we enter in the account all cheques received, and take from the account all cheques paid. We shall also have several contra entries every month, recording cash takings paid in or cash drawn out when required for office use. We therefore have in our Cash Book a bank balance (as per the Cash Book).

The bank are also keeping a record of our Bank Account, and they too enter into our account every day what is paid in and what is drawn out. At the end of any day they will gladly tell us our bank balance (as per the bank).

(2) Why Do the Cash Book Figure and the Bank's Figure Disagree?

There are three reasons why these figures are rarely the same:

(*a*) One party may lack knowledge of the actions performed by the other.

(*b*) There is always an unavoidable delay between one party doing something and the other party knowing about it.

(*c*) Errors often occur.

The idea of a Bank Reconciliation Statement is to discover these three sorts of difference, put right anything that is wrong, and draw up a logical explanation of the remaining differences, which are not wrong, but are delayed from being right by the time lag.

Consider the following information from A. Dealer's Cash Book and Bank Statement:

CASH BOOK (BANK COLUMN ONLY)

Dr.							Cr.
19..				19..			
Feb. 1	To Balance	225·00		Feb. 2	By Green	47·60	
10	„ Ambrose	50·75		14	„ Howard	28·50	
17	„ Bloggs	62·62		19	„ Ives	36·70	
28	„ Crayford	73·50					

A rough calculation shows that the balance on this Cash Book is 299·07—a debit balance.

BANK STATEMENT

A. Dealer in account with Barclay's Bank Limited

Date	Details	Dr.	Cr.	Balance
19..				
Feb. 1	Balance Forward			225·00
2	Green	47·60		177·40
12	Ambrose		50·75	228·15
16	Howard	28·50		199·65
16	Charges	5·25		194·40
17	Bloggs		62·62	257·02
28	Bank of England (bonds)		12·58	269·60

A careful look at these two accounts will show:

(*a*) The balances do not agree. 299·07 according to the Cash Book, 269·60 according to the Bank Statement.

(*b*) Both accounts did agree on February 1st, so the problem is quite recent. Sometimes we may find a time lag lasting months, usually because someone has failed to bank a cheque.

(*c*) Ives's cheque sent to him on February 19th has not yet been paid in by Ives. He may be a sole trader who only bothers to go to the bank once a week or so. On the other hand, it may have blown down the back of the radiator when someone opened the window. This is one example of the time lag.

(*d*) Crayford's cheque received by February 28th, that is today, has been paid in by Dealer but is not recorded on the Statement. This is another kind of time lag; the bank will probably credit it tomorrow to the account.

(*e*) The bank has charged Dealer 5·25 Bank Charges. Dealer did not know about this deduction from his funds, but now he does know he should clearly put it right by deducting it from his Bank Account.

(*f*) The bank has received some interest from the Bank of England for Dealer. Dealer has not been told about this increase in his funds but now that he knows he will obviously enter it into his Cash Book.

(*e*) and (*f*) are examples of a lack of knowledge existing between Dealer and his bankers. Dealer did not know that the bank had taken away, nor received on his behalf, these moneys.

(3) How to Draw Up a Bank Reconciliation Statement

In examinations we are sometimes asked to reconcile the two balances using all the items that are outstanding, but in business the following is the programme:

(*a*) Compare the two accounts and note all the items of disagreement, as we have done in (*a*)—(*f*) in the last section.

(*b*) Adjust all items that can be put right in the Cash Book—items which are only wrong because of our lack of knowledge of what the bankers have done.

(*c*) Reconcile the rest in a reasonable statement, starting with one balance and finishing with the other.

If we cannot reconcile them there must be some mistake, either on our part or on the bank's part. Carefully scrutinize every figure. (The author once went heavily 'in the red' because his bankers paid the mortgage twice every month for six months. A bad figure on the Standing Order for payment was being read by one Clerk as 'Pay on the 1st' and by another clerk as 'Pay on the 7th'.)

Our calculations now look like this:

REVISED CASH BOOK (BANK COLUMNS ONLY)

Dr. 19..				Cr. 19..			
Feb. 1	To Balance	225·00		Feb. 2	By Green	47·60	
10	„ Ambrose	50·75		14	„ Howard	28·50	
17	„ Bloggs	62·62		19	„ Ives	36·70	
28	„ Crayford	73·50		28	„ Bank Charges	5·25	
28	„ Interest Received	12·58		28	„ Balance	306·40	
		424·45				424·45	
Mar. 1	To Balance	306·40					

BANK RECONCILIATION STATEMENT

(as at February 28th)

Balance as per Cash Book	306·40
Add back the cheque not yet presented	36·70
(because the bank has not yet been asked for the money)	343·10
Deduct the Crayford cheque not yet cleared	73·50
(because the bank are not yet crediting us with the money)	
Balance as per Bank Statement	269·60

Clearly we have been able to explain the disagreement successfully. Bank Reconciliation Statements are typed out neatly and filed away for inspection when required.

EXERCISES SET XXIII

(4) Bank Reconciliation Statements

No. 1. On June 30th W. Evans's Cash Book showed a bank balance of 404·18, but at the same date the monthly statement from his bank showed a balance of 420·64.

The difference between the two balances was found to be due to the following:

(*a*) On June 10th a charge of 0·40 for foreign exchange commission had been made by the bank. Evans had not entered this in his Cash Book.

(*b*) An annual subscription of 5·00 had been paid by a banker's Standing Order on June 25th.

(*c*) Cheques for 25·80 and 37·19 issued by Evans had not been presented for payment.

(*d*) A cheque for 41·13 from A. Jones paid into the bank on June 15th had been returned marked 'No Account'. No entry of this dishonour had been made in the Cash Book.

You are asked to open Evans's Bank Account in his Cash Book with the opening balance given above, 404·18; to enter such items as have been omitted; to find the new balance that results, and to draw up a Bank Reconciliation Statement to reconcile this new balance with the balance given on the Bank Statement.

(*R.S.A.—Adapted*)

No. 2. The following shows the entries in T. Fitt's Cash Book in March:

19..				19..			
Mar.	1	To Balance at bank brought forward	115·00	Mar.	5	By Drawings—self	20·00
	16	„ Brown	25·00		15	„ Noah	80·00
	25	„ Abel	185·00			„ Oliver	25·00
	31	„ Warner	286·00		29	„ Rigg	95·00
						„ Lee	15·00
					31	„ Balance at bank carried forward	376·00
			611·00				611·00

Early in April he received this statement from his bank:

T. FITT: IN ACCOUNT WITH THE LOANSHIRE BANK LIMITED

Date	Particulars	Debit	Credit	Balance
Mar. 1	Balance forward			115·00
5	Self—T. Fitt	20·00		95·00
17	Sundries		25·00	120·00
18	Oliver	25·00		
18	Noah	80·00		15·00
26	Sundries		185·00	200·00
28	Cheque returned unpaid	25·00		175·00
31	Charges	4·00		171·00
31	Lee	15·00		156·00

Draw up a Cash Book, starting with the present balance of 376·00 and correct such differences as are caused by a lack of knowledge of the bank's activities. Then reconcile the revised cash balance with the balance at the bank in a Bank Reconciliation Statement.

No. 3. On December 31st the Woodlands Girls' School Fund Cash Book showed a balance at the bank of 47·12, whereas the Bank Statement showed a balance of 32·51. On checking these against one another it was found that Mrs. Austerberry, the Treasurer, had entered a cheque for 40·12 in the Cash Book as 40·13. This cheque was paid out to 'War on Want'. Two cheques paid into the school fund had not yet been credited by the bank. These were from A. Governor, 5·50, and from A. Parent, 7·00. The bank had charged 2·12 for keeping the account for the six months ending December 31st, and this had not been entered in the Cash Book. Get the Cash Book right first and then do the Bank Reconciliation Statement.

No. 4. On July 31st R. Heron's Cash Book shows a balance at the bank of 263·19. On asking the bank for a statement he finds it shows that he has 333·11. On checking he sees the following differences: he has forgotten to write 0·50 off his Cash Book for a standing order, and the bank have also charged him 2·76 charges. Two cheques sent to R. Blood 27·51, and B. Thunder 45·67, have not yet been presented by them.

You are asked (*a*) to put the Cash Book right where it is wrong; (*b*) to make out a Bank Reconciliation Statement for the remaining items.

No. 5. On August 31st J. Trueman asks his bank for a statement. It shows a balance of cash at the bank 162·95, whereas according to his Cash Book he has exactly 200·00 at the bank. He finds that a cheque for 149·95 which he sent on August 30th to P. Brown has not yet been presented by Brown, and also that two cheques paid into the bank for 160·00 and 27·00 have not yet been credited by the bank. These cheques were from J. Jones and R. Elvidge. Reconcile the two balances.

No. 6. On March 31st, J. Cooper's Cash Book showed a balance of 450·00 and his Statement of Account from the bank showed a balance in his favour of 800·00. On comparing the statement with his Cash Book he found that the following entries in the Cash Book had not yet been entered on the statement:

Cheques paid in on March 31st, 160·00
Cheques drawn up to March 31st, 350·00

and the following entries on the statement had not yet been entered in his Cash Book:

Bank Charges 20·00
Payment direct to the bank by a debtor 180·00

You are asked (*a*) to draw up a new Cash Book balance bearing in mind such of the above figures as are relevant; (*b*) to reconcile this new Cash Book balance with the bank balance shown above.

(*R.S.A.—Adapted*)

No. 7. The following are copies of the Bank Column of R. Miller's Cash Book and of his Bank Statement as rendered by the bank. You are asked to bring the Cash Book up to date and reconcile the remaining items, in a well-presented Bank Reconciliation Statement.

CASH BOOK (BANK COLUMNS ONLY)

Dr. 19..			19..		Cr.
June 20	To Balance	198·40	June 21	By A	6·56
25	,, C	28·46	23	,, B	17·32
30	,, E	14·60	29	,, D	29·54
			30	,, Balance	188·04
		241·46			241·46
July 1	To Balance	188·04			

R. Miller in account with Royal Bank Ltd.

19..	Details	Dr.	Cr.	Balance
June 20	Balance			198·40
23	Cheque	6·56		191·84
25	Sundries		28·46	220·30
29	Cheque	29·54		190·76
30	Charges	4·65		186·11
30	Credit transfer		17·55	203·66

No. 8. F. Graham's Cash Book showed a balance of 540·18 cash at bank on December 31st. On that date his bank pass book showed a balance of 525·96 cash at bank. The difference arose as follows:

Cheques drawn by F. Graham for 28·77 in favour of Smith and 72·16 in favour of Williams had not been presented by them for payment and 99·71 received on December 31st was not shown in the pass book until January 2nd. The bank charged 15·44 interest which had not been entered in the Cash Book.

You are required to prepare a Reconciliation Statement in correct form.

No. 9. On August 31st R. Herd's Cash Book shows a balance at the bank of 268·70. The Bank Statement on the same date shows 350·14. On carefully checking the two statements he finds:

(*a*) Two cheques sent to B. Disraeli and K. Gladstone during the month, for 72·12 and 31·10 have not yet been presented by them.

(*b*) The takings paid in on August 31st have not yet been entered. These were 18·60.

(*c*) Bank Charges of 2·98 have been deducted by the bank without notice, and commission for 0·20, has been deducted also by them. This had been forgotten in the Cash Book.

Reconcile the two balances.

No. 10. On January 1st, R. Jones has a balance at the bank, according to his Cash Book, of 300·15. He asks his bank for a statement and is told that he has a balance of 478·84. He is also able to discover that the bank charged him 4·12 Bank Charges, and had collected from the Treasury interest on his War Loan amounting to 160·00. A cheque for 22·81 sent by Jones to a supplier,

Best Biscuits Ltd., on December 31st had not yet been presented by them.
You are asked: (*a*) to correct the Cash Book; (*b*) to reconcile the amended
Cash Book with the Bank Statement.

No. 11. Barnaby's Cash Book for July was as follows:

19..				19..			
July	1	To Balance	525·75	July	2	By Cromer & Co.	25·45
	4	„ Cash Sales	50·00		10	„ Folkstone Ltd.	47·77
	7	„ Jones & Co.	366·75		22	„ Drawings	25·00
	24	„ Cash Sales	60·15		27	„ Lee & Co.	48·56
	31	„ B. Smith	42·65		29	„ Zenith Ltd.	29·65
					29	„ Charges	0·50

His bank statement showed:

19..				19..			
July	17	To Folkstone	47·77	July	1	By Balance	600·50
	18	„ Cromer & Co.	25·45		4	„ Sundries	50·00
	19	„ Hugh & Co.	54·45			„ Sundries	366·75
	22	„ Drawings	25·00		24	„ Sundries	60·15
	22	„ Toffer	20·30			„ Credit transfer	
	29	„ Charges	0·50			(Peters)	40·45

You are asked to correct the Cash Book for items which are the result of
Barnaby's not knowing what the bank had done, and then to do a Bank
Reconciliation Statement for the remaining items.

No. 12. From the following prepare a Bank Reconciliation Statement as at
June 30th, after first bringing the Cash Book up to date if this is required:

J. JONES & CO.

CASH BOOK ON JUNE 30TH, 19..

19..				19..			
June	4	To Bank Loan	500·00	June	1	By Balance	227·10
	11	„ R. Gee	3·20		8	„ T. Smith	40·60
	30	„ L. Mitre	4·00		15	„ R. Port	4·96
					29	„ B. Lemon	62·10

BANK STATEMENT AS AT JUNE 30TH, 19..

Date		Particulars	Debit	Credit	Balance
June	1			(Red)Dr.	227·10
	4	Loan		500·00	272·90
	8	Sundries	40·60		232·30
	11	„		3·20	235·50
	16	Bank of S. Africa Div.		12·40	247·90
	29	Sundries	62·10		185·80
	30	Charges	0·50		185·30

CHAPTER TWELVE

ANALYTICAL OR COLUMNAR DAY BOOKS

(1) Introduction

Where a firm has departments, or lines of goods which are distinctive from other lines, the proprietor may prefer to calculate the profits on each department separately. This is to prevent good work in one department hiding bad work in another. One department may be well run by an efficient departmental manager who is careful to keep costs as low as possible and to buy astutely when prices are right. Another department may be run very badly, its buying policy weak, with articles of poor value for the price, and its sales only maintained because of the low profit margin added. Such a department may actually be running at a loss, yet because of the good work done in other departments the weakness is hidden. The business as a whole is making reasonable profits.

Such weak points in a firm can be discovered if Departmental Accounts are kept. This will be discussed more fully in Chapter Twenty-seven, page 345, the section on Departmental Accounts. Before we can prepare such accounts we must provide the figures, and this means analysis of the Purchases, Sales, and Returns made by the departments. We can then discover what each department has bought and sold.

(2) Columnar Sales and Purchases Rulings

A simple Day Book is written on Journal Paper, but the two money columns are not equally important. One column is used only for collecting together the items that occur on one invoice, or for deducting Trade Discount. The other column is the important one that is used to post the original entry into the Ledger Accounts.

With an analytical or columnar Day Book, extra columns are added to analyse the amounts relating to separate departments. In the specimen paper shown here we have allowed only five analysis columns, but in business as many as thirty-eight columns can be provided. Naturally this makes a very large book indeed, and if the Day Book is typewritten a very long carriage on the typewriter is desirable. Such analysis work lends itself to mechanization since the carriage can be adjusted to stop exactly where it is required, and registers can also be employed to add the amounts entered into the columns.

Fig. 99 shows such an analysis book for a garage. Sales are analysed under five headings, and the columns can be totalled to produce the

Date	Details	Petrol and Oil	New Vehicles	Repairs	Acces-sories	Parts	F	Details	Total
19.. July 1	Moore & King								
	5 gallons petrol	1·85						1·85	
	4 pints oil	0·45						0·45	
	De-mister				3·25			3·25	
							L. 27		5·55
1	Lewis & Co.						L. 25		
	Mercedes-Benz		1,328·00						1,328·00
2	Colt & Lewis								
	5,000-mile service			4·50				4·50	
	Plugs, etc.					2·65		2·65	
	Spot Lamp				4·76			4·76	
							L. 13		11·91
		2·30	1,328·00	4·50	8·01	2·65	c/f		1,345·46

Fig. 99. A Columnar Sales Day Book

departmental figures required. The ordinary Day Book work is unchanged. We still record the invoice details in the details column, carry them straight through to the end column if there is only one item on the invoice, or add them up in the second column from the edge of the paper if there are several items. The extra columns simply help us, as they did in the Petty Cash Book, to collect into sub-totals information we require about each department of the firm.

At the end of the page the totals of the columns are carried forward to the next page, but before we do this it is usual to *cross-tot*. This gives us a useful check on the arithmetical work performed.

When columnar Sales and Purchases Books become very cumbersome separate books can be used for each department; so can separate Sales Accounts instead of the Departmental Sales Account shown in Fig. 100.

(3) Posting the Totals of an Analysis Book

As the month goes by we post the various invoices to the debtors' accounts, but when we come to the end of the month the sales total for the month is posted to a special type of Sales Account, a Departmental Sales Account. Here is an example, but the figures are not those shown in Fig. 99 since clearly July 2nd is not the last day of the month.

Page Centre   SALES ACCOUNT (CREDIT SIDE ONLY)

Date	Petrol and Oil	New Vehicles	Repairs	Acces-sories	Spare Parts	L. 162 Total
July 31	1,786·50	5,678·00	987·50	325·60	1,473·50	10,251·10

Fig. 100. A Columnar Sales Account

Purchases Day Books and Returns Books can be ruled in similar styles to provide departmental figures for Purchases, Purchases Returns, and Sales Returns.

EXERCISES SET XXIV

(4) Analysis Day Books

No. 1. Give the ruling of a Sales Book suitable for a business divided into three departments and insert three specimen entries, supplying your own dates, names, etc.

No. 2. Give the ruling of a Purchases Book for a businessman who buys silk, cotton, and woollen goods, so that he may ascertain his total monthly purchases of each class of goods, as well as the gross total. Make three specimen entries.

No. 3. Rock N. Roll is a retailer selling gramophones, wireless sets, and musical instruments, and keeps a separate Purchases Account for each department. You are asked to prepare a suitable Purchases Day Book in columnar form and enter in it the following purchases:

19..
Mar. 1 Bought from Adam & Co. 6 Violins at 30·00 each less 10% trade discount.
12 Bought from Benjamin's Ltd 12 Gramophones at 15·50 each.
18 Bought from Caleb & Co. 3 'Cellos at 40·00 each, plus 3·50 for carriage.
21 Bought from Abel Swinger a job lot of Saxophones for 89·00.
29 Bought from Western Radios 3 'Spacetuner' Wireless sets at 20·00 each, less 15% trade discount.

Rule off the Day Book at the end of the month and insert the totals.

(*R.S.A.—Adapted*)

No. 4. B. Whittington is in business as a wholesale florist. He deals in four main classes of goods: seeds, bulbs, cut flowers, and pot plants. Record the following invoices in a suitable Sales Day Book—analysed for these four departments:

19..
Oct. 3 R. Mulligan purchases goods as follows:
1 gross assorted flower seeds	= 4·75
1 gross assorted vegetable seeds	= 3·75
5 cwts. bulk Daffodils	= 12·25

10 M. Bews purchases goods as follows:
6 boxes cut Chrysanthemums	= 9·50
12 boxes cut Roses	= 14·50
3 gross Iris bulbs (packets of 12)	= 10·40

17 R. Peachey purchases goods as follows:
40 boxes cut Scabious	= 36·50
20 gross packets flower seeds	= 75·00
20 gross packets vegetable seeds	= 65·00

27 M. Lupin purchases goods as follows:
6 boxes cut Chrysanthemums	= 9·50
1 gross pot plants (various)	= 16·00
1 gross flower seeds	= 4·75

No. 5. Floris Brandt runs a business which has four departments: stationery, confectionery, chemists' sundries, and toys. He keeps a Purchases Day Book on the columnar basis which analyses the purchases under these four headings. Enter the following invoices on special paper ruled up for the purpose and total the book at the end of the month:

19..

Aug.   4 R. Rector sold Brandt goods as follows:
5 gross packets envelopes at 1·10 gross	= 5·50
2 gross writing pads at 1·65 gross	= 3·30
3 dozen dolls at 0·20 each	= 7·20
2 dozen 'Mini Model' cars at 0·15 each	= 3·60

12 B. Vicar sold Brandt goods as follows:
6 jars liquorice drops at 0·35 jar	= 2·10
10 jars fruit drops at 0·30 jar	= 3·00
4 dozen packets Snacktime chocolates at 0·05	= 2·40
2 gross aspirin tubes at 1·55 gross	= 3·10

18 A. Priest sold to Brandt goods as follows:
20 packets cough tablets at 0·08 each	= 1·60
1 gross infants' dummies at 0·20 dozen	= 2·40

29 G. Monk sold to Brandt as follows:
1 gross bars chocolate at 0·03	= 4·32
1 gross bars chocolate at 0·06	= 8·64
2 gross memo pads at 1·25 gross	= 2·50

Insert appropriate folio numbers in suitable places.

(*East Anglian Examination Board—Adapted*)

CHAPTER THIRTEEN

THE BANK CASH BOOK

(1) Introduction

As a firm grows larger the problems of controlling the firm grow too, especially that of finding enough good workers. This does not mean that reliable workers are not available, or that workers are more dishonest than they used to be. It means that the number of posts available to workers has increased and they are able to pick and choose their firms, and demand higher wages as a result. If we can devise schemes which permit us to use less skilled or less reliable labour we can keep the wage bill down.

The Bank Cash Book is such a device. It gives efficient control of the cash, enabling Head Office to see what is happening in all branches at the shortest possible notice, and to descend suddenly upon branches where they suspect inefficiency or even crime.

(2) The Principle of the Bank Cash Book

The basic idea of the Bank Cash Book, which replaces the Three-column Cash Book, is that the cashier does not disburse cash at all, and if he receives any he pays it into the bank as if it was a cheque. Any cash that has to be paid out will be dealt with through the Petty Cash Book, on the Imprest System.

If this is how we intend to deal with the cash, then the cash column in the Three-column Cash Book will not be required at all, and may be used for another purpose which will be illustrated shortly.

The cashier is now receiving money, probably from daily takings in the tills, and possibly from debtors, but that money will be banked each night in full, probably in the night safe of the local bank. Head Office usually has an arrangement with the bank that if the daily takings are not banked in the night safe, Head Office will be informed at once. This enables Head Office to send someone down to see the branch manager immediately.

Head Office will also watch the amounts of the daily takings. If a particular day's takings seem lower than usual, or if takings generally are declining, Head Office will investigate. There may be a thousand and one reasons: the manager is stealing the money; the assistants are not ringing up the tills for the right amounts; the manager is bad-tempered, and is alienating customers; the shop is facing cut-price

175

Debit side (receipts)

Date	Details	Folio	Discount Allowed	Details	Bank
19.. Jan. 1	To Balance	B/d			378·65
1	,, D. Williams	L. 79		7·35	
1	,, Grout & Co.	L. 26	1·40	12·60	
1	,, Cash Sales	L. 34		45·32	65·27
2	,, R. Jones	L. 45		28·35	
2	,, P. Masters	L. 49	1·65	4·25	
2	,, Cash Sales	L. 34		65·75	98·35
4	,, J. Cornwell	L. 27		179·50	
4	,, D. Davis	L. 29	8·50	14·75	
4	,, R. Morgan	L. 38		12·65	
4	,, Cash Sales	L. 34		48·72	255·62
			11·55		797·89
			L. 81		
5	To Balance	B/d			626·64

Credit side (payments)

Date	Details	Folio	Discount Received	Details	Bank
19.. July 3	By Marshall & Co.	L. 62	1·55	27·45	27·45
4	,, M. Fox	L. 33		4·62	
4	,, T. Green	L. 37	3·35	7·35	
4	,, M. Larkin	L. 42		127·65	
4	,, Petty Cash	P.C.B. 5		4·18	
4	,, Balance	c/d			143·80 626·64
			4·90		797·89
			L. 82		

Fig. 101. The Bank Cash Book

competition from other shopkeepers. This is the way to control a business—to investigate immediately all unusual matters, from every possible point of view.

(3) Layout of the Bank Cash Book

The difference between this book and the Three-column Cash Book is that cash will not be handled at all, except as daily takings to be paid into the bank. This means that the cash column is not needed and may be used instead as a details column for bank payments, the total paid into the bank being the only figure to appear in the bank column. This is a great advantage since it enables us to compare the bank figures very easily with the Bank Statement sent to us by the bank. The Bank Statement usually has the amount paid in, both cheques and cash, lumped together in one figure as Sundries. It is a great help to have this one figure, lumped together, also in our Cash Book.

The lines ruled across the details column are for the addition of the day's total for the bank. Usually the last item on the debit side will be the daily cash takings as the tills are cashed up at the end of the day and paid into the bank.

In all other respects the Bank Cash Book is exactly like the Three-column Cash Book.

(4) The Cash Book as a Book of Original Entry

In discussing the books of Original Entry we have not yet considered the position of the Cash Book. It is unusual in that it is both a book of Original Entry, and a part of the Ledger.

It is a book of Original Entry because documents—cheques and receipts—are entered directly into it. The Cash Book therefore constitutes the prime entry for cheques and receipts. There is no real need to Journalize cash, since the Cash Book is itself the Day Book. For very formal matters, like the purchase of valuable assets for cash, a Journal Entry would probably be done in order to record the serial number, if any, of the asset purchased.

The entries in the Petty Cash Book are similarly original entries, and yet form part of the Ledger itself. The Petty Cash Book is an extension of the Cash Account, to cover small cash receipts and disbursements.

Exercises Set XXV

(5) The Bank Cash Book

No. 1. Write up a trader's Bank Cash Book from the following information:
19..
May 1 Balance as per Cash Book 727·65; total paid in 97·65, consisting of 47·65 from M. Jones in full settlement of his debt of 50·00, and 50·00 cash sales; cheques drawn: R. Fowler 16·75, M. Lewis 13·25.

2 Total paid in 127·65, all cash sales; cheque drawn: Urban Council 25·25; Petty Cash 5·00.

3 Total paid in 127·32, consisting of cheques from M. Cantor, 7·32, in full settlement of his debt of 8·00; and R. Lessor, 45·00. The rest was cash takings; cheques drawn: T. Clive 4·75, R. Loosely 7·62.

Balance off the book and bring down the balance. Insert appropriate folio numbers in suitable places.

No. 2. Write up a trader's Bank Cash Book from the following:

19..

July 1 Balance as per Cash Book 691·75; total paid in 84·62, consisting of cheques from R. Roper, 5·75, P. Lucas, 6·87, and cash sales 72·00; cheques drawn: A. Landlord 40·50.

2 Cheques drawn: J. Morgan 52·75.

3 Total paid in 176·25, consisting of a cheque for 15·25 from R. Lauder and the rest cash sales; cheques drawn: Petty Cash 8·75.

4 Total paid in 75·65, of which there were cheques from T. Sampson 4·35 and D. Lyler 11·30; the rest was cash sales; cheques drawn: M. Gyler 64·50.

No. 3. Write up a trader's Bank Cash Book from the following information:

(*a*) his balance at the bank at the close of business on May 27th, according to his Cash Book, was 872·53;

(*b*) the counterfoils of his Paying-in Book give these details:

19..

May 28 Total paid in 203·30, consisting of cash from sales 45·30, a cheque from B. Bath for 60·50, and a cheque from L. Poole for 97·50; Poole's cheque was accepted in full settlement of 100·00 owed by him.

30 Total paid in 44·15, consisting entirely of cash from sales.

31 Total paid in 80·60, consisting of cash from sales 39·00 and a cheque from H. Winton for 41·60.

(*c*) The counterfoils of his cheque book show:

19..

May 28	J. Battle and Co. Ltd.	298·65
	30 W. Thorley and Co.	195·00
	31 Petty Cash	26·30
	Self	50·00
	Elton's Garage	17·65

The cheque to Thorley and Co. was accepted in full settlement of 200·00 owing to them. The cheque to Elton's Garage was for petrol, oil, and maintenance of the delivery van for the previous month, and no previous record of this transaction had gone through the books.

The details columns of the Cash Book should indicate clearly which Ledger Account is to be debited or credited in respect of each entry. Rule off and balance the Cash Book as at the close of business on May 31st.

(*R.S.A.—Adapted*)

No. 4. The Cash Book of Thomas, a wholesaler, shows a balance at the bank of 876·55 on January 1st. He pays all receipts into the bank and pays all payments by cheque except for Petty Cash items. Enter the following items in correct date order and balance off the account. Invent suitable folio numbers for each item.

Receipts in Receipts Book

Jan.	1	Nigel and Co.	Cheque	177·55	Discount	7·45
	5	Ravel and Co.	„	85·60	„	3·40
	7	Purcell and Co.	„	77·25	„	2·25
	11	Mozart Ltd.	„	145·65	„	6·35

Cash Sales from Till

Jan.	2	134·60
	6	127·50
	8	138·80
	10	78·50

Cheques Drawn

Jan.	1	Haji and Co.	42·75	Discount	1·15
	2	Nartey and Co.	30·65		
	3	M. Thompson	7·85	„	1·15
	5	R. Fidler	19·73		
	6	L. Shane	16·45		
	8	R. Mackay	12·75		
	10	S. Lucas	113·75	„	5·25
	11	R. Theron	14·60		

CHAPTER FOURTEEN

MORE ABOUT DEPRECIATION

(1) A 'True and Fair View' of the Assets

Depreciation is the reduction in value of an asset as a result of fair wear and tear. As an asset loses value we reduce the book valuation of it in line with our estimate of the loss. In Chapter Six we saw how to do this by means of a simple Journal Entry. We now need to learn a little more about depreciation, a fairly complex subject, where book-keeping merges into accountancy.

The accounting principle which motivates accountants to try different methods of depreciation, is that we are seeking in our accounting to achieve a 'true and fair view' of the position of the business. As far as Limited Companies are concerned in Great Britain, this is positively required by law. The Companies' Act requires all businesses to keep accounts in such a way as to give a 'true and fair view' of the Company's affairs. This 'true and fair view' requires two things:

(a) The assets must be valued on the books at a fair value so far as we can estimate it.

(b) If a loss has been suffered it must be charged against the profits— to do otherwise would overstate the profitability of the business.

Applying these two rules to the problem of depreciation, we see that if an asset wears out the loss suffered as a result of wear and tear must be written off the profits. At the same time the asset will be reduced in value to show only its present value now that it has been partly worn out.

There are about eight different methods of calculating depreciation, but for *Book-keeping Made Simple* we will discuss the three commonest methods. These are:

(a) The Straight Line or Equal Instalment Method
(b) The Diminishing Balance Method
(c) The Revaluation Method

(2) The Equal Instalment Method

The accountant first calculates the amount of the annual charge for depreciation necessary to reduce the asset to its scrap value, or residual value, over the lifetime of the asset. To do this we use the following formula:

$$\text{Annual Charge} = \frac{\text{Cost Price less Scrap Value}}{\text{Estimated lifetime in years}}$$

Example: A motor vehicle is purchased for 750·00 on January 1st. It is estimated that it will need replacing in four years and will then fetch 250·00 on trade-in. Using the formula, we have:

$$\text{Annual Charge} = \frac{750\cdot00 - 250\cdot00}{4}$$

$$= \frac{500\cdot00}{4}$$

$$= 125\cdot00$$

The asset will be depreciated by four equal instalments of 125·00 and will then be reduced on the books to a value of 250·00. The Motor Vehicle Account will look like this:

MOTOR VEHICLE ACCOUNT   L. 11

Year 1				Year 1			
Jan. 1	To Rex Garages	J. 1.	750·00	Dec. 31	By Depreciation	L. 17	125·00
				31	,, Balance	c/d	625·00
			750·00				750·00
Year 2				Year 2			
Jan. 1	To Balance	B/d	625·00	Dec. 31	By Depreciation	L. 17	125·00
				31	,, Balance	c/d	500·00
			625·00				625·00
Year 3				Year 3			
Jan. 1	To Balance	B/d	500·00	Dec. 31	By Depreciation	L. 17	125·00
				31	,, Balance	c/d	375·00
			500·00				500·00
Year 4				Year 4			
Jan. 1	To Balance	B/d	375·00	Dec. 31	By Depreciation	L. 17	125·00
				31	,, Balance	c/d	250·00
			375·00				375·00
Year 5							
Jan. 1	To Balance	B/d	250·00				

Fig. 102. Depreciation by the Straight Line Method

Advantages and Disadvantages of the Method

Advantages: (*a*) It is straightforward and easily understood.

(*b*) It writes the asset down over a definite period to a predicted minimum value below which the business would not normally keep the asset.

Disadvantages: (*a*) Whenever new assets are bought or old assets are sold the depreciation for the asset must be recalculated.

(*b*) There is an increasing charge to the Profit and Loss Account over the years, because the repairs on an old machine increase. As the depreciation charge is steady the total cost—depreciation plus repairs—must increase over the years. This offends against another book-keeping principle that we should try to even out the burden to Profit and Loss Account over the years from the use of the same asset.

(*c*) There is no provision made for replacing the asset when it is worn out. This is discussed later in the chapter.

(3) The Diminishing Balance Method

Under this method the asset is depreciated by a fixed percentage every year on the diminishing balance of the account. This is a very simple method since recalculation is not required when additions or sales take place during the year.

Example: A firm's depreciation policy for motor vehicles requires the book-keeper to write 25 per cent off the diminishing balance of the asset every year. Show the Depreciation Account for a motor vehicle valued at 750·00 bought on January 1st, 19...

The Motor Vehicles Account will appear as follows:

MOTOR VEHICLES ACCOUNT   L. 11

Year 1				Year 1			
Jan. 1	To Rex Garages	J. 1.	750·00	Dec. 31	By Depreciation L. 17		187·50
				31	„ Balance c/d		562·50
			750·00				750·00
Year 2				Year 2			
Jan. 1	To Balance	B/d	562·50	Dec. 31	By Depreciation L. 17		140·63
				31	„ Balance c/d		421·87
			562·50				562·50
Year 3				Year 3			
Jan. 1	To Balance	B/d	421·87	Dec. 31	By Depreciation L. 17		105·47
				31	„ Balance c/d		316·40
			421·87				421·87
Year 4				Year 4			
Jan. 1	To Balance	B/d	316·40	Dec. 31	By Depreciation L. 17		79·10
				31	„ Balance c/d		237·30
			316·40				316·40
Year 5							
Jan. 1	To Balance	B/d	237·30				

Fig. 103. Depreciation by the Diminishing Balance Method

Advantages and Disadvantages of the Diminishing Balance Method

Advantages: (*a*) It is straightforward and recalculations are not required when new assets are purchased or old assets sold.

(*b*) The charge against the profits for the use of the asset is more even over the years, since the diminishing charge for depreciation offsets the increasing charge for repairs.

Disadvantages: (*a*) The asset is never completely written off.

(*b*) Where a very short life is normal for an asset the percentage method is unsatisfactory, since the percentage required to write the asset off is very high. For instance, to write off 100·00 completely over three years requires a 90 per cent depreciation rate, i.e. 90·00 the first year, 9·00 the second year, and 0·90 the next year. This charge is so uneven as to be unsatisfactory.

(*c*) Again there is no provision for replacing the asset at the end of its useful life.

(4) The Revaluation Method

With some businesses it is quite impossible to treat depreciation by the normal method. For instance, a farmer can hardly say with certainty 'This old cow has declined by 20 per cent this year'. She may have had two fine calves this year. Where a firm has many loose tools, for instance shovels, spades, hoes, and rakes for a landscape gardening firm, it is often difficult to depreciate these items.

The sensible method in these cases is the revaluation method. This may result in a loss, a depreciation charge, or a profit—an appreciation in value caused by a rise in the asset's value. (See top of page 184.)

19.. Dec. 31	Depreciation Account Dr. To Herd Account Being decrease in value of herd during year	L. 7 L. 5	660·00	660·00

Fig. 104. Depreciation on Revaluation

HERD ACCOUNT   L. 5

19.. Jan. 1 To Balance	B/d	12,725·00	19.. Dec. 31 By Depreciation 31 „ Balance	L. 7 c/d	660·00 12,065·00
		12,725·00			12,725·00
19.. Jan. 1 To Balance	B/d	12,065·00			

Fig. 105. An Asset Account that has been revalued (see example, page 184)

Example: Farmer Giles's herd was valued at 12,725·00 on January 1st by the local valuer called in for the purpose. On December 31st the same valuer estimated the herd to be worth 12,065·00. Show the depreciation entry and the Herd Account. See Figs. 104 and 105 (page 183).

(5) Leaving Assets on the Books at Cost Price

A change has come over the established methods of depreciation since the Companies' Act of 1948, which introduced the requirement for companies that assets must be shown on the Balance Sheet at 'cost price less accumulated depreciation to date'. In Figs. 102 and 103 we see that the depreciation is written off the asset, so that the book value of the asset quite rightly reduces as the years pass. In these circumstances with long-lived assets we may lose sight of what the asset originally cost and thus be unable to comply with the requirement of the Companies' Act outlined above.

One way of overcoming this difficulty is to credit the depreciation, not in the Asset Account, but in a separate Provision for Depreciation Account, which collects the depreciation over the years, leaving the asset on the books in the Asset Account at cost price. The two accounts would look like this at the end of the third year, using the example illustrated previously in Fig. 102:

MOTOR VEHICLES ACCOUNT   L. 11

19.. Jan. 1 To Rex Garages J. 1 750·00	

PROVISION FOR DEPRECIATION ON MOTOR VEHICLES ACCOUNT   L. 12

	19.. Dec. 31 By Motor Vehicles 125·00 19.. Dec. 31 „ „ „ 125·00 19.. Dec. 31 „ „ „ 125·00

Fig. 106. Leaving the Asset on the books at Cost Price

The value of the asset at any given time is therefore the book-value (i.e. cost price), less the accumulated depreciation to date.

In this case it would be:

Cost price	750·00
Less depreciation	375·00
Present value of asset	375·00

which is the same as the balance on the Asset Account shown in Fig. 102 at the end of the third year.

(6) Providing for the Replacement of an Asset

Unfortunately depreciation in the way we have described does nothing at all to provide cash to replace an asset when it finally becomes obsolete or worn out. Depreciation reduces the profit available for the use of the proprietor, but it leaves this undistributed wealth in the business. Since uncommitted wealth has a way of getting used up in the ordinary conduct of the business, it is unwise to leave this wealth lying about. Sooner or later someone will put it to use in an 'extravagant' way. To purchase extra equipment, replace existing assets, or pay higher wages out of money that should be accumulating for the purchase of new main machinery in the future, is an extravagance the business cannot afford.

Prudent managers therefore take a second step in depreciation policy. Not only do they write depreciation off the profits in the Profit and Loss Account and thus reduce the value of the asset as already shown—**they also invest an equal amount of money in securities outside the business**. When the day comes to replace the asset the investments can be sold to provide the purchase price of the new equipment. This prevents the wealth accumulating inside the firm where anyone who notices it can find a use for it. The Journal Entry for this type of investment might read:

19.. Dec. 31	Plant and Machinery Replacement Investment Account Dr. To Bank Account Being cash invested at this date	125·00	125·00

Fig. 107. Investing to Provide for Renewal of Machinery

The asset, cash at bank, has been reduced and the portion given up has been replaced by a further asset, investments, which will not be touched until the order for new machinery is placed. A further point is that these investments will earn profits which can be reinvested to enlarge the portfolio of investments available for sale by the proprietors when required. This type of fund is called a **Sinking Fund**.

(7) Leases—A Special Case of the Straight-line Method

When we purchase the lease of a property, we purchase the right to live in that property for a given number of years, after which time it is returnable to the landlord. The commonest period for a long-term lease is 99 years, but some leases are now being given for 999 years. Short leases are very common too.

If we purchase a lease for 5,000·00 which has twenty years to run, we should write off one-twentieth of its value every year, that is 250·00 each year. This is called **amortizing the lease**, that is, writing off the dead part of the life of the lease. *This is treated here as a special case of the Straight-line Method of Depreciation, but more advanced treatments are possible.*

Two other points worth mentioning on leases are Dilapidations and Lease Replacement Sinking Funds.

Dilapidations

When a property is returned to the landlord he is entitled to demand that it be in as good a condition as when he leased it to us. For this reason leaseholders often put away certain sums each year to provide for any dilapidations that may need to be put right when the property is returned.

Lease Replacement Sinking Funds

When we surrender our lease we shall have to find alternative property, or pay a lump sum to renew the lease if the landlord is prepared to renew it. To provide for this, sums of money are invested each year to provide the necessary cash when it is required. The method is the same as the one described in the previous section (see 6, p. 185).

Exercises Set XXVI

(8) Depreciation

No. 1. On January 1st a firm bought a machine for 1,800·00. Its probable working life was estimated at ten years and its probable scrap value at the end of that time at 200·00. It was decided to write off depreciation by the fixed instalment method. Show the Machinery Account for the first two years.

(R.S.A.—Adapted)

No. 2. L. Jericho has a machine on his books which he purchased on July 1st, 19.., for 3,000·00. He depreciates it at a rate of 10 per cent per annum on December 31st of every year. In 19.. this is based on cost price, but in subsequent years it is based on the value at the start of the year (i.e. he uses the diminishing balance method). Show the Machinery Account for years 1, 2, and 3, bringing down the balance each year.

(*East Anglian Examination Board—Adapted*)

No. 3. A and B who set up in partnership as builders on January 31st, 19.., had a motor van the value of which was 200·00. On February 1st, 19.. (next day), the firm bought (for cash) a further motor van for 800·00 and a car for 600·00.

It is decided to write off depreciation at 20 per cent per annum on the reducing balance system.

On January 31st, two years later, the car was sold for 450·00 (cash).

You are asked to prepare the Motor Vehicles Account as it would appear in the partnership books for each financial year ended January 31st, year 1 and year 2, showing the amount written off as depreciation each year.

No. 4. G. Cresswell buys machinery on January 1st, 19.., valued at 720·00. The scrap value in ten years time is expected to be 170·00. If depreciation is written off by equal instalments every December 31st, show the Machinery Account for the years 1, 2, and 3.

No. 5. A Farmer has a herd valued at 15,750·00 on March 31st, 19... One year later, when he has the herd revalued, it is only valued at 13,275·00. Show the Journal Entry for the depreciation, and the 'Herd Account' for the year, balanced off and brought down.

No. 6. Gardening Ltd. use great quantities of small tools whose working life is fairly short. All purchases of such tools are entered in the Loose Tools Account, but the stock of loose tools is valued on December 31st of each year. On January 1st, 19.., they were valued at 415·00. New tools to the value of 227·00 were added in the year, on June 30th. On December 31st the stock of loose tools to be carried forward to the next year was valued at 440·00. Show the Journal Entry for depreciation and the Loose Tools Account for the year.

No. 7. A business buys an asset which it depreciates at the rate of 10 per cent per annum on a reducing basis. The original cost was 8,000·00 on January 1st, 19... Show the Asset Account for years 1, 2, and 3.

No. 8. On January 1st, year 1, Abacus Ltd. purchased two motor lorries (1 and 2) for 1,200·00 each, and on January 1st, year 2, purchased a third (3) at the same price.

On January 1st, year 3, lorry 1 was sold for 750·00 and replaced on the same day by a new lorry (4) which cost 1,500·00. Depreciation at the rate of 20 per cent per annum, calculated on the cost price, is credited each year to a 'Provision for Depreciation' Account, and the balance on the Motor Lorries Account represents the original cost of the lorries which have not been sold.

Show the entries in the Motor Lorries Account and in the Provision for Depreciation Account for years 1, 2, and 3.

(*R.S.A.—Adapted*)

CHAPTER FIFTEEN

THE WAGES BOOK AND WAGES SYSTEMS

(1) Introduction

Wage payment has become more and more involved in recent years as most countries introduce some elements of welfare, paid for by deductions from the pay packet. Liability to pay Income Tax has also increased as world wage levels have risen and the activities of governments in providing public education and other facilities have grown. Some sort of 'Pay As You Earn' system of taxation is necessary for lower income earners, who cannot be expected to save up a year's tax and pay it in one lump sum. An employer must keep a clear record of the wage earned, the deductions for welfare payments (called in Great Britain the 'National Insurance Scheme'), the P.A.Y.E. tax deductions, and other deductions of a voluntary nature. In many firms these include charitable contributions or contributions for sports club facilities. Britain's P.A.Y.E. scheme is shortly to be improved by a 'Tax Credit' system.

(2) The Traditional Wages Book

A traditional Wages Book is illustrated in Fig. 108. A careful study of the columns will show the student how the final sums due to the employee have been calculated, and what other payments must be made to outside bodies like the Commissioners of Inland Revenue and charitable organizations.

(3) Modern Wages Systems

The systems to be described in this section have been developed in recent years to provide complete records of wages payments without repetition of work.

For a satisfactory wages system three things are essential:

(a) A wages book providing the sort of information shown in Fig. 108.

(b) An individual record for each employee which can be referred to whenever the employee queries his pay for any reason. It would not be satisfactory to show an employee the Wages Book itself for he can then see what other people earn; this can be embarrassing and can lead to bad relations between staff.

Fig. 108 The Wages Book

No	Name of Employee	Earnings				Tax Details to Date						Deductions					Net Pay	Refunds	Total Payable
		Basic	Overtime	Other	Gross Pay	Gross to Date	Tax Free	Taxable Pay	Tax Due	Tax Paid	Refunds	Tax	National Insurance	Other Ins.	Voluntary	Total Deducts			
1	R. Brewer	10.50	8.60	0.40	19.50	138.66	138.66	—	—	—	—	—	0.95	—	0.01	0.96	18.54	—	18.54
2	T. Jones	10.50	8.60	1.50	20.60	142.40	82.40	60.00	11.70	8.50	—	3.20	0.95	—	0.01	4.16	16.44	—	16.44
3	V. Smith	17.50	1.50	1.40	20.40	168.20	90.60	77.60	13.25	9.20	—	4.05	0.95	—	0.01	5.01	15.39	—	15.39
4	M. Stanton	10.50	7.50	0.40	18.40	142.40	142.40	—	—	—	—	—	0.95	—	0.01	0.96	17.44	—	17.44
5	R. Vickery	10.50	8.60	0.40	19.50	140.50	140.50	—	—	—	—	—	0.95	—	0.01	0.96	18.54	—	18.54
6	G. White	23.50	—	4.75	28.25	172.60	90.60	82.00	14.10	10.60	—	3.50	0.95	—	0.01	4.46	23.79	—	23.79
		83.00	34.80	8.85	126.65							10.75	5.70	—	0.06	16.51	110.14	—	110.14

Figures for management to be used in controlling costs and fixing selling prices

Sums due to Income Tax Authorities

National Insurance Stamps

Donations to charities

Cash to be collected from bank for wage packets

Sums due to employee in wage packet

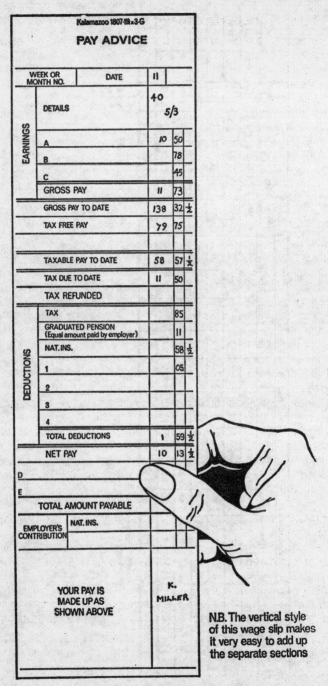

Fig. 109 (a). A Wages Advice Note

(*c*) An advice note to go into the wage packet of the employee; or information which may be written on the packet.

Clearly it would be a great advantage if these could all be prepared at once, without any rewriting from the Wages Book to the individual record and the wage packet.

There are many such systems, but the one described here is by courtesy of Kalamazoo Ltd.

A flat board giving a good writing surface is supplied to the wages clerk. This board is called the **Copy-Writer**, and has at the top a series of studs which engage with holes in the paper placed on the board. As the illustrations show, a set of ten advice notes is first laid on the Copy-Writer with the holes punched at the top engaging with the studs to keep the advice notes steady. A sheet of carbon is laid over the advice note and over this is placed the Wages Book in loose leaf form. This is called the **Pay Roll** form, and in the example shown is written in the opposite way to that of the Wages Book shown in Fig. 108, so that the calculations are vertical instead of horizontal. This vertical system saves 20 per cent of addition and subtraction time because it is the natural way to work. Cross-totting is never as easy as long-totting.

Over the Pay Roll sheet is placed a further piece of carbon and the individual record sheet of the employee. These sheets are ruled to give twenty-six weeks of the employee's records, and are stored in a locked index when not required. Any employee who wishes to query his pay can then be shown his own record without seeing those of other employees.

The clever part of the whole system is the positioning of this individual record sheet on top of the Pay Roll sheet and the advice notes. If it is positioned so that the next clean space on the individual record is over the next clean space on the Pay Roll and advice sheet, then whatever is written on the individual record sheet will be carbon copied without any further effort on to the Pay Roll and advice note below.

We thus have three records printed at once, and a copying error is impossible. The individual record returns to its locked index. The Pay Roll is totalled to give the managerial figures required for total wages and cost records.

The advice slips are torn off across the perforations and folded in batches of ten before being separated and used to prepare the wage packets.

This is a good example of the type of improvement that can be made in a book-keeping system by the expert accountant. At present over three million people in Great Britain alone are paid by the Kalamazoo system.

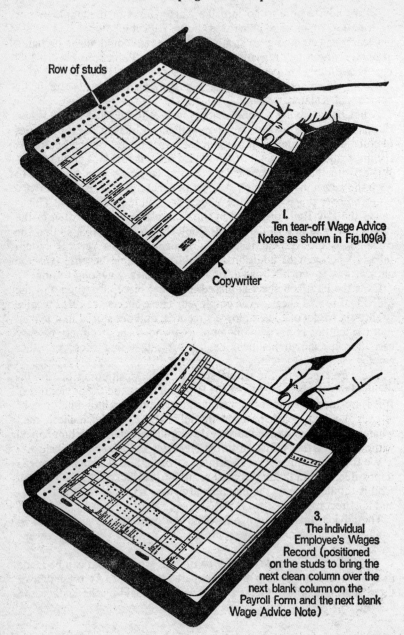

Row of studs

I.
Ten tear-off Wage Advice
Notes as shown in Fig.109(a)

Copywriter

3.
The individual
Employee's Wages
Record (positioned
on the studs to bring the
next clean column over the
next blank column on the
Payroll Form and the next blank
Wage Advice Note)

Fig. 109 (*b*). A Modern

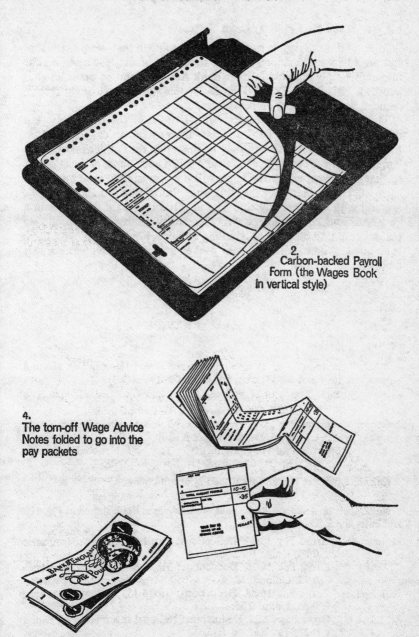

2.
Carbon-backed Payroll
Form (the Wages Book
in vertical style)

4.
The torn-off Wage Advice
Notes folded to go into the
pay packets

Wages System

(4) Wages and the Credit Transfer System

More and more people today receive nothing in their wages envelope but an advice note similar to that described in the last section. The money is simply credited to their Bank Accounts and no actual cash is handled. This is the Credit Transfer system and it is strongly recommended as the best way to pay wages.

The basic idea is this: the pay roll is done in the usual way, but instead of going to the bank to draw the pay roll in cash and notes, from which the wage packets may be prepared, the cashier takes to the bank a list of the employees' names. Against each name is the sum due to that employee, which the bank will now transfer to the employee's account. The cashier gives the bank an authorization to debit the firm's account with the total pay roll. The firm has thus paid the wages in a very safe and economical way. No security guards are needed; no tedious counting of notes or handling of coins. For the employee, there is no queuing up to collect his pay packet, and no chance of spending it before he gets home.

EXERCISES SET XXVII

(5) Wages Books

No. 1. Rule up a Wages Book similar to the Wages Book in Fig. 108 and enter the following details (invent any figures not supplied):

M. High   Gross Pay 17·55. Deductions: National Insurance 0·95, Sports Club 0·15, Dr. Barnardo's 0·05, Refund 0·55.

J. Outred   Gross Pay 17·00. Deductions: National Insurance 0·95, Sports Club 0·15, Dr. Barnado's 0·10.

C. Davies   Gross Pay 17·30. Deductions: Tax 1·50, National Insurance 0·95, Sports Club 0·15, Dr. Barnado's 0·05.

Calculate the Net Pay and total the important columns.

No. 2. Rule up a Wages Book similar to the Wages Book shown in Fig. 108 and enter the following details:

D. Bennett   Gross Pay 13·54. Deductions: Tax 1·70, National Insurance 0·85, Union 0·22.

T. Watts   Gross Pay 14·26. Deductions: Tax 0·55, National Insurance 0·95, Union 0·28.

R. Rogerson   Gross Pay 16·88. Deductions: Tax 4·15, National Insurance 0·85, Union 0·35.

M. Lloyd   Gross Pay 12.25. Deductions: National Insurance 0·95, Union 0·22; Tax Refund 1·73.

Calculate the Net Pay and total the important columns.

No. 3. Rule up a Wages Book similar to the Wages Book shown in Fig. 108 and enter the following details:

R. Lawrence   Gross Pay 27·62. Deductions: Tax 7·30, National Insurance 0·95, Union 1·62, Charities 0·16.

T. Gold   Gross Pay 25·88. Deductions: Tax 6·32, National Insurance 0·95, Union 1·62, Charities 0·23.

M. Silva   Gross Pay 42·75. Deductions: Tax 11·15, National Insurance 0·95, Union 1·62, Charities 0·25.

A. Copper   Gross Pay 28·34. Deductions: Tax 7·55, National Insurance 0·95, Union 1·62, Charities 0·16.

Calculate the Net Pay and total the important columns.

No. 4. Rule up a Wages Book similar to the one in Fig. 108 and enter the following details:

E. Nartey   Gross Pay 15·65. Deductions: Tax—nil, National Insurance 0·85, Union 0·33, Refund of Tax 4·27.

G. Haji   Gross Pay 17·25. Deductions: Tax 2·35, National Insurance 0·95, Union 0·33.

K. Khamis   Gross Pay 17·35. Deductions: Tax 3·25, National Insurance 0·85, Union 0·33.

H. Bwanamkubwa   Gross Pay 16·85. Deductions: Tax 1·85, National Insurance 0·85, Union 0·33.

Calculate the Net Pay and total the important columns.

CHAPTER SIXTEEN

BOOK-KEEPING TO 'FINAL ACCOUNTS'—PART ONE: THE TRIAL BALANCE

(1) Introduction—What are Final Accounts?

In a free enterprise society businessmen go into business with the idea of making profits, which are the reward of enterprise. But whatever the society, people are likely to be best served in the long run if the utmost economic gain can be achieved at the smallest economic cost.

Final Accounts enable us to check on the conduct of our enterprise, and to discover whether it is being run efficiently. A great variety of statistical control figures can be deduced from the Final Accounts, which enable us to check on our business. Is the manager embezzling the money? Are the staff stealing the stock? Is Mrs. Jones, the buyer, an old fuddy-duddy? Does Brown, the office manager, collect too many pretty young typists? Does the dog-lover in the Pet's Corner hold a bigger stock of expensive dog-collars than the public will ever buy? These are the sort of questions you should be able to answer from studying a set of final accounts. If you are able to answer them correctly someone should give you a bonus for promoting the efficiency of the business.

To begin with we will learn the simplest type of Final Accounts: a Trading Account followed by a Profit and Loss Account. The starting-point for these two accounts is the Trial Balance. We prepare from the Trial Balance a Trading Account and a Profit and Loss Account, and by the time we have finished, we have a very much smaller Trial Balance which we then rearrange into a Balance Sheet.

(2) A Closer Look at the Trial Balance

A real understanding of Final Accounts must be based first of all on a real understanding of the Trial Balance. Before we try to draw up Trading and Profit and Loss Accounts we must be quite sure we can always draw up a Trial Balance from any given set of figures.

Consider the following Trial Balance, which has had notes added on each line:

R. JONES

TRIAL BALANCE

(as at December 31st, 19..)

Ledger Accounts	Notes	Dr.	Cr.	Notes
Premises Account	Asset	6,490·00		
Capital Account			16,100·00	Liability
Debtors:				
R. Johnson Account	Asset	4,000·00		
M. Thompson Account	Asset	1,506·00		
Creditors:				
R. Lupin Account			120·00	Liability
M. Chuzzlewit Account			360·00	Liability
Plant and Machinery Account	Asset	2,500·00		
Office Furniture Account	Asset	1,600·00		
Cash Account	Asset	300·00		
Bank Account	Asset	200·00		
Bad Debts Account	Loss	100·00		
Carriage in Account	Loss	100·00		
Commission Paid Account	Loss	664·00		
Discount Allowed Account	Loss	100·00		
Discount Received Account			60·00	Profit
Rent and Rates Account	Loss	200·00		
Carriage Out Account	Loss	60·00		
Salaries Account	Loss	360·00		
Warehouse Wages Account	Loss	520·00		
Rent Received Account			90·00	Profit
Stock at January 1st, 19..	Trading Account Item.	2,100·00		
Purchases Account	Trading Account Item.	3,200·00		
Sales Account			7,500·00	Trading Account Item.
Purchases Returns Account			90·00	Trading Account Item.
Sales Returns Account	Trading Account Item	20·00		
Drawings	Special Item	300·00		
		24,320·00	24,320·00	

In abbreviated form these notes can be condensed into the following groups:

TRIAL BALANCE	Dr.	Cr.
	(a) Assets	Liabilities
	(b) Losses	Profits
	(c) 3 Trading Items	2 Trading Items
	(d) Drawings	

The student here has the key to a real understanding of the Trial Balance. The following points are important:

(a) *Assets and Liabilities.* If an account is an Asset Account it must have a debit balance and come in the debit column. The moment it ceases to have a debit balance it crosses over the columns and becomes a liability. The best example of this is the Bank Account. The moment it ceases to be an asset, because we draw a cheque that is greater than the money on deposit, the account becomes a bank overdraft and becomes a liability. As fast as the bank computer prints its warning sign about the overdraft, the Bank Account crosses from the debit column to the credit column of the Trial Balance.

In the same way capital is nearly always a liability, but when the proprietor loses all his capital, and develops a **deficit on Capital Account**, the Capital Account ceases to have a credit balance. It crosses over from the credit side to the debit side, becoming an asset of the business—but a rather unsatisfactory one. The next thing that usually happens is that the proprietor goes out of business, or is bankrupted and forced out of business.

(b) *Losses and Profits.* These are the items which will be taken into account in the Final Accounts when we try to work out the profitability or otherwise of the business. Some of them will go into the Trading Account with the Trading Account items shown in part (c) but most of them will be dealt with in the Profit and Loss Account. (It is a pity we call it the 'Profit and Loss Account'; 'Loss and Profit' Account would be so much more sensible. The losses are the debits and the profits are the credits.) When asked to arrange a list of balances into a Trial Balance, the student can be sure that any losses will be debit balances and any profits will be credit balances.

(c) *Trading Account Items.* A full explanation will be given of these items in the next chapter. For the present the student should learn by heart the layout of these accounts in the Trial Balance, which is shown below:

TRADING ACCOUNT ITEMS IN THE TRIAL BALANCE

Dr.	Cr.
Stock at beginning of year	—
Purchases	Sales
Sales Returns	Purchases Returns

(d) *Drawings.* This is a rather special item. It actually represents some of the future profits drawn out. As profits are added to the capital, which is always a credit item, drawings will clearly be a debit item. A full discussion of what is implied by drawings is given later in 'Drawings and Interest on Drawings'.

(3) Causes of Confusion in the Trial Balance

There are one or two confusing items in a Trial Balance. A word of warning will save you hours of looking for mistakes.

(a) *Returns In and Returns Out*. One of these is a debit balance and one is a credit balance.

Returns In is the return of something we have sold, which the purchaser is dissatisfied with. It is therefore Sales Returned, and is a debit balance, as shown in the chart in 2 (c) above.

Returns Out is the return of something we do not want that we have purchased previously. It is therefore Purchases Returned and is a credit balance as shown in 2 (c) above.

(b) *Carriage In and Carriage Out*. If Returns In and Returns Out are on opposite sides of the Trial Balance it seems as if Carriage In and Carriage Out ought to be on opposite sides too. This is very deceptive, but in fact both are *losses* and must therefore be debit balances. Carriage In and Carriage Out have to be kept separate because one is dealt with in the Trading Account and one in the Profit and Loss Account. Carriage In is explained on p. 209, Carriage Out on p. 218. Remember then, Carriage In and Carriage Out are both debit balances.

(c) *Provisions for Bad Debts and Provisions for Depreciation*. These are dealt with in due course, but for the present it is important to realize that they are not losses. They do not come into the debit column. In fact they are sums of profit tucked away in anticipation of bad debts and wear and tear on assets. They really belong to the owner of the business since they are some of his profits earned in years gone by. They must be put in the credit column, and a full discussion of them follows in the chapter on Adjustments (p. 262 and p. 272).

Now consider the following example:

Example: Prepare a Trial Balance from the following balances which were extracted from the books of R. Gosling on May 31st. 19..:

Trade Expenses	920·50
Sales	2,800·00
Purchases	1,060·00
Cash in Hand	60·65
Freehold Property	2,800·00
Sundry Debtors	800·50
Stock in Trade at start	1,380·75
Sundry Creditors	500·95
Bank Overdraft	2,100·85
Plant and Machinery	2,000·00
Returns Inward	100·30
Discount Received	100·90
Capital	3,620·00
Rent and Rates	220·00
Office Expenses	780·00
Loan from A. Friend	1,000·00

A quick check through will enable us to write the following notes by each item, and prepare the Trial Balance.

TRIAL BALANCE
(as at May 31st 19..)

Name of Account	Note	Dr.	Cr.
Trade Expenses	Loss	920·50	
Sales	Trading Account item		2,800·00
Purchases	Trading Account item	1,060·00	
Cash in Hand	Asset	60·65	
Freehold Property	Asset	2,800·00	
Sundry Debtors	Asset	800·50	
Stock in Trade at start	Trading Account item	1,380·75	
Sundry Creditors	Liability		500·95
Bank Overdraft	Liability		2,100·85
Plant and Machinery	Asset	2,000·00	
Returns Inwards (Sales Returns)	Trading Account item	100·30	
Discount Received	Profit		100·90
Capital	Liability		3,620·00
Rent and Rates	Loss	220·00	
Offices Expenses	Loss	780·00	
Loan from A. Friend	Liability		1,000·00
		10,122·70	10,122·70

The student should now prepare several Trial Balances from the information given in the exercises that follow, so that he develops facility at placing these balances properly in the Dr. or Cr. columns.

EXERCISES SET XXVIII

(4) The Trial Balance

No. 1. Prepare a Trial Balance from the following details taken from R. George's Ledger on December 31st.

Sundry Debtors	6,750·00
Sundry Creditors	500·00
Premises	24,000·00
Furniture and Fittings	6,000·00
Rates	300·00
Cash in Hand	150·00
Cash at Bank	600·00
Capital	32,700·00
Drawings	750·00
Purchases	40,000·00
Sales	57,500·00
Returns Inwards	2,100·00
Returns Outwards	3,425·00
Factory Wages	2,250·00
Carriage Inwards	250·00
Carriage Outwards	100·00
Salaries	1,500·00 (cont. on p. 201)

Rent received	1,150·00
Stock, January 1st	10,000·00
Insurance	425·00
Bad Debts	100·00

No. 2. The following is the list of a trader's accounts at March 31st. Take out the Trial Balance.

Bad Debts Account 540·00
Carriage Inwards 327·00
Discount Received 385·00
Lighting and Heating Account 480·00
Factory Wages 2,925·00
Office Salaries 609·00
Rent Account 1,900·00
Sales Account 16,391·00
Drawings 766·00
Debtors: A. Jones 620·00, B. Brown 1,000·00
Creditors: C. Richards 1,250·00
Postage Account 200·00

Bank Account 319·00
Discount Allowed 536·00
General Expenses Account 196·00
Machinery 5,500·00
Motor Vehicles Account 800·00
Purchases Account 9,216·00
Returns Outwards 436·00
M. Tyler's Capital Account 9,072·00
Stock at April 1st last 1,600·00

(*R.S.A.—Adapted*)

No. 3. The following is the list of Peter Hyde's accounts at March 31st. Prepare the Trial Balance.

Stock at April 1st last 15,000·00
Sales Account 85,000·00
Carriage Inwards 100·00
Rents and Rates 375·00
Postage Account 25·00
Printing and Stationery 80·00
Bank Interest Paid 30·00
Creditor: C. Bryant 5,000·00
Cash in Hand 100·00
Machinery and Plant 50,000·00
Carriage Out 50·00
Drawings 1,000·00

Purchases Account 75,000·00
Factory Wages Account 2,500·00
Repairs 250·00
Insurance 150·00
Travelling Expenses Account 150·00
Discount Received 50·00
Debtors: R. Cross 5,000·00, B. Thomas 5,000·00
Bank Overdraft 8,000·00
Buildings 34,000·00
Capital 90,860·00
Advertising 100·00

No. 4. The following is a list of a trader's accounts at March 31st. Take out a Trial Balance.

Bad Debts 1,080·00
Bank Account 638·60
Discounts Received 750·90
Travelling Expenses 190·60
Machinery 11,000·00
Motor Vehicles 1,600·00
Purchases 18,450·50
Returns Outward 860·50
M. Jones's Capital 18,144·00
Stock at April 1st last 3,962·00
Creditor: A. Richards 2500·50

Light and heating 654·50
Repairs to plant 1,052·00
General Expenses 190·20
Redecorations 960·50
Factory Wages 5,850·50
Salaries 1,200·50
Rents Account 3,800·00
Sales Account 32,404·00
Drawings 750·00
Debtors: R. Thomas 1,240·00, B. Brown 2,000·00
Postage Account 40·00

No. 5. From the following prepare B. Perkins's Trial Balance, as at December 31st:

Capital	300,000·00
Rates and Insurance	2,200·00
Light and Heat	2,000·00
Purchases	186,000·00
General Factory Expenses	3,000·00
Sales	342,000·00
Stock at beginning of year	60,000·00
Postage	700·00
Office Expenses	500·00
Bank Loan	6,600·00
Returns In	3,000·00
Returns Out	6,000·00
Cash in Hand	600·00
Machinery	50,000·00
Office Salaries	15,000·00
Warehouse Wages	22,800·00
Discount Received	3,000·00
Creditors	18,600·00
Debtors	32,400·00
Carriage In	1,200·00
Bad Debts	1,800·00
Commission Received	600·00
Motor Vehicles	3,700·00
Furniture	40,200·00
Premises	180,000·00
Goodwill (asset)	38,400·00
Cash at Bank	3,300·00
Investment in Harrow Ltd.	30,000·00

No. 6. In a Trial Balance you are asked to prepare, the following items appear. Copy out and complete:

Name of Account	Does it go in the Dr. or Cr. Column?	Why?
1. Motor Vehicles 2. Creditor A. Jones 3. Capital 4. Light and Heat Account 5. Rent Received Account 6. Drawings		

No. 7. A. Jaffa extracts the following balances from his Ledger on December 31st. Present them in the form of a Trial Balance.

Cash in Hand	25·00
Cash at Bank	625·00
Sales	7,265·00
Purchases	2,350·00
Motor Vehicles	1,250·00
Rent and Rates	125·00
Light and Heat	60·00
Carriage In	50·00
Carriage Out	35·00
Opening Stock at January 1st	1,825·00
Commission Received	135·00
Capital	8,000·00
Drawings	850·00
Returns Outwards	160·00
Returns Inwards	165·00
Warehouse Wages	1,520·00
Office Salaries	980·00
Debtors	2,365·00
Creditors	565·00
Furniture and Fittings	800·00
Land and Buildings	4,600·00
Loan from Bank (borrowed on December 30th)	1,500·00

(*East Anglian Examination Board—Adapted*)

No. 8. M. Lucas extracts the following balances from his Ledger on December 31st. Present them in the form of a Trial Balance.

Capital at July 1st	18,000·00
Rent and Rates	350·00
Purchases	15,500·00
Audit Fee	250·00
Sales	25,500·00
Stock at July 1st	5,000·00
Telephone	100·00
Bank Overdraft	550·00
Returns Inward	250·00
Returns Outward	500·00
Cash in Hand	50·00
Machinery	5,000·00
Salaries	1,250·00
Factory Wages	1,900·00
Discount Received	250·00
Creditors	1,550·00
Debtors	2,700·00
Carriage Outwards	100·00
Bad Debts	150·00
Commission Received	50·00
Furniture	5,600·00
Premises	5,000·00
Goodwill	3,200·00

No. 9. The following Trial Balance has been prepared from R. Joiner's books by an inefficient book-keeper. You are asked to rewrite it correctly.

Trial Balance (as at Feb. 28th, 19..)	Dr.	Cr.
Capital at start		6,000·00
Premises	3,400·00	
Drawings		350·00
Plant and Machinery	750·00	
Stock at March 1st		1,500·00
Office Furniture, March 1st	100·00	
Insurance	25·00	
Office Salaries		190·00
Factory Wages	220·00	
Bank Loan	100·00	
Cash at Bank	10·00	
Bad Debt	35·00	
Discount Allowed		30·00
Debtors and Creditors	220·00	180·00
Returns Inwards		20·00
Returns Outwards	40·00	
Purchases and Sales	1,700·00	2,230·00
Repairs	30·00	
Rent Paid	30·00	
Commission Received		60·00
	6,660·00	10,560·00

No. 10. The following Trial Balance of a sole trader is incorrect, although it adds up to the same total on both sides.

TRIAL BALANCE
(as at June 30th, 19..)

	Dr.	Cr.
Capital at July 1st	8,950·50	
Drawings		1,050·50
Stock at July 1st	3,725·00	
Purchases	23,100·25	
Sales		39,425·25
Wages and Salaries	6,205·00	
Lighting and Heating	310·00	
Equipment	3,600·00	
Carriage Outwards		230·50
Returns Inwards	105·00	
Provision for Bad Debts	350·50	
Returns Outwards		290·00
Discount Allowed	285·75	
Discount Received		315·75
Rent, Rates, and Insurance	1,115·00	
Motor Vehicles	1,475·00	
Cash in Hand	110·00	
Sundry Creditors	4,925·25	
Sundry Debtors		13,920·25
Bank Overdraft	975·00	
	55,232·25	55,232·25

Draw up a corrected Trial Balance.

(R.S.A.—Adapted)

CHAPTER SEVENTEEN

BOOK-KEEPING TO 'FINAL ACCOUNTS'—PART TWO: THE TRADING ACCOUNT

(1) The Profit on a Simple Transaction

Imagine a simple transaction. I buy a bar of chocolate for 0·04 and sell it for 0·05. Clearly the profit on trading is 0·01, for profit is the difference between cost price and selling price.

The very simple Trading Account recording this set of transactions would read as follows:

TRADING ACCOUNT

(for year ending December 31st, 19..)

To Purchases	0·04	By Sales	0·05
„ Gross Profit	0·01		
	0·05		0·05

Note these points:

(*a*) Every Trading Account must bear at the top the phrase (*for* ....
ending .... 19..). In this case it was a year ending on December 31st.

(*b*) The Profit at the end of a Trading Account is called the **Gross Profit** which means 'Fat Profit' or 'Overall Profit'. The reason will be made clear later.

(*c*) The Gross Profit is the difference between the selling price and the cost of the sales.

(2) Final Accounts and Closing Journal Entries

In Chapter Six (on Journal Entries), the only common type of Journal Entry that was not discussed was a Closing Journal Entry. These are used to close off the Nominal Accounts and to transfer their balances to the Trading Account or the Profit and Loss Account.

Consider the Sales Account in the Trial Balance of Chapter Sixteen (2) page 197. It has a credit balance of 7,500·00. When we transfer this to the Trading Account in order to work out the Gross Profit, we close off the Sales Account.

Here it is before and after closure.

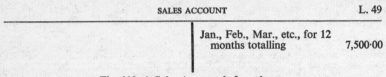

Fig. 110. A Sales Account before closure

| 19..
Dec. 31 | Sales Account   Dr.
    To Trading Account
Being transfer of Sales figure to
Trading Account to determine
gross profit | L. 49
L. 186 | 7,500·00 | 7,500·00 |

Fig. 111. A Closing Journal Entry

SALES ACCOUNT   L. 49

Dec. 31 To Trading Account	7,500·00	Jan., Feb., Mar., etc., for 12 months totalling	7,500·00
	7,500·00		7,500·00

Fig. 112. The Sales Account closed off for the year

The result of this Closing Entry is that the Sales Account no longer has a balance on it, it is clear, and therefore vanishes from the Trial Balance. Its place has been taken by the entry in the Trading Account which now reads:

TRADING ACCOUNT   L. 186
(for year ended December 31st, 19..)

| | By Sales | 7,500·00 |

Fig. 113. Starting the Trading Account

In every transfer into the Trading Account we shall be doing the same sort of Closing Entry, clearing off completely the balances on the Nominal Accounts we close, and transferring their balances to the Trading Account.

(3) The True Sales Figure

We now have an entry for sales in our Trading Account which reads 7,500·00. But is this the true sales figure for our business? Did we really sell 7,500·00 worth of goods? If we are going to find the Gross Profit we must know the correct purchase price and the correct selling price.

This figure of 7,500·00 is not the correct sales figure because there were some Sales Returns. Looking back to the Trial Balance again, page 197, we find that the Sales Returns Account has a balance of 20·00 on it. It looks like this:

SALES RETURNS ACCOUNT   L. 65

Jan., Feb., Mar., etc., coming to a total of 20·00	

Fig. 114. The Sales Returns Account before closure

Clearly this should be closed off and the entry transferred to the Trading Account. Sticking to the rules of strict double entry we must this time debit the Trading Account and credit the Sales Returns Account. This will clear the Sales Returns Account and leave the Trading Account looking like this:

TRADING ACCOUNT   L. 186
(for year ending December 31st, 19. .)

To Sales Returns	20·00	By Sales	7,500·00

Fig. 115. Sales on the Trading Account (by strict Double Entry)

In fact this is very awkward, for it leaves us not knowing quite what the sales figure really was; we have to do some mental arithmetic to find out. For the sake of greater clarity, and 'good style', we adopt a little trick. Instead of debiting the Trading Account with the 20·00 returns we *deduct* these returns from the credit side. Since deducting them from the credit side is exactly the same as adding them to the debit side, we still keep a good double entry. We have, in order to get a really clear picture of the sales for the year, abandoned strict double entry. All students should appreciate that **clear presentation is the vital thing in Final Accounts. We must be able to see the important figure instantly.**

Our Trading Account now looks like this:

TRADING ACCOUNT   L. 186
(for year ending December 31st, 19. .)

	By Sales	7,500·00
	Less Returns	20·00
	Net Turnover	7,480·0

Fig. 116. Trading Account showing the true Sales Figure

The Turnover of a Business

In the Trading Account of Fig. 116 we have now brought out one of the vital figures of business. Whenever a business is bought or sold one of the important things to be taken into account in determining the price is the turnover figure, or **net turnover**. The word 'net' means 'clean', and implies that the returns have been deducted from the sales figure to give a clear figure of actual turnover.

Why is turnover so important? Naturally it reflects the 'busy-ness' of the business. If a business is prosperous, the public are buying and the proprietor will make good profits. If a business has only a small turnover it offers poor prospects to the purchaser, so that he will not pay a high price for it. Some businessmen specialize in curing the ills of bad businesses; they take over a firm cheaply because it has a poor turn-over, improve it and restore it to good heart. They then sell it at a profit. It now offers a new owner a good prospect of profitability.

The reason we adopt the good style shown in Fig. 116 is because it brings out clearly the net turnover figure.

(4) The True Purchases Figure

Having found the true sales figure we now have to discover what these sales cost us, because the Gross Profit is the difference between the sales figure and the **cost of the sales**. To find the cost of the sales is much more difficult than finding the true sales figure, because some of the things that we sold were purchased last year, and the purchases figure on the Purchases Account does not include them. They are to be found on the Stock Account. We must build up our idea on the **Cost of Sales** figure in stages.

(5) Finding the Cost of the Sales
Stage I of Finding the Cost of Sales—Finding the Net Purchases Figure

This is the same as the calculation of the true sales figure. Referring back to the Trial Balance on page 197 we find that the Purchases Account and the Purchases Returns Account are as follows:

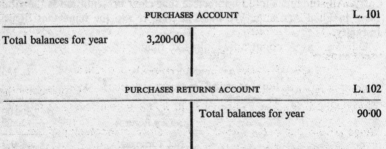

PURCHASES ACCOUNT		L. 101
Total balances for year	3,200·00	

PURCHASES RETURNS ACCOUNT		L. 102
	Total balances for year	90·00

Fig. 117. Purchases Account and Purchases Returns Account before closure

Closing these off in the same way as before, and adopting the good style used to produce the sales figure, we now have a Trading Account that reads:

TRADING ACCOUNT   L. 186
(for year ending December 31st, 19..)

To Purchases	3,200·00	By Sales	7,500·00
Less Returns	90·00	*Less* Returns	20·00
Net Purchases	3,110·00	Net Turnover	7,480·00

Fig. 118. Stage I—Finding the Net Purchases Figure

Stage II of Finding the Cost of Sales—Carriage In and Other Increases in the Purchase Price

We must now deal with the difficulty referred to in (4) above. Is the figure shown in Fig. 118 the true purchases figure? In fact it is not, because the goods that we purchased probably cost us more than this. In the Trial Balance we find that Carriage In was 100·00 for the year. Carriage In is the carriage paid on goods coming into the business, which have been purchased at an **ex works** price. If we pay 100·00 for goods ex works, and pay 5·00 delivery charges, the true purchase price is 105·00. Everyone who buys a car finds to his disgust that a charge for delivery is added to the price quoted by the dealer. The true purchase price of the car is the list price plus the delivery charge.

Carriage In is not the only charge that may be added, another very common one is Customs Duty on imported goods. These again represent an increase in the purchase price, and should really be added to the purchases figure.

If we now transfer the Carriage In to the Trading Account by a Closing Journal Entry we have:

TRADING ACCOUNT   L. 186
(for year ending December 31st, 19..)

To Purchases	3,200·00	By Sales	7,500·00
„ Carriage In	100·00	*Less* Returns	20·00
	3,300·00	Net Turnover	7,480·00
Less Returns	90·00		
Net Purchases	3,210·00		

Fig. 119. Stage II—Taking Carriage In into account

NOTE: The best place to add the Carriage In is as shown in the illustration. It is added in business life *before* we even think of returns.

Stage III of Finding the Cost of Sales—Stock at Beginning of Year

We now have a figure of 3,210·00 for the net purchases figure. Is this the cost price of the goods we sold? Unfortunately not, because if we are running our business sensibly we shall sell off goods that are already in stock at the beginning of the year before we sell off the purchases we are buying in January, February, etc. Most businesses operate a first-in, first-out system of dealing with Stock, to clear goods before they depreciate. Stage III of finding the Cost of Sales figure involves transferring the Opening Stock at January 1st, valued on the Trading Account at 2,100·00, to the Trading Account. This is why the figures for Purchases in Figs. 118 and 119 were indented a little, to have a clear line for the addition of this stock and the net purchases figure. We have now:

TRADING ACCOUNT   L. 186
(for year ending December 31st, 19. .)

To Opening Stock		2,100·00	By Sales	7,500·00
„ Purchases	3,200·00		*Less* Returns	20·00
„ Carriage In	100·00			
			Net Turnover	7,480·00
	3,300·00			
Less Returns	90·00			
Net Purchases		3,210·00		
Total Stock Available		5,310·00		

Fig. 120. Stage III—Taking account of Stock at Start

NOTE: The phrase 'Total Stock available' accurately describes the sum of 5,310·00 since this is the stock we had at the beginning of the year, plus the stock purchased (and not returned) during the year. It is therefore the stock that has been available during the present year.

Stage IV of Finding the Cost of Sales—Closing Stock

We now come to one of the vital things in Final Accounts, the adjustment needed for closing stock. Stock valuation is a subject of sufficient importance to merit a chapter by itself, and is dealt with in Chapter Twenty-one, page 241. All we need say here is that stock still in hand at the close of the financial year, must be counted, valued, and totalled up. This gives us the valuation of stock in hand that has not been sold.

Having found the stock figure, which must be given to us in any exercise we do on the Trading Account, but which in real life must be found by actually taking stock, we need to bring this figure into the Trading Account. Here again good style is important. First let us look at the Stock Account as it is at present:

STOCK ACCOUNT   L. 37

19. .			19. .		
Jan. 1	To Balance	2,100·00	Dec. 31	By transfer to Trading Account	2,100·00

Fig. 121. The Stock Account with Opening Stock closed off to Trading Account

Taking the new figure for closing stock as 1,560·00, we must now record this stock figure on the Stock Account because it is one of the assets of the business. This requires a Journal Entry debiting the Stock Account with the stock value 1,560·00. Here is this Journal Entry:

19.. Dec. 31	Stock Account Dr. To Trading Account *Being stock at close of year recorded* *in books at this date*	L. 37 L. 186	1,560·00	1,560·00

Fig. 122. Journalizing Closing Stock

and the Stock Account now reads as follows:

STOCK ACCOUNT   L. 37

19..
Jan. 1 To Balance
Dec. 31 „ New Stock
          Valuation
	2,100·00
	
	1,560·00
		19..
		Dec. 31 By Transfer to
		          Trading Account
			2,100·00

Fig. 123. Re-opening Stock Account with the Closing Stock Figure

When we do the other half of the double entry we should, according to strict double entry, credit the Trading Account with the closing stock. This will unfortunately spoil the clarity of the figures we are trying to produce. What we want to bring out clearly is the cost of the stock sold. If we deduct the closing stock from the total stock available we shall produce the cost of the stock sold, for what is not left in stock must have been sold. As the stock and the purchases are at cost price we shall have the sales at cost price, i.e. the cost of stock sold. Our Trading Account now looks like this:

TRADING ACCOUNT   L. 681
(for year ending December 31st, 19..)

To Opening Stock
„ Purchases
„ Carriage In
 	
     Less Returns
 	
Net Purchases
 	
Total Stock Available
     Less Closing Stock
 	
Cost of Stock Sold
	
	3,200·00
	100·00
	
	3,300·00
	90·00
	
		2,100·00
		
		3,210·00
		
		5,310·00
		1,560·00
		
		3,750·00
			By Sales
			     Less Returns
			
			Net Turnover
				7,500·00
				20·00
				
				7,480·00

Fig. 124. Bringing out the Cost of the Stock Sold

Stage V of Finding the Cost of Sales—Factory or Warehouse Expenses

The last stage in finding the Gross Profit is to enter in the Trading Account any items of expenses which are better dealt with there than in the Profit and Loss Account. This is one of those grey areas, neither black nor white, where people often argue about whether expenses should go in the Trading Account at all, and if so, which.

Probably the best guide is that the Profit and Loss Account should be kept for the selling and administrative expenses. Any expense which is concerned with the production or warehousing of the goods should be dealt with at this stage in the Trading Account. Later we shall learn how to keep a Manufacturing Account, but at present the best policy is to put such items in the Trading Account.

The only expense of this type in our Trial Balance is the Warehouse Wages Account, 520·00.

When we close the Warehouse Wages Account and transfer the wages to the Trading Account we finish up with the following Trading Account which shows us the Gross Profit on trading clearly and easily. The cost of sales, deducted from the sales figure, gives us the Gross Profit.

TRADING ACCOUNT   L. 186

(for year ending December 31st, 19..)

To Opening Stock		2,100·00	By Sales		7,500·00
„ Purchases	3,200·00		*Less* Returns		20·00
„ Carriage In	100·00				
			Net Turnover		7,480·00
	3,300·00				
Less Returns	90·00				
Net Purchases		3,210·00			
Total Stock Available		5,310·00			
Less Closing Stock		1,560·00			
Cost of Stock Sold		3,750·00			
To Warehouse Wages		520·00			
Cost of Sales		4,270·00			
Gross Profit (transferred to					
Profit and Loss Account)		3,210·00			
		7,480·00			7,480·00

Fig. 125. A Trading Account in Good Style

The Profit and Loss Account is now open and looks as follows:

PROFIT AND LOSS ACCOUNT   L. 187

(for year ending December 31st, 19..)

	By Gross Profit (transferred	
	from Trading Account)	3,210·00

Fig. 126. Starting the Profit and Loss Account with the Gross Profit

(6) Some Definitions Connected with the Trading Account

The following definitions are worth learning:

Gross Profit—Gross Profit is the difference between the net sales of the business, and the cost of these sales.

Cost of Stock Sold—is the cost of the stock we had at first, plus the cost of the net purchases, minus the cost of the unsold portion of the stock.

Cost of Sales—is the cost of the stock sold, plus the expenses of handling that stock.

The Turnover of a Business—is the net sales, that is the sales less sales returns.

The student should now practise preparing Trading Accounts in good style, to bring out the net turnover and the cost of sales.

EXERCISES SET XXIX

(7) Trading Accounts

No. 1. From the following particulars prepare the Trading Account of J. Weaver for the year ended December 31st, 19. . :
Sales 27,056·50; Purchases 15,275·75; Sales Returns 156·50; Purchases Returns 175·75; Stock January 1st 1,765·50; Stock December 31st 1,854·40.

No. 2. From the following particulars prepare the Trading Account of C. Cooper for the year ended December 31st, 19. . :
Stock January 1st 1,279·65; Purchases 47,326·55; Purchases Returns 1,306·55; Sales 75,263·25; Sales Returns 1,263·25; Stock December 31st 2,735·50; Factory Wages 2,746·50.

No. 3. Prepare the Trading Account of A. S. Brewis for the year ended December 31st, 19. . :
Stock January 1st 525·65; Cash Purchases 3,725·50; Credit Purchases 7,256·40; Carriage In 275·65; Returns Outwards 426·50; Cash Sales 5,650·50; Credit Sales 9,672·50; Returns Inwards 72·50; Stock December 31st 675·75.

No. 4. Prepare a Trading Account for the year ended December 31st, 19. . for J. Lyons from the following information:
Opening Stock 1,706·50; Purchases 5,726·50; Carriage In 126·50; Customs Duty on Imported Purchases 586·50; Purchases Returns 276·25; Closing Stock 1,409·20; Wages of warehouse workers 1,479·50; Warehouse expenses 826·45; Sales 12,265·30; Sales Returns 205·50.

No. 5. At December 31st, 19. ., the Trial Balance of E. Randall contained the following items:

Stock at January 1st, 19. .	2,785·00
Purchases	6,908·00
Sales	7,642·00
Returns Outwards	195·00

Returns Inwards	262·00
Warehouse Wages	700·00
Wages Owing	20·00
Import Charges	126·00

Randall's Stock at December 31st, 19.., was valued at 4,440·00. Prepare the Trading Account for the year ending December 31st, 19...

(*R.S.A.—Adapted*)

No. 6. The following figures relating to a dressmaking business were extracted from the Trial Balance taken out on March 31st, 19... From them select those items you consider should be used in the Trading Account of the business and prepare this account for the quarter ended on that date.

Sales for the quarter	8,000·00
Purchases of cloth, etc.	2,554·00
Purchases of sewing machines	380·00
Carriage on goods sold	47·00
Returns to and allowances from suppliers	54·00
Purchases of cardboard boxes, wrapping paper, etc.	30·00
Office heating and lighting	103·00
Heating and lighting of workrooms	212·00
Office salaries and expenses	872·00
Workroom Wages	1,650·00
Advertising	200·00
Rent and rates (three-quarters workroom, one-quarter office)	480·00
Electric power for machines	150·00
Carriage on purchases	32·00
Discounts allowed	36·00
Discounts received	50·00
Stocks of cloth, etc.:	
January 1st, 19..	600·00
March 31st, 19..	766·00

(*R.S.A.—Adapted*)

No. 7.

(*a*) From the following information prepare the Trading Account of W. Wigg for the year ending June 30th, 19..:

Stock at start	2,400·00
Purchases	15,205·00
Sales	20,860·00
Stock at close	3,840·00
Returns Outwards	185·00
Returns Inwards	860·00
Manufacturing Wages	2,896·00
Carriage Inwards	524·00

(*b*) If the Stock at June 30th, 19.., had been valued at 3,000·00, what would the gross profit have been?

(*R.S.A.—Adapted*)

No. 8. Give the effect of *each* of the following errors on the *Gross Profit* of a business, stating exactly by how much the Gross Profit will be increased or decreased. If you think there would be no change write 'None'.

(*a*) The Sales Returns Book was over-added by 20·00.

(*b*) The entries in respect of an invoice for goods bought totalling 60·00 were omitted from the books.

(*c*) Carriage on sales had been entered in the Ledger Account as 121·00 instead of 112·00.

(*d*) The closing stock was under-valued by 649·00.

(*e*) Carriage on purchases had been entered in the Ledger Account as 189·00 instead of 198·00.

(*f*) An amount of 80·00 in respect of goods returned to a supplier was entered in the Sales Book instead of the Purchases Returns Book.

(*R.S.A.—Adapted*)

CHAPTER EIGHTEEN

BOOK-KEEPING TO 'FINAL ACCOUNTS'—PART THREE: THE PROFIT AND LOSS ACCOUNT

(1) A Revised Trial Balance

Consider what has happened to the Trial Balance drawn up in Chapter Sixteen (2), page 197.

Because of the transfer of items to the Trading Account, a number of the balances shown on that Trial Balance have been cleared off completely, and, as a result, have disappeared from the Trial Balance. In

R. JONES

TRIAL BALANCE

(as at December 31st, 19..)

Ledger Account	Notes	Dr.	Cr.	Notes
Premises Account	Asset	6,490·00		
Capital Account			16,100·00	Liability
Debtors:				
R. Johnson Account	Asset	4,000·00		
M. Thompson Account	Asset	1,506·00		
Creditors:				
R. Lupin Account			120·00	Liability
M. Chuzzlewit Account			360·00	Liability
Plant and Machinery Account	Asset	2,500·00		
Office Furniture Account	Asset	1,600·00		
Cash Account	Asset	300·00		
Bank Account	Asset	200·00		
Stock Account	Asset	1,560·00		
Bad Debts Account	Loss	100·00		
Commission Paid Account	Loss	664·00		
Discount Allowed Account	Loss	100·00		
Discount Received Account			60·00	Profit
Rent and Rates Account	Loss	200·00		
Carriage Out Account	Loss	60·00		
Salaries Account	Loss	360·00		
Rent Received Account			90·00	Profit
Drawings Account	Special Item	300·00		
Gross Profit (on Profit and Loss Account)			3,210·00	Profit
		19,940·00	19,940·00	

Fig. 127. A Revised Trial Balance

addition, one of the accounts shown on that Trial Balance has changed from one figure to another, and has also changed its character. This is the Stock Account, which formerly was a Nominal Account with a balance of 2,100·00. It was a Nominal Account because the 2,100·00 was there 'in name only', in fact this stock had been sold and replaced by other stock purchased in the year. At first we transferred this 2,100·00 to the Trading Account, leaving the Stock Account clear for a short while, but then we reopened it with the closing stock. This closing stock is not a nominal figure, it is real. (Anyone who likes to check it can count the stock and value it.) It is therefore an asset, but, of course, tomorrow we begin a new year and we shall start selling our stock, so that the real figure today of 1,560·00 will soon become a nominal figure again. To be really clear about this is a vital part of understanding the stock. Our figure of 1,560·00 is an asset for today, but it will soon become a Nominal Account again, when dealings in stock change the real stock figure from 1,560·00 to some other figure.

The Trading Account items, and the losses that are best dealt with in the Trading Account have disappeared from the Trial Balance, and have been replaced by the Gross Profit, which starts off the Profit and Loss Account.

(2) Finding the Net Profit—Stage I—Transferring the Losses

On the Trial Balance opposite we still have a number of Nominal Accounts, which are either losses or profits. The Loss Accounts are all debit balances. When we clear these accounts off we credit them, to clear the balances from the accounts, and hence from the Trial Balance, and debit the loss in the Profit and Loss Account.

A typical entry would be:

19.. Dec. 31	Profit and Loss Account Dr. To Bad Debts Account Being Bad Debts transferred to Profit and Loss Account	L. 187 L. 44	100·00	100·00

Fig 128. Transferring a Loss to the Profit and Loss Account

The Bad Debts Account now looks like this:

BAD DEBTS ACCOUNT   L. 44

19.. July 4 To R. Smith Oct. 17 „ M. Pierce	60·00 40·00	19.. By transfer to Profit and Loss Account	100·00
	100·00		100·00

Fig. 129. A Loss Account closed

After similar entries in the Journal to close off the other Loss Accounts we have a Profit and Loss Account like this:

PROFIT AND LOSS ACCOUNT   L. 187
(for year ending December 31st, 19. .)

To Bad Debts	100·00	By Gross Profit (transferred	
„ Commission Paid	664·00	from Trading Account)	3,210·00
„ Discount Allowed	100·00		
„ Rent and Rates	200·00		
„ Carriage Out	60·00		
„ Salaries	360·00		

Fig. 130. Losses transferred to the Profit and Loss Account
Note: Carriage Out—like most selling expenses—appears in the Profit and Loss Account.

(3) Finding the Net Profit—Stage II—Transferring the Profits

It is now the turn of the profits to be transferred into the Profit and Loss Account. At present these Nominal Accounts which are profits have credit balances. To clear them and transfer the profits to the Profit and Loss Account we must debit the Nominal Account and credit Profit and Loss Account. A typical Journal Entry would be:

19. . Dec.31	Discount Received Account Dr. To Profit and Loss Account Being discount received in year transferred to Profit and Loss Account	L. 154 L. 187	60·00	60·00

Fig. 131. Transferring a Profit to the Profit and Loss Account

and the Discount Received Account would then be clear as in Fig. 132.

DISCOUNT RECEIVED ACCOUNT   L. 154

19. . Dec. 31 To Profit and Loss Account	60·00	19. . Jan., Feb., etc., Sundry Discount totalling	60·00
	60·00		60·00

Fig. 132. A Profit Account closed off

After all the profits had been transferred in this way, the final Profit and Loss Account would be as Fig. 133 opposite.

(4) Closing the Drawings Account

When we have determined the Net Profit of the business the profit belongs to the proprietor, and he may appropriate it for his private use. Since the average small trader has no private means other than the capital invested in his business, he will probably have been drawing

PROFIT AND LOSS ACCOUNT L. 187
(for year ending December 31st., 19..)

To Bad Debts	100·00	By Gross Profit (transferred	
„ Commission Paid	664·00	from Trading Account)	3,210·00
„ Discount Allowed	100·00	„ Discount Received	60·00
„ Rent and Rates	200·00	„ Rent Received	90·00
„ Carriage Out	60·00		
„ Salaries	360·00	Total Profits	3,360·00
Total Expenses	1,484·00		
To Net Profit (transferred to			
Capital Account)	1,876·00		
	3,360·00		3,360·00

Fig. 133. A Profit and Loss Account in Good Style

sums of money for private purposes during the year. These sums are really drawings in expectation of profits made, and he has therefore already appropriated a good deal of the profit for his private use.

The Net Profit is transferred to the owner's Capital Account as shown in Fig. 134.

CAPITAL ACCOUNT L. 11

	19..	
	Jan. 1 To Opening Balance	16,100·00
	Dec. 31 „ Profit and Loss	
	Account	1,876·00

Fig. 134. The Net Profit transferred to the proprietor's Capital Account

We now want to close the Drawings Account, by transferring the total to the proprietor's Capital Account. The Journal Entry is as follows:

19..				
Dec. 31	Capital Account	L. 11	300·00	
	To Drawings Account	L. 69		300·00
	Being Drawings for year transferred			

Fig. 135. Closing the Drawings Account

The Drawings Account is now closed, and consequently no longer appears on the Trial Balance.

DRAWINGS ACCOUNT L. 69

19..				10..		
Mar. 31	To Bank	C.B. 1	75·00	Dec. 31 By transfer to		
June 30	„ „	C.B. 7	75·00	Capital Ac-		
Sept. 30	„ „	C.B. 12	75·00	count	L. 11	300·00
Dec. 31	„ „	C.B. 15	75·00			
			300·00			300·00

Fig. 136. The Drawings Account closed

The Capital Account can now be ruled off and brought down ready for the new financial year.

CAPITAL ACCOUNT   L. 11

19..			19..		
Dec. 31	To Drawings	300·00	Jan. 1	To Opening Balance	16,100·00
31	,, Balance	17,676·00	Dec. 31	,, Profit and Loss Account	1,876·00
		17,976·00			17,976·00
			19..		
			Jan. 1	To Balance	17,676·00

Fig. 137. The Final Entries in the Capital Account

Our double entry book-keeping has now been brought to a successful conclusion and all that is needed is to marshal the assets in a clear and well-presented Balance Sheet.

EXERCISES SET XXX

(5) Profit and Loss Accounts

No. 1. From the following figures prepare T. Stebbing's Profit and Loss Account for the half year ended June 30th, 19..:

Gross profit	1,276·50
Discount allowed	24·25
Discount Received	136·55
Bad Debts	4·25
Rent and Rates	26·50
Light and Heat	25·25
Packing and Delivery Expenses	35·60
Commission Received	106·50
Salaries	375·00

No. 2. From the following particulars prepare M. Fletcher's Profit and Loss Account for the year ended December 31st, 19..:

Gross Profit from Trading	7,246·50
Selling Expenses	1,245·50
Salaries	2,365·25
Discount Allowed	252·65
Discount Received	286·40
Rent, Rates, and Insurance	426·50

No. 3. R. Dwyer's Trial Balance contains the following items other than assets and liabilities. From them prepare his Profit and Loss Account for year ending December 31st, 19..:

Gross Trading Profit	11,260·00
Salaries	3,450·50
Selling Expenses	426·50
Package Materials	1,425·55
Rent, etc.	1,846·50
Discount Received	47·85
Discount Allowed	143·50 (See next page)

Salaries of 64·50 are due to a member of staff who is absent and these are to be included in the Profit and Loss Account.

No. 4. From the following particulars prepare the Trading Account and then the Profit and Loss Account of R. Mildred, for the year ending June 30th, 19..:

Stock at start, July 1st, 19..	1,760·55
Discount allowed	17·50
Insurance Premiums	4·15
Salaries	426·50
Purchases	4,550·50
Returns Outwards	12·14
Printing and Stationery	25·88
Rent and Rates	442·25
Sales	8,516·60
Returns Inwards	16·85
General Expenses	325·15
Telephone Account	25·50
Stock, June 30th, 19..	1,585·65
Discount Received	2·05
Interest paid on loans	30·55
Light and Heat	24·65

No. 5. From the following list of balances you are required to prepare the Trading and Profit and Loss Accounts for the year ending March 31st, 19.., of Robert Dingley, a wholesale merchant:

Returns Outwards	180·00
Carriage Outwards	210·00
Sales	47,810·00
Wages and Salaries	5,600·00
(Half to Trading Account; half to Profit and Loss Account)	
Returns Inwards	210·00
Commission Paid	1,800·00
Commission Received	220·00
Carriage Inwards	360·00
Motor Van Expenses	120·00
Stock, April 1st, 19..	5,500·00
Purchases	34,000·00
Bank Interest and Charges	115·00
Rent, Rates, and Insurance	1,140·00
General Expenses	1,850·00
Bad Debts	210·00
Discount Allowed	120·00
Discount Received	680·00

In preparing your account you should note the following:

(*a*) Stock on March 31st, 19.., was valued at 4,835·00.
(*b*) *No* Trial Balance or Balance Sheet is required.

(*R.S.A.—Adapted*)

No. 6. From the following prepare R. Mowler's Trading and Profit and Loss Accounts for the quarter ended September 30th, 19.., using such of the figures as you think should be used:

Capital	75,000·00
Rent and Rates	1,050·00
Purchases	46,500·00
Audit Fee	750·00
Sales	85,500·00
Stock at July 1st, 19..	15,000·00
Telephone	300·00
Bank Overdraft	1,650·00
Returns Inwards	750·00
Returns Outwards	1,500·00
Cash in Hand	150·00
Machinery	15,000·00
Salaries	3,750·00
Factory Wages	5,700·00
Discount Received	750·00
Creditors	4,650·00
Debtors	8,100·00
Carriage Outwards	300·00
Bad Debts	450·00
Commission Received	150·00
Furniture, July 1st, 19..	16,800·00
Premises, July 1st, 19..	45,000·00
Goodwill (this is an asset)	9,600·00

Stock at September 30th, 19.., was valued at 20,250·00.

CHAPTER NINETEEN

BOOK-KEEPING TO 'FINAL ACCOUNTS'—PART FOUR: THE BALANCE SHEET

(1) The Residue of the Trial Balance

The Trial Balance originally given in Chapter Sixteen (2), page 197, and revised in Chapter Eighteen (1), page 216, has now been reduced still more. By closing off further accounts and transferring them to the Profit and Loss Account we have caused all the accounts with debit balances, which were losses, to disappear from the Trial Balance, and all the accounts with credit balances, which were profits, to do likewise.

We have also closed off the Drawings Account into the Capital Account. The Capital Account, a liability of the business, has therefore changed from its original balance of 16,100·00 to a new balance of 17,676·00, since we now owe the proprietor not only what he put into the business but also the profit resulting from the year's activities, which has been added to Capital Account.
year's activities, which has been added to Capital Account.

As a result of these activities the Trial Balance now contains only the residual items which will continue into the next year's business—the assets and liabilities of the firm which will go on being used, or honoured, over the course of the next year. The problem now is to present these

R. JONES

TRIAL BALANCE

(as at December 31st, 19..)

Ledger Accounts	Notes	Dr.	Cr.	Notes
Premises Account	Asset	6,490·00		
Capital Account			17,676·00	Liability
Debtors:				
R. Johnson Account	Asset	4,000·00		
M. Thompson Account	Asset	1,506·00		
Creditors:				
R. Lupin Account			120·00	Liability
M. Chuzzlewit Account			360·00	Liability
Plant and Machinery Account	Asset	2,500·00		
Office Furniture Account	Asset	1,600·00		
Cash Account	Asset	300·00		
Bank Account	Asset	200·00		
Stock Account	Asset	1,560·00		
		18,156·00	18,156·00	

Fig. 138. The Residue of the Trial Balance

in such a way as to show 'a true and fair view' of the business to anyone interested in it. This means to *the owner*, the *prospective buyer*, should the owner be thinking of selling, or anyone else interested, like the Tax Authorities. Our Trial Balance now looks as in Fig. 138 (see page 223).

(2) History Makes a Mess of Things—The Balance Sheet Reversed

In Chapter One (7), page 5, it was pointed out that by a strange quirk of history it has become usual to write the Balance Sheet the wrong way round in Great Britain and countries associated with her. The historical circumstances are worth noting.

Simon Stevin of Bruges invented the Balance Sheet in the sixteenth century. He called it a 'Statement of the Affairs' of the business, a phrase which we still use today in connexion with Single Entry, dealt with in Chapter Twenty-five, page 314. Unfortunately, in taking the totals of the Assets and Liabilities out of the books he crossed them over and wrote them down with the assets on the right-hand side and the liabilities on the left. We don't quite know why he did this, probably he was thinking of it as if he were posting the Cash Book. It was quite wrong, but as the Balance Sheet is only a sheet of paper, not part of the real books, it doesn't make any difference, except that it is misleading to the student.

What made matters worse was that the British Parliament, not knowing its book-keeping, passed an Act which made this type of Balance Sheet the law of Great Britain. The Company Act of 1856 included, in Table B, a set of model articles which referred to a Balance Sheet which 'shall be presented to the members at the Annual General Meeting in the form annexed to this table, or as near thereto as the circumstances permit' (Article 72, 1856 Act). The Balance Sheet given was in Simon Stevin's form, with the assets on the right-hand side, and the liabilities on the left-hand side.

A British Act of Parliament, even when it makes absolute rubbish, is so revered a document that we all obey it. Other nations, which have less respect for formal nonsense, produce their Balance Sheets in the sensible form; as the accounts appear in the Trial Balance; with the assets on the left-hand side and the liabilities on the right-hand side. Fortunately British policies do change in time, and harmonization with the EEC countries may yet produce a British balance sheet in correct style.

Remember, then, that although it makes no difference at all it is customary in Great Britain and associated countries to put the Balance Sheet with sides reversed: assets on the right, liabilities on the left.

(3) The Order of Permanence and the Order of Liquidity

In Chapter One the student prepared a number of Balance Sheets with the assets and liabilities arranged in the Order of Liquidity, that is to say with the most liquid assets first. An alternative order is the Order of Permanence, with the least liquid assets first. In order to make these two orders clear, the Balance Sheet of R. Jones is presented twice. Note that the changes in the Capital Account have been brought into the Balance Sheet. This is a useful and popular idea, showing the owner exactly how his new capital figure was derived.

R. JONES

BALANCE SHEET

(as at December 31st, 19. .)

Order of Liquidity

CURRENT LIABILITIES			CURRENT ASSETS	
Sundry Creditors		480·00	Cash in Hand	300·00
			Cash at Bank	200·00
			Sundry Debtors	5,506·00
LONG-TERM LIABILITIES		0·00	Stock	1,560·00
				7,566·00
CAPITAL			FIXED ASSETS	
At Start		16,100·00	Office Furniture	1,600·00
Add			Plant and	
Profits	1,876·00		Machinery	2,500·00
Less			Premises	6,490·00
Drawings	300·00			10,590·00
		1,576·00		
		17,676·00		
		18,156·00		18,156·00

Fig. 139. A Balance Sheet in the Order of Liquidity

R. JONES

BALANCE SHEET

(as at December 31st, 19. .)

Order of Permanence

CAPITAL			FIXED ASSETS	
At Start		16,100·00	Premises	6,490·00
Add			Plant and	
Profits	1,876·00		Machinery	2,500·00
Less			Office Furniture	1,600·00
Drawings	300·00			10,590·00
		1,576·00		
		17,676·00		
			CURRENT ASSETS	
			Stock	1,560·00
LONG-TERM LIABILITIES		0·00	Sundry Debtors	5,506·00
			Cash at Bank	200·00
			Cash in Hand	300·00
CURRENT LIABILITIES				
Sundry Creditors		480·00		7,566·00
		18,156·00		18,156·00

Fig. 140. A Balance Sheet in the Order of Permanence

The really important thing to achieve with a Balance Sheet is that the assets are well displayed whichever order you choose. The two methods, the Order of Liquidity and the Order of Permanence, are simply the reverse order of one another. The student should think seriously about where to place each asset and each liability. It is clear that cash is the most liquid asset we have, for the word 'liquid' means 'in cash form'. Cash at bank is the second most liquid asset—we can easily obtain the cash if we want it by drawing it out. Which is more liquid, stock or debtors? This is debatable. Debtors have a contractual obligation to pay you. Has anyone a duty to buy your stock? Since the answer is 'No', we usually consider Debtors as more liquid than Stock. Similarly the fixed assets are more, or less, easily convertible into cash, and become more fixed and permanent as we move through the list shown.

(4) For Which Type of Business is Each Method Suitable?

Banks always use the Order of Liquidity, because liquidity is very important to a bank. It is a basic idea of banking that depositors shall be able to obtain their money whenever they ask for it. A bank is therefore at pains to maintain its assets in a sufficiently liquid form to meet every requirement of depositors.

Limited companies other than banks usually marshal their assets and liabilities in the Order of Permanence. The strength of a company is often reflected in the material wealth of assets it controls. One can never be sure though, and a large proportion of fixed assets may leave the firm short of working capital, or liquid capital. These matters are discussed later in Chapter Twenty-six, page 320, on Interpretation of Balance Sheets.

Sole traders and partnerships may be presented in either form; both are equally correct.

(5) Book-keeping to Final Accounts

The student should now prepare a large number of exercises to the Final Accounts level. There are still many things to learn about Final Accounts, but we must first consolidate our present knowledge. Every time the student begins to prepare a set of Final Accounts from a Trial Balance he should be prepared to do it first in rough. He should then make a really neat set of Final Accounts, perfect in layout and style, from his rough copy. The student who acquires real facility at these exercises will find himself able to do the rough work, and get his Balance Sheet to balance, in about twenty minutes. A really neat fair copy then takes about ten minutes to write out. Headings and sub-totals can be made to look attractive with suitable underlining in red (a ball-point pen is best).

EXERCISES SET XXXI

(6) Simple Final Accounts

No. 1. Here is the Trial Balance of A. Tacitus's books. From it prepare his Trading Account, Profit and Loss Account, and Balance Sheet.

TRIAL BALANCE
(as at March 31st, 19..)

Stock at Start	5,560·00	
Debtors and Creditors	5,954·00	2,772·00
Freehold Land and Buildings	3,756·00	
Carriage In	398·00	
Purchases and Sales	16,722·00	22,394·00
Bad Debts	300·00	
Motor Vehicle Expenses	130·00	
Office Repairs Account	130·00	
Returns—In and Out	550·00	1,466·00
Fixtures and Fittings	1,500·00	
Motor Vans	1,600·00	
Office Expenses	750·00	
Capital at April 1st last year		12,730·00
Bank Loan		1,038·00
Drawings	750·00	
Salaries and Commissions	1,650·00	
Depreciation	220·00	
Carriage Out	280·00	
Cash in Hand	150·00	
	40,400·00	40,400·00

Closing Stock on March 31st, 19..: 4,500·00

No. 2. Here is the Trial Balance of N. Carter's books on December 31st, 19... You are asked to prepare the Trading Account, Profit and Loss Account, and a Balance Sheet at this date for the year that has just passed.

	Dr.	Cr.
Debtors and Creditors	4,500·25	2,420·75
Plant and Machinery	9,300·00	
Purchases and Sales	8,500·55	15,000·00
Capital at January 1st, 19..		30,000·00
Premises	11,000·00	
Cash in Hand	500·95	
Bank Overdraft		600·55
Discount Allowed and Received	250·35	300·25
Bad Debts	340·00	
Motor Vehicles	2,000·00	
Commission Paid	1,300·00	
Insurance Premiums	110·00	
Office Furniture	3,000·00	
Stock on January 1st, 19..	4,500·00	
Rent and Rates	320·00	
Fees to Lawyers for Debt Collection	180·00	
Returns—In and Out	150·00	60·55
Office Salaries	430·00	
Wages (to go in Trading Account)	1,500·00	
Light and Heat	500·00	
	48,382·10	48,382·10

Stock at the end of December: 3,900·00.

No. 3. Here is the Trial Balance of P. Holden at March 31st, 19... You are to prepare his Trading Account and Profit and Loss Account for the year ending March 31st, 19.., and his Balance Sheet at that date.

	Dr.	Cr.
Office Salaries	635·25	
Discount Allowed and Received	35·75	95·25
Rent	410·50	
Capital		3,925·00
Debtors and Creditors	785·50	1,600·75
Cash	485·65	
Plant and Machinery	635·00	
Stock at April 1st previous year	1,700·00	
Carriage Inwards	75·35	
Carriage Outwards	130·00	
Purchases and Sales	3,335·00	5,000·25
Premises	1,085·00	
Cash at Bank	1,085·75	
Drawings	315·00	
Returns—In and Out	110·25	202·75
	10,824·00	10,824·00

Stock on March 31st, 19.., was valued at 1,775·50.

No. 4. Mr. R. Teasdale is in business as a master tailor. On December 31st, 19.., he takes out his Trial Balance as shown below. Prepare his Trading Account, Profit and Loss Account, and Balance Sheet.

	Dr.	Cr.
Stock at January 1st, 19..	1,350·00	
Purchases and Sales	12,500·00	18,500·00
Returns—In and Out	25·50	40·50
Carriage In	22·50	
Carriage Out	40·00	
Factory Wages	1,250·50	
Factory Light and Heat	120·00	
Premises	4,000·00	
Plant and Machinery	2,800·00	
Motor Vehicles	1,800·00	
Debtors and Creditors	200·75	2,300·50
Office Expenses	2,161·75	
Office Salaries	200·00	
Commission Paid	200·00	
Bad Debts Recovered		25·00
Cash	10·00	
Capital		5,815·00
	26,681·00	26,681·00

Closing stock was valued at 1,900·00.

No. 5. Here is T. Lauder's Trial Balance as at December 31st, 19... You are asked to prepare his Trading Account, Profit and Loss Account, and Balance Sheet as at that date.

	Dr.	Cr.
Capital		8,900·00
Cash	4·00	
Cash at Bank	3,250·00	
Stock at January 1st, 19..	4,500·00	
Sales Returns and Sales	1,000·50	29,500·50
Purchases and Purchases Returns	17,500·25	119·75
Debtors and Creditors	5,990·00	10,000·00
Discount Allowed and Received	500·50	100·00
Factory Wages	1,200·50	
Carriage Inwards	120·00	
Power and Heat for Office	2,075·25	
Rent and Rates	1,500·75	
Miscellaneous Expenses	500·50	
Salaries	1,428·00	
Drawings	2,000·00	
Office Expenses	800·00	
Freehold Premises	1,500·00	
Motor Vehicles	2,000·00	
Fixtures and Fittings	2,600·00	
Depreciation	350·75	
Interest and Commission Received		200·75
	48,821·00	48,821·00

The stock at the end of the year was valued at 2,500·00.

No. 6. Mr. Pinch's Trial Balance is as follows on December 31st, 19... Prepare his Trading Account, Profit and Loss Account, and Balance Sheet in good style.

	Dr.	Cr.
Opening Stock	1,950·50	
Capital		6,376·50
Carriage on Sales	25·50	
Sundry Expenses	300·00	
Purchases and Sales	25,000·25	34,000·50
Returns—In and Out	85·50	35·25
Salaries	700·50	
Cash	25·75	
Land and Buildings	2,534·00	
Plant and Machinery	3,000·00	
Office Furniture	1,850·00	
Commission paid to Travellers	760·50	
Cash at Bank	2,875·00	
Rent and Rates	40·50	
Factory Wages	1,850·00	
Discount Allowed and Received	26·00	125·00
Debtors and Creditors	3,000·00	3,676·75
Light and Heat	190·00	
	44,214·00	44,214·00

Stock at the end of the year: 3,000·00.

No. 7. Prepare a Trading Account, Profit and Loss Account, and Balance Sheet from the Trial Balance below as at December 31st, 19...

	Dr.	Cr.
Capital		36,000·00
Travellers' Salaries and Commissions	3,948·00	
Drawings	2,800·00	
Office Furniture	1,400·00	
Purchases and Purchases Returns	20,884·00	1,696·00
Sales and Sales Returns	728·00	59,936·00
Cash in Hand	884·00	
Cash at Bank	4,960·00	
Stock at January 1st, 19..	4,584·00	
Salaries	2,512·00	
Sundry Debtors and Creditors	14,788·00	6,792·00
Discount Received		72·00
Factory Wages	15,424·00	
Freehold Factory, January 1st, 19..	10,000·00	
Rent and Rates	2,776·00	
Carriage In	924·00	
Carriage Out	1,296·00	
Factory Expenses	2,896·00	
Factory Fuel	3,180·00	
Plant and Machinery	9,600·00	
Office Expenses	912·00	
	104.496·00	104,496·00

Closing stock was valued at 5,716·00.

No. 8. Here is T. Lowe's Trial Balance as at December 31st, 19... You are asked to prepare his Trading Account, Profit and Loss Account, and Balance Sheet as at that date.

	Dr.	Cr.
Sales Returns and Sales	756·50	28,680·50
Capital		8,960·00
Cash	2,254·50	
Purchases and Purchases Returns	15,340·75	126·25
Cash at Bank	3,210·00	
Stock at January 1st, 19..	4,256·00	
Warehouse Wages	2,340·00	
Debtors and Creditors	6,300·50	10,500·50
Discount Allowed and Received	730·75	228·25
Carriage Inwards	115·50	
Power, Light, and Heat for machines	2,300·00	
Rent and Rates	1,250·00	
Miscellaneous Expenses	521·50	
Salaries	730·00	
Drawings	2,100·00	
Office Expenses	630·00	
Freehold Premises	1,300·00	
Leasehold Premises	2,300·00	
Fixtures and Fittings	1,760·00	

Depreciation Leasehold	200	
Depreciation Freehold	200	
	400·00	
Interest Received		100·50
	48,596·00	48,596·00

The stock at the end of the year was valued at 4,000·00.

CHAPTER TWENTY

CAPITAL AND REVENUE EXPENDITURE AND RECEIPTS

(1) Introduction

Whenever we spend money we exchange it for some useful good or service, but the benefit received from the expenditure varies in duration. If we buy a filing cabinet it may last thirty years, and still give quite satisfactory service at the end. If we buy a stamp and stick it on a letter it will last a much shorter time.

The difference between these two types of expenditure is the difference between capital expenditure and revenue expenditure. It is of fundamental importance in understanding Final Accounts, because it is the key that decides whether to write off the expenditure as a loss or to carry it forward to next year as an asset.

(2) Capital and Revenue Expenditure Defined

Capital Expenditure. This is expenditure on fixed assets which last a long time and permanently increase the profit-making capacity of the business.

Revenue Expenditure. This is expenditure on items which are useful to the business, but are used up in less than one year, and therefore only temporarily increase the profit-making capacity of the business. Such expenses include goods for resale.

The chief difference between the two types is the length of time the expenditure is of benefit to the business and since we have to draw a line somewhere the sensible line to draw is at one year. If a good, or a service, lasts *less than one year it is revenue expenditure*. If it lasts *longer than one year it is capital expenditure*.

Examples of Capital and Revenue Expenditure

Capital Expenditure	Revenue Expenditure
Purchase of factory	Wages of factory workers
,, ,, machines	Oil to lubricate machines
,, ,, electric motors	Power to drive the motors
,, ,, new vehicles	500-mile service at garage
,, ,, loose tools	Screws to be used in repair jobs
New set of garage doors	Repairs to padlock on door

Example of a Doubtful Case

Brewer redecorates his premises at a cost of 500·00. He calculates this will last for five years. Is it capital or revenue expenditure? It is a little difficult to say. We will discuss the answer to this question later in the chapter (page 234).

(3) Capital and Revenue Receipts

When the business receives money it is again of two sorts. It may be a capital receipt, a contribution by the proprietor, either to start the business off or to increase the funds available to it. It might be a mortgage or a loan which brings money into the business of a capital nature, but in this case it is not the owner of the business but some other investor who is supplying the capital.

Alternatively the receipt may be a revenue receipt, one which is truly a profit of the business. It may be rent received, or commission received, or it may be cash for sales of goods made that day, or at some previous time. In each case the receipt should be taken to the Revenue Account, for it is a revenue receipt. What, then, is the Revenue Account?

(4) The Revenue Account

The name Revenue Account is a general term in book-keeping for the accounts where the profit or loss of the business is determined. Revenue expenses are losses of the business and must therefore go to the debit side of the Revenue Account; revenue receipts are profits of the business and must therefore be taken to the credit side of the Revenue Account.

In fact, the name Revenue Account is only used today for professional firms: doctors, dentists, lawyers, and accountants are some of the commonest. Such firms cannot really talk about profits and losses. It would be comical and unprofessional to say, 'We made 3·50 out of Mrs. Jones's liver this morning.' Such professional firms talk about 'fees' and 'expenses' instead of profits and losses.

The complete list of Revenue Accounts looks like this:

Names given to the Revenue Account

(*a*) Revenue Account—for professional firms.
(*b*) Trading Account and Profit and Loss Account—for merchants.
(*c*) Manufacturing, Trading, and Profit and Loss Accounts—for manufacturing firms.
(*d*) Income and Expenditure Accounts—for clubs and non-profit-making societies.

Each of these types of firm is dealt with in the course of this book and in each case the distinction between capital and revenue expenditure is important.

(5) Importance of Distinguishing between the Two Types of Expenditure and Receipt

In most countries today an annual check-up on the business is required by law, to discover how profitable it has been. This is necessary because every government is an interested party in the business, wanting to collect tax revenues from the proprietor. In order to ensure that the owner arrives at a fair and accurate profit figure, he is required by law to abide by certain rules and regulations in preparing his Final Accounts figure.

At the root of these rules lie the distinctions between capital and revenue receipts and expenditure. If a receipt is a revenue receipt it must have added to the profitability of the firm and should therefore be included in the calculation of profits. If it is left out, then the profit will be understated and the Income Tax Authorities will be cheated of the government's lawful share.

If an item of expenditure is a revenue expense the benefit derived from it was used up completely during the year, and clearly should be counted as a deduction from the profits. If an item of expenditure is a capital expense, its benefit lasts more than a year, perhaps for ever (like buying the freehold of a piece of land), and clearly it should not be counted as a loss to the business.

To define exactly the nature of a revenue expense leads to many difficulties. Entertaining a business friend may justifiably be regarded as an expense of the business. But if you agree to entertain him in return for him inviting you back later you are clearly both evading the law in order to dodge taxation.

This is a rather extreme example, but doubtful cases arise all the time. We have already referred to one such case on page 232: Brewer redecorates his premises at a cost of 500·00 and estimates that this will last five years. Is this capital expenditure or revenue expenditure? The crucial point here is: does this expenditure increase the value of Brewer's assets? To the extent that it does it is capital expenditure. If it merely maintains the premises so that they retain their present value it is revenue expenditure—which seems likely to be the case here.

Since it lasts longer than a year, this revenue expenditure has to be treated as an adjustment. Adjustments are dealt with fully in Chapter Twenty-two, page 250.

(6) The Rules with Capital and Revenue Items

To deal properly with capital and revenue items a businessman must abide by the following rules:

Rule 1. **Let every Revenue Account for the year in question carry every penny of loss that the business has suffered, and every penny of gain that the business has achieved; no more and no less.**

It follows from this rule that if we have not paid some item which we should have paid—like rent or wages or salaries—we should still count in the expense as if it had been paid, otherwise we shall overstate our profits. Conversely, if some payment is due to us, like commission that we should have received, we must still count this in as profit, and must *adjust* the commission received to take account of this receipt that has accrued. Chapter Twenty-two is about adjustments and explains fully how to make allowances for all accrued payments due.

It follows equally clearly from Rule 1 that if we have made some payment in advance for next year, it would be unfair to include that payment in this year's losses. We must adjust the loss to account for the overpayment, since this year cannot fairly be expected to carry next year's losses. Conversely, any profits received now which properly belong to next year must be disregarded. In Club Accounts there are always some members who pay their subscriptions in advance. If a member pays next year's subscription in December we must hold this 'profit' of the club over until next year; it cannot be counted in this year's receipts. Chapter Twenty-two deals fully with Payments in Advance.

Rule 2. **Every Balance Sheet must carry the assets at their fair value at the date shown on the Balance Sheet, while the liabilities must also be stated at their correct figure.**

If an asset has worn out a little since last year we must depreciate it to its proper value, writing the loss off the profits as depreciation. An interesting case is the asset **debtors**. It is well known that some debtors do not pay, either because fate is unkind to them or because they are rogues. We must provide for possible Bad Debts even though we do not know they have actually occurred, and deduct this provision from the debtors' figure to show the debtors at their true value. All these matters are dealt with in Chapter Twenty-two.

(7) The Capitalization of Revenue Expenditure

There is one particular type of expenditure that is of great interest because it involves an obvious revenue expense that has to be treated as a capital expense. Consider these two examples:

Example 1. A machine, purchased for 1,000·00 is erected by our own fitters and maintenance men while the factory is closed on a public holiday. The cost of this in wages is 230·00.

Clearly wages is a revenue expense, but in this case the wages have been added to the value of the machine. The value of the machine as we purchased it is 1,000·00. The value of the machine installed in its place is 1,230·00 for it cost us 1,000·00 and 230·00 to install.

Let us say that at present the Wages Account looks like this:

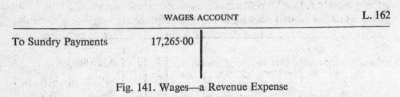

WAGES ACCOUNT   L. 162

To Sundry Payments	17,265·00		

Fig. 141. Wages—a Revenue Expense

Included in the figure of 17,265·00 is 230·00 which has been paid to the workers but which is not really a revenue expense. It has to be removed from the Wages Account and capitalized. A simple Journal Entry will record the purchase of the asset and capitalize the revenue expense. Here it is:

19..				
July 12	Machinery Account Dr.	L. 2	1,230·00	
	To Thompson Tools Co.	L. 71		1,000·00
	,, Wages Account	L. 162		230·00
	Being purchase of Machine No. LZ.			
	123 and erection at this date			

Fig. 142. Capitalization of a Revenue Expense

The Wages Account will now appear as shown below. Notice particularly that the amount to be written off the profits at the end of the year for the Revenue Expense, Wages, has been reduced by 230·00. This 230·00 has not been lost—it is still in the business, embodied in the asset, machinery.

WAGES ACCOUNT   L. 162

To Sundry Payments	17,265·00	By Machinery	J. 1 230·00

Fig. 143. Wages Account adjusted to the true 'loss' figure

Example 2. Jones is a builder, but weather is poor and his men are unable to proceed with his present building jobs. He decides to alter his own premises, enlarging the shop front, redesigning display counters, and altering storage facilities, shelving, etc. This involves the following expenses: (*a*) materials 280·00; (*b*) labour 320·00—but it increases the value of the building by 1,000·00. Capitalize the revenue expenses.

This is an exercise in double entry:

(*a*) The asset, premises, has increased in value by 1,000·00.

(*b*) Materials (Purchases Account) has lost 280·00, the Wages Account has 320·00 on it that should not be there, and Jones has made 400·00 profit on the men's work. This will be treated as a capital profit and be credited in the Capital Account.

We would do the following Journal Entry:

19.. Nov. 27	Premises Account	L. 12	1,000·00	
	To Purchases Account	L. 27		280·00
	„ Wages Account	L. 33		320·00
	„ Capital Account	L. 187		400·00
	Being the capitalization of revenue expenses on improving the property			

Fig. 144. Improving the Capital Assets by Revenue Expenditure

(8) Revenue Expenses that Show Up as Reduced Stock

There is one type of business loss that never appears directly in either the Trading or Profit and Loss Accounts. That is the type of loss which has the effect of reducing the stock. Consider these cases:

(*a*) A customer in a china shop breaks a plate accidentally. She offers to pay, but the owner refuses to allow her to do so as it was a pure accident. The broken plate is put in the dustbin. Such a loss would not appear in the Profit and Loss Account because it already appears in the Trading Account. When we count the stock, the plate will not be there. We will therefore take account of it and to write it off the Profit and Loss Account would be to take account of it twice.

(*b*) A greengrocer has some tomatoes go bad over the week-end. There is no need to take account of this loss, as it will be taken into account when we value the stock.

(*c*) A furniture dealer has to reduce the price of a piano because of a bad mark sustained in moving it. This loss will be taken into account when the piano is valued as part of the stock.

EXERCISES SET XXXII

(9) Capital and Revenue Expenditure

No. 1. The following items appear in R. Smith's books for this year:

Telephone expenses 24·00; Salaries for office workers 850·00; New weighing machines for shop 54·10; New counters 20·00; Wages of men fitting the counters 5·00.

Would you call each of these a capital or a revenue expense? Say where you would expect to find each of them when the Final Accounts of the year and the Final Balance Sheet have been completed.

No. 2. The Newtown Zoological Company Ltd. has the following expenses during the current year. Copy them out and put a tick in the appropriate column:

Expenses		Revenue Item	Capital Item	Trading Account	Profit and Loss Account	Balance Sheet
(a) Purchased gorilla	5,000·00					
(b) Paid keepers' wages	950·00					
(c) Hire of loudspeaker equipment	30·00					
(d) Built monkey house	2,800·00					
(e) Repairs to aquarium air pumps	5·00					

No. 3. On December 31st you begin work on your Final Accounts. The owner of your business, Mr. Watchit, points out to you that crockery valued at 12·10 was destroyed last year after an accident in the shop, but you have made no note of this loss in the Profit and Loss Account. Explain to him why none is necessary.

No. 4. A.B. Ltd. purchased a machine ex works for 2,350·00. They paid carriage of 85·00, and wages to their own fitters for erecting the machine on a Sunday, 75·00. Show the capitalization of these revenue expenses and the purchase of the new machine, by doing a Journal Entry and posting it to the Ledger. The machine is on credit from Wormco Engineering Ltd.

No. 5. M. Stove's expenses in the first month of business include the following: (1) Purchase of motor van 500·00. (2) Postage and stationery 20·00. (3) Purchase of typewriter 28·00. (4) Purchase of goods for resale 180·00. (5) Repairs to garage lock 0·25. (6) Teas for staff 0·65.

Say which you think are capital expenses and which are revenue expenses, and make a list of those he would still have on his books in twelve months' time.

No. 6. Rapidfloors Ltd., a firm of linoleum manufacturers, have the following expenses on their books. Copy out this list and tick in the appropriate column.

Expenses		Type of Expense		Position in Final Accounts		
		Revenue Item	Capital Item	Trading Account	Profit and Loss Account	Balance Sheet
(a) Painting machine	8,200·00					
(b) Paper and string	26·10					
(c) Building new canteen	15,000·00					
(d) Wages of workers building canteen	5,000·00					
(e) Wages of workers making lino	12,000·00					
(f) Pitch (raw material) purchased	2,800·00					

No. 7. Your employer suggests to you that as fruit and vegetables to a total value of 150·00 have been wasted during the year because they became over-ripe and unfit for sale, you should debit these losses in the Profit and Loss Account. Would you accept the suggestion or not? Justify your answer.

No. 8. Funfair Ltd. employ maintenance staff who, in busy times, act as attendants in the fun fair, and in less busy times do repair work—repainting side shows, installing new items, etc. On analysing their working time at the end of the season the following was discovered:

(*a*) Wages earned while acting as attendants 5,800·00.

(*b*) Wages earned while repairing existing parts of the fair during slack times 2,200·00.

(*c*) Wages earned while erecting a new sideshow—the water chute 1,800·00.

Do you consider these to be capital or revenue expenses? Explain where they would appear in the Final Accounts.

No. 9.
(*a*) In keeping the books of a business, why is it important to distinguish between capital expenditure and revenue expenditure?

(*b*) In connexion with the business of a restaurant proprietor, state whether you consider the following to be capital expenditure or revenue expenditure, giving your reasons:

(i) Purchase of a new electric cooker.
(ii) Charge for hire of a refrigerator.
(iii) Cost of structural alterations to the dining-room to increase seating capacity.
(iv) Cost of repainting the kitchen and the outside of the premises.

(*R.S.A.—Stage I*)

No. 10.
(*a*) What is meant by the two terms capital expenditure and revenue expenditure?

(*b*) Name *two* types of capital expenditure and *two* types of revenue expenditure.

(*c*) A. Smartfoot has his premises redecorated externally at a cost of 200·00. He estimates that this will only be necessary once every four years. Discuss whether this is capital or revenue expenditure.

(*East Anglian Examination Board—Adapted*)

No. 11. A stray dog chases a cat into your employer's china shop, smashing a quantity of cut-glass ware. Some time later, when the Trading Account for the period has been prepared, your employer complains that the figure for the net profit must be incorrect as he remembers the considerable damage which took place but no entry appears in the Final Accounts in respect of it. What explanation would you give him?

(*R.S.A.—Adapted*)

No. 12.
(*a*) R.S. deals in typewriters and accessories. State whether the following items of expenditure are capital or revenue expenditure, giving reasons for your answer:

(i) Purchase of two typewriters as stock-in-trade and two for office use.
(ii) Repairs to office adding-listing machine.
(iii) Fire insurance premiums on warehouse.

(*b*) A firm's Profit and Loss Account included an item of 500·00 for repairs and alterations to premises. If it is decided to capitalize one-half of this expenditure, what would be the effect on the Balance Sheet of the firm?

No. 13. W. Tanner Ltd. owned freehold business premises of which the book value on January 1st, 19.., was 10,000·00. During that year the company engaged Builders Limited to repair, paint, decorate, and build extensions to these premises. The invoice from Builders Limited, dated November 30th, 19.., showed repairs 80·00, painting and decorating 170·00, and cost of building extensions 1,500·00. (This invoice was paid on December 7th by cheque.) The company also purchased adjoining premises during the year for the sum of 4,000·00 which was paid by cheque on December 16th, 19...

Make the entries in the company's Ledger to record the above transactions.

(*University of London 'O' Level—Adapted*)

No. 14. Give *three* examples of capital expenditure that might be undertaken by a garage proprietor, and *three* examples of Revenue Expenditure that might be undertaken by a café owner.

Smartfront Ltd. spend 600·00 improving and redecorating their shop premises. It is estimated that the improvements, which are of a permanent nature, represent two-thirds of the total cost. The redecorations are estimated to last five years and are to be held in a Decorations in Suspense Account. At present the 600·00 spent is to be found as follows: 300·00 in the Wages Account, having been paid to the firm's workers, and 300·00 in Purchases Account, having been spent on building materials.

You are asked to show the Journal Entry or Entries recording these matters.

(*East Anglian Examination Board—Adapted*)

CHAPTER TWENTY-ONE

THE VALUATION OF STOCK

(1) Introduction—The Importance of Correct Stock Valuation

In Chapter Seventeen the position of stock was discussed as part of the Trading Account. The valuation of closing stock is very important, since it affects the Gross Profit figure. If we overvalue closing stock we will overstate our profits, and if we undervalue closing stock we will understate our profits. Moreover, since closing stock appears on the Balance Sheet, an incorrect stock figure means an incorrect Balance Sheet. Since businesses are bought and sold on the basis of a Balance Sheet, the deliberate misrepresentation of a stock figure is fraudulent. Many purchasers of businesses insist upon an independent valuation of the stock by a disinterested third party.

Accurate stock valuation is therefore essential for the production of an honest Trading Account and an honest Balance Sheet. On what basis should stock be valued?

(2) The Basis of Stock Valuation

The case of Freeman Hardy & Willis v Ridgway, 1969, laid it down that the best basis on which to value stock is as follows:

Stock should be valued at cost price or current selling price, whichever is the lower.

Let us examine this proposal. To value stock at cost price, that is, what it cost us when we bought it, seems a fair enough idea. To value it at selling price would not be very wise, because it would mean we were taking a profit on it while it was still in our hands. Before we sell it the price may fall again, and our so-called profit would have disappeared. Prudent businessmen never take a profit until they have actually realized it. If current stocks rise in value on the market, ignore the price change until you actually sell and realize the profit.

Now consider what happens if the value of our stock falls. The traditional caution of businessmen has always led them to accept a loss when it was reasonably certain to occur, but never to anticipate a profit. It used to be thought that if the purchase price of stock to replace items sold fell, then this replacement price was the best valuation to place upon existing stock. However the case of Freeman Hardy and Willis v Ridgway 1969 changed this rule, and said that if the selling price was above the original cost price the goods must be valued at cost price. A lower value than cost price could only be placed on stock if the

241

current **selling** price fell below cost. This might happen where goods deteriorated, for example.

The result is that the professional accountancy bodies have changed their rule to read 'stock should be valued at cost price, or current selling price whichever is lower.' The student should learn this basis of valuation by heart.

(3) Stock-taking at the End of the Financial Year

The process of valuing stock can be an arduous one, for it involves the physical checking of the stock, pricing it at cost price or current selling price, multiplying the price by the number of units in stock, and adding the totals.

To reduce the work as much as possible it is usual to hold a stock-taking sale. This has a dual purpose. First it reduces the physical number of items to be counted, and second, it gives the proprietor an opportunity to appraise the stock. An astute owner will notice many significant things about his stocks at sale-time. Certain lines will be found to have sold badly—the shop is cluttered up with huge supplies of slow-moving items. This may be due to the personal foibles of the buyer concerned. He may be 'terribly interested' in Polynesia and have the art department littered with Easter Island statuettes that do not command a ready sale. She may be an old 'fuddy duddy', buying lines that were the rage thirty years ago. Some lines may be traditional ones that the shop has always sold, but times have changed. The elimination of these slow-moving lines, clearing the shelves for newer, more popular, items will improve the profitability of the business.

One effect of stock-taking sales is that they reduce the expected rate of Gross Profit. A slow-moving line may be cut to clear it from stock. It will still probably make a profit, but a much lower profit than was originally hoped. We shall see when we come to consider Gross and Net Profit percentages that this causes a fall in the Gross Profit percentage. We may have to remove that 'fuddy duddy' buyer to stop the same thing happening next year—dismiss her, promote her, demote her, but see that she doesn't buy any more. This may seem harsh, but if our competitors force us out of business other employees will suffer too.

(4) A Stock Valuation Question

Consider the following case:

A firm's stock records show—

19..		Quantity	Cost price
January 1st	Stock	2,500	1·50 each
January 1–31	Purchases	3,000	1·65 ,,
February 1–28	Purchases	3,000	1·70 ,,
March 1–31	Purchases	1,000	1·45 ,,
January 1–31	Sales	4,000	2·50 ,,
February 1–28	Sales	3,500	2·55 ,,
March 1–31	Sales	1,500	2·25 ,,
March 31st	Stock	?	value?

The firm's policy is to sell all stock in strict rotation, first in, first out. Current selling price of similar items of stock at March 31st, 2·20 each.

You are to discover:

(*a*) The value to be placed on closing stock.

(*b*) The Gross Profit for the 3-month period.

Calculations. We shall need to calculate all the figures for the Trading Account, but first deal with section (*a*).

Calculation of Value of Closing Stock:

$$
\begin{aligned}
\text{Stock at Start} &= 2{,}500 \text{ units} \\
\text{,,\ Purchased} &= 7{,}000 \text{ ,,} \\[2pt]
\hline
\text{,,\ Available} &= 9{,}500 \text{ ,,} \\
\textit{Less}\ \text{Sales} &\quad\ 9{,}000 \text{ ,,} \\[2pt]
\hline
\therefore \text{Closing Stock} &= \quad\ 500 \text{ ,,}
\end{aligned}
$$

These must have been part of the most recent batch bought, which cost 1·45 each. As the current selling price is 2·20 we must value this stock at the lower figure.

$$
\begin{aligned}
\therefore \text{Value of Closing Stock} &= 500 \times 1\cdot45 \\
&= 725\cdot00
\end{aligned}
$$

Other calculations:

Opening Stock = $2{,}500 \times 1\cdot50 = 3{,}750\cdot00$

$$
\begin{aligned}
\text{Purchases} &= (3{,}000 \times 1\cdot65) + (3{,}000 \times 1\cdot70) + (1{,}000 \times 1\cdot45) \\
&= 4{,}950\cdot00 + 5{,}100\cdot00 + 1{,}450\cdot00 \\
&= 11{,}500\cdot00
\end{aligned}
$$

$$
\begin{aligned}
\text{Sales} &= (4{,}000 \times 2\cdot50) + (3{,}500 \times 2\cdot55) + (1{,}500 \times 2\cdot25) \\
&= 10{,}000\cdot00 + 8{,}925\cdot00 + 3{,}375\cdot00 \\
&= 22{,}300\cdot00
\end{aligned}
$$

We are now able to proceed with section (*b*).

TRADING ACCOUNT
(for quarter ending March 31st, 19..)

To Opening Stock	3,750·00	By Sales	22,300·00
,, Purchases	11,500·00		
Total Stock Available	15,250·00		
Less Closing Stock	725·00		
Cost of Sales	14,525·00		
Gross Profit	7,775·00		
	22,300·00		22,300·00

Therefore: Gross Profit = 7,775·00

The student might usefully amuse himself with following through exactly what happens when stock is overvalued, or understated. Using the above Trading Account as an example, if the Closing Stock is overvalued—say at 800·00—this will reduce the cost of sales and increase the Gross Profit:

Hence *overvalued stock = overstated profits*

Undervalued stock has the reverse effect:

Hence *undervalued stock = undervalued profits*

Carrying the idea a step further, what will happen next year?

In the next year, this year's closing stock becomes next year's opening stock. Therefore overstated profits this year will be followed by understated profits next year.

In tabulated form we have:

Error	Effect on this year	Effect on next year
Overstated Stock	Overstated Profits	Understated Profits
Understated Stock	Understated Profits	Overstated Profits

We shall see later that this is an important explanation of statistical differences between the years. (See Chapter Twenty-six, page 323(*g*), on Interpretation of Final Accounts.)

(5) Delays in Stock-taking

It is often difficult to take stock on exactly the right day of the year. It may be too big a job for one evening and we may not wish to shut the store for a whole day. To overcome this difficulty we can take stock at any time we like that is conveniently near the last day of the financial year, and then adjust the stock figure for any incoming or outgoing stock in the interval between stock-taking and the end of the year. Consider the following case:

Example. A firm decides to do its stock-taking on December 27th, which is a public holiday. It finds its stock on that date is 7,826·00. In the four remaining days of the year the following transactions take place:

Goods purchased and entered into stock	= 835·00
Credit sales at selling prices	= 556·00
Cash sales at selling prices	= 334·00
Returns from a customer taken back into stock =	12·00
(These returns were valued at selling price.)	

The firm adds 33⅓ per cent to its cost prices to obtain its selling prices.

Calculations:

There are a number of points to discuss here, but we will deal with each as we come to it.

(*a*) Stock on December 27th = 7,826·00
(*b*) Stock purchases   = 835·00
                    ───────
                    8,661·00

(As this stock is at cost price it is clearly correct to add it on to the stock at December 27th, since it will be in stock on December 31st.)

(*c*) Cash Sales and Credit Sales. Here we have a problem. These sales are clearly part of the December 27th stock which has been disposed of and will not be in stock on December 31st. We must therefore deduct them—but at cost price.

NOTE: Students who are not very good at commercial arithmetic may not appreciate that $33\frac{1}{3}$ per cent added on to cost price is the same as 25 per cent deducted from Selling Price. Here is the explanation:

$$\text{Cost Price} + \text{Profit} = \text{Selling Price}$$
$$\therefore \quad 100\% \quad + 33\frac{1}{3}\% = \quad 133\frac{1}{3}\%$$

If we want to remove $33\frac{1}{3}$ per cent from $133\frac{1}{3}$ per cent it is not one-third but one-quarter of it. There are $4 \times 33\frac{1}{3}$ per cent in $133\frac{1}{3}$ per cent.
    The full rule is:

$$\frac{1}{2} \text{ on to cost price} = \frac{1}{3} \text{ off selling price}$$
$$\frac{1}{3} \quad \text{,,} \quad \text{,,} \quad = \frac{1}{4} \quad \text{,,} \quad \text{,,}$$
$$\frac{1}{4} \quad \text{,,} \quad \text{,,} \quad = \frac{1}{5} \quad \text{,,} \quad \text{,,}$$
$$\frac{1}{5} \quad \text{,,} \quad \text{,,} \quad = \frac{1}{6} \quad \text{,,} \quad \text{,,} \quad \text{etc.}$$

For percentages that do not easily change to this type of proper fraction (like 40 per cent) we find the cost price by this formula:

$$CP = \frac{SP}{140} \times 100$$

i.e. the CP is $\frac{100}{140}$ths of the SP

Returning to our example:
    Cash Sales + Credit Sales $\times \frac{3}{4}$

$$= \frac{556 + 334}{4} \times 3 = \frac{890}{4} \times 3 = 667\cdot50$$

Deducting these sales at cost price we have

$$
\begin{array}{r}
8,661\cdot00 \\
667\cdot50 \\
\hline
= 7,993\cdot50
\end{array}
$$

(d) Returns have to be added back at COST PRICE $= \quad 9\cdot00$

Valuation to be placed on Stock $8,002\cdot50$

EXERCISES SET XXXIII

(6) Stock Valuation

No. 1. John Dillon, a merchant in malting barley, prepared his Trading Account for the year ended December 31st, 19.. On that date his stock consisted of 200 tons bought at varying prices: 20 tons at 19·50 a ton, 80 tons at 20·00 a ton, and 100 tons at 19·75 a ton. At the same date, December 31st, 19.., the current selling price was 28·50; 5 tons of his stock, originally costing 20·00 per ton, had overheated and were sold for cattle feed at 15·00.

Draw up a statement showing how Dillon should value, for his Trading Account, his unsold stock of barley on December 31st, 19...

(*R.S.A.—Adapted*)

No. 2. The following information is available from Jones & Co.'s stock records:

19..		Quantity	Price
January 1st	Stock	3,000	0·75
January 1–31	Purchases	4,000	0·77
February 1–28	Purchases	4,000	0·79
January 1–31	Sales	4,500	1·10
February 1–28	Sales	3,500	1·15
February 28th	Stock	?	

(*a*) State the usual basis of stock valuation at the end of any trading period.

(*b*) Work out the quantity and value of the stock on February 28th, 19.., given that the current selling price of stock was 1·20 but that 100 units were shopsoiled and valued as only likely to fetch 0·75.

No. 3. (*a*) On what basis is stock valued at the end of the financial year? (*b*) Hans Memling had on January 1st, 19.., a stock of 3,000 pairs of shoes valued at cost price (1·00 each). During January he sold 1,800 pairs and bought 2,500 pairs at 1·10 each. In February he bought a further 2,500 at 1·05 and sold 3,000 pairs. At the end of February he still has 100 pairs of the January 1st stock unsold. These are in an unfashionable colour and he decides to dispose of them for 0·75 per pair. The shoes bought in February have not yet been offered to his customers. Calculate the value of his stock on February 28th, 19...

(*East Anglian Examination Board—Adapted*)

No. 4. A trader, dealing in a single standard article, follows strictly the rule of selling his goods in the order in which he has bought them. On January 1st, 19.., his stock was 1,000 articles, which had cost him 0·75 each. His subsequent purchases were: January 30th, 2,000 articles at 0·83 each; February 27th, 2,000 articles at 0·85 each; March 16th, 2,000 articles at 0·87 each. His sales were: January, 2,400 articles at 1·05 each; February, 2,000 articles at 1·03 each; March, 1,800 articles at 1·04 each. Damaged articles are sold off at half their cost price. On March 31st he had 80 damaged articles, 20 purchased in January and 60 in February.

Show the trader's Trading Account for the quarter ended March 31st, 19...

(*R.S.A.—Adapted*)

No. 5. A trader had in stock on March 1st 10,000 articles at 0·35 each. During March he purchased a further 14,000 costing 0·38 each, but was given an allowance of 0·10 each on 1,000 of these because they arrived in a damaged condition. His sales during the month, made in strict rotation, were 15,000 undamaged articles at 0·55 each and 680 of the damaged articles at 0·45 each. He now feels that the remaining damaged articles will only fetch 0·25 each, and values his stock accordingly.

Show the Trading Account of the trader for the month of March. (Goods are sold in strict rotation—first in, first out.)

(*R.S.A.—Adapted*)

No. 6. The following information was extracted from a firm's stock records:

19..		Quantitty	Price
January 1st	Stock	2,000 articles	0·75 each
January 1–31	Purchases	3,000 ,,	0·88 ,,
February 1st to March 31st	Purchases	1,000 ,,	0·95 ,,
January 1–31	Sales	4,000 ,,	1·05 ,,
February 1st to March 31st	Sales	1,500 ,,	1·10 ,,
March 31st	Stock	500 ,,	

(*a*) Assuming that the current selling price on March 31st was 1·15, prepare the firm's Trading Account for the above three months. (Articles were sold in the same order as that in which they were purchased.)

(*R.S.A.—Adapted*)

No. 7. From the following figures you are required to prepare an estimate of J. Wilson's stock at cost price on June 30th, 19...:

Stock (January 1st, 19..) at cost	2,600·00
Purchases from January 1st to June 30th, 19..	15,400·00
Returns Outwards	350·00
Sales	17,850·00
Returns Inwards	280·00
Goods given away for advertising purposes at cost	100·00

J. Wilson adds 40 per cent to his cost prices to obtain selling prices.

(*R.S.A.—Adapted*)

No. 8. A firm sells its goods for cash and on credit; it adds 33⅓ per cent to its purchase prices to obtain the selling prices.

The stock of the concern, at cost, on December 27th, 19. , amounted to 5,320·00. In the remaining three working days of the financial year the following transactions took place:

Purchases at cost	424·00
Credit sales at selling prices	124·00
Cash sales at selling prices	120·00

Goods previously sold to a customer for 12·00 were returned by him, undamaged, and taken back into stock.

Prepare a statement showing the value of the firm's stock at December 31st, 19...

(*R.S.A.—Adapted*)

No. 9.

(*a*) It is sometimes said that stock should be valued at 'cost or current selling price, whichever is the lower'. What is meant by this?

(*b*) B. & M. Sellers are retailers whose financial year closed on Thursday March 31st, 19... It was found convenient to take stock on the following Saturday afternoon when the business was closed. From the following information calculate the value of the stock at the close of business on March 31st, 19..:

Stock at cost on Saturday, April 2nd, 19..	2,862·00
Cost of goods delivered by suppliers on April 1st and 2nd and taken into stock	426·00
Sales on April 1st	145·00
Sales on April 2nd	220·00
Credit to customers (at sale price) for goods returned on April 1st	40·00

NOTE: The business earns 20 per cent Gross Profit on *selling price*.

No. 10. A trader began stock-taking for the year ended March 31st, 19.., on that date. He did not complete the stock-taking until the close of business on April 4th, 19.., when he ascertained the value of stock at cost price as 3,896·00.

The following information is available for the period April 1st to 4th, 19..:

Purchases included in stock figure	304·00
Sales of goods not included in stock figure	460·00

Goods invoiced to a customer on March 31st, 19.., at 80·00 but held in the warehouse pending instructions as to delivery, were included in the stock figure. Percentage of Gross Profit on sales is 25.

Draw up a statement to show the correct value of stock at cost price on March 31st, 19...

(*London University 'O' level—Adapted*)

No. 11. From the following figures you are required to prepare an estimate of a trader's stock at May 31st, 19..:

Stock at January 1st, 19.. (at cost)	4,000·00
Purchases from January 1st to May 31st, 19..	33,000·00
Sales from January 1st to May 31st, 19..	42,000·00
Goods given away for advertising purposes	300·00 (at cost price)

The trader adds 33⅓ per cent to his cost prices to ascertain his selling prices.

No. 12. On May 4th, 19.., a fire occurred on the premises of a trader and part of the stock-in-trade was destroyed. From the following information estimate the value at cost price of the stock destroyed:

Stock at cost price on April 1st, 19..	4,670·00
Purchases April 1st to May 4th, 19..	5,842·00
Sales April 1st to May 4th, 19..	7,345·00
Value at cost price of stock salvaged	1,426·00

Percentage of Gross Profit on sales is 20.

(*University of London 'O' level—Adapted*)

CHAPTER TWENTY-TWO

ADJUSTMENTS IN FINAL ACCOUNTS

(1) Introduction—Why are Adjustments Necessary?

The aim of a good book-keeper is to provide a 'true and fair view' of the profitability and present state of the business. The Revenue Accounts display profitability, the Balance Sheet displays the present state. If there is any item which is incorrectly stated in either the Revenue Accounts or the Balance Sheet, then these records will not give 'a true and fair view' of the business.

The purpose of adjustments is to clear up all such outstanding details and bring the books into perfect order.

The main adjustments necessary are:

(1) Payments in advance by the firm.
(2) Payments in advance to the firm.
(3) Accrued expenses owed by the firm.
(4) Accrued receipts due to the firm.
(5) Bad debts.
(6) Provision for bad debts.
(7) Provision for discounts.
(8) Depreciation of assets.
(9) Depreciation of goodwill.

Before beginning a detailed discussion of these the student is advised to commit to memory this vital phrase:

The purpose of adjustments is to produce a perfectly accurate set of Final Accounts for the period under review, and a perfectly honest Balance Sheet as at the present date.

(2) Adjustments No. 1—Payments in Advance by the Firm

Certain expenses are nearly always paid in advance. The best example is insurance since the insurance cover only begins on payment of the premium and then runs for a given period, usually one year. Rent is often payable in advance, so are rates.

If we use insurance as an example, consider the following Insurance Account which we propose to close off into the Profit and Loss Account.

19..			
Jan. 1	To Balance	60·00	
June 30	„ Fire Insurance	18·00	
Sept. 30	„ Motor Vehicles	102·00	

Fig. 145. Expenses, some of which are in Advance

How much of these insurance expenses apply to the present year, assuming that they are all annual premiums? Clearly all the 60·00 on January 1st, 19.., has been used up by December 31st, 19.., and may fairly be treated as a loss. The Fire Insurance premium of 18·00 on June 30th, 19.., has only been half consumed; the insurance company has still to cover us for a further six months. 9·00 of this 18·00 has to be treated as an expense of the year, the other 9·00 is an asset at present— it will become an expense of next year.

The 102·00 paid for Motor Vehicle Insurance on September 30th has only been one-quarter used up by December 31st, 19... 76·50 of this is an asset; the insurance company owes us cover for this amount. The 25·50 is a loss for the present year.

Our adjustment now reads as follows: instead of 180·00 being transferred to the Profit and Loss Account as a loss, only 60·00 + 9·00 + 25·50 = 94·50 should be transferred, leaving 85·50 still on the Insurance Account as an asset of the business.

The Journal Entry for this will be:

19..				
Dec. 31	Profit and Loss Account Dr. To Insurance Account Being Insurance Premiums for year transferred	L. 66 L. 61	94·50	94·50

Fig. 146. Transferring the Adjusted Amounts

and the Insurance Account now looks like this:

19..			19..		
Jan. 1	To Balance	60·00	Dec. 31	By Profit and Loss	
June 10	„ Fire Insurance	18·00		Account	94·50
Sept. 30	„ Motor Vehicles	102·00	31	„ Balance	85·50
		180·00			180·00
19..					
Jan. 1	To Balance	85·50			

Fig. 147. A Nominal Account that has become a temporary asset account

Notice that the Nominal Account, which has carried our losses on insurance for the year, is at present carrying a balance that is in effect an asset. It must appear on the assets side of the Balance Sheet, since the insurance company are virtually debtors for this amount of cover.

(NOTE: Some theoreticians argue that a Nominal Account cannot have a real balance, and say the correct thing to do is to transfer this balance to a Suspense Account for Balance Sheet purposes. This is a highly academic rule 'more honoured in the breach than in the observance'.)

The Balance Sheet will now have this balance on the assets side, under Current Assets. The best place is to put it as the most liquid item, since it is so liquid *you have already spent it.*

BALANCE SHEET
(as at December 31st, 19. .)

FIXED ASSETS	
CURRENT ASSETS	
Stock	
Debtors	
Cash	
Insurance in Advance	85·50

Fig. 148. The most liquid asset

In examination work, where a student is working from a Trial Balance without the actual accounts, it is usual to show the adjustment on the Trading Account or Profit and Loss Account itself, by indenting the main figure. The Profit and Loss Account in this case would look as follows:

PROFIT AND LOSS ACCOUNT   L. 161
(for year ending December 31st, 19. .)

To Insurance	180·00	
Less Amount Paid in Advance	85·50	
	94·50	

Fig. 149. The best way to show Adjustments for Examination Purposes

The payment in advance must still be shown on the Balance Sheet as in Fig. 148.

(3) Adjustments No. 2—Payments in Advance to the Firm

If payments in advance by the firm should not be counted as losses of the present year, but regarded as assets carried over to the next year for use in the coming months, it seems only logical that payments in advance to the firm for services not yet rendered should not be treated as profits, but carried forward to the next year as liabilities.

Taking the example of insurance used in (2), on page 250, from the insurance company's point of view the position will be the reverse of payments in advance by the firm. They have received premiums, of perhaps 1,000,000·00. Of this figure, let us imagine that 250,000·00 represents premiums received in advance. Clearly only 750,000·00 should be transferred to the Revenue Account, the rest remaining on the books as a liability to the policy-holders. It will become a profit in the course of the coming year. Such an account might look like this after closure:

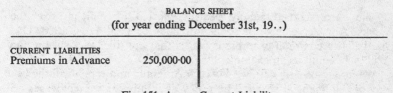

PREMIUMS RECEIVED ACCOUNT			L. 195
Dec. 31 To Revenue Account	750,000·00	By Sundry Premiums	1,000,000·00
„ Balance	250,000·00		
	1,000,000·00		1,000,000·00
		By Balance	250,000·00

Fig. 150. A Nominal Account that has temporarily become a liability

When the credit balance is taken into the Balance Sheet it will look like this:

BALANCE SHEET
(for year ending December 31st, 19..)

CURRENT LIABILITIES	
Premiums in Advance	250,000·00

Fig. 151. A very Current Liability

EXERCISES SET XXXIV

(4) Payments in Advance

No. 1. Lomax's Rent Account shows payments made to his landlord on January 3rd, March 31st, June 26th, September 25th, and December 20th, 19.., of 100·00 each time. The rent is 100·00 per quarter. Show the Rent Account for the year, including the transfer to Profit and Loss Account on December 31st, 19...

No. 2. Phillipson's Insurance Account shows annual insurance payments as follows: Fire Policy on January 1st, 26·50; Motor Vehicles on March 31st, 124·00; Life Assurance on June 30th, 36·00. Show the Insurance Account for the year, including the transfer to Profit and Loss Account on December 31st, 19...

No. 3. The Swinging Hypnotists' Club had a credit balance on its Subscriptions Account of 225·00, which represented subscriptions in advance, on January 1st, 19... During the year subscriptions of 6,255·00 were received, but 255·00 of this was in advance for the next year. Show the Subscriptions Account, including the amount transferred to the club's Income and Expenditure Account (this is the same as the Profit and Loss Account, and is explained later, on page 304).

No. 4. Robson & Co. receive commissions on the sales executed for Yamachita & Co.: 2½ per cent commission on cost price on accepting the authority to sell, and 2½ per cent on selling price when the sale is made. If they are unable to sell, the commission on cost price is returnable. They therefore do not count such commission as profit until they have made the sale.

On January 1st, 19.., there was 326·00 of such commission outstanding as profit earned, but subject to the 'returnable' clause. During the year other commission came to 5,786·00 and on December 31st there was 525·50 outstanding again.

Draw up the Commissions Received Account and thus show how much was transferred as profit to the Profit and Loss Account.

(5) Adjustments No. 3—Accrued Expenses Owed by the Firm

Sometimes we are not in advance with our payments but in arrears. Rent may be accrued due, or commission to travellers may be accrued due.

The word 'accrued' simply means 'collected' or 'built up' over the weeks. Any accruals must sooner or later be paid and settled. One particularly common example is wages that are due. We will use the Wages Account as an example.

Wages are usually paid weekly or fortnightly, and rarely will the last day of the financial year fall on a pay day. Suppose we pay wages on Fridays and the last Friday in the year is December 27th. Workers who work on the 28th, 29th, 30th, or 31st will not be paid for these four days until Friday, January 3rd. We must therefore adjust for these four days, otherwise this year will only be covering 361 days and next year will have 369 days.

To make this adjustment clear, consider the Wages Account as it is at present.

WAGES ACCOUNT	L. 75
19.. Dec. 27 52 weekly payments coming to a total of 17,216·50	

Fig. 152. Wages Account before Adjustment

The 17,216·50 is the amount paid out by the cashier in wages over the weeks of the year. It would not be on the account in one piece as shown here, but there would be fifty-two entries, one for each week in the year. Is this figure the correct figure to show in the Trading Account for wages for the year? Clearly it is not, because there are still four days of the year to adjust. Suppose the wages due are 227·50 for these four days?

Then the total figure to be transferred to the Trading Account is
17,216·50, plus 227·50 = 17,444·00. The Journal Entry will read:

19.. Dec. 31	Trading Account Dr. To Wages Account Being wages for year transferred	L. 95 L. 75	17,444·00	17,444·00

Fig. 153. Closing Wages Account

and the wages account will now have a credit balance. Like all credit

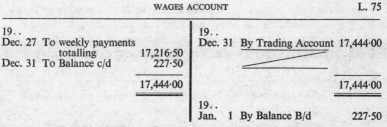

WAGES ACCOUNT   L. 75

19.. Dec. 27 To weekly payments totalling Dec. 31 To Balance c/d	17,216·50 227·50	19.. Dec. 31 By Trading Account	17,444·00
	17,444·00		17,444·00
		19.. Jan. 1 By Balance B/d	227·50

Fig. 154. The Wages Due shown as an outstanding Balance

balances this is a liability and will appear on the Balance Sheet as shown
below:

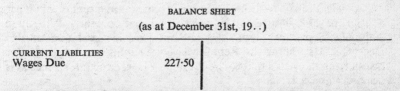

BALANCE SHEET
(as at December 31st, 19. .)

CURRENT LIABILITIES
Wages Due   227·50

Fig. 155. An Accrued Expense appearing on the Balance Sheet

As with all adjustments we have achieved a dual aim. The charge
against the profits for wages has been adjusted to the exact figure for
365 days, while the liability due to the workers for their efforts in the
last four days of the year appears on the Balance Sheet as a current
liability.

What effect does this credit balance have next year? On January 3rd,
19.., we shall pay a full week's wages, say 500·00. These wages will be
recorded in the Cash Book and posted over to the debit side of Wages
Account. The credit balance of 227·50 will automatically reduce the
amount of 500·00 to a figure of 272·50 which will be the charge for wages
for the three days of the new year. If the student feels that these figures
have been badly chosen, since on the four days of the old year less wages
are paid than in the three days of the new year, he should remember that

those four days include Saturday and Sunday—two non-working days in most countries. The Wages Account now looks as follows:

WAGES ACCOUNT   L. 75

19..				19..			
Jan. 3	To Cash	C.B. 1	500·00	Jan. 1	By Balance	B/d	227·50

Fig. 156. The first week's wages in the New Year

(6) Adjustments No. 4—Accrued Receipts Due to the Firm

Expenses may have accrued that we owe to other firms, but clearly the reverse can also be true. Receipts that the firm should have received for goods or services supplied this year may still be outstanding at the end of the year. It would be unfair in principle to let next year receive the benefit of this year's work. We should include these profits, even if they have not actually arrived, as if they had done so. This means we must adjust our Revenue Accounts. Rent received is a good example of this type of adjustment. Many firms sub-let spare rooms in their buildings to smaller businesses and thus earn valuable rent. If such a sub-tenant is in arrears with his rent, and we feel quite sure he will pay, this rent should be included. What is needed in the Profit and Loss Account is a full year's rent from the sub-tenant, even if he has not paid in full.

Example. P. Brown sub-let a room to Homeless at a rent of 25·00 per quarter, payable in arrears: Homeless paid rent on March 27th, June 29th, and September 30th, but had not paid his next quarter due December 31st. Show the Rent Received Account for the year, after transferring the year's rent to the Profit and Loss Account. Homeless is deemed to be reliable.

Clearly the profit for the year on this tenancy is 100·00 and this figure should be carried to the Profit and Loss Account. The Rent Received Account will therefore look as follows:

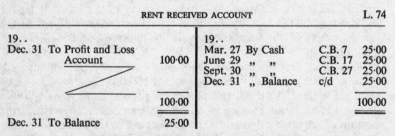

RENT RECEIVED ACCOUNT   L. 74

19..				19..			
Dec. 31	To Profit and Loss Account		100·00	Mar. 27	By Cash	C.B. 7	25·00
				June 29	„ „	C.B. 17	25·00
				Sept. 30	„ „	C.B. 27	25·00
				Dec. 31	„ Balance	c/d	25·00
			100·00				100·00
Dec. 31	To Balance		25·00				

Fig. 157. A profit that has accrued as an asset

This balance will appear as a current asset on the Balance Sheet.

EXERCISES SET XXXV

(7) Accrued Expenses and Accrued Receipts

No. 1. P. Carter, a retailer, sub-lets the flat over his shop at an annual rent of 156·00 payable quarterly in arrear. During the year the tenant paid rent due from him on March 23rd, June 25th, and September 30th, but at December 31st had not paid the quarter's rent due. Show the Rent Account in P. Carter's Ledger, after the preparation of his Profit and Loss Account for the year.

(R.S.A.—Adapted)

No. 2. From the following information prepare the Electricity Account in the Ledger of L. Welsh, a manufacturer:

Amount due at January 1st, 19..	64·35
Payments during the year	
January 15th	64·35
April 20th	54·25
July 17th	42·35
October 15th	47·55

The bill for electricity supplied during the three months ended December 31st was 82·50 and not paid until January 19th, 19 ... Two-thirds of the net cost is to be charged to the Manufacturing Account and one-third to Profit and Loss Account. Balance the account on December 31st, 19...

(R.S.A.—Adapted)

No. 3. At January 1st, 19.., T. Tennant owed a quarter's rent, 20·00, in respect of business premises that he occupied.

During the next twelve months he paid 20·00 by cheque on each of the following dates: January 4th, March 26th, June 25th, and December 27th.

(*a*) Prepare Tennant's Rent Account as it would appear after his Profit and Loss Account for the year ending December 31st, 19.., had been drawn up.

(*b*) What entry relating to rent should appear in his Balance Sheet dated December 31st, 19..?

(R.S.A.—Adapted)

No. 4. H. & C. Ltd. erect lifts and repair them. Their Repairs Revenue Account has a debit balance of 728·00 at January 1st, 19.., for repairs effected the previous year and not yet paid for. During the year 9,878·60 was paid by customers for repairs work, and at December 31st it was calculated that 1,020·45 was outstanding for repairs already executed. Show the Repairs Revenue Account for the year, after transferring the correct profit to the Trading Account.

Show also the entry in the Balance Sheet as at December 31st for the Repairs Account.

Exercises Set XXXVI

(8) Final Accounts Exercises on Payments in Advance and Accrued Expenses

No. 1. On January 1st, 19.., the Rates Account of C. Cooper showed a prepayment of 200·00. During the year ending December 31st, 19.., he paid 450·00 for rates and 2,122·00 in respect of salaries. At the end of the year Cooper calculated that a further 28·00 was owing for salaries and that the rates were then prepaid to the extent of 185·00.

(*a*) Show the Salaries and Rates Accounts after the preparation of the annual Profit and Loss Account.

(*b*) What difference would there have been in Cooper's profits if the amounts in advance or accrued at the *end* of the year had not been allowed for?

(*R.S.A.—Adapted*)

No. 2. C. Cone began business on April 1st, 19.., and ended his first financial period on December 31st, 19... Rent, due at 50·00 per quarter on June 30th, September 30th, and December 31st, was paid on the due dates except that the rent due on December 31st was not paid until January 3rd, 19... Rates paid were 52·45 for the half-year ended September 30th, 19.. (paid April 1st, 19..) and 55·80 for the half-year to the following March 31st, 19.. (paid October 1st, 19..).

Prepare the Rent and Rates Account as it would appear in C. Cone's books for the period of nine months ended December 31st, 19.., and balance it, showing the amount chargeable to the Profit and Loss Account for the period.

(*R.S.A.—Adapted*)

No. 3. A firm has in its Ledger a combined Rent and Rates Account, which on July 1st, 19.., read:

RENT AND RATES

19..			19..		
July 1	To Balance B/d being rates prepaid to September 30th	40·00	July 1	To Balance B/d being rent due June 24th	100·00

The transactions affecting this account, which took place during the following financial year ending June 30th, were:

(*a*) Rent due on June 24th, 19.., 100·00 was paid by cheque on July 4th.

(*b*) Rent due on September 29th, 19.., 100·00, was paid by cheque on the due date.

(*c*) Rates for the half-year October 1st, 19.., to March 31st, 19.., 85·00, were paid by cheque on October 31st.

(*d*) Rent due on December 25th, 19.., 100·00, was paid by cheque on December 22nd, 19...

(*e*) Rent due on March 25th, 19.., 100·00, was paid by cheque on April 5th, 19...

(*f*) Rates for the half-year April 1st, 19.., to September 30th, 19.., 85·00, were paid on May 1st, 19...

(*g*) On June 18th, 19.., the usual reminder that a quarter's rent, 100·00, was due and payable on June 24th was received from the landlord. This payment had not been made when the financial year ended on June 30th.

You are required to copy the heading and opening balances in the firm's Rent and Rates Account, as given above, to complete the account for the financial year ended June 30th, 19.., and to rule it off and balance it at the close of business on that date, after doing the Final Accounts entries.

No. 4. Here is the Trial Balance of Gerard Eliasson on December 31st, 19... You are asked to prepare his Trading Account and Profit and Loss Account for the year, and his Balance Sheet as at this date, bearing in mind the adjustments given below the Trial Balance.

TRIAL BALANCE
(as at December 31st, 19..)

	Dr.	Cr.
Cash in Hand	27·50	
Cash at Bank	2,465·00	
Purchases and Sales	8,248·25	13,612·50
Returns—In and Out	112·25	48·25
Stock at January 1st, 19..	780·00	
Wages	450·00	
Salaries	580·00	
Light and Heat	420·00	
Commission Received		650·25
Rent Received		130·00
Telephone Expenses	120·50	
Insurance	250·00	
Motor Vehicles	1,250·00	
Land and Buildings	4,000·00	
Plant and Machinery	1,400·00	
Loan from Southern Bank		3,000·00
Interest Paid	150·50	
Capital		2,813·00
	20,254·00	20,254·00

NOTES:

(*a*) At December 31st, 19.., stock was valued at 1,250·00.
(*b*) Insurance has been paid in advance for 19.. 50·00.
(*c*) Interest is due on the loan from the bank 30·00.

(*East Anglian Examination Board—Adapted*)

No. 5. Prepare a Trading Account, Profit and Loss Accounts, and Balance Sheet from B. Murray's Trial Balance as at March 31st, 19...

	Dr.	Cr.
Capital (B. Murray)		5,000·00
Cash	25·00	
Bank	11,075·00	
Premises	2,000·00	
Motor Vehicles	850·00	
Plant and Machinery	1,270·00	
Factory Wages	866·50	
Office Salaries	735·25	
Factory Light and Heat	124·50	
Office Light and Heat	38·50	
Commission Received		594·00
Loan from R. Cambridge		2,406·00
Office Expenses	27·25	
Stationery	164·00	
Discount Allowed and Received	27·00	36·75
Purchases and Sales	7,246·00	18,294·75
Sales Returns and Purchases Returns	124·00	146·75
Drawings (B. Murray)	600·00	
Stock at April 1st, 19..	1,320·00	
Debtors and Creditors	2,136·50	2,279·75
Carriage In	100·00	
Carriage Out	28·50	
	28,758·00	28,758·00

Stock at the end of the year was valued at 1,400·00. 43·50 is owing for factory wages and is to be included in the above accounts. Commission amounting to 26·00 has not yet been received, but is to be included as part of the year's profits.

No. 6. Mrs. Brown runs a small clothing factory and on December 31st, 19.., takes out the following Trial Balance. From it prepare her Trading Account, Profit and Loss Account, and Balance Sheet. There are some adjustments given below:

	Dr.	Cr.
Stock at January 1st, 19..	1,800·00	
Purchases and Sales	42,300·00	58,725·00
Returns—In and Out	125·00	1,300·00
Carriage In	100·50	
Carriage Out	265·50	
Factory Wages	3,200·50	
Factory Light and Heat	400·75	
Land and Buildings	7,500·00	
Plant and Machinery	6,500·00	
Motor Vehicles	1,800·00	
Debtors and Creditors	2,400·25	1,800·50
Office Expenses	230·00	
Office Salaries	370·50	
Commission Paid	400·00	
Commission Received		40·50
Cash	850·00	
Capital		6,377·00
	68,243·00	68,243·00

Closing stock was valued at 4,270·00.
Wages due amounted to 100·00.
An amount is owing for office expenses 30·00.
A sum is due to Mrs. Brown for commission amounting to 26·50.

No. 7. Prepare a Trial Balance from the following balances extracted from the books of R. Lasham on March 31st, 19.., and then produce a Trading Account, a Profit and Loss Account, and a Balance Sheet:

Discount Allowed	21·00
Discount Received	26·75
Returns Inward	55·75
Returns Outward	30·00
Purchases	700·00
Sales	1,200·00
Bank Overdraft	125·50
Creditors	140·00
Debtors	545·50
Cash in Hand	10·00
Rent and Rates	80·75
Premises (Freehold)	2,500·00
Stock at April 1st, 19..	350·00
Machinery	1,000·00
Carriage Charges on Sales	69·25
Capital Account	4,850·00
Office Wages	1,263·00
Travellers' Salaries	500·00
Drawings Account	440·00
Commission Received	1,163·00

You should also take into account the following adjustments:

(a) Rent and rates due 16·25.
(b) Office wages due 17·00.
(c) Travellers' salaries paid in advance 50·00.
(d) Commission received in advance 17·00.
(e) The stock on hand at March 31st amounted to 467·00.

(9) Adjustments No. 5—Bad Debts

One of the important figures on a Balance Sheet is the **Sundry Debtors** figure. This shows how much our debtors owe us, and naturally appears on the assets side of the Balance Sheet. At the end of the financial year, before the debtors figure is brought into the Balance Sheet, all debts should be scrutinized to see whether they are in fact good debts. If we leave a bad debtor on our books, and pretend that the debt is good, we are breaking both our rules. Rule 1 said that we must admit and write off every loss that has been suffered in the year. Rule 2 says we must have an honest Balance Sheet. Neither rule will be observed if we allow a bad debt to persist into the new year.

Any debt revealed in our scrutiny as being bad, should be written off to the Bad Debts Account as already described in Chapter Six (see page 104). This will leave us with a true valuation of the debtors on our Balance Sheet, and the Bad Debts Account will be written off the profits, so that the full loss for the year has been accepted.

(10) Adjustments No. 6—Provision for Bad Debts

We may have achieved a true debtors figure, but is it also a 'fair' view? Even the best debtor can become a bad debtor if fate knocks unkindly on his door. Someone will die, or be maimed for life, or become seriously ill, and his affairs will deteriorate over the next few months. Every business suffers a percentage of bad debts, and the average businessman knows roughly what percentage of bad debts is normal for his type of business.

If we intend to be perfectly accurate in our figure for the debtors, we should adjust for this expected percentage of bad debts. This is one of the finer points of book-keeping and the student should follow this example with care.

Example. R. Brown's debtors total 4,260·00 and it is usual in his trade for 5 per cent of debts to prove to be bad. Brown decides to provide this amount out of his profits for the year.

Method. 5 per cent of 4,260·00 = 213·00
Brown must write off 213·00 from his profits as shown below:

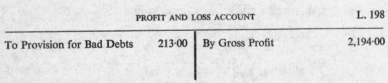

PROFIT AND LOSS ACCOUNT			L. 198
To Provision for Bad Debts	213·00	By Gross Profit	2,194·00

Fig. 158. Providing for Bad Debts that have not yet occurred

This means he must debit the Profit and Loss Account. But which account must be credited? Will Jones die, or Smith, or Bryant? Will Higgins get ill, or will it be Morris? Clearly Brown cannot tell, and yet he has to credit some account. The solution to the problem is to credit a Nominal Account, the Provision for Bad Debts Account. This account is best regarded as a liability to the proprietor. It is his profits that have been taken and tucked away in this Provision Account where he cannot spend them. When bad debts occur in the first few months of the year, the profits set aside from last year will offset the loss suffered, so that the new year is not suffering last year's bad debts.

The really ingenious part of this arrangement is the way it is dealt with on the Balance Sheet. We have charged the 213·00 to the Profit and Loss Account so that the current year has suffered the loss. We have this credit balance on the Provision for Bad Debts Account. As it is a credit balance we should expect it to appear on the liabilities side of the Balance Sheet, thus:

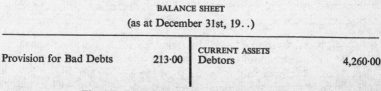

BALANCE SHEET
(as at December 31st, 19. .)

Provision for Bad Debts	213·00

CURRENT ASSETS
Debtors 4,260·00

Fig. 159. Provision for Bad Debts is a liability

In fact it is much better style to take it over to the assets side as a deduction from the asset, debtors. When we do this we make it perfectly clear to anyone reading the Balance Sheet that although the debtors' balances actually total 4,260·00, we only expect to collect 4,047·00. This gives a 'true and fair view' of the asset, debtors.

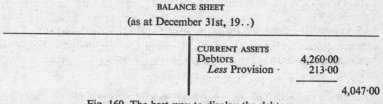

BALANCE SHEET
(as at December 31st, 19. .)

CURRENT ASSETS
Debtors   4,260·00
  Less Provision ·   213·00
                       ─────────
                       4,047·00

Fig. 160. The best way to display the debtors

(11) What Happens to the Provision for Bad Debts in the Next Year?

Consider the present provision as shown in the last section. It has a credit balance. It represents a liability to the proprietor for profits earned,

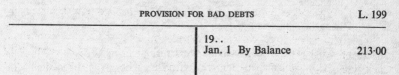

PROVISION FOR BAD DEBTS   L. 199

19. .
Jan. 1 By Balance   213·00

Fig. 161. The Provision for Bad Debts Account

but retained in the business in case bad debts occur.

Next year we shall suffer some bad debts, and at the end of the year the provision we shall need will certainly not be 213·00. It would be a very rare chance that our debtors figure for one year should be exactly the same as the debtors figure twelve months later. As the provision is tied to the debtors figure it must vary from year to year.

Method I

The simplest way to deal with this problem is to **write the bad debts off the Provision Account and not off the Profit and Loss Account**, on December 31st next. We can then make a new charge to profits for the new provision. There are three possibilities, one of which is highly improbable.

(*a*) The bad debts could be less than the provision at present of 213·00.
(*b*) The bad debts could be exactly 213·00.
(*c*) The bad debts could be more than the present provision.

Example (*a*). The next year R. Brown suffers bad debts of 132·00 and on December 31st his debtors balances are 3,850·00.

If we write the bad debts off against the provision and not against the Profit and Loss Account we will debit them in the Provision Account as we close off the Bad Debts Account. This figure of 132·00 deducted from 213·00 leaves a balance of 81·00 still in the Provision Account.

This year we need 5 per cent of 3,850·00 which is 192·50. As we already have 81·00 in the provision for Bad Debts Account we only need to take 111·50 from the profits in the Profit and Loss Account. When this sum is debited to Profit and Loss Account and credited to Provision Account we have an account which balances off with exactly the right provision.

PROVISION FOR BAD DEBTS ACCOUNT   L. 199

19..			19..		
Dec. 31	To Bad Debts	132·00	Jan. 1	By Balance	213·00
31	,, Balance c/d	192·50	Dec. 31	,, Profit and Loss Account	111·50
		324·50			324·50
			Jan. 1	By Balance B/d	192·50

Fig. 162(*a*). The Old Provision changed to the new figure (case (*a*))

Example (*b*). Too unlikely to be worth illustrating.

Example (*c*). Going a further year with this account R. Brown suffers serious bad debts due to an economic slump. The total bad debts are 426·50 and his roll of debtors totals 5,900·00. Brown decides to increase the provision to 10 per cent of the debtors figure. This time the bad debts transferred to the Provision for Bad Debts Account use up the entire provision of 192·50 and leave an unsatisfied loss of 234·00. This

will have to be written off the Profit and Loss Account. As we also
need a new provision of 590·00 (10 per cent of the debtors) we have to
write off 824·00 from the Profit and Loss Account into the Provision
for Bad Debts Account. This will then have exactly the right balance
for the new provision.

PROVISION FOR BAD DEBTS ACCOUNT L. 199

19..			19..		
Dec. 31	To Bad Debts	132·00	Jan. 1	By Balance	213·00
31	,, Balance c/d	192·50	Dec. 31	,, Profit and Loss Account	111·50
		324·50			324·50
Year 2			Year 2		
Dec. 31	To Bad Debts	426·50	Jan. 1	By Balance B/d	192·50
31	,, Balance	590·00	Dec. 31	,, Profit and Loss Account	824·00
		1,016·50			1,016·50
			Jan. 1	By Balance	590·00

Fig. 162(*b*). The old Provision changed to the new Provision figure (case (*c*))

Method II

An alternative way to deal with the bad debts next year is to keep the
Bad Debts Account and the Provision for Bad Debts Account quite
separate. At the end of the year the total of the Bad Debts Account is
written off to the Profit and Loss Account by a closing Journal Entry.

The Provision for Bad Debts Account is now adjusted to the new
provision. In Fig. 162 the old provision was changed from 213·00 to
192·50. Since Bad Debts are being treated separately from the Provision
for Bad Debts, we now have:

PROVISION FOR BAD DEBTS ACCOUNT L. 199

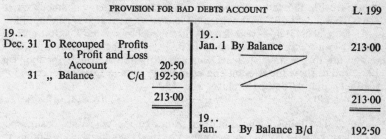

19..				19..		
Dec. 31	To Recouped Profits to Profit and Loss Account		20·50	Jan. 1	By Balance	213·00
31	,, Balance	C/d	192·50			
			213·00			213·00
				19..		
				Jan. 1	By Balance B/d	192·50

Fig. 163(*a*). The old Provision changed to the new figure—case (*a*)

Note that the Profit and Loss Account will suffer the same burden
as before, but in a different way.

METHOD I: PROFIT AND LOSS ACCOUNT   L. 175

19..		
Dec. 31 To Provision for Bad		
Debts	111·50	

METHOD II: PROFIT AND LOSS ACCOUNT   L. 175

19..		19..	
Dec. 31 To Bad Debts	132·00	Dec. 31 By Recovered Provision	
		for Bad Debts	20·50

Fig. 163(*b*). The effect on the Profit and Loss Account

EXERCISES SET XXXVII

(12) Bad Debts and Provision for Bad Debts

No. 1.

(*a*) At January 1st, 19.., the balance of the Provision for Bad Debts Account of J. Moore stood at 250·00. During that year bad debts amounting to 96·00 were incurred and at December 31st a balance of 280·00 was carried forward. In the next year 35·00 was received in respect of a debt previously written off and a loss of 122·00 for bad debts was suffered, but Moore decided to reduce his provision to 270·00.

You are to prepare the Provision for Bad Debts Account for years 1 and 2.

(*b*) Assuming that at the end of the second year Moore's debtors amounted to 5,400·00, give the entry in the Balance Sheet of that date in respect of them.

(R.S.A.—Adapted)

No. 2. The balance sheet of J. Wilson, dated January 1st, 19.., gave his total debtors as 6,500·00 and there was a provision of 8 per cent against bad debts. During the following year the bad debts written off amounted to 486·00, but a debt of 126·00 written off in a previous year was paid in full.

At December 31st, a year later, Wilson's debtors were 7,000·00 and he decided to increase his provision to 10 per cent of that amount.

You are to prepare the Bad Debts and Provision Accounts for the year 19.., and to show the relevant entries in the Profit and Loss Account and in the Balance Sheet dated December 31st, 19...

(R.S.A.—Adapted)

No. 3. The following information relates to the wholesale business of Tupman. Show the account or accounts which you would expect to find in his Nominal Ledger to record the information for the year ended December 31st, 19...

(NOTE: Personal accounts are not required.)

January 1st, 19... The provision for bad and doubtful debts amounts to 425·00. The following debts were written off as irrecoverable on December 31st, 19..:

T. Wardle	27·50
W. Jingle	3·24
K. Trotter	18·75

On September 18th, 19.., 4·12 was received in respect of a debt previously written off as irrecoverable. When the Final Accounts were being prepared it was decided to increase the provision for bad and doubtful debts to 480·00.

(*R.S.A.—Adapted*)

No. 4. At December 31st, 19.., a firm's debtors totalled 2,600·00 and its Provision for Bad Debts Account amounted to 120·00. It was decided to write off as irrecoverable debts of 140·00, and to carry forward a provision of 5 per cent of the debtors.

Prepare the Provision Account for bad and doubtful debts, the entries in the Profit and Loss Account, and the entry for debtors on the Balance Sheet at December 31st, 19...

(*R.S.A.—Adapted*)

No. 5. On January 1st, 19.., the Sales Ledger of T. & Co. showed the following debtors:

Smith	250·00
Brown	128·00
Jones	22·00
Robinson	230·00
Williams	140·00

T. & Co. had a Bad Debts Provision equal to 10 per cent of the total debts outstanding. Trading continued during the year 19.. with these and other customers, except that there were no sales to Jones and Robinson; the former made no payment in respect of the amount due from him, while Robinson paid only 200·00 during the year. On December 31st, 19.., (*a*) it was found that the Sales Ledger debit balances, including those due from Jones and Robinson, totalled 952·00; (*b*) it was decided to write off as bad debts the amounts then due from Jones and Robinson; and (*c*) it was decided to adjust the Bad Debts Provision to 8 per cent of the remaining debts.

You are asked to show the entries recording the above in the appropriate *impersonal* Ledger Accounts for the financial year ended December 31st, 19.., including the entries in the firm's Profit and Loss Account for the year.

No. 6. On January 1st, 19.., the Sales Ledger of Barber & Co. showed the following debtors:

White	400·00
Grey	160·00
Brown	32·00
Green	66·00
Pink	24·00

A Bad Debts Provision of 10 per cent of these debts was set up (worked out to the nearest 1·00). Trading continued with these and other debtors during the year, but Brown and Green were not dealt with again, nor did they pay any money. Pink paid 12·00 off his debt and was sold further goods, value 8·00.

On December 31st, 19.. :

    (*a*) The total debtors figure including Brown and Green was 698·00.

    (*b*) It was decided to write off Brown and Green as bad debts.

    (*c*) Pink was written down as a partially bad debt—to half his present value.

    (*d*) A new provision of 8 per cent of the bad debts still outstanding was to be made (calculated to the nearest 1·00).

Show the Impersonal Accounts affected, including the Profit and Loss Account.

                                                (*R.S.A.—Adapted*)

No. 7. Alexander Skeen, a merchant, has the following arrangements in respect of bad debts: the balances in his Sales Ledger of all debtors who fail, during any trading year, to discharge their indebtedness are charged to the Bad Debts Account as soon as Skeen is sure that recovery is unlikely. As a result of experience he also maintains a Provision for Bad Debts Account at 3 per cent of his total of sundry debtors at the date of his Final Accounts. This provision is varied upwards or downwards at the end of each trading year in accordance with changes in the sundry debtors total.

In his Balance Sheet as at January 1st, 19.., the gross total of his sundry debtors was 3,700·00, and the balance of his Provision for Bad Debts Account corresponded with this. During 19.., the following events occurred:

Feb. 10 Skeen received from the trustee in bankruptcy of J. Wilcox, who owed him 54·00 (still standing as a debit in the Sales Ledger), a first and final dividend of 0·50 in the 1·00.

Apr. 8 On January 1st, 19.., H. Watkins owed Skeen 87·00. Skeen is now advised by his own solicitor that Watkins has emigrated and that there is no hope of receiving anything from him.

July 22 During 19.., the account of T. Norie had been written off as a bad debt. Norie's solicitor now sends in a cheque for 78·00, being payment in full of the debt itself, 75·00 plus 3·00 as interest by way of compensation.

Dec. 15 Preparatory to drawing up his Final Accounts for the year, Skeen writes off the following small debts: A. Chivers 6·00, W. Hartley 8·00, and F. Bickersdyke 12·00.

Dec. 19 Skeen receives from his own solicitor an account for 8·40, charges in connexion with debt recovery during the year.

On December 31st, 19.., the total of sundry debtors' balances still open in the Sales Ledger was 2,900·00.

You are required to write up the Bad Debts, Provision for Bad Debts, Interest and Legal Charges Accounts in Skeen's Ledger for the year 19.., and to show how the relevant items would appear in his Profit and Loss Account for the year.

(R.S.A.—Adapted)

No. 8. The books of Francis McCarthy, a wholesale dealer in toys, showed the following balances at the close of business on December 31st, 19..:

	Dr.	Cr.
Capital at January 1st, 19..		7,161·00
Stock at January 1st, 19..	2,795·00	
Purchases	32,329·75	
Sales		43,237·50
Warehouse Wages	1,625·00	
Office Salaries	1,927·00	
Travellers' Salaries and Commission	1,425·00	
Customs Duty on Imported Purchases	317·00	
Carriage Outwards	430·00	
Returns Inwards	218·50	
Returns Outwards		74·75
Rent, Rates, and Insurance	2,170·00	
Fixtures and Fittings	900·00	
Discount Allowed	315·75	
Discount Received		284·75
Sundry Debtors	5,132·00	
Sundry Creditors		2,390·00
Drawings	1,200·00	
General Expenses	496·00	
Balance at Bank	1,321·00	
Cash in Hand	115·00	
Carriage Inwards	468·00	
Provision for Bad Debts		37·00
	53,185·00	53,185·00

You are required to draw up McCarthy's Trading and Profit and Loss Accounts for the year ended December 31st, 19.., and his Balance Sheet as at that date, taking into account the following:

(a) On December 31st, 19.., his unsold stock was valued at 4,385·00.

(b) During the year bad debts, as they occurred, had been debited to the Provision for Bad Debts Account. Additional provision should be made, to bring the balance of this account up to 100·00.

(c) The rent of the offices is 1,400·00 a year, and the quarterly instalment due on December 24th, 19.., has not been paid.

(R.S.A.—Adapted)

No. 9. Here is B. Irving's Trial Balance on March 31st, 19... You are asked to prepare, in good style, the Trading Account, Profit and Loss Account, and Balance Sheet of his business:

	Dr.	Cr.
Cash in Hand	125·00	
Cash at Bank	7,235·00	
Purchases and Sales	5,990·00	12,726·50
Stock at April 1st, 19..	2,362·00	
Debtors and Creditors	1,780·00	4,368·50
Returns—In and Out	27·00	140·00
Carriage In	36·00	
Carriage Out	48·00	
Plant and Machinery	2,300·00	
Power for Plant and Machinery	124·00	
Factory Light and Heat	36·25	
Factory Rent and Rates	180·60	
Office Light and Heat	28·75	
Office Rent and Rates	100·40	
Wages	2,426·00	
Salaries	1,368·00	
Factory Manager's Wages	1,150·00	
Office Manager's Salary	1,250·00	
Commissions Received		1,160·75
Provision for Bad Debts		70·25
Capital		8,101·00
	26,567·00	26,567·00

Closing Stock = 3,820·00. You are to increase the Bad Debts Provision to 120·00.

(R.S.A.—Adapted)

No. 10. Here is M. Milwaukee's Trial Balance at December 31st, 19... Prepare his Trading Account, Profit and Loss Account, and Balance Sheet, taking into account the adjustments below:

	Dr.	Cr.
Stock at Start	1,540·00	
Rent and Rates	216·50	
Purchases and Sales	2,131·00	5,336·00
Packing Materials	154·00	
Debtors and Creditors	595·00	525·27
Plant and Tools (at cost)	1,000·00	
Cash at Bank	458·75	
Capital Account		3,300·83
Interest Received		177·65
Provision for Bad Debts		28·00
Office Salaries	208·50	
Light and Heat	104·00	
Power for Machines	230·00	
Wages and Returns Outwards	2,356·00	76·00
Drawings	450·00	
	9,443·75	9,443·75

(*a*) Closing stock was valued at 2,000·00.

(*b*) Of the debtors 95·00 are reckoned to be definitely bad. After writing these off a provision of 5 per cent of outstanding debts is to be set aside out of profits.

(*c*) Office salaries due are 32·00.

(13) Adjustments No. 7—Provisions for Discounts

Another source of possible misconception about debtors arises from the discounts that may be taken by our debtors if they pay promptly. If we are allowing debtors to deduct discount, the valuation placed on debtors will be misleading if we do not provide for this discount.

The provision for discount is very similar indeed to the provision for bad debts, but when calculating the amount to be provided we use the **Net Debtors** figure, that is **Debtors less Provision for Bad Debts**. Since we have provided for the bad debts these debtors will not qualify for discount, since they are not going to pay promptly.

Example. R. Brown's debtors total 4,260·00 on December 31st, 19... He provided for 5 per cent of possible bad debts and a further 2½ per cent of discount to be allowed to debtors.

Calculation: 5 per cent of Bad Debts = 213·00.

This figure gives a net figure of 4,047·00:

$$2\tfrac{1}{2} \text{ per cent of } 4,047{\cdot}00 = 101{\cdot}18$$

The Journal Entry will be:

19..
Dec. 31
	Profit and Loss Account Dr.
	    To Provision for Discount
	        Account
	Being 2½% of Net Debtors provided
	    to cover discounts
		L. 17
		L. 25
			101·18	

				101·18

Fig. 164. Providing for Discount

and the Balance Sheet entry for debtors now reads:

BALANCE SHEET (ASSETS SIDE ONLY)

(as at December 31st, 19..)

CURRENT ASSETS		
Debtors		4,260·00
Less Bad Debts Provision	213·00	
and Discount Provision	101·18	
		314·18
		3,945·82

Fig. 165. Providing a True Debtors Figure

Similar but opposite entries could be devised so that the businessman reduces the creditors figure. If he intends to pay promptly it seems only sensible that he should offset the losses he is taking into account on his debtors with a little profit on his creditors' accounts. Unfortunately this offends against that book-keeping principle *never anticipate a profit, always anticipate a loss*. The cautious businessman will therefore not accept this profit because it is unrealized, and this is why provisions for profit on discount receivable are rarely seen.

(14) Adjustments No. 8—Depreciation of Assets

The entries for depreciation have already been dealt with fully in Chapter Fourteen. These entries are often required as adjustments, since the normal time for depreciating assets is at the end of the year when the Final Accounts are being prepared. The student should note that if asked, in a note at the foot of a Trial Balance, to adjust for depreciation on an asset, he should deduct the depreciation entry from the profits in the Profit and Loss Account and from the stated value of the asset in the Trial Balance. If depreciation is merely included in the Trial Balance, and not in the footnotes, he should write the depreciation off in the Profit and Loss Account, but there is no need to reduce the book value of the asset; it will already have been reduced.

(15) Goodwill, and Depreciation of Goodwill

Goodwill is a valuation placed upon a going concern over and above the value of the assets forming it. It is paid by the buyer to the seller in expectation of profits to be made, which result directly from the hard work of the former owner. It is sensible that the buyer should pay for the assets, premises, stock, etc., which he takes over. Why should he pay an extra sum for goodwill?

Imagine that Mr. Jones buys Smith's business and opens shop on January 1st. The doorbell rings as Roberts, a regular customer of Smith's, enters the shop. 'Twenty cigarettes please, Joe—Hullo—where *is* Joe?' Mr. Jones will explain that Joe has retired from business but that he will be very happy to serve him in future. The profit on that packet of cigarettes came from Smith's hard work and the goodwill borne him by the people in the area.

Goodwill—an Intangible Asset

Goodwill is often called an intangible asset. You cannot actually touch this asset, but it really does exist. The people who have had business relations with Smith will continue to deal with Jones because they are used to the idea that this shop is efficiently run. It is for this intangible benefit that Jones pays a lump sum of money as compensation to the previous owner. The value of goodwill is a matter for negotiation between the parties when a business changes hands. The seller will demand a good price for the goodwill, the buyer will offer less, and by a process of haggling the bargain will finally be struck.

Depreciation of Goodwill

Since goodwill is not a real asset in the normal meaning of the word 'real', it is frequently written off over the first few years of the business's new lease of life. There is no *necessity* to write off goodwill if the business is making steady profits, since steady profits are a sign of public goodwill. The goodwill must therefore still be as valuable as, or more valuable perhaps than, the original purchase value.

If goodwill is to be written down, then it cannot be written off the Profit and Loss Account, because it is not a revenue loss. It is a decision by the proprietor to reduce the stated value of his assets. This must be met out of his own pocket by a capital loss, in other words the amount written off is taxable for Income Tax purposes. It is what we call an appropriation of profit, not a charge against the profits and will therefore be debited either to the Capital Account or to the Appropriation Account (see page 279), and not to the Profit and Loss Account.

The Journal Entry will be as in Fig. 166.

19.. Dec. 31	Capital Account Dr. To Goodwill Account Being Goodwill reduced at this date	400·00	400·00

Fig. 166. Writing down the value of goodwill

The Paradox of Goodwill

Accountants sometimes speak of the paradox of goodwill. A paradox is an apparent contradiction. We have on our books, when we take over a business, an asset at a high valuation called goodwill. In fact the public bears us no goodwill at all, for they do not even know that we exist. As the years go by, if we adopt the policy of writing off the intangible asset by a series of appropriations of profit, our goodwill gradually reduces until it is written off completely. At the same time, the public have now learned to know us; they realize our goods or services are reliable and they now bear us some goodwill. Here is the paradox of goodwill: it is valued at a high figure on the books when it is worthless, and at nothing on the books when it is very valuable.

EXERCISES SET XXXVIII

(16) Final Accounts with all Types of Adjustment

No. 1. From the following abridged Trial Balance of M. Montgomery dated December 31st, 19.., prepare his Profit and Loss Account for the year, and his Balance Sheet at that date. You should note that:

(*a*) Rates 20·00 were prepaid, and 50·00 was owing by Montgomery's tenant.

(*b*) The machinery balance is to be depreciated by 10 per cent and the additions by 5 per cent.

(*c*) 100·00 is to be written off the goodwill. (Debit to Capital Account.)

TRIAL BALANCE

(at December 31st, 19. .)

	Dr.	Cr.
Rates	200·00	
Salaries	284·00	
Heating, Lighting, etc.	176·00	
Insurance	49·00	
Advertising	260 00	
General Expenses	137·00	
Drawings	1,010·00	
Cash in Hand	16·00	
Trade Debtors	1,104·00	
Stock at December 31st, 19. .	2,618·00	
Machinery	2,000·00	
Machinery Additions	500·00	
Land and Buildings	3,000·00	
Goodwill	500·00	
Gross Profit		2,026·00
Discount		135·00
Rent		150·00
Bank Loan		150·00
Trade Creditors		393·00
Capital Account (January 1st, 19. .)		9,000·00
	11,854·00	11,854·00

(*R.S.A.—Adapted*)

No. 2. After his Trading Account has been prepared for the year ended December 31st, 19. ., a manufacturer's position is as follows:

	Dr.	Cr.
Trading Account, Gross Profit		5,250·75
Plant and Machinery	3,290·00	
Stock at December 31st, 19. .	410·50	
Debtors	1,625·75	
Creditors		1,180·25
Capital at January 1st, 19. .		3,965·50
Discount Allowed	223·25	
Discount Received		183·50
Salaries and Office Expenses	1,160·00	
Rent, Rates, and Insurance	865·50	
Carriage Outwards	120·00	
Bad Debts	85·00	
Goodwill	1,035·00	
Drawings	850·00	
Cash at Bank	895·00	
Petty Cash	20·00	
	10,580·00	10,580·00

Draw up the manufacturer's Profit and Loss Account for the year, and a Balance Sheet as at December 31st, 19. ., taking into consideration:

(*a*) Depreciation on Plant and Machinery which is to be provided for at 10 per cent of its original cost, 4,000·00.

(*b*) Rent, 400·00 a year, of which the quarterly instalment due December 25th, 19. ., is unpaid.

(*c*) 335·00 to be appropriated for the reduction of goodwill. (Debit to Capital Account.)

No. 3. The following Trial Balance was extracted from the books of Donald Haig. You are required to draw up the Trading Account and Profit and Loss Account of the business for the year ending September 30th, 19. ., and a Balance Sheet as at that date.

TRIAL BALANCE

(at September 30th, 19. .)

	Dr.	Cr.
Stock at start on October 1st	4,200·00	
Purchases and Sales	12,386·50	16,286·00
Returns	186·00	682·50
Wages	1,536·75	
Carriage on Purchases	580·25	
Salaries	570·00	
Advertising	706·50	
Carriage on Sales	320·00	
Rates and Taxes	528·50	
Heating and Lighting	619·00	
Bad Debts	599·00	
Insurance	78·00	
Debtors and Creditors	3,500·00	4,750·50
Capital		11,050·00
Drawings	1,600·00	
Cash in Hand	28·50	
Cash at Bank	130·00	
Goodwill	1,200·00	
Land and Buildings	4,000·00	
	32,769·00	32,769·00

You should take the following into account:

(*a*) The stock in hand on September 30th, 19. ., was valued at 5,221·00.

(*b*) The lands and buildings are to be depreciated by 5 per cent.

(*c*) Salaries 50·00 are owing.

(*d*) Rates have been pre-paid to the extent of 40·00.

(*e*) Goodwill is to be reduced by 600·00. (Debit to Capital Account.)

(*R.S.A.—Adapted*)

No. 4. M. Martindale carries on business as a retailer. On December 31st, 19.., the following Trial Balance was extracted from his books:

TRIAL BALANCE
(at December 31st, 19..)

	Dr.	Cr.
Goodwill	343·00	
Premises	7,600·00	
Debtors and Creditors	1,600·00	2,755·00
Wages	1,296·00	
Rent		170·00
General Expenses	1,308·00	
Bad Debts	206·00	
Discount	175·00	
Commission	278·00	
Purchases and Sales	17,439·00	27,453·00
Capital at January 1st, 19..		9,500·00
Drawings	2,675·00	
Cash	126·00	
Bank	5,210·00	
Stock at January 1st, 19..	2,400·00	
Carriage Outwards	472·50	
Salaries	325·50	
Loan Interest	80·00	
Loan (Midland Bank Ltd.)		2,000·00
Advertising	97·00	
Returns Inwards and Outwards	365·00	276·00
Carriage Inwards	158·00	
	42,154·00	42,154·00

(*a*) On December 31st, 19.., the value of stock in hand was estimated at 2,300·00.

(*b*) Two-thirds of the wages is to be charged to the Trading Account and one-third to the Profit and Loss Account.

(*c*) The goodwill is to be written off in full. (Debit to Capital Account.)

(*d*) A provision for bad debts of 5 per cent of the debtors figure is to be made.

(*e*) A provision for discount of 2½ per cent of the net debtors is to be made.

You are to prepare the Trading Account and Profit and Loss Account for the year ending December 31st, 19.., and the Balance Sheet as at that date.

CHAPTER TWENTY-THREE

PARTNERSHIP ACCOUNTS

(1) Introduction—Why take a Partner?

There are several reasons why sole traders combine together to form partnerships. The chief advantages are:

(*a*) Increased capital, permitting the business to expand more rapidly than is possible by the 'ploughing back' of profits earned.

(*b*) The responsibility of control no longer rests with one person. This makes possible holidays and free week-ends, and reduces the worry the sole trader experiences at times of ill-health.

(*c*) Wider experience is brought to the firm and some degree of specialization is possible; this is particularly true of professional partnerships. A physician and a surgeon may form a partnership; or lawyers with experience in different fields—divorce, criminal law, commercial law—may combine to offer a more comprehensive service to the public.

(*d*) Very often a young man teams up with an older man. The young man has his health and strength; his partner has the capital and the experience. Together they make a satisfactory team.

(2) The Partnership Act of 1890

Even when the partners agree now, the possibility always exists that they will disagree later. This has led to a very complicated and ancient case law on partnership matters which was finally codified by the Partnership Act of 1890. This Act is very short, containing only fifty sections, but it is a very good example of an Act of Parliament. Any British student who is not familiar with the layout of an Act of Parliament is strongly advised to buy a copy of this one from his local bookseller and study it. Naturally it covers the entire range of possible dispute between partners, but the main book-keeping features are contained in section 24 and are briefly as follows:

(*a*) All the partners are entitled to contribute equally to the capital. They must share equally the profits of the business, and must contribute equally to the losses.

(*b*) No partner is entitled to a salary for his part in the activities of the firm.

(*c*) No partner is entitled to interest on his capital.

(*d*) Where a partner loans money to the firm over and above his capital he shall be entitled to interest at 5 per cent per annum.

(*e*) Any partner may see and copy the books of the partnership which must be kept at the ordinary place of business.

(*f*) No new partner may be introduced without the general consent of all the partners.

These rules, and others, apply in any dispute where there is no clear evidence of what agreement the partners originally made. This evidence does not have to be written evidence; it can be implied from a course of conduct over the years. For instance, if two partners had for many years divided their profits two-thirds and one-third, this would imply that they had originally agreed to share the profits in this way. This fact would go against a partner who now claimed that profits should be shared equally.

(3) The Partnership Deed

To avoid the ruling of the Partnership Act, partners must agree among themselves and should preferably draw up an agreement in writing. The Partnership Deed should cover most of the following points:

(*a*) The amount of capital to be provided by each partner.

(*b*) The ratio of sharing profits and losses.

(*c*) The date at which the partnership shall begin, and the duration of the partnership.

(*d*) The amount of any salaries payable to partners.

(*e*) How much each partner shall be allowed to draw in anticipation of profits.

(*f*) Whether interest shall be allowed on capital and if so, whether it shall also be charged on drawings.

(*g*) What arrangements shall be made in the event of the death of a partner.

(*h*) How disputes shall be settled, i.e. by arbitration or some other method.

(*i*) What arrangements shall be made in the event of the admission of a new partner.

(4) The Capital of the Partnership

Since the capital of a partnership business forms an important part of the original agreement, it is desirable to preserve the original capital on the books as evidence of the capital position at the start. This means that the original capital shall not be varied, as sole trader capital varies, by the addition of profits to the Capital Account or the subtraction of losses from the Capital Account. Instead, each partner has a new account opened called a Current Account, to which profits can be credited and from which losses and drawings can be subtracted. It follows that each partner now has three accounts opened in his name:

(*a*) A Capital Account, which records the original capital.

(*b*) A Current Account, which records changes in the original capital as a result of the activities of the firm.

(*c*) A Drawings Account, which records the amounts drawn out.

Since the Capital Accounts are fixed, they will appear on the Balance Sheet every year, and will be added together to show the total initial capital. The Balance Sheet on the liabilities side, in the order of permanence, therefore begins:

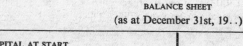

BALANCE SHEET
(as at December 31st, 19. .)

CAPITAL AT START		
H. Brown	4,000·00	
R. Brown	2,000·00	
	6,000·00	

Fig. 167. The original Capital of a Partnership

(5) The Final Accounts of a Partnership Business

The Trading Account and Profit and Loss Account of a partnership business are exactly the same as those of a sole trader's business. Perhaps the only point worth noting here is that, where a partner loans the business sums of money over and above his capital, the interest on this loan will be charged to the Profit and Loss Account exactly like any other type of interest, but instead of actually being paid out it will be credited to the partner's Current Account, which is discussed on page 284.

The main changes in Partnership Accounts begin when the partners start to appropriate the profits. We now have a much more complex appropriation which requires an Appropriation Account.

(6) The Appropriation Account of a Partnership

The Appropriation Account will be opened as in Fig. 168 by the transfer of the Net Profit to the credit side of the Appropriation Account. The following entries, in the order shown, may be required on the debit side, to authorize various appropriations to the partners' Current Accounts, or to implement agreed policies of the partners.

(*a*) *Goodwill.* If the partners have agreed to write down the value of goodwill, then the Appropriation Account will be debited and goodwill credited.

(*b*) *Partnership Salaries.* If either partner is authorized by the Partnership Deed to draw a salary for his efforts in the business, this will have a first claim on the profits after goodwill. This requires a debit to the Appropriation Account, the amount being credited to the partner's Current Account.

(*c*) *Interest on Capital.* Partners who have agreed to allow interest on capital are really withdrawing their profits in a slightly different way from the agreed ratio for sharing profits. The idea is to give some bias to favour the partner who has contributed the greater share of capital. Where partners have contributed equal capital sums, and share profits equally, there will be no point in deciding to give each other interest on capital at some agreed percentage. Where the capital contributed is unequal, the partners may well feel that interest on capital is desirable. The partner who has invested 5,000·00 will receive, at 6 per cent, interest amounting to 300·00. The partner who has invested only 1,000·00 will receive interest amounting to 60·00. The unequal payments represent fair rewards for the unequal services rendered.

(*d*) *Sharing the Residue of the Profit.* Whatever the Net Profit, considerable inroads into it may have been made by these earlier appropriations, leaving a residue to be shared in the agreed proportions. If there is no agreement, then the Partnership Act of 1890 states that these profits must be shared equally.

A typical Appropriation Account might look as follows:

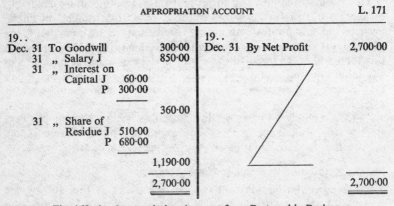

APPROPRIATION ACCOUNT   L. 171

19..				19..		
Dec. 31	To Goodwill		300·00	Dec. 31	By Net Profit	2,700·00
31	„ Salary J		850·00			
31	„ Interest on					
	Capital J	60·00				
	P	300·00				
			360·00			
31	„ Share of					
	Residue J	510·00				
	P	680·00				
			1,190·00			
			2,700·00			2,700·00

Fig. 168. An Appropriation Account for a Partnership Business

Interest on Drawings

The reward earned by partners is a share of the profits of the firm. Since profits are not calculated until the end of the year the partners may withdraw moneys in expectation of profits, in the same way as sole traders do. An element of unfairness creeps in here if these drawings are unequal. One partner may withdraw large sums early in the year, or throughout the year. The other may withdraw smaller sums, or not

draw anything until later in the year. To equalize the position between
the two partners some firms charge interest on drawings. This interest
is usually calculated in a second money column on the Drawings Account, and then sub-totalled into the main column on the Account as
shown below:

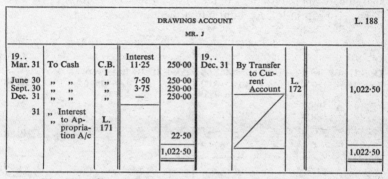

Fig. 169. A Drawings Account with interest charged at 6 per cent

The interest which is being entered in the main column for the year is
the total interest the business is entitled to recoup from Mr. J. As this
interest is recouped it must be credited to the Appropriation Account,
to enable the partners to share it out in the same ratio as that in which
they agreed to share profits.

An Appropriation Account might therefore look like this:

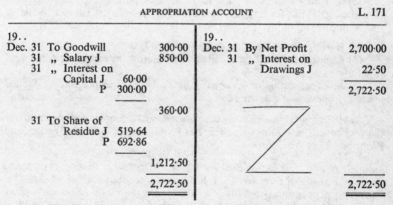

Fig. 170. An Appropriation Account with Interest on Drawings

What Happens When there is only a Loss to Appropriate?

When a business is running at a loss, the loss will have to be appropriated to the partners. It makes no difference to the Appropriation

Account. We still write off goodwill if this is agreed, and there is a very strong case for doing so. If we are making a loss, then we have lost public goodwill and should not have goodwill as an asset on the books. We still give the partners their salaries and interest on capital. Each of these appropriations increases the loss to be suffered, which is then shared between the partners in the way that they share profits or losses.

The Appropriation Account might therefore look like this:

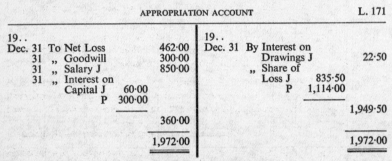

APPROPRIATION ACCOUNT   L. 171

19..				19..			
Dec. 31	To Net Loss		462·00	Dec. 31	By Interest on		
31	„ Goodwill		300·00		Drawings J		22·50
31	„ Salary J		850·00		„ Share of		
31	„ Interest on				Loss J	835·50	
	Capital J	60·00			P	1,114·00	
	P	300·00					1,949·50
			360·00				
			1,972·00				1,972·00

Fig. 171. Appropriating a Loss

EXERCISES SET XXXIX

(7) The Appropriation Account

No. 1. Hayes and Harlington are in partnership. On June 30th, 19.., their Capital Accounts (unchanged since July 1st in the previous year) are: Hayes 15,000·00, Harlington 10,000·00. Their deed of partnership provides that, after the Net Profit for any year has been ascertained, the balance available will be applied as follows:

(*a*) Harlington will receive a salary of 1,200·00.

(*b*) Each partner will be credited with interest on capital at 6 per cent per annum.

(*c*) After providing for (*a*) and (*b*), the remaining balance is to be divided equally between the partners.

You are required to draw up the partnership Appropriation Account for the year ended June 30th, 19... The Net Profit, as shown by the Trading and Profit and Loss Account, was 6,250·00.

No. 2. Arthur and Brian Buckley are in partnership, sharing profits and losses in the ratio of three to two. It has been agreed that interest on capital at 5 per cent per annum should be allowed. Some years ago Brian had loaned the business 400·00, but agreed that as from July 1st, 19.., this should be converted to capital, though it was still to carry interest at 4 per cent per annum. The interest on this sum for the whole year is to be charged to Appropriation Account. At the same date Arthur introduced 600·00 new capital. Before sharing loan and capital interest and allowing Brian a salary of 150·00, the divisible profit for the year was 931·00. From the following details prepare

the Appropriation Section of their Profit and Loss Account for the year
ending December 31st, 19.. :

	Arthur	Brian
Capital Account balances (At start)	3,000·00	2,000·00

(*R.S.A.—Adapted*)

No. 3. Sybrandt and Cornelis are in partnership. They have a written
agreement which says:

(*a*) Partnership capitals shall carry interest at 10 per cent per annum.
(*b*) Cornelis shall have a salary of 750·00 per annum.
(*c*) Goodwill shall be reduced each year by 20 per cent.
(*d*) Profits over and above those required for the first three clauses shall
be shared, two-thirds to Sybrandt and one-third to Cornelis.

Capitals are: Sybrandt 5,000·00, Cornelis 1,000·00. Goodwill is valued at
2,000·00. Show the Appropriation Account (i.e. the Appropriation Section of
the Profit and Loss Account) if the profits at December 31st, 19.., were
4,000·00.

(*East Anglian Examination Board—Adapted*)

No. 4. Nelson, Blake, and Hardy are partners in carrying on a business
under an agreement which provides that, after allowing interest on capital
(but not on Current Accounts) at 5 per cent per annum, and partnership
salaries of 700·00 to Nelson and 500·00 to Blake, the remaining profit is to be
shared one-fourth to Nelson and three-eighths each to Blake and Hardy.

The Net Profit for the year ended March 31st, 19.., was 6,400·00 before
providing partnership salaries or interest on capital. The balances on the
partners' capital accounts on April 1st, 19.., were: Nelson 4,000·00, Blake
3,000·00, and Hardy 1,000·00, and there was no further contribution of
capital during the year.

(*a*) You are required to prepare the Appropriation section of the firm's
Profit and Loss Account for the year ended March 31st, 19...

(*b*) Why do partnership agreements sometimes direct, as in this case, that
interest on capital shall be provided before ascertaining divisible profits?

(*R.S.A.—Adapted*)

No. 5. At January 1st, 19.., G. Wilson owned a business in which he had
10,000·00 capital. As from July 1st, 19.., W. Gibbs came in as a partner on
the following terms:

(*a*) Wilson's capital was to remain unchanged and Gibbs was to bring in
1,800·00.
(*b*) Interest at 5 per cent per annum was to be allowed on both capitals
from the start of the partnership.
(*c*) Gibbs was to be credited with a salary of 1400·00 per annum.
(*d*) Profits, after charging interest and salary, were to be divided: Wilson
two-thirds, and Gibbs one-third.

At December 31st, 19.., the Net Profit available for division before charging the partnership interest and salary was 1,475·00. You are required to
prepare the partnership's Appropriation Account.

(*R.S.A.—Adapted*)

(8) The Current Accounts of the Partners

On page 278 we saw that the Capital Accounts in a partnership business are not varied every year by the addition of profits or the deduction of losses. Instead, these fluctuations in capital are recorded in a Current Account for each partner. A Current Account, as its name implies, is one that varies from day to day, although in fact entries are few in the partners' Current Accounts.

At the beginning of the year a Current Account will either be clear, or have a balance on it. This balance may be a debit balance or a credit balance, according to the policy pursued the previous year by the partner. If the partner has been prudent, withdrawing only such sums as he feels sure will be covered by the profits, then at the year's end the profits appropriated to him will exceed his drawings, and leave him with a credit balance. If the partner has been rash, withdrawing more heavily than the business justifies in expectation of profits, the sums appropriated to him will leave him with a deficit on his Current Account, that is, a debit balance. Here are two such Current Accounts:

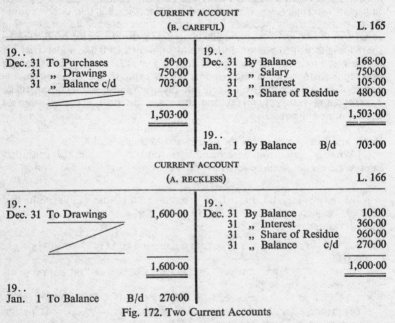

CURRENT ACCOUNT

(B. CAREFUL)   L. 165

19..			19..			
Dec. 31	To Purchases	50·00	Dec. 31	By Balance		168·00
31	,, Drawings	750·00	31	,, Salary		750·00
31	,, Balance c/d	703·00	31	,, Interest		105·00
			31	,, Share of Residue		480·00
		1,503·00				1,503·00
			19..			
			Jan. 1	By Balance	B/d	703·00

CURRENT ACCOUNT

(A. RECKLESS)   L. 166

19..			19..			
Dec. 31	To Drawings	1,600·00	Dec. 31	By Balance		10·00
			31	,, Interest		360·00
			31	,, Share of Residue		960·00
			31	,, Balance	c/d	270·00
		1,600·00				1,600·00
19..						
Jan. 1	To Balance	B/d 270·00				

Fig. 172. Two Current Accounts

On these two accounts the student can follow the normal entries in a Current Account. They include the following:

(*a*) An opening balance, which may be either a debit or credit balance.
(*b*) Various appropriations of profit on the credit side. These include

salaries, interest on capital, and shares of the residue of the profit. One that is not shown in either of these Current Accounts is interest on a loan. This would be credited in the Current Account after being debited in the Profit and Loss Account as explained on page 279.

(c) Various drawings, *in cash* or *in kind*, on the debit side. These have not been dealt with before, so a word of explanation is required.

We know that **drawings in cash** are taken, either in cash from the till, or by cheque from the bank. They therefore appear on the credit side of the Cash Book, either in the Cash Account or the Bank Account, and are posted into the proprietors' Drawings Accounts. These accounts are closed off into the partners' Current Accounts at the end of the financial year. The Closing Entry will be as follows:

19.. Dec. 31	Current Account B. Careful To Drawings Account B. Careful Being drawings for year transferred	L. 165 L. 150	750·00	 750·00

Fig. 173. Closing off the Drawings Account

When posted to the Drawings Account this will clear the account and the debit entry in the Current Account as shown in Fig. 172 will set off the money already drawn out against the profits appropriated to the partner.

Drawings in kind means drawings in goods, or perhaps even drawings of assets out of the business. Businessmen often take home stock or surplus assets for their own use, and without payment. The goods are simply charged to the debit side of Current Account and set off against the profits earned. If we debit the Current Account in this way we must credit some other account. If the item taken home is an asset we shall treat it in the same way as the disposal of any other worn-out asset, removing it at its book value from the books, and adjusting depreciation if necessary.

If the item taken home is goods for resale, a difficulty arises. We cannot call them sales, for the partners naturally take the goods at cost price, and if cost price sales are mixed up with ordinary sales it spoils the Gross Profit percentage figure. We shall see later that this is a very valuable control figure which we do not wish to distort. The best thing to do, since we cannot credit the Sales Account, is to credit the Purchases Account. This means that the goods purchased and now taken by the proprietor or partners are removed from the Purchases Account; **they did not buy them for the business but for themselves, and they pay for them by setting off these purchases against their profits in the Current Account.** This explains the first line of Careful's Current Account in Fig. 172.

(*d*) A closing balance on the Current Account, which may be either a debit or credit balance.

The nature of the Current Account balance is something which needs a little further explanation. The Current Account is that part of the partner's capital which has accumulated since the business began and which is permitted to fluctuate.

What does Careful's Current Account balance of 703·00 represent? It is a credit balance, a liability of the business, and represents accumulated capital which the business owes to Careful.

What does Reckless's Current Account balance of 270·00 represent? It is a debit balance, an asset of the business, and represents an overdraft of profits by Reckless which he owes to the business. For the present we will show it as a Current Asset of the business.

EXERCISES SET XL

(9) Current Accounts of Partners

No. 1. Messrs. Wilson and Brown are in partnership, sharing profits and losses: Wilson three-fifths, Brown two-fifths. Their fixed capitals are: Wilson 8,000·00, Brown 5,000·00. The partnership agreement provides that interest of 5 per cent per annum shall be paid on fixed capital and that Brown is to receive a salary of 400·00 per annum and 2 per cent commission on the balance of trading profit *after* charging his salary, but *before* charging interest on capital.

The balances on the Current Accounts at January 1st, 19.., are: Wilson credit 420·00, Brown credit 350·00.

Drawings during the year: Wilson 2,000·00, Brown 1,800·00.

The trading profit for the year ended December 31st, 19.., was 5,400·00.

Prepare the Current Account of each partner for the year ended December 31st, 19...

(R.S.A.—Adapted)

No. 2. Hebron and Haifa are in partnership with capitals of 5,000·00 and 1,000·00 respectively. The partnership deed provides that:

(*a*) Haifa is entitled to a salary of 600·00 per annum.

(*b*) Each gets 6 per cent interest on capital per annum.

(*c*) The remaining profits are shared three-quarters to Hebron, one-quarter to Haifa.

Each partner has a Current Account to which all items of personal income arising from the firm are posted, and against which any drawings, either of cash or goods, are charged.

Show Haifa's Current Account for the year 19... On January 1st, 19.., he had a credit balance of 182·00. During the year he drew 1,040·00 in cash and took home goods valued at 84·00. Profits for the year were 4,000·00.

(East Anglian Examination Board—Adapted)

No. 3. The partnership agreement between L. Hemp, T. Wool, and M. Cotton contains the following provisions:

(*a*) The partners' fixed capitals shall be: Hemp 12,000·00, Wool 10,000·00, and Cotton 8,000·00.

(*b*) Wool and Cotton are to receive salaries of 800·00 and 600·00 respectively.

(*c*) Interest on capital is to be calculated at 6 per cent per annum.

(*d*) Hemp, Wool, and Cotton are to share profits and losses in the ratios 3 : 2 : 1.

(*e*) No interest is to be charged on drawings or Current Accounts.

On January 1st, 19.., the balances on Current Accounts were: Hemp Cr. 700·00, Wool Cr. 400·00, and Cotton Dr. 100·00.

During the year the drawings were: Hemp 2,500·00, Wool 1,800·00, and Cotton 1,200·00.

The Profit and Loss Account for the year showed a profit of 8,900·00 before charging interest on capital or on partners' salaries.

Show the Capital and Current Accounts of Hemp, Wool, and Cotton, as at December 31st, 19.., after division of the profit.

(*R.S.A.—Adapted*)

No. 4. At January 1st, 19.., G. Watson owned a business in which he had 10,000·00 capital. As from July 1st, 19.., S. Holmes came in as a partner on the following terms:

(*a*) Watson's capital was to remain unchanged and Holmes was to bring in 2,300·00 of which 500·00 was to be credited to his current account.

(*b*) Interest at 5 per cent *per annum* was to be allowed on both capitals from the beginning of the partnership.

(*c*) Holmes was to be credited with a salary of 700·00 per annum.

(*d*) Profits, after charging interest and salary, were to be divided between Watson, two-thirds, and Holmes, one-third.

Holmes withdrew 450·00 on August 1st, 325·00 on September 30th, and 325·00 on November 30th. At December 31st, 19.., the Net Profit available for division before charging the partnership interest and salary was 1,485·00.

You are required to prepare the Current Account of S. Holmes.

No. 5. David and Peter Fitch are in partnership, sharing profits and losses in the ratio of three to two. It has been agreed that interest on capital at 5 per cent per annum should be allowed. Some years earlier Peter loaned the business 500·00 but agreed that as from July 1st, 19.., this should be converted to capital, though it was still to carry interest at 4 per cent per annum. The interest on this sum for the whole year is to be charged to Appropriation Account. At the same date David introduced 700·00 new capital. The divisible profit for the year, before charging loan and capital interest, and before allowing Peter a salary of 500·00, was 1,281·00. From the following details prepare the Appropriation Section of their Profit and Loss Account and the Current Accounts of the brothers for the year ending December 31st, 19..:

[See over]

	David	Peter
Capital Account balances (January 1st, 19..)	3,000·00	2,000·00
Current Account balances (January 1st, 19..)	236·00 (Cr.)	48·00 (Dr.)
Drawings (June 30th, 19..)	350·00	215·00
Drawings (November 30th, 19..)	270·00	208·00

(R.S.A.—Adapted)

(10) The Balance Sheet of a Partnership

It has already been said that Partnership Accounts differ from Sole Trader Accounts in that the Capital Accounts do not vary, Current Accounts being used instead to record fluctuations in the partners' holdings in the firm.

It follows that the Capital Accounts, as shown in Fig. 167, are merely added together as a sub-total on the Balance Sheet. The Current Accounts will perhaps both have credit balances, in which case they can be shown added together as a second sub-total. If one is a debit balance, or if both are, the debit balances will appear on the assets side of the Balance Sheet. The partner is overdrawn on Current Account, and appears as a debtor of the business.

Here is a typical Partnership Balance Sheet, arranged in the order of permanence:

G. GOLD AND S. SILVER

BALANCE SHEET

(as at December 31st, 19..)

CAPITALS			FIXED ASSETS		
Gold	20,000·00		Land and Buildings	27,000·00	
Silver	8,000·00		Plant and		
		28,000·00	Machinery	13,000·00	
			Furniture and		
CURRENT ACCOUNTS			Fittings	3,000·00	
Gold	1,000·00				
Silver	800·00				43,000·00
		1,800·00	CURRENT ASSETS		
			Stock	2,856·00	
LONG-TERM LIABILITY			Debtors	5,000·00	
Mortgage		20,000·00	*Less* Prov.	500·00	
CURRENT LIABILITIES					
Creditors	1,750·00			4,500·00	
Wages Due	450·00		Cash at Bank	1,544·00	
		2,200·00	„ in Hand	100·00	
					9,000·00
		52,000·00			52,000·00

Fig. 174. A Partnership Balance Sheet

EXERCISES SET XLI

(11) The Final Accounts of Partnerships

NOTE: In working Final Accounts exercises for partnerships, it is always advisable to do the Appropriation Account and the Current Accounts so that the Balance Sheet figures can easily be derived from the available information, even though the question may not ask for them.

No. 1. Arthur and Brian Woods are in partnership sharing profits and losses in the proportions three-fifths and two-fifths respectively. The following is their abridged Trial Balance as at June 30th, 19..:

	Dr.	Cr.
Gross Profit		5,020·00
Carriage Outwards	390·50	
Bank Charges	30·50	
Rates	410·00	
Salaries	1,050·00	
Insurance	280·00	
Heating and Lighting	460·75	
Car Expenses	200·25	
Debtors and Creditors	3,000·00	2,700·75
Provision for Bad Debts		100·00
Bank Overdraft		500·75
Capital Accounts:		
Arthur		6,000·00
Brian		5,000·00
Drawings:		
Arthur	850·00	
Brian	900·00	
Current Accounts:		
Brian	35·75	
Arthur		76·50
Cash in hand	50·25	
Stock	3,740·00	
Machinery	4,000·00	
Premises	4,000·00	
	19,398·00	19,398·00

You are required to prepare the firm's Profit and Loss Account for the year ended June 30th, 19.., and the Balance Sheet as at that date, paying attention to the following:

(*a*) Depreciation is to be written off the machinery at the rate of 10 per cent.

(*b*) The premises have been over-depreciated by 500·00 (treat this as appreciation).

(*c*) Of the car expenses 50·00 is to be charged to each of the partners.

(*d*) The provision for bad debts is to be increased by 50·00.

(*e*) 150·00 is due in respect of salaries.

(*f*) A salary of 550·00 is to be credited to Brian.

(*g*) The partners are to be credited with interest on the above capital balances at the rate of 5 per cent.

(*R.S.A.—Adapted*)

No. 2. The following trial balance was extracted from the books of the partnership of Bath and Wells at December 31st, 19.., after the profit for the year had been ascertained:

	Dr.	Cr.
Capital Accounts (January 1st, 19..):		
Bath		1,900·00
Wells		1,440·00
Current Accounts (January 1st, 19..)		
Bath		520·00
Wells		30·00
Drawings during year:		
Bath	800·00	
Wells	700·00	
Profit and Loss Account		1,860·00
Cash in Hand	15·00	
Balance at Bank	1,660·00	
Goodwill	400·00	
Furniture and Fittings	740·00	
Sundry Debtors and Creditors	310·00	190·00
Rent Accrued		80·00
Stock	1,404·00	
Provision for Bad Debts		34·00
Insurance Prepaid	25·00	
	6,054·00	6,054·00

You are required to draw up the Balance Sheet of the partnership as at December 31st, 19.., having regard to the following notes:

(*a*) The furniture and fittings have been depreciated by 60·00 during the year.

(*b*) Wells is entitled to be credited with a salary of 200·00 before the division of the profit.

(*c*) The balance of the profit or loss is to be divided between Bath and Wells in the proportion of three-quarters and one-quarter respectively.

(*d*) In preparing the Balance Sheet, you are to group the assets and liabilities so that the totals can be clearly seen of (i) the fixed assets, (ii) the current assets, and (iii) the current liabilities.

(*R.S.A.—Adapted*)

No. 3. Peele and Mellis conduct a merchanting business in partnership on the following terms:

(*a*) Interest is to be allowed on partners' Capital Accounts at 6 per cent per annum.

(*b*) Peele is to be credited with a partnership salary of 750·00 per annum.

(*c*) The balance of profit in any year is to be shared equally by the partners.

After preparing their Trading and Profit and Loss Account for the year ended March 31st, 19.., but before making any provision for interest on capital or for Peele's partnership salary, the following balances remained on the books:

	Dr.	Cr.
Capital Accounts:		
Peele (as on April 1st previous year)		1,000·00
Mellis (as on April 1st previous year)		2,000·00
Current Accounts:		
Peele		220·50
Mellis		100·50
Drawings Accounts:		
Peele	890·50	
Mellis	500·50	
Profit and Loss Account—Net Profit for year		4,500·00
Stock at March 31st, 19..	1,400·00	
Goodwill Account	1,000·00	
Plant and Machinery, at cost	3,000·00	
Plant and Machinery, depreciation		600·00
Fixtures and Fittings, at cost	1,800·00	
Fixtures and Fittings, Depreciation		948·00
Trade Debtors and Creditors	3,500·00	850·50
Loan from H. Oldcastle, and accrued interest		2,120·50
Rent accrued due at March 31st, 19..		150·00
Insurance unexpired at March 31st, 19..	94·00	
Cash at Bank, Current Account	305·00	
	12,490·00	12,490·00

It is agreed by the partners to reduce the book value of goodwill by writing off 250·00 at March 31st, 19.. (to be charged to the Appropriation section of the Profit and Loss Account).

You are asked to prepare the Appropriation section of the firm's Profit and Loss Account and the partners' Current Accounts for the year ended March 31st, 19.., together with the Balance Sheet as on that date.

(*R.S.A.—Adapted*)

No. 4. The following Trial Balance was extracted from the books of the partnership of Haig and Grant who share profits and losses: Haig three-fifths and Grant two-fifths.

TRIAL BALANCE
(at September 30th, 19. .)

	Dr.	Cr.
Stock (at start of financial year)	4,202·00	
Purchases and Sales	12,386·00	16,286·00
Returns	186·00	683·00
Wages	1,536·50	
Carriage on Purchases	580·50	
Salaries	570·50	
Advertising	706·50	
Carriage on Sales	320·00	
Rates and Taxes	528·00	
Heating and Lighting	619·00	
Bad Debts	599·00	
Insurance	76·00	
Debtors and Creditors	3,500·00	4,750·00
Capital:		
Haig		7,050·00
Grant		4,000·00
Drawings:		
Haig	900·00	
Grant	700·00	
Cash in Hand	28·00	
Cash at Bank	131·00	
Motor Vans	1,200·00	
Land and Buildings	4,000·00	
	32,769·00	32,769·00

You are required to draw up the Trading and Profit and Loss Account of the partnership for the year ending September 30th, 19. ., and a Balance Sheet as at that date.

You should take the following into account:

(*a*) The stock in hand on September 30th was valued at 5,221·00.
(*b*) The vans are to be depreciated by 10 per cent.
(*c*) Salaries, 50·00, are owing.
(*d*) Rates have been pre-paid to the extent of 40·00.

(*R.S.A.—Adapted*)

No. 5. Messrs. King and Snagsby are in business as retailers and on December 31st, 19.., the balances on their books were as shown below:

	Dr.	Cr.
Capital Accounts:		
King		1,500·00
Snagsby		1,000·00
Current Accounts:		
King (as on December 31st previous year)	150·50	
Snagsby (as on December 31st previous year)		250·50
Drawings Account:		
King	800·00	
Snagsby	800·00	
Carriage Inwards	120·25	
Discounts Received		210·75
Fixtures and Fittings (as on December 31st previous year)	2,100·00	
General Expenses	596·00	
Interest on Loan	60·00	
Lighting and Heating	280·75	
Loan, A. Horden		2,000·00
Motor Vehicles (as on December 31st previous year)	2,950·00	
Motor Expenses	926·75	
Purchases	4,960·25	
Rent, Rates, and Insurance	1,540·00	
Returns Outwards		356·25
Sales		11,100·00
Stock (as on December 31st previous year)	3,060·00	
Trade Creditors		1,590·75
Bank Overdraft		336·25
	18,344·50	18,344·50

NOTES.

(*a*) On December 31st, 19.., stock was valued at 2,784·00.

(*b*) Motor vehicle licences in advance on December 31st, 19.., amounted to 50·00.

(*c*) Fixtures and fittings to be depreciated by 8 per cent and motor vehicles by 450·00.

(*d*) Snagsby is to be credited with a commission of 2 per cent on sales for the year and the balance of profits (or losses) shared equally between the partners.

From the foregoing information you are asked to prepare the firm's Trading and Profit and Loss Account for the year ended December 31st, 19.., and Balance Sheet as on that date.

(*R.S.A.—Adapted*)

No. 6. A. Forsyth and B. Gordon are in partnership as manufacturers and on December 31st, 19.., the balances in their books were as follows:

	Dr.	Cr.
Capital Accounts:		
A. Forsyth		6,500·00
B. Gordon		4,400·00
Current Accounts:		
A. Forsyth (January 1st, 19..)		50·50
B. Gordon (January 1st, 19..)		100·75
Drawings Accounts:		
A. Forsyth	789·00	
B. Gordon	1,050·00	
Bank Overdraft		650·25
Debtors and Creditors	2,805·50	1,915·50
Stock at January 1st, 19..	3,945·00	
Purchases and Sales	20,952·50	34,202·25
Wages	6,022·00	
Carriage Inwards	628·25	
Discounts Allowed and Received	131·75	90·50
Rent Received		120·25
Heating and Lighting	1,655·00	
Rates and Taxes	678·50	
Salaries	1,222·50	
Insurance	149·00	
Bad Debts	233·00	
Carriage on Sales	410·00	
Cash in Hand	58·00	
Fixtures	700·00	
Motor Vehicles	1,000·00	
Machinery	3,500·00	
Land and Buildings	2,000·00	
Returns Inwards	100·00	
	48,030·00	48,030·00

NOTES: On December 31st, 19.., the unsold stock was valued at 4,267·00. The fixtures and motor vehicles are each to be depreciated by 10 per cent. The firm's tenant owes one-quarter's rent, 40·00.

Insurance is owing, 21·00.

A bad debts provision of 200·00 is to be created.

Gordon is to be credited with a salary of 300·00 and the balance of profits (or losses) is to be divided equally.

From the above information you are asked to prepare the firm's Trading and Profit and Loss Account for the year ended December 31st, 19.., and its Balance Sheet as on that date.

(*R.S.A.—Adapted*)

No. 7. The following Trial Balance was extracted from the books of Messrs. Tree and Branch, wholesalers, who share profits and losses three-quarters and one-quarter respectively. Prepare the Trading Account and Profit and Loss Account for the year ending December 31st, 19.., and the Balance Sheet as at that date.

TRIAL BALANCE
(as at December 31st, 19..)

	Dr.	Cr.
Capital Accounts, January 1st, 19..:		
Tree		10,000·00
Branch		4,000·00
Drawings:		
Tree	1,750·00	
Branch	1,250·00	
Current Accounts, January 1st, 19..:		
Tree		500·00
Branch		300·00
Trade Debtors and Creditors	4,520·00	5,420·25
Warehouse Wages	3,200·00	
Office Salaries	1,500·00	
Stock at January 1st, 19..	6,334·00	
Purchases and Sales	10,472·00	22,232·75
Returns In and Out	361·00	547·25
Bank Balance	2,641·00	
Cash in Hand	142·25	
Lighting and Heating:		
Warehouse (¾) Office (¼)	470·00	
Rates:		
Warehouse (¾) Office (¼)	248·00	
Freehold Premises	6,500·00	
Fixtures and Fittings	1,440·00	
Vehicles	1,600·00	
Stationery	156·75	
Sundry Expenses	64·00	
Postage and Telephone	136·00	
Insurance	60·50	
Discounts	248·00	426·75
Provision for Bad Debts		125·00
Bad Debts incurred during 19..	72·00	
Vehicle Expenses	386·50	
	43,552·00	43,552·00

In preparing the accounts provide for the following items which have not yet been passed through the books:

(*a*) Stock at December 31st, 19.., was valued at 4,400·00.

(*b*) Fixtures and fittings are to be depreciated by 5 per cent and vehicles by 10 per cent.

(*c*) Rates prepaid amount to 64·00.

(*d*) Insurance unexpired amounts to 10·00.

(*e*) Provision for bad debts at December 31st, 19. ., to be $2\frac{1}{2}$ per cent of trade debtors total.

(*f*) Five per cent interest on the partners' capital and a salary of 1,000·00 for Branch are to be charged to the Appropriation section of the Profit and Loss Account.

CHAPTER TWENTY-FOUR

THE ACCOUNTS OF CLUBS AND NON-PROFIT-MAKING ORGANIZATIONS

(1) Non-Profit-making Organizations

People join together for a multitude of reasons in voluntary organizations: for mutual entertainment, for protection, or for professional
reasons. There are sports clubs, trade unions, consumer co-operatives,
political associations, automobile associations, and many more. The
richness of any society lies partly in the variety of the voluntary
organizations it promotes.

From the book-keeping point of view the aim of such organizations
is the pursuit of some interest other than financial gain, so that they
may all be termed non-profit-making organizations. Yet associations of
this sort must have funds to promote their activities, and these funds
must be honestly accounted for. The official elected for this purpose is
called the Treasurer, one of the key figures on the committee which is
elected to run the club. The others are the Secretary, responsible for
organizing the club's activities, and the Chairman, or President, who
controls the meetings.

The Treasurer's functions are to collect subscriptions, disburse such
funds as are needed in the course of the activities, and report to the
members when required, but especially at the Annual General Meeting
—an important occasion in the club's life. At this meeting the activities
of the club are reviewed, criticisms are voiced, or praise is accorded the
Committee. The Treasurer submits suitable Final Accounts to the
members, supported by an audited statement approved by two members
who were elected as auditors at the previous Annual General Meeting.
In this chapter we shall clarify the form of Final Accounts suitable for
clubs. Before we do so we must first consider the ordinary records of
club receipts and payments.

(2) The Cash Book of a Club

Clubs rarely keep a full set of Ledger Accounts, but some clubs are
very large indeed and need just as huge an organization as any other
large scale business. For example, the Automobile Association of
Great Britain has an annual budget in excess of 7,000,000·00. It employs
patrolmen, inspection staff, legal advisers, and operates a chain of
regional headquarters. The Co-operative Movement is one of the

Date	Details	Subscriptions	Competitions	Refreshments	Sundries	Total
Jan. 1	To Balance				37·45	37·45
7	" Subscriptions	14·00				14·00
7	" Raffle Proceeds		1·60			1·60
7	" Refreshment Sales			3·46		3·46
7	" Fine (broken cups)				0·10	0·10
14	" Subscriptions	22·00				22·00
14	" Raffle Proceeds		2·15			2·15
	And so on throughout year					
Dec. 28	To Subscriptions	2·00				2·00
28	" Raffle Proceeds		1·78			1·78
28	" Children's Party Tickets				4·55	4·55
		79·00	55·00	27·60	76·25	237·85
					46·20	46·20
Jan. 1	To Balance					

Date	Details	Equipment	Competitions	Refreshments	Sundries	Total
Jan. 7	By Raffle Prize		0·75			0·75
7	" Postage				0·04	0·04
	" Prizes for Children's Party		4·65			4·65
14	" Raffle Prize		0·55			0·55
14	" Refreshment Costs			0·75		0·75
14	" Catering (Party)			18·12		18·12
	And so on throughout year					
Dec. 28	By Table Tennis Equipment	7·75				7·75
28	" Balance in Hand				46·20	46·20
		27·75	15·10	56·00	139·00	237·85

Fig. 175. The Analysis Cash Book of a Club

greatest voluntary organizations in the world. In Great Britain trade exceeds one billion pounds a year. Such huge organizations can hardly conduct their affairs with a penny notebook, yet many club treasurers in small clubs do exactly that, while bigger clubs usually have just a Cash Book with analysis columns. We shall see that even very small clubs must analyse their receipts and payments once a year for the Annual General Meeting, so that we may say the analytical Cash Book is the basic club record, or book of original entry. Such a book is shown in Fig. 175.

In this type of book the Treasurer keeps a record of all sums received and paid, and analyses them into various sub-headings as he goes along. He can add up the columns and cross-tot each page of the book to check that he is doing the work correctly and at any given time the balance in hand can be easily found.

A Treasurer who has no such book but merely keeps a record of the cash received and paid in an ordinary cash notebook will have to analyse the notebook at the end of the year, to find the totals spent under various headings. In this way he arrives at the same result as the Treasurer with a more sophisticated ruled book. From either method the Treasurer can prepare the Receipts and Payments Account.

(3) The Receipts and Payments Account

Definition. The Receipts and Payments Account is the simplest way a Treasurer can account for the funds of a non-profit-making organization. It is a statement of receipts and payments, drawn up from an analysis of the club's Cash Book.

The Receipts and Payments Account for the club whose Cash Book is shown in Fig. 175 is shown in Fig. 176.

RECEIPTS AND PAYMENTS ACCOUNT
QUEENSWOOD COMMUNITY ASSOCIATION
(year ending December 31st, 19..)

RECEIPTS			PAYMENTS		
Jan. 1	Cash in Hand	37·45		Purchase of Equipment	27·75
	Subscriptions	79·00		Competition Expenses	15·10
	Competition Proceeds	55·00		Refreshment Expenses	56·00
	Refreshment Sales	27·60		Sundry Expenses	92·80
	Sundry Receipts	38·80	Dec. 31	Cash in hand	46·20
		237·85			237·85
Jan. 1	Cash in Hand	46·20			

Fig. 176. Final Accounts for the A.G.M.

Notice that the Sundry Receipts and Sundry Expenses totals are not quite the same as those in the Cash Book. On the receipts side the opening balance, shown as a receipt to help the cross-tots to come right in the Cash Book, is shown separately. On the payments side the closing balance is similarly shown separately. The Sundry Receipts and Sundry Expenses have therefore been reduced by these amounts.

Membership Appraisal of the Receipts and Payments Account

The Treasurer will stand up at the Annual General Meeting and go through the points that are of interest. Firstly, the club has a better balance at the end of the year than it had at the start. He will offer to produce the 46·20 in hand, but as probably most of it will be in the bank he will perhaps produce the bank book and the odd cash in hand. The club has purchased equipment valued at 27·75 during the year. There are eighty-five members of whom seventy-two have paid their subscriptions and seven have paid for next year in advance.

It will then be up to the members to criticize the accounts. There are serious drawbacks to this type of account from the accounting point of view, but before we discuss these let us see what an astute member might notice from this report.

(*a*) The club paid 56·00 for refreshment materials—loaves of bread, sandwich fillings, etc.—yet they only sold 27·60 worth of refreshments. Where did the rest go? Are there a lot of members who eat refreshments but don't pay? Do the committee take home refreshments not consumed? Perhaps these extra refreshments are eaten by visiting teams? (A reasonable enough explanation.)

(*b*) Who are the thirteen members who enjoy club facilities but do not pay subscriptions?

(*c*) The club spent only 27·75 on new equipment but 92·80 on Sundry Expenses. What were these expenses and how were they incurred?

These and similar questions will be explained by the Treasurer, no doubt to the satisfaction of the members. (Note: The Simplex *Accounts Book for Club Treasurers* is available from George Vyner Ltd., Holmfirth, Huddersfield.)

EXERCISES SET XLII

(4) Receipts and Payments Accounts

No. 1. The following sums of money were received and paid by the Treasurer of the Coronation Croquet Club during the season April–September, 19... On April 1st the club had a Cash Balance of 40·65 brought forward from the year before.

Moneys received: Subscriptions 126·00; Visitors' fees 16·00; Refreshment sales 48·55; Sales of ties and blazer badges 22·35; Lottery receipts 38·95.

Moneys spent: Postage 4·65; Refreshment expenses 31·15; Gift to groundsman 10·50; New hoops, mallets, and balls 18·90; Secretary's honorarium 10·50; Treasurer's honorarium 5·25; Prizes and trophies 32·55; Lottery printing 0·65; Lottery prize 25·00.

Draw up the Receipts and Payments Accounts for the year, for submission to the Annual General Meeting on September 30th, 19... Bring out clearly the Cash Balance on September 30th.

(East Anglian Examination Board—Adapted)

No. 2. The following particulars relate to the Hole in The Road Club for the year ended December 31st, 19... The treasurer presents the information to the members in the form of a Receipts and Payments Account. You are required to draw up this account.

Cash Balance:	
January 1st	10·50
December 31st	9·26
Bank Balance:	
January 1st	60·00
December 31st	28·72
Payments:	
Refreshments	141·10
New Games Equipment	19·00
Rent to September 30th	90·00
Rates	25·00
Printing	15·58
Stationery	28·12
Postage	17·00
Repairs to Games Equipment	12·10
Lighting and Heating	51·50
Wages	120·60
Dance Expenses	53·60
Competition Prizes	14·30
Receipts:	
Subscriptions	332·10
Sale of Dance Tickets	73·18
Competition Fees	20·00
Sale of Refreshments	130·10

(R.S.A.—Adapted)

No. 3. The Arthurian England Archaeological Society has the following Receipts and Expenses during the summer season 19..:

Receipts: Subscriptions 176·00; Donations 250·00; Collections at 'digs' 127·30; Sale of refreshments 37·50; Raffle (surplus artifacts) 27·80.

Payments: Rights to dig on land 50·00; Hire of barrows, etc., 25·00; Small tools 12·50; Refreshment purchases 28·50; Report printing 75·00; Wages of student labour 25·50; Transport costs 72·50; Carbon 14 test charges 36·20.

Draw up the Receipts and Payments Account and calculate the balance in hand.

No. 4. The New University Mountaineering Club has the following Receipts and Expenses during the summer season 19..:

Receipts: Student membership fees 86·50; Grant from College 500·00; Collection for Alpine trip 178·75; Dance proceeds 38·50; Annual Dinner tickets 145·50.

Payments: Use of Alpine huts and equipment 75·00; Camping fees 32·50; Transport 126·50; Purchase of ropes, etc., 56·50; Guide books 2·55; Refreshments 56·50; Dance expenses 18·25; Dinner expenses 98·50.

Draw up the Receipts and Payments Account and calculate the balance in hand.

(5) Limitations of the Receipts and Payments Account

For a variety of reasons the Receipts and Payments Account is unsatisfactory as a record of the club's activities, and only very small clubs would produce their accounts in this way at the Annual General Meeting. The chief objections are:

(*a*) There is no record of the club's initial assets apart from cash in hand. Where a club had at the start of the year premises or equipment of value it is unsatisfactory to have no mention of this at the Annual General Meeting.

(*b*) Similarly, and more importantly, there is no record of the assets owned by the club at the end of the year. If a club has equipment it should be shown as a list of assets on a Balance Sheet.

(*c*) There is no mention of liabilities outstanding. The members must ask the Treasurer about outstanding bills, and payments in advance to the club.

(*d*) The members cannot see whether a profit or loss was made on the year's activities. In club accounts it is not usual to call profits and losses by these names. It is not the business of clubs to make profits out of the membership, the aim is rather to provide amenities with funds mutually subscribed, whether by subscription or by lotteries and similar harmless fund-raising techniques. We therefore use the phrase 'surplus' for profits, and 'deficiency' for losses. Members have either contributed more than necessary, leaving a surplus, or less than necessary, leaving a deficiency of funds.

We are therefore faced with the usual Final Accounts problems—how to present a 'true and fair view' of the club's affairs. The solution is to present a more sophisticated set of Final Accounts than the Receipts and Payments Account. These are the Income and Expenditure Account and a Balance Sheet as at the date of the Annual General Meeting. Sometimes a Trading Account is also produced if sales of drinks, etc., are considerable.

(6) The Accumulated Fund of a Club

Just as the phrase 'Profits and Losses' is not an appropriate one for non-profit-making organizations, so the word 'capital' is not really appropriate either. 'Capital' has acquired implications that are distasteful to many societies, co-operative societies, for example. So the gentler phrase 'Accumulated Fund' has come to be used for the capital fund of a club. It describes exactly how the fund is collected over the years.

The calculation of the Accumulated Fund is one that gives many students difficulty, yet it is quite simple. The Accumulated Fund, like the Capital Fund of a sole trader, can be calculated by the formula: **Total Assets less External Liabilities**.

What the club owned at the beginning of the year, less what it *owed* at the start of the year, gives the Accumulated (or Capital) Fund at the beginning. It is exactly like doing the arithmetic for an opening Journal Entry. The Accumulated Fund occupies the same position as the capital on the Balance Sheet. Like the Capital Account it is increased by the surplus (profit) which is added to it, or decreased by the deficiency (loss) which is deducted from it.

Example. The Space Exploration Society was set up some years ago to promote an interest in astronomy and space research. On January 1st, 19.., it had assets as follows: Premises 2,000·00; Telescopes, etc., 1,800·00; Furniture and Fittings 500·00; Cash at bank 380·50; Cash in hand 23·50; Subscriptions were due from fifteen members at 5·00 each, and seventeen members had paid next year's subscriptions in advance at 5·00 each; A printer's bill for 15·75 was due. It would be set out as follows, and would appear on the Balance Sheet as Accumulated Fund at the beginning of the year.

TOTAL ASSETS		
Premises		2,000·00
Telescopes		1,800·00
Furniture and Fittings		500·00
Cash at Bank		380·50
Cash in Hand		23·50
Subscriptions due		75·00
		4,779·00
LESS LIABILITIES		
Subscriptions in Advance	85·00	
Printing Bill	15·75	
		100·75
Accumulated Fund		4,678·25

(7) Trading Accounts of Clubs

It is quite common to prepare a number of Trading Accounts to show the results of a particular aspect of the club's activities. For instance, a Bar Trading Account for clubs with licensed premises is very common, especially since stocks would enter into the calculations. Similarly, a Trading Account on refreshments or on dances and socials might be presented as a preliminary account for Final Accounts.

(8) The Income and Expenditure Account

This is the main account for Final Accounts of a club. It is exactly
like the Profit and Loss Account of a sole trader except that the final
result is called a **surplus**, or a **deficiency**, not a Net Profit or Net Loss.
Once again we must state the period 'for year ending, etc.' and we must
be careful to do adjustments so that the revenue expenses and revenue
receipts are only those for the period concerned. Capital items do not
enter into a Revenue Account, so that any equipment purchased does
not appear in the Income and Expenditure Account but goes straight
to the Balance Sheet.

Example. The Woodlands Old Girls' Association was formed some
years ago, and at January 1st, 19.., had assets and liabilities as follows:
premises 250·00; games apparatus 50·00; cash at bank 50·00; cash
42·00; Subscriptions were due from three members at 2·00 each and
were paid in advance for next year by seven members, at 2·00 each. The
treasurer produces the following Receipts and Payments Account for
19.. on December 31st.

RECEIPTS AND PAYMENTS ACCOUNT

(for year ending December 31st, 19..)

RECEIPTS		PAYMENTS	
Balance of Cash in Hand	42·00	Rent of Ground	10·00
Subscriptions	250·00	Groundsmen's Tips	25·00
Profit on Dances	40·00	Purchase of Equipment	60·00
Hire of Pitches	5·00	Donation to School Funds	100·00
		Balance in Hand	142·00
	337·00		337·00

You are asked to prepare the Income and Expenditure Account and
the Balance Sheet at December 31st, 19.., bearing in mind that (*a*)
subscriptions in advance were £25, and (*b*) the groundsman was owed
£5 for preparing new hockey posts.

The solution is given in Fig. 177 and 178, but the calculation of the
Accumulated Fund at start is as follows:

TOTAL ASSETS	
Premises	250·00
Games Apparatus	50·00
Cash at Bank	50·00
Cash in Hand	42·00
Subscriptions Due	6·00
	398·00
LESS LIABILITIES	
Subscriptions in Advance	14·00
Accumulated Fund at Start	384·00

Notice particularly that subscriptions in advance are a liability, since we owe the members one year's entertainment, etc., in return for their subscriptions.

The task is now to prepare the Income and Expenditure Account and the Balance Sheet, from the receipts and payments we have been given. Since the Receipts and Payments Account is an analysed Cash Book, and this Cash Book has never been posted to any Ledger Accounts, it follows that the profits are on the debit side. They have never been

WOODLANDS OLD GIRLS' ASSOCIATION

INCOME AND EXPENDITURE ACCOUNT

(for year ended December 31st, 19..)

To Rent		10·00	By Subscriptions		250·00
„ Groundsman's Tips	25·00		*Less* Subscriptions in Arrear		
Add amount due	5·00		on January 1st		6·00
		30·00			244·00
To Donation to School Funds		100·00	*Add* Subscriptions in		
„ Surplus (transferred to			Advance on January 1st		14·00
Accumulated Fund)		138·00			258·00
			Less Subscriptions in		
			Advance on December 31st		25·00
					233·00
			„ Profit on Dances		40·00
			„ Hire of Pitches		5·00
		278·00			278·00

Fig. 177. An Income and Expenditure Account

BALANCE SHEET

(as at December 31st, 19..)

ACCUMULATED FUND			FIXED ASSETS		
At Start	384·00		Premises		250·00
Add Surplus	138 00		Games Apparatus	50·00	
		522·00	*Add* New Apparatus	60·00	
					110·00
					360·00
CURRENT LIABILITIES			CURRENT ASSETS		
Subscriptions in Advance	25·00		Cash at Bank	50·00	
Groundsman's Tip	5·00		Cash in Hand	142·00	
		30·00			192·00
		552·00			552·00

Fig. 178. A Club's Balance Sheet

posted over to the credit side of the profit accounts as in an ordinary business. Similarly the losses are on the credit side, having never been posted to the debit side of expense accounts. The resulting Income and Expenditure Account and Balance Sheet are as shown on page 305. The figures for the Balance Sheet come from three places: (*a*) the opening Accumulated Fund calculation, (*b*) the capital expenditure in the Receipts and Payments Account, and (*c*) the surplus of the Income and Expenditure Account.

The student should note carefully how this improved set of Final Accounts clarifies the position to the members. We now have a clear picture of the surplus collected during the year. We can also see what the assets are, and whether there are any outstanding liabilities. We have adjusted the receipts and payments to the exact figures for the year, and have carried our surplus to the Accumulated Fund.

EXERCISES SET XLIII

(9) Club Final Accounts

No. 1. The New Town Association began activities on January 1st, 19.., and the following is a summary of its transactions for that year:

Receipts:		
Subscriptions		350·50
Net Income from Dances and Whist Drives, etc.		120·50
Deposit Interest		5·00
		476·00
Payments:		
Rent of Premises	151·50	
Rates	40·50	
Lighting, Heating, etc.	52·50	
Purchase of Savings Certificates	120·00	
	364·50	
Balance in Hand at December 31st, 19.. (including 86·00 in Post Office Savings Bank)		111·50

One quarter's rent, 50·50, is due at December 31st, 19.., and 10·00 for a coal bill is not paid; Subscriptions received include 25·00 in advance for 19..; Rates in advance at December 31st, 19.., were 15·00.

You are asked to prepare the Association's Income and Expenditure Account for the year and its Balance Sheet on December 31st, 19...

(R.S.A.—Adapted)

No. 2. The following is the Receipts and Payments Account of a social club for the year ended December 31st, 19...

RECEIPTS AND PAYMENTS ACCOUNT

RECEIPTS		PAYMENTS	
To Balance (January 1st, 19..)	31·00	By Games Equipment	24·00
Subscriptions:		,, Printing, Postages, and	
Current Year	272·00	Stationery	13·50
Previous Year	12·00	,, Periodicals	18·50
,, Profit on Refreshments	35·00	,, Competition Prizes	12·25
,, Competition Fees	18·00	,, Sundry Expenses	20·75
		,, Wages	78·00
		,, Rent	120·00
		,, Rates	37·00
		,, Balance	44·00
	368·00		368·00

(*a*) Prepare the club's Income and Expenditure Account and Balance Sheet having regard to the following:

(i) Subscriptions due but unpaid for current year amounted to 18·00.

(ii) The club had furniture and games equipment at the beginning of the year valued at 80·00, and this is to be depreciated by 20 per cent. (No depreciation is to be written off additions made during the year.)

(iii) Of the rates payment, 13·00 was in respect of next year.

(*b*) State the amount of the society's Accumulated Fund as at December 31st, 19...

(R.S.A.—Adapted)

No. 3. The Willesden Green Retired Teachers' Association began its activities on January 1st, 19... On December 31st, 19.., the Treasurer, Miss Sandon, prepared a list of receipts and payments as follows:

Receipts:		
Subscriptions	425·00	
Net Income from Dances, etc.	235·00	
Deposit Interest	10·00	
		670·00
Payments:		
Rent of Club-house	230·00	
Rates Paid in Year	50·00	
Lighting and Heating	65·00	
Purchase of Savings Certificates	100·00	
		445·00
Balance in Hand (of which 200·00 is in the Post Office Savings Bank)		225·00

The following points were given in a report:

One quarter's rent 76·50 was due on December 31st but not paid; 10·00 was due for an electricity bill; Subscriptions received included 30·00 for the coming year which had been paid in advance; Rates in advance were 15·00.

You are asked to assist Miss Sandon to prepare the club's Income and Expenditure Account and a Balance Sheet at that date.

No. 4. The Treasurer of the sports club of your firm provided the following analysis of his receipts and payments during the year ended December 31st, 19... From it, and the notes given below, draw up the club's Income and Expenditure Account as it should have been presented to the members on December 31st.

Receipts:	
Subscriptions:	
Current Year	295·00
Previous Year	14·00
Profit on Refreshments	46·00
Competition Fees	17·50
Payments:	
New Games Equipment	18·90
Printing, Postage, and Stationery	14·50
Periodicals	16·30
Competition Prizes	10·50
Sundry Expenses	25·00
Wages	70·75
Rent	140·00
Rates	46·00

NOTES:

(*a*) Subscriptions due but unpaid for the current year amount to 22·50.

(*b*) The club furniture and games equipment at the beginning of the year was valued at 105·00. It is to be written down—ignoring additions during the year—by 20 per cent.

(*c*) At January 1st, 19.., rates paid in advance amounted to 12·00, and of the rates payment made during the year 13·00 was in respect of the following year.

No. 5. (*a*) Distinguish briefly between (i) a Receipts and Payments Account, (ii) an Income and Expenditure Account, and (iii) a Profit and Loss Account.

(*b*) The following is a summary of the receipts and payments of the West End Cricket Club for the period from the date of formation on January 1st, 19.., to December 31st, 19...

Subscriptions	234·00	Purchase of Land	700·00
Gate Money	124·10	Purchase of Refreshments	123·15
Sales of Refreshments	162·15	Equipment	62·00
Loan secured on Land	600·50	Printing, Stationery, etc.	21·15
		Travelling Expenses	18·14
		Sundry Expenses	22·16
		Club-house—paid on account	150·00
		Balance (c/d)	24·15
	1,120·75		1,120·75

Prepare the Income and Expenditure Account of the club for the year ended December 31st, 19.., and the Balance Sheet at that date, taking into consideration the following:

(*a*) There is an unpaid account for provisions amounting to 12·80.
(*b*) Subscriptions received included 10·00 paid in advance.
(*c*) The stock of provisions on hand at December 31st, was valued at 8·00.

(*R.S.A.—Adapted*)

No. 6. After the passing of certain entries for the calculation of the profits or losses on the restaurant and bar, the Trial Balance of the Bluewater Sailing club on December 31st, 19.., is as follows:

	Dr.	Cr.
Club Motor Launch	850·00	
Members' Subscriptions Received		3,140·00
Capital Fund at January 1st, 19..		7,230·00
Club Sailing Boats	1,200·00	
Hiring Fees Received for Club Boats		620·50
Leasehold Premises	5,000·00	
Maintenance Expenses of Launch and Club Boats	240·50	
Furniture and Equipment	800·00	
Cash in Hand	25·00	
Balance at Bank	600·00	
Stock of Wines and Spirits	105·50	
Racing Entrance Fees Received		335·50
Cost of Racing Prizes	103·50	
Salaries of Secretary and Office Assistant	1,650·75	
Sundry Creditors		294·00
Printing and Stationery	90·75	
Wages of Club Boatman	520·00	
General Expenses	223·00	
Rates	325·50	
Loss on Restaurant Catering	185·50	
Profit on Bar		380·00
Office Expenses, Postages and Telephone	80·00	
	12,000·00	12,000·00

You are required to draw up the club's Income and Expenditure Account for the year, and a Balance Sheet as at December 31st, 19.., taking the following into account:

(*a*) The motor launch, the fleet of club boats, and the furniture and equipment should all be depreciated by 10 per cent.
(*b*) On January 1st, 19.., the club's lease had twenty years to run, and a proportionate amount for the current year should be written off the Leasehold Premises Account.
(*c*) Members' subscriptions for the current year, amounting to 60·00 were in arrear and unpaid on December 31st, 19...

No. 7. The following is the Trial Balance of the Greensward Cricket and Social Club on December 31st, 19...

	Dr.	Cr.
Accumulated Fund at January 1st, 19..		2,136·00
Club-house	2,000·00	
Club-room Equipment	420·00	
Sports Equipment	270·00	
Sale of Refreshments		243·00
Purchase of Refreshments	185·50	
Interest Free Loan from a Member		500·00
Subscriptions Received for Current Year		370·00
Subscriptions Outstanding for Previous Year	5·00	
Receipts from Club-room Games		182·50
Maintenance of Games and Sports Equipment	42·50	
Postages	76·50	
Insurance	18·75	
Sundry Expenses	48·25	
Printing and Stationery	80·50	
Wages	208·50	
Cash at Bank	62·25	
Cash in Hand	13·75	
	3,431·50	3,431·50

Prepare:

(*a*) An account to show the profit or loss on sale of refreshments, and

(*b*) The Income and Expenditure Account for the year ended December 31st, 19.., and a Balance Sheet at that date.

The following notes are to be taken into consideration:

(*a*) Sports equipment is to be depreciated at 20 per cent per annum and club-room equipment at 10 per cent per annum.

(*b*) Subscriptions, 15·00, are due for the current year and not yet paid.

(*c*) There is an unpaid account for provisions (refreshments) amounting to 12·00.

(*d*) The stock of provisions (refreshments) on hand at December 31st, 19.., was 16·00.

(*e*) Subscriptions from previous year still outstanding are now to be written off as a bad debt.

(*R.S.A.—Adapted*)

No. 8. Last year the Treasurer of an archery club received 325·00 on account of subscriptions, of which 40·00 represented subscriptions in advance for this year. This year 340·00 was received on account of subscriptions. Of this sum 25·00 represented subscriptions for the previous year which, on January 1st, were in arrear, and 20·00 represented subscriptions in advance for the coming year. Subscriptions in arrear for this year 19.. at December 31st were 15·00 and it may be assumed that none of the subscribers in arrear will fail to pay in due course.

Give a statement showing the amount that should be credited in the club's Income and Expenditure Account for the current year, on account of subscription income, and how this amount is arrived at.

(R.S.A.—Adapted)

No. 9. The New Social Club was founded on January 1st, 19... On the same day ten Life Members subscribed 5·50 each and it was agreed that this revenue should be spread evenly over five years. The annual subscription for each Ordinary Member was fixed at 1·10. At January 1st three years later, seven of the hundred Ordinary Members still owed their subscriptions for the previous year. During this year twelve new members were enrolled who paid their subscriptions. By the end of the year all dues except those of three members for this year had been received.

Prepare the Life Members' Subscription Account and one for the Ordinary Members as they would appear after the Income and Expenditure Account for the year had been closed. Bring out clearly any balances on January 1st of the fifth year.

(R.S.A.—Adapted)

No. 10. (*a*) In what respects does an Income and Expenditure Account differ from a Receipts and Payments Account?

(*b*) From the following details and the notes attached relating to the Westshire Tennis Club, prepare the Final Accounts of the Club for the year ended December 31st, 19..:

On January 1st, 19.., the club's assets were: Freehold club-house 1,000·00; Equipment 70·00; Club subscriptions in arrear 8·00; Cash in hand and balance at bank 76·00. The club owed 40·00 to Caterer's Ltd. for Christmas dance catering.

SUMMARY OF RECEIPTS AND PAYMENTS FOR 19..

RECEIPTS		PAYMENTS	
Subscriptions	164·00	Catering—Christmas Dance	
Locker Rents	10·00	(Caterer's Ltd.)	40·00
Receipts from Dances and		This Year's Dances and Socials	95·00
Social	139·00	Band Fees—Dances	25·00
Sales of Used Match Tennis		New Lawn Mower	53·00
Balls	15·00	Repairs to Tennis Nets	19·00
Sale of old Lawn Mower	8·00	Match Tennis Balls	31·00
		Match Expenses	17·00
		Repair and Decoration of	
		Club-house	65·00

NOTES: (*a*) The book value on January 1st, 19.., of the old lawn mower sold during the year was 3·00.

(*b*) The club has 40 members and the subscription is 4·00 per annum. The subscriptions received in 19.. included those in arrear for the previous year

(*c*) On December 31st, 19.., 11·00 was owed to Playfair Ltd. for tennis balls supplied.

(*d*) Equipment as at December 31st, 19.., is to be depreciated by 15 per cent.

(*e*) Tennis balls are regarded as revenue expenditure.

(University of London 'O' Level—Adapted)

No. 11. The following figures were taken from the records of the Riverside Club for the year 19...

Prepare:

    (*a*) The Receipts and Payments Account.

    (*b*) The Income and Expenditure Account of the club for the year ended December 31st, 19...

Receipts:	
Members' Subscriptions	690·00
Sale of Refreshments	2,021·00
Sundry Receipts	140·00
Payments:	
Suppliers of Refreshments	1,434·00
Wages	650·00
Rent, Rates, and Insurance	250·00
Repairs and Renewals	213·00
Purchase of New Furniture for Lounge	205·00
Sundry Expenses	126·00

NOTES: All receipts and payments were passed through the club's Bank Account.

Members' Subscriptions in Arrear at January 1st, 19.., and paid during 19..	60·00
Members' Subscriptions in Arrear at December 31st, 19..	35·00
Cash at Bank, January 1st, 19..	131·00
Rates Paid in Advance at December 31st, 19..	26·00
Estimated depreciation on Club Furniture and Fixtures for the year 19..	72·00
Purchases of Refreshments during the year	1,540·00
Stocks of Refreshments at January 1st, 19..	138·00
Stocks of Refreshments at December 31st, 19..	156·00

(N.B. Necessary calculations must be shown clearly either above or below the accounts.)

                                               (*University of London 'O' Level—Adapted*)

No. 12. The assets and liabilities of the Happy Venturers' Football Club on January 1st, 19.., were: Cash in hand 20·00; Cash at bank 130·00; Bar stocks 310·00; Furniture and fittings 560·00; Subscriptions due for the previous year 20·00.

On December 31st, 19.., the office cash record showed:

Cash drawn out from Bank	900·00
Wages paid:	
Cleaners	400·00
Barman	350·00
Postage and Sundry Expenses	75·00

The bank paying-in slips showed:

Subscriptions received 490·00 (this includes the amount owing for the previous year)

Receipts from Dances and Socials	126·50
Receipts from Bar	2,850·50

Cheque-book counterfoils showed:

Rent	320·75
Rates and Insurance	204·75
Lighting and Heating	46·50
Expenses of Dances and Socials	75·00
Cash for Office Use	900·00
Purchase of Stocks for Bar	1,440·00

The annual subscriptions to the club were 2·00 per member.
Ten members were in arrears for one year's subscriptions.
Insurance 14·00 was prepaid.
It was decided to depreciate furniture and fittings by 10 per cent.
Stock in the bar at December 31st was valued at 246·00.

Prepare the Income and Expenditure Account of the club for the year ended December 31st, 19.., and a Balance Sheet as at that date. Calculations must be shown in the accounts or immediately below them.

(N.B. In preparing the accounts show the profit made on the bar and on the dances and socials.)

(University of London 'O' Level—Adapted)

CHAPTER TWENTY-FIVE

THE INCREASED NET-WORTH METHOD OF FINDING PROFITS: SINGLE ENTRY OR INCOMPLETE RECORDS

(1) Introduction

We have now learned how to calculate the profits of the three simple types of business organization: the sole trader, the partnership, and the non-profit-making club. We have assumed that the sole trader and the partnership keep proper book-keeping records, and that the club treasurer keeps a Cash Book which can be analysed. We have not yet dealt with the Final Accounts of a Limited Liability Company, since these are more complex, and will be dealt with in Chapter Twenty-nine, page 363. But before we proceed we must pick up a loose thread we have ignored until now. This is the calculation of the profits of a small business whose owner keeps either no record of transactions at all, or incomplete records. This type of book-keeping is called **single entry**, to distinguish it from double entry book-keeping. This system amounts to no system at all, for the proprietor cannot keep more than a rough check on his financial affairs.

Many small businesses are run successfully by relatively untrained people. One does not need higher education to succeed in business—a tough character and a capacity for hard work are more important. Establishing the right business in the right place is even more vital. The ideal thing is to discover some bottle-neck situation in a commercial or industrial activity which can be relieved by the type of service you can supply.

How does the self-made man, who conducts his entire affairs without written records, face up to the problem of discovering the profitability of his business? Years ago he would not have bothered; he would judge it by the gradual increase in worldly goods with which he was endowed. Today the Revenue Authorities of whatever country he lives in will require an annual assessment of his affairs, so that they can decide the government's share of that income.

(2) Profit as an Increase in Net Worth

The businessman who does not keep written records can see, as the years go by, a gradual increase in the assets of his business. An airline operating in the South of England began twenty-one years ago with a single Puss Moth aircraft, and now has a capital of four million pounds. Where did this increased wealth come from? It was accumulated over the years by the profitable activities of the sole pilot who founded it. He did not withdraw all the profits he made, but he clearly must have lived on these profits by drawing some of them. The rest were retained in the business—for buying new aircraft and premises, building booking offices, and so on.

Profit can therefore be measured as an increase in the **net worth** of a business. The net worth of a business is the value of the business to the owner of the business. Consider this example:

Example 1. John Trader sets up in business on January 1st, 19. ., as a hawker. He has a van, value 60·00, weighing machines and shelving worth 10·00, and he buys stock valued at 30·00. He keeps no records, but on December 31st he has two vans, value 120·00 and 45·00, scales and other equipment worth 25·00, and stock valued at 80·00. He has 245·00 in the bank, and a cash float of 15·00. He has given his wife 10·00 per week and has used about 4·00 per week for personal expenses. During the year an aunt left him a legacy of 100·00 which he put into the business. How do we calculate the profits of the business?

First we have to discover the net worth of the business at the beginning and end of the year, and see whether there has been an increase. To do this we need a Balance Sheet for each of the days mentioned, but the term 'Balance Sheet' is not a satisfactory one here, for it implies that there are Ledger Accounts, with balances on them. It is better to call such a Balance Sheet by another name: **Statement of Affairs.** Here is the Statement of Affairs for January 1st, 19. . :

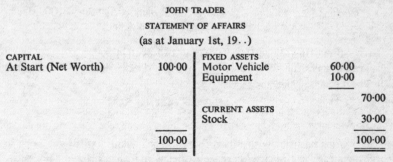

JOHN TRADER

STATEMENT OF AFFAIRS

(as at January 1st, 19. .)

CAPITAL		FIXED ASSETS		
At Start (Net Worth)	100·00	Motor Vehicle	60·00	
		Equipment	10·00	
				70·00
		CURRENT ASSETS		
		Stock		30·00
	100·00			100·00

Fig. 179. The Opening Net Worth

From this Statement of Affairs we can see that on January 1st the net worth of the business to John Trader was 100·00.

The second Statement of Affairs is as follows:

JOHN TRADER

STATEMENT OF AFFAIRS

(as at December 31st, 19. .)

CAPITAL		FIXED ASSETS		
At Close (Net Worth)	530·00	Motor Vehicles	165·00	
		Equipment	25·00	
				190·00
		CURRENT ASSETS		
		Stock	80·00	
		Cash at Bank	245·00	
		Cash in Hand	15·00	
				340·00
	530·00			530·00

Fig. 180. The Closing Net Worth

It is clear that the net worth of John Trader's business to him has increased from 100·00 to 530·00. This increase in net worth has come from the profits he has made over the year. He is now surrounded by more worldly goods than he had previously, because of the profits he has made.

(3) Calculating the Profits by the Increased Net-worth Method

The calculations are as follows:

(*a*) Calculate the increase in net worth by drawing up two Statements of Affairs as shown in (2), page 315, and subtracting the opening net worth from the closing net worth. In our example:

Closing Net Worth — Opening Net Worth = 530·00 — 100·00
∴ *Increase in Net Worth* = 430·00

(*b*) Adjust this figure to take account of drawings.
Trader gave his wife 10·00 per week and also drew 4·00 per week himself.

∴ *Drawings* = 14·00 × 52
= 728·00

If Trader had not withdrawn this money it would still have been in the business, so that the increase in net worth would have been more noticeable.

∴ *True Increase in Net Worth* = 430·00 + 728·00
= 1,158·00

(*c*) Adjust this figure for any increases or decreases of net worth that can be explained by something other than profits.

In this case a legacy of 100·00 explains some of the increase in Net Worth. This 100·00 did not come from profits but from a source outside the business. Therefore we have:

$$Profit\ for\ Year = True\ Increase\ in\ Net\ Worth - Legacy$$
$$= 1,158·00 - 100·00$$
$$= 1,058·00$$

This is the profit on which John Trader should pay tax.

The student will see that such a calculation depends upon the honest valuation of the assets and an honest revelation of the sums drawn. Clearly it is easy for Trader to falsify the figures in the hope of evading tax, but the Tax Authorities of all countries are able to compare the profits earned in all similar businesses, and a trader who appears to be making less than normal profits is subjected to careful investigation of his affairs. A common method of dealing with the type of trader who will not give reasonably honest figures is to assess him at a very high tax figure. When he protests that he is quite unable to pay such a high tax the Revenue Authorities point out politely that they are only too willing to be more reasonable with him, provided that he will be more reasonable with them, and give them the true figures.

(4) Adjustments with the Increased Net-worth Method

Just as in all other Final Accounts there may be adjustments to consider here. Before drawing up the two Statements of Affairs we would question the proprietor on the valuations he is placing on his assets. For instance, if the motor vehicle was valued at the end of the year at the same value as at the beginning, we would point out that it must have depreciated. The adjustments tend to be taken into account directly, by reducing the value of the asset on the Statement of Affairs. This particularly affects the asset, debtors, since it will be necessary to ensure that the proprietor is not including debts he knows to be bad. We would also point out to him that he should take into account some provision for bad debts that may arise.

EXERCISES SET XLIV

(5) Finding Profits by the Increased Net-worth Method

No. 1. The following Statements of Affairs have been drawn up to give the financial position as on January 1st, 19.., and December 31st, 19.., respectively, of A. Brogan, who keeps his books on a single entry basis:

STATEMENT OF AFFAIRS
(as at January 1st, 19..)

CAPITAL		FIXED ASSETS		
At Start	4,470·00	Fixtures		470·00
CURRENT LIABILITIES		CURRENT ASSETS		
Creditors	531·00	Debtors	1,755·50	
		Stock	2,520·00	
		Cash	255·50	
				4,531·00
	5,001·00			5,001·00

STATEMENT OF AFFAIRS
(as at December 31st, 19..)

CAPITAL			FIXED ASSETS		
At close		6,007·00	Fixtures		440·00
CURRENT LIABILITIES			CURRENT ASSETS		
Creditors	678·00		Debtors	2,300·00	
Wages Due	25·00		Stock	2,800·00	
			Cash at Bank	850·00	
		703·00	Cash in Hand	320·00	
					6,270·00
		6,710·00			6,710·00

Brogan has transferred 100·00 a month regularly from his business Bank Account to his private Bank Account by way of drawings, and has taken 25·00 of stock for his private use. The alteration in the value of the fixtures represents depreciation. Calculate Brogan's profits for the year.

(*R.S.A.—Adapted*)

No. 2. A. Rover is in the entertainments profession. He has little time to keep books and relies solely on his memory for receiving fees and paying his way. Once a year he consults his accountant on his financial position. They draw up the following figures for 19..:

	January 1st	December 31st
Cash in Hand	27·50	162·75
Cash at Bank	427·50	2,380·25
Instruments and Electronic Equipment	400·00	1,200·00
Motor Vehicles	280·00	850·00
Debts Due by A. Rover	62·75	320·50
Fees Due to A. Rover	12·25	230·50

Capital contributed during year (and partly responsible for his extra assets) as a result of a legacy and prize award, 1,000·00.

Drawings for personal support during year, 620·00.

You are asked to draw up a Statement of Affairs as at December 31st, and to show your calculations of the profit made during the year.

No. 3. On January 1st, 19.., T. J. Wise began business by paying 800·00 into a Bank Account. He did not keep complete books of account, and used the Bank Account for both his private and business expenses. On March 31st, 19. ., Wise wished to ascertain his profit or loss for the quarter. On that date his cash in hand was 10·00 and the balance at the bank 275·00. Stock-in-trade was valued at 840·00 and a motor van at 450·00. Trade creditors were 496·00 and trade debtors 189·00. Rent, 25·00, was prepaid, and an account for electricity, 19·00, was outstanding.

An examination of bank withdrawals disclosed that 258·00 of these were for private expenses. Wise had also taken 217·00 for private expenses out of the business takings before paying them into the bank. The motor van was brought into the business during the quarter at the same figure as its valuation on March 31st, 19. ..

Prepare a statement to show the profit or loss of the business for the quarter ended March 31st, 19...

(University of London 'O' Level—Adapted)

No. 4. On January 1st, 19. ., A. Singleton decided to go into business. His only asset was a bank balance of 1,000·00. For the next six months he kept no books except a Cash Book.

At June 30th, 19. ., his cash balance was 45·00 and his bank balance 215·00. Singleton estimated his debtors at 640·00, stock-in-hand at 700·00, and he had a van worth 400·00. His creditors amounted to 950·00. During the half-year he had drawn 530·00 for his personal expenses.

(*a*) Draw up a statement showing the profit or loss Singleton had made by June 30th, 19...

(*b*) State two items of information, which you consider important, that Singleton cannot ascertain from the statement you have prepared.

(R.S.A.—Adapted)

No. 5. A trader began business on January 1st, 19. ., his position then being—Assets: Land and buildings 7,500·00; Fixtures and fittings 550·00; Balance at bank 1,750·00. Liabilities: Loan on mortgage of land and buildings 5,000·00.

He traded for a year, drawing nothing out of the business for his personal use, and paying in no additional capital. His position on December 31st, 19. ., was—Assets: Land and buildings 7,500·00; Fixtures and fittings 550·00; Delivery van 650·00; Sundry debtors 445·00; Stock 970·00; Balance at bank 1,445·00; Cash in hand 115·00. Liabilities: Loan on mortgage of land and buildings 5,000·00; Sundry creditors 875·00.

You are required to calculate his profit or loss for the year.

(R.S.A.—Adapted)

No. 6. On January 1st, 19. ., A. Alexander began business in premises valued at 1,500·00 and with a bank balance of 500·00. On December 31st, 19. ., his financial position was as follows: Creditors 250·00; Debtors 360·00; Cash in hand 40·00; Stock 500·00. His rates were prepaid by 10·00 and during the year he had withdrawn for his private use 390·00.

Calculate the profit made by Alexander after he had depreciated his premises by 10 per cent per annum.

(R.S.A.—Adapted)

CHAPTER TWENTY-SIX

THE INTERPRETATION OF FINAL ACCOUNTS: STATISTICAL CONTROL FIGURES

(1) Introduction—Controlling a Business

The businessman who has successfully prepared a set of Final Accounts from an accurate set of records has completed the routine book-keeping functions; but if he is astute enough to pursue his accounting a little further he can discover many useful facts about the trends of his business affairs. Is the business expanding or contracting? Is it more profitable than last year or less profitable? Has the manager been stealing the cash? Do the shop assistants take home the stock? Do they give it away free to relations and friends? Are some lines more profitable than others?

The chief matters to be dealt with in this chapter are:

(a) **The Gross Profit Percentage** and its significance to the proprietor.

(b) **The Net Profit Percentage** and its significance to the proprietor, including **Expense Ratios to Turnover.**

(c) **The Rate of Stock Turnover** and its significance to the proprietor.

(d) **The Interpretation of a Balance Sheet** including the significance of the following to the proprietor:

    (i) Capital owned
    (ii) Capital employed
    (iii) Fixed capital
    (iv) Floating capital
    (v) Liquid capital
    (vi) Net Working capital
    (vii) Solvency and insolvency
    (viii) Overtrading
    (ix) The return on capital invested.

The student should particularly note the control of his business that can be achieved by a proprietor who understands what is happening to these control ratios and percentages. By indicating that something is wrong with his business they can lead him to discover what is wrong, and apply the remedy before the business has suffered irreparable damage.

(2) The Gross Profit Percentage

This is the percentage of Gross Profit that we make upon Sales, or a better phrase is Net Turnover. The term Net Turnover means *sales less returns*, and the Net Turnover of the business is itself an important statistic about any enterprise. The formula for the Gross Profit Percentage is therefore:

$$Gross\ Profit\ Percentage = \frac{Gross\ Profit}{Net\ Turnover} \times 100$$

Consider the following Trading Account:

TRADING ACCOUNT
(for year ending December 31st, 19..)

To Opening Stock		1,450·00	By Sales	27,900·00
„ Purchases	13,800·00		Less Returns	400·00
Add Carriage In	450·00			
			Net Turnover	27,500·00
	14,250·00			
Less Returns	700·00			
Net Purchases		13,550·00		
Total Stock Available		15,000·00		
Less Closing Stock		2,000·00		
Cost of Stock Sold		13,000·00		
To Warehouse Expenses		2,500·00		
Cost of Sales		15,500·00		
Gross Profit		12,000·00		
		27,500·00		27,500·00

Fig. 181. A Trading Account

The Gross Profit Percentage on this Trading Account is:

$$\frac{Gross\ Profit}{Net\ Turnover} \times 100$$
$$= \frac{12,000}{27,500} \times 100$$
$$= \frac{43·63}{11)480}$$
$$= 43·6\%$$

Supposing that next year the firm does twice as much business? Would it need to purchase twice as many purchases? Would it expect to pay out twice as many expenses? Would it expect to make twice as much profit? Of course we cannot answer a 'yes' with absolute confidence to all these questions, but generally speaking the answer will be 'roughly yes'. If we sell twice as many goods we would expect to buy twice as many goods. For the sake of this argument we will assume that every-thing simply doubles. Next year the Gross Profit Percentage works out as follows:

$$\frac{Gross\ Profit}{Net\ Turnover} \times 100$$

$$= \frac{24,000}{55,000} \times 100$$

$$= \frac{480}{11}$$

$$= 43 \cdot 6\%$$

You will see that it is the same answer as we had before, and this is the vital thing about the Gross Profit Percentage: it is a constant. It ought to come out the same every year providing our business is running in the same way. We say, in a scientific way:

Gross Profit Percentage = K (Constant)

(Scientists can't say C for Constant; it already stands for Celsius.)

It is important to work your Trading Account out the same way from year to year. If it is not prepared in a similar manner each year, the different items introduced will prevent you comparing the Gross Profit Percentages.

What Can be Wrong When the Gross Profit Percentage Falls?

Remember, year by year, the Gross Profit Percentage should be constant. Supposing we find that it has fallen? There could be many possible explanations.

(*a*) The manager, or the staff, are stealing the cash takings. This will reduce the sales figure and the profits will fall. The cash is being diverted into the manager's pocket, or someone else's pocket. What can we do about it? We can query the matter with the manager, let him know we are watching the situation. This may be enough. We might point out that it must be very expensive driving that huge car. How does he do it on his money? If it appears unlikely that he is responsible we can watch the assistants. Who has the luxurious handbag or the ex-pensive new clothes? How does she do it on her money?

(*b*) Perhaps someone is stealing the stock? One of the good things about stock-taking is that it discovers losses of stock. A low stock figure means a high cost of sales figure and a lower Gross Profit. Who takes the stock home? Two pounds of sugar and a quarter of tea every night for a year makes quite a big hole in the stock. A very common practice of dishonest shop assistants is to help their friends to free goods. A packet of cigarettes to each boy friend soon stops the Gross Profit Percentage being K.

(c) If neither (a) nor (b) is the cause, stock might be getting lost in other ways. For instance, breakages due to clumsiness in the crockery department transfer some of the stock to the dustbin. Bad buying of perishables has the same effect—we throw away the tomatoes that go bad, the cheese that gets stale, the cakes that go dry. If we don't actually throw them away we have to sell them cheaply and that still means the profit on them is lost.

(d) Another type of bad buying, in the clothing and footwear trades especially, concerns the out-of-touch buyer who is behind the times and *will* buy lines that have to be reduced in the sales because we can't get rid of them in any other way. We have to keep our fashion buyers young in heart or their work will adversely affect the Gross Profit Percentage.

(e) A quite legitimate explanation for the falling Gross Profit Percentage may be that the cost of goods to us has risen and we have been slow to pass this on to the public. It may be because we have poor control in our pricing department, or because competition from more efficient traders prevents us from raising prices. Sometimes governments regulate prices by law and force the trader to accept lower profit margins. A government tax may be levied but because of the demand in our particular market we are unable to pass the tax on and must suffer it ourselves. The astute businessman will at least be ready with his plans to recoup these losses as soon as the law, or the market situation, changes.

(f) The expense items on the Trading Account may be the cause of the trouble. Is the manager taking on more staff than he needs? Perhaps the light and heat bill has risen violently. Is it a hard winter? If it is, there is nothing we can do about it. If it is not, perhaps the staff have brought in electrical appliances without our knowledge and are eating hot buttered toast with our electricity. In this case we will order the bright fellow who thought of the idea to take his toaster home again.

(g) It may be that the stock is wrongly valued. As explained in Chapter Twenty-one, an error in stock valuation affects the Gross Profit. If we overvalue our closing stock we overvalue the Gross Profit; but the next year, when that closing stock has become the opening stock, we undervalue our Gross Profit. This double action produces a drop in the Gross Profit Percentage compared with the previous year.

What Can Cause a Rise in Gross Profit Percentage?

If the types of inefficiency described in the last section cause a fall in Gross Profit Percentage, then an improved efficiency in these directions will cause a rise in Gross Profit Percentage. Honesty over the cash takings will keep the cash sales figure up, and hence the Gross Profit

Percentage will improve. A manager who takes over and at once detects sharp practice by assistants with cash takings or stock, will similarly improve the percentage. If he improves the buying, or eliminates breakages, or is quick to pass on increased prices to the customer, he will keep up the Gross Profit Percentage.

What action should we take in this event? Clearly we should reward him. That is what a bonus is all about; it is a reward for efficiency in the line of duty.

(3) Gross Profit Percentage on Cost

A very similar figure to the Gross Profit Percentage on turnover is the Gross Profit Percentage on cost. This is calculated as follows:

$$Gross\ Profit\ Percentage\ on\ Cost = \frac{Gross\ Profit}{Cost\ of\ Stock\ sold} \times 100$$

In the Trading Account shown in Fig. 182 we would get:

$$\frac{12,000}{13,000} \times 100$$
$$= 92\%$$

The Trader concerned is actually making a 92 per cent profit on the goods he buys to sell again, but some of this profit is being eroded by expenses and overheads.

A common example of this sort of thing is where a shopkeeper sells you something for 10·00 that cost him 5·00. He may say to you, 'I get 5·00 of the sales price, i.e. 50 per cent.' In fact, of course, he is making a profit of 5·00 on an original outlay of 5·00 which is not 50 per cent but 100 per cent. In this way he hides the true profit from the simple customer.

(4) Absolute and Relative Changes

It is important to understand the difference between absolute and relative changes. Absolute changes mislead many proprietors into thinking that their businesses are doing quite well when in fact serious weaknesses have begun to creep in. Relative changes, that is to say ratio, or percentage, changes, throw up quite clearly the true picture of what is happening. Consider the following case:

Mr. A. owns a business and gives the following figures for two successive years:

	Year 1	Year 2
Turnover	10,000·00	20,000·00
Gross Profit	2,500·00	4,000·00

He speaks very highly of his manager who has increased the profits from 2,500·00 to 4,000·00 and describes him as 'dynamically successful'. Criticize this assessment of the manager.

Mr. A. is looking at the absolute changes in gross profits, that is, at the actual figures themselves. It is true that profits have risen from 2,500·00 to 4,000·00. But in fact the turnover has doubled. When we work out the relative changes we find:

Year 1   *Gross Profit Percentage* $= \dfrac{2,500}{10,000} \times 100 = 25\%$

Year 2   *Gross Profit Percentage* $= \dfrac{4,000}{20,000} \times 100 = 20\%$

In fact these extra profits have been made at a greater cost than the earlier profits, and diminishing returns have begun to set in. This does not mean that the manager is necessarily incapable, but he is not quite as brilliant as Mr. A. thinks. If Mr. A. lets him go ahead and expand the business still further he may get to the point fairly quickly where he is overtrading and profits will begin to fall back. The relative figure, the Gross Profit Percentage, sounds a note of early warning about the trend of the business, and could save Mr. A.'s business if he paid attention to it and restrained the enthusiasm of his manager with a word of warning about the dangers ahead.

Exercises Set XLV

(5) Gross Profit Percentage

No. 1. (*a*) State, briefly and clearly, what you understand by the term Net Turnover in relation to the business of a retailer.

(*b*) A trader had in stock on February 1st 300 articles costing 2·00 each. During the month he bought 900 more of these articles at the same price and sold 510 at 3·00 each, of which 10 were returned. Draw up a statement showing the Gross Profit earned and express the Gross Profit as a percentage of the turnover.

(*R.S.A.—Adapted*)

No. 2. (*a*) Describe the method of calculation and explain the significance of the ratio of Gross Profit to Sales in a retail business.

(*b*) A retailer sells only three types of commodity which should give him, respectively, Gross Profit ratios of 22½ per cent, 20 per cent, and 17½ per cent on sales, i.e. an average of 20 per cent.

On preparing a Trading Account at the end of his latest financial year, he finds that the ratio of Gross Profit to sales is only 18 per cent.

You are asked to give three possible circumstances, any of which would account for the apparent shortage as compared with the expected result, and explain why each would operate to reduce the ratio.

(*R.S.A.—Adapted*)

No. 3. On preparing the Trading Account of T. Weave, a retailer, for the financial year ended March 31st, 19.., it was found that the ratio of Gross Profit to sales was 15 per cent, whereas for the previous financial year the corresponding ratio had been 25 per cent. State, with your reasons, whether or not the following may have contributed to cause the decline:

(*a*) The stock at March 31st, 19.., was under-valued.

(*b*) The cost of a new delivery van had been included in the purchases for the year ended March 31st, 19.., and charged to Trading Account.

(*c*) The sales for the year ended March 31st, 19.., showed a decline compared with the previous year.

(*d*) In both years T. Weave and his family had been supplied with goods from the shop but the value of these goods had not been recorded in the books of the business.

(*e*) The stock at March 31st, 19.., included a number of items which were soiled and at this stock-taking had been written down in value by one-half of their cost.

No. 4. H. Anderson is a wholesale dealer in British and imported toys. His Trial Balance on June 30th, 19.., was as follows:

	Dr.	Cr.
Capital at Start		22,000·00
Motor Vehicles	9,500·00	
Balance at Bank	3,100·00	
Drawings	2,400·00	
Motor Vehicles Expenses	840·00	
Rates	1,000·00	
Warehouse Wages	3,750·00	
Fixtures and Fittings	3,250·00	
Purchases (Dr.) and Sales (Cr.)	94,900·00	120,830·00
Cash in Hand	650·00	
Carriage Outwards	730·00	
Returns Outwards		875·00
Stock at Start	9,325·00	
General Wages and Salaries	8,325·00	
Carriage and Freight Inwards	1,105·00	
Discounts Allowed	380·00	
Discounts Received		610·00
General Expenses	895·00	
Customs Duty on Imported Purchases	945·00	
Returns Inwards	830·00	
Insurance	115·00	
Debtors (Dr.) and Creditors (Cr.)	9,000·00	8,300·00
Bad Debts	75·00	
Rent	1,500·00	
	152,615·00	152,615·00

Taking note of the facts that Anderson's unsold stock at June 30th, 19.., was valued at 9,150·00, and that the item 'warehouse wages' should be dealt with in the Trading Account, you are required:

(*a*) To choose from the above figures those that would appear in Anderson's Trading Account for the year ended June 30th, 19.., and to draw up this account.

(*b*) To express the Gross Profit as a percentage (correct to 1 decimal place) of the cost price of goods sold.

(*c*) To state the amount of Anderson's turnover for the year.

(*d*) To express the Gross Profit as a percentage of this turnover.

NOTE: *No Profit or Loss Account or Balance Sheet is required.*

(*R.S.A.—Adapted*)

(6) The Net Profit Percentage

The Net Profit is the clear profit left after the office and selling expenses have been deducted from the Gross Profit. If we wish to check on the efficiency of the office and sales sides of our business, the ratio that gives us a clear picture of the trends shown is the Net Profit Percentage. This is found by the formula:

$$Net\ Profit\ Percentage = \frac{Net\ Profit}{Turnover} \times 100$$

Consider Fig. 182, a Profit and Loss Account which follows from the Trading Account, Fig. 181.

PROFIT AND LOSS ACCOUNT
(for year ending December 31st, 19..)

To Salaries	1,450·00	By Gross Profit	12,000·00
„ Light and Heat	1,300·00	„ Commission Received	1,180·00
„ Insurance	850·00	„ Rent Received	250·00
„ Advertising	2,400·00		
„ Depreciation	450·00		13,430·00
„ Bad Debts	650·00		
	7,100·00		
„ Net Profit	6,330·00		
	13,430·00		13,430·00

Fig. 182. A Profit and Loss Account

The Net Profit Percentage here is calculated as follows:

$$Net\ Profit\ Percentage = \frac{6,330}{27,500} \times 100$$
$$= \frac{1,266}{55}$$
$$= 23\cdot0\%$$

Once again we would expect the Net Profit Percentage to be constant, that is to remain roughly the same from year to year providing we always prepare our Profit and Loss Account in the same way. It follows that any significant change in Net Profit Percentage, say 2 per cent or more, would be investigated to discover the cause.

Suppose that last year the Net Profit Percentage was 26·5 per cent and this year it has fallen to 23 per cent. This is a significant fall and we must find the reason.

What Can Have Caused a Fall in the Net Profit Percentage?

If the Gross Profit Percentage is steady, but the Net Profit Percentage has fallen the fault must lie in the expenses or profits shown on the Profit and Loss Account. We should examine each expense item carefully, working out an **Expense Ratio to Turnover**, for this year and the previous year. This is quite simple and involves a calculation:

$$\frac{Expense}{Turnover} \times 100$$

So for Salaries it would be:

$$\frac{Salaries}{Turnover} \times 100$$

$$= \frac{1,450}{27,500} \times 100$$

$$= \frac{58}{11}$$

$$= 5\cdot3\%$$

By comparing this with the similar figure for the previous year we may discover some increase in expense. Perhaps the manager has taken on more staff than are really necessary? Similar expense ratios may reveal other causes of the change. Perhaps the advertising has been excessive? An increased advertising budget did not yield proportionately higher sales. Perhaps insurance rates have risen, and have not been passed on to the consumer in higher prices? The profits on the credit side may show some falling off from the previous year. Have we received less commission than previously, or less rent? These will also affect Net Profit Percentage.

When we discover the cause of the fall in Net Profit Percentage we must take the necessary action to correct the profitability of the business. This means we must reduce the expenses that are soaring, or increase the receipts that have been declining. If such action is impossible, we must pass the increased cost on to the final consumer.

Interim Final Accounts

Some firms find the annual check-up on Gross Profit and Net Profit Percentage too long a period to wait before correcting undesirable trends. The quicker we can discover adverse variations, the quicker we can take steps to put them right. For this reason many firms prepare interim Final Accounts, say at three-monthly intervals. A quick check every three months on Gross and Net Profit Percentages keeps management and staff informed of the dynamic trends of the business.

EXERCISES SET XLVI

(7) Gross and Net Profit Percentages

No. 1. In making a comparison between two successive years of his business, N. Peters notices the following matters:

	Year 1	Year 2
Turnover	65,000·00	75,000·00
Gross Profit	15,900·00	17,560·00
Net Profit	3,800·00	9,600·00

Present these two sets of results in such a way as to make a comparison, and state any conclusions you can draw.

No. 2. At January 1st, 19.., D. Dickinson valued his stock in hand at 3,925·00. For the ensuing year he made the following estimates: Sales 12,500·00; Returns inwards 500·00; Carriage inwards 275·00; Manufacturing wages 2,200·00; Purchases 5,500·00. Dickinson's Gross Profit ratio on all his sales was 17½ per cent.

(*a*) Prepare Dickinson's Estimated Trading Account, showing the value of his stock at December 31st, 19...

(*b*) To what amount must Dickinson limit his revenue expenditure to ensure at least a 10 per cent return on his capital of 6,000·00?

(*R.S.A.—Adapted*)

No. 3. T. is proposing to set up in business as a retailer and is negotiating for a shop, the rent of which is 450·00 per annum and rates 375·00 per annum. He expects that he will need to employ an assistant at a wage of 8·00 per week, and that the incidental expenses of the business will be 50·00 per annum. The rate of Gross Profit he expects is 25 per cent on sales (before deducting expenses or wages). Assuming that T. will make a Net Profit of 1,000·00 and that at the end of the year he will have a stock of 500·00, draft a *pro-forma* Trading and Profit and Loss Account for the first year.

(*R.S.A.—Adapted*)

No. 4. The statement below summarizes the trading results of B. Barnaby, a wholesaler, for the year ended December 31st, 19..:

Sales (*less* returns)		20,000·00
Less Cost of Goods Sold		12,000·00
Gross Profit		8,000·00
Less Assistants' Wages	4,200·00	
„ Other Expenses	2,500·00	
		6,700·00
Net Profit for the year		1,300·00

During the next year Barnaby hopes to expand his business, and estimates that he will be able to increase his sales to 30,000·00, maintaining the rate of Gross Profit.

To handle the additional trade, he expects to have to employ two more assistants costing 550·00 each in wages. Of his total expenses those costing 800·00 would not increase, but he estimates that the others would increase in proportion to the increase in sales.

Prepare for B. Barnaby a statement, similar in form to the summary given above, showing the estimated results for the next year.

(*R.S.A.—Adapted*)

No. 5. Two friends, Guppy and Jobling, are engaged in preliminary discussions with a view to setting up in business as retailers. It is agreed that Net Profits and Losses are to be shared between them in the ratio of two-thirds to Guppy and one-third to Jobling. They further estimate that:

(*a*) The Net Profit for the first year will be sufficient for Jobling to get 500·00 as his share of it.

(*b*) Rent, assistants' wages, and other expenses will amount to 1,800·00 for the first year.

(*c*) The ratio of Gross Profit will be 20 per cent of the sales.

(*d*) The stock at the end of the first year will be 1,500·00.

You are asked to show (giving your calculations):

(*a*) The value of sales necessary to produce the required Net Profit.

(*b*) The amount of purchases for the year.

(*R.S.A.—Adapted*)

No. 6. For the trading year ended December 31st, 19.., the figures in a merchant's Trading Account are: Stocks, January 1st, 4,355·00, and December 31st, 1,365·00; Sales 80,405·00; Purchases 47,330·00; Returns inwards 405·00; Returns outwards 320·00. In his Profit and Loss Account the summarized net debits for general, administrative, and distributive expenses are 20,000·00.

(*a*) You are required:

(i) To draw up the merchant's abridged Trading and Profit and Loss Account for the year ended December 31st, 19...

(ii) To state the cost price of the goods sold.

(iii) To state the amount of the merchant's turnover for the year.

(iv) To state the percentage rate of *Gross Profit* on cost.

(v) To state the percentage rate of *Gross Profit* on turnover.

(vi) To state the percentage rate of *Net Profit* on turnover.

(*b*) On the assumption that during the following year turnover will increase by 25 per cent, that the percentage rate of Gross Profit will remain unchanged, and that overhead charges (i.e. general, administrative, and distributive expenses) will increase by 4 per cent for every increase of 10,000·00 in turnover over the 19.. figure, you are required to draw up an estimated Trading and Profit and Loss Account for the year ended December 31st of the next year.

(*R.S.A.—Adapted*)

No. 7. A firm has two branches selling exactly the same range of goods; one in Sheffield, the other in Manchester. The following figures are drawn from the records of these branches:

		Year 1	Year 2
Gross Profits	Sheffield	27,000·00	29,000·00
	Manchester	84,000·00	80,000·00
Net Profits	Sheffield	18,000·00	19,300·00
	Manchester	37,000·00	42,000·00
Turnover	Sheffield	108,000·00	116,000·00
	Manchester	252,000·00	200,000·00

You are asked to draw up the Gross Profit Percentage and Net Profit Percentage for each branch for the two years and hence criticize their performances and those of their managers. The Trading and Profit and Loss Accounts may be assumed to have been prepared in a consistent manner.

No. 8. In making a comparison between two successive years of trading F. Taylor, a trader, has the following information:

	Year 1	Year 2
Turnover	46,000·00	54,000·00
Gross Profit	15,180·00	16,200·00
Net Profit	5,520·00	6,760·00

Present these results in such a way as to make a comparison between the two years and state the conclusions you draw from the comparison.

(London University 'O' Level—Adapted)

No. 9. What conclusions do you draw from the following statements relating to the accounts of W. Ames, a sole trader, after the books have been closed and the Final Accounts prepared?

(*a*) F. James's Account in the Sales Ledger has a debit balance.
(*b*) The Capital Account has a debit balance.
(*c*) There is a credit balance on the Rates Account.
(*d*) There is a debit balance on the Packing Materials Account.
(*e*) There is a debit balance on the Insurance Account.
(*f*) The Bank Account in the Cash Book has a credit balance.
(*g*) There is a debit balance on the Advertising Account.

No. 10. What conclusions do you draw from the following information about R. Lord's business?

(*a*) R. Coombe's Account in the Purchases Ledger has a credit balance.
(*b*) T. Low's Account in the Sales Ledger also has a credit balance.
(*c*) There is a debit balance on the Advertising Account on January 1st, the first day of his financial year.
(*d*) There is a credit balance on the Rent Account on the same day.
(*e*) The Bank Account in the Cash Book has a credit balance.

(8) Turnover and Rate of Turnover, or Rate of Stock Turnover

We have already defined turnover as the net sales of a business, i.e. *sales less returns.* Another figure that can easily be confused with turnover is the **Rate of Turnover**, sometimes called the **Rate of Stock**

Turnover. This is quite a different idea from turnover, but it is a most important concept which every student should understand.

Stock turnover is a very important thing, because it is at the point where stock turns over that the profits are made. We say that stock has turned over when it has been sold and replaced with new stock. In Chapter One we learned about **circulating assets**, which revolve from stock to debtors to cash and back to new stock again. Every revolution of this circle yields a profit. If we want to double our profits, one way is to double the rate of stock turnover.

The rate of stock turnover is always expressed as a number. To say that the rate of stock turn is six means that the stock turns over six times in a year. Is this a good rate of stock turn? Or is it a poor rate of stock turn? We can't possibly say until we know the product we are discussing. If a grocer turned over his stock of eggs six times a year they would be in stock for an average of two months each. This hardly makes them new-laid eggs by the time they are consumed. On the other hand, grand pianos tend to be a slow-moving line and do not deteriorate if kept in stock two months. Some classes of goods are very 'perishable', like newspapers, which must be turned over every day if they are to be sold at all.

Calculating the Rate of Stock Turnover

Two formulae which give the same answer are:

$$1.\ Rate\ of\ Stock\ Turn = \frac{Cost\ of\ Stock\ Sold}{Average\ Stock\ at\ Cost\ Price}$$

$$2.\ Rate\ of\ Stock\ Turn = \frac{Net\ Turnover}{Average\ Stock\ at\ Sales\ Price}$$

Use formula 1 for the moment. If you find the average stock, and divide it into the amount of stock sold at cost price, you will find out how often the stock turns over in each trading period.

The average stock is found by taking opening stock + closing stock and dividing by two. If quarterly stock figures are available we can add up the four quarterly figures and divide by four.

Using the Trading Account of Fig. 181 we find that the average stock comes out to 1,725.

$$\frac{1,450 + 2,000}{2} = \frac{3,450}{2} = 1,725$$

As the cost of stock sold is 13,000 it follows that

$$Rate\ of\ Stock\ Turn = \frac{13,000}{1,725}$$

$$= \frac{520}{69}$$

$$= 7\cdot5\ times\ per\ year$$

Whether this is a good rate of stock turnover we cannot say, but it means that goods are in stock for roughly seven weeks on average. For some classes of goods this might be a good rate of stock turn. For fresh fish, or spring flowers, it would hardly do.

EXERCISES SET XLVII

(9) Rate of Stock Turnover

No. 1. A trader carries an average stock valued at cost price, of 2,000·00 and turns this over five times per year. If he marks his stock up by 25 per cent on cost price, what is his Gross Profit for the year?

No. 2. A trader carries an average stock valued at cost price of 6,250·00 and turns this over four times a year. If his mark-up is 20 per cent on cost, and his overheads came to 2,800·00, what is the Net Profit for the year?

No. 3. A retailer carries an average stock valued at cost price of 600·00. His rate of stock turn is 150, his average profit is 10 per cent on cost, and his overheads and running expenses come to 6,500·00. What is his Net Profit for the year?

No. 4. H.J. is in business as a retailer and during the year ended December 31st, 19.., the average value of his stock at cost price was 8,000·00. He turned this over four times, at an average mark-up of 25 per cent. His fixed expenses were 3,000·00 and his variable expenses 10 per cent of the turnover. Calculate H.J.'s profit or loss for the year. If he had turned over his stock only three times during the year, by how much would his profit or loss have been affected?

(R.S.A.—Adapted)

No. 5. L.P. & Co. Ltd. are a firm of wholesalers. Their average stock is valued at 12,000·00 at cost, and is turned over four times in each trading year at an average mark-up of 50 per cent on cost. The firm's fixed, or standing, charges are 8,000·00 and their variable expenses are 20 per cent of the turn-over. Calculate (*a*) the firm's profit for the year, and (*b*) the profit if the stock is turned over five times in a year. What conclusion would you draw from the difference in the amount of profit?

(R.S.A.—Adapted)

No. 6. During the year 19.., J. W. Hardman made a Gross Profit of 25 per cent on a turnover of 21,600·00 and a Net Profit of 12 per cent on turn-over. His rate of turnover of stock for the year was 10.

For the following year Hardman estimates that he can increase his rate of turnover of stock to 14, while carrying the same average stock, by reducing his prices by 5 per cent on selling price. If he does this, his ratio of expenses to turnover will be reduced by 2 per cent.

Calculate:

(*a*) Hardman's Gross Profit for 19...
(*b*) Hardman's Expenses for 19...
(*c*) Hardman's Net Profit for 19...

and then calculate to the nearest 1·00:

> (*d*) Hardman's estimated Sales for the following year.
> (*e*) Hardman's estimated Gross Profit for the following year.
> (*f*) Hardman's estimated Expenses for the following year.
> (*g*) Hardman's estimated Net Profit for the following year.
>
> (*London University 'O' Level—Adapted*)

No. 7. During 19. . Harper made a Gross Profit of 20 per cent on sales. His total turnover was 42,000·00. His Net Profit was 12½ per cent on turnover, and his rate of stock turn was 6.

During the next year Harper estimates that he can increase his rate of stock turn to 10, while carrying the same average stock, if he reduces his prices by 10 per cent, and this should also bring him a reduction in expenses of 2½ per cent on turnover.

Calculate:

> (*a*) Gross Profit for 19. . .
> (*b*) Net Profit for 19. . .
> (*c*) Expenses for 19. . .

and then calculate, to the nearest 1·00, for the following year:

> (*d*) His estimated Sales.
> (*e*) His estimated Gross Profit.
> (*f*) His estimated Expenses.
> (*g*) His estimated Net Profit.

Would it be worth his while to carry out this policy?

No. 8. The following details relate to J.B.'s business for the year ended December 31st, 19. . :

Sales	33,984·00
Sales Returns and Allowances	380·00
Stock (January 1st, 19. .) valued at cost price	1,378·00
Stock (December 31st, 19. .) valued at cost price	1,814·00
Gross Profit for the year	8,068·00

Calculate:

> (*a*) The turnover for the year.
> (*b*) The cost of goods sold during the year.
> (*c*) The amount of purchases for the year.
> (*d*) The rate of turnover of stock for the year.
> (*e*) The percentage of Gross Profit to turnover (to nearest whole number).

(10) Terminology Used in the Interpretation of the Balance Sheet

Balance Sheets are not always well presented and the first task of any investor wishing to decide whether a business is sound or not is to arrange the Balance Sheet in good style. Good style for a Balance Sheet involves grouping the assets in the way shown in Chapter One of this book, either in the *Order of Liquidity* or the *Order of Permanence*. The groups are as shown in the following example, so that we bring out clearly the Current Assets, Fixed Assets, Current Liabilities, Long-term Liabilities, and Capital or Net Worth.

For the purpose of recapitulation these groups are defined as:

Current Assets. Those assets which are held in the business with a view to their conversion into cash in the ordinary course of the firm's profit-making activities.

Fixed Assets. Those assets which are retained in the firm for use by the proprietor and his employees, because they permanently increase the profit-making capacity of the business.

Current Liabilities. Those liabilities which will fall due for payment fairly quickly, and certainly within less than one year.

Long-term Liabilities. Those liabilities which will not fall due immediately, but which will gradually be repaid over an agreed period greater than one year.

Capital. The Net Worth of the business to the owner of the business; that portion of the owner's wealth which he has invested in the business either originally or by leaving past profits to accumulate in the service of the firm.

Fig. 183 shows a typical Balance Sheet which will serve as a basis for discussion.

M. ERASMUS

BALANCE SHEET

(as at December 31st, 19..)

CAPITAL			FIXED ASSETS		
At Start	24,000·00		Premises	7,400·00	
Add Net			Plant and		
Profit	4,500·00		Machinery	14,000·00	
Less			Motor Vehicles	3,800·00	
Drawings	6,000·00				
		−1,500·00			25,200·00
		22,500·00	CURRENT ASSETS		
			Stock	8,898·00	
LONG-TERM LIABILITIES			Debtors	3,704·00	
Bank Loan		10,000·00	Bank Moneys	650·00	
CURRENT LIABILITIES			Cash in Hand	48·00	
Creditors		6,000·00			
					13,300·00
		38,500·00			38,500·00

Fig. 183. A Balance Sheet

By careful consideration of this Balance Sheet the reader may learn more phrases which are commonly used in business to help in the interpretation of Final Accounts. A mastery of these terms enables an investor to make sound judgements about the business whose affairs are being considered.

The new terms are:

(*a*) **Fixed Capital.** This is capital tied up in fixed assets, and in the case of M. Erasmus the fixed capital is 25,200·00. The significance of fixed capital is that it is sunk into the business and cannot be regained without seriously affecting the conduct of the business. If Erasmus tries to realize this fixed capital by selling motor vehicles or plant and machinery, the distribution or production of the firm's products will be hampered. If he tries to sell the premises he will be out in the street.

(*b*) **Floating Capital** or **Circulating Capital.** This is capital tied up in current assets, which can be realized more easily and without interfering with the conduct of the business; indeed that is what we are in business for—to turn over stock and make profits as the stock turns into cash.

(*c*) **Liquid Capital.** The term 'liquid' in economic matters means 'in cash form'. The liquid capital is that portion of the assets that are available as cash, or near cash. In this case it is 4402·00, the total of cash, bank moneys and debtors.

(*d*) **Working Capital.** This is the most important of these four terms— one of the most vital concepts in business. It is that portion of the capital invested in the business which is left to run the business *after providing the fixed capital*. Once a firm has bought its premises, plant and machinery, etc., it still needs working capital to run the business, to pay wages and sundry expenses. One might really say that having expended all the capital expenditure one still needs funds for revenue expenditure. The 13,300·00 that Erasmus has left after paying for his fixed assets is clearly something to do with working capital, but the real way to find working capital is as follows:

$$Working\ Capital = Current\ Assets - Current\ Liabilities$$
$$= 13,300·00 - 6,000·00$$
$$= 7,300·00$$

A firm should never allow itself to run short of working capital. This is a very common reason for failure in business. If you allow your firm to buy too many fixed assets (called **over-capitalization**), then you are forced to borrow from the bank to find your working capital and this will probably cost you 2 per cent more than Minimum Lending Rate, say 8 or 9 per cent interest. This means that the bank is creaming off most of your profits, and in fairly competitive trades this may leave you unable to earn a fair reward for yourself. A wise investor never buys shares in a firm that is short of working capital.

What is a reasonably safe working capital? It is generally agreed that 1:1 is a minimum working capital ratio, that is, the ratio of current assets to current liabilities. This is found by:

$$Working\ Capital\ Ratio = \frac{Current\ Assets}{Current\ Liabilities}$$

and in this case comes to
$$\frac{13,300}{6,000} = 2\cdot2 \text{ times}$$

This is perfectly satisfactory. So important is the working capital figure considered to be that many Limited Companies publish their Balance Sheets with the current liabilities taken over and deducted from the assets side. This is illustrated in the section on Company Accounts, page 369.

Here is another ratio: the liquid capital ratio or **acid test ratio.**
$$Liquid\ Capital\ Ratio = \frac{Current\ Assets - Stock}{Current\ Liabilities}$$
$$= \frac{4,402}{6,000} = 0\cdot73 \text{ times}$$

The name 'acid-test ratio' is used to show that this is the critical test of solvency. Can the firm, with its present cash and debtors (due to pay within the month) meet its current liabilities (due for payment within the month)?

This is very interesting because it shows how weak this firm is as far as liquid assets go. Most of its current assets are stock.

(*e*) **External Liabilities.** These are the liabilities owed to persons outside the business, and that means both current liabilities and long-term liabilities, in this case 16,000·00.

(*f*) **Capital Owned.** This is the Net Worth of the business, the value of the business to the owner of the business. In this case it is 22,500·00.

(*g*) **Capital Employed.** This is a very important figure. It is the total capital being used in the business, no matter to whom it belongs. Clearly this business is worth 38,500·00, because it has that many assets. Who has provided the capital to buy 38,500·00-worth of assets? The owner, Erasmus, has provided 22,500·00, but he is also employing the bank's money, 10,000·00 and his creditors' money 6,000·00, making 38,500·00 in all.

Unfortunately this is not the correct figure for capital employed, because if we can claim that Erasmus is using his creditors' capital it must also be true that Erasmus's debtors are using Erasmus's money for their own business. We therefore have:

Capital Employed = Total Value of Assets Less Debtors

(11) Appraising a Balance Sheet

We are now ready to discuss the Balance Sheet. Is the business whose Balance Sheet we are considering in a healthy state or an unhealthy state?

Is Erasmus solvent? This means can he pay his debts, or at any rate such debts as are likely to be presented to him in the near future? The answer is that he has 6,000·00 of such debts likely to be presented to him and he has 13,300·00 of current assets. He will therefore probably be able to pay his debts as they fall due, but there is just a little worry over liquidity. He should really sell some of that stock to improve his liquidity position. He i s solvent; the business is reasonably reliable.

Is he overtrading? Overtrading is a term used to describe a situation where the trader is tending to run short of working capital. He has over-capitalized, bought too many fixed items and left himself short of cash for revenue expenses. Here again Erasmus is just a little shaky. That stock figure is the worry, but he is probably safe enough. That bank loan is a long-term liability so that it isn't likely to be repaid in less than three years. If we say that 3,300·00 of it is due this year then that makes 9,300 Erasmus might have to pay back this year. He has 13,300 to do it with, providing he can sell that stock all right?

What was the return on Capital Invested? The capital invested by Erasmus on January 1st was 24,000·00. This earned him 4,500·00 in profits.

$$The\ Return\ on\ Capital\ Invested = \frac{4,500}{24,000} \times 100$$
$$= 18·75\%$$

This was a very satisfactory return. If Erasmus had invested in the ordinary type of savings account he would scarcely have got more than 6 per cent. It was certainly worth while being in business.

Conclusion. Erasmus should watch events closely. He should not buy any more fixed assets at present, but should do his utmost to improve the liquidity position of his business by (*a*) increasing sales, (*b*) restricting drawings. 6,000·00 of drawings last year was too much—he is living beyond his means, and probably this explains the slight weakness in the business.

EXERCISES SET XLVIII

(12) Balance Sheet Interpretation, and General Questions on the Interpretation of Final Accounts

No. 1. Here is F. Clement's Balance Sheet. You are to answer the questions below (with calculations if needed).

BALANCE SHEET
(as at December 31st, 19. .)

CURRENT LIABILITIES			CURRENT ASSETS		
Creditors		3,000·00	Cash	24·00	
LONG-TERM LIABILITIES			Bank	326·00	
Bank Loan		5,000·00	Debtors	1,850·00	
CAPITAL			Stock	4,450·00	
At Start	12,000·00				
Less Drawings	3,000·00				6,650·00
	————		FIXED ASSETS		
	9,000·00		Motor Vehicles	1,400·00	
Add Net Profit	2,250·00		Plant and Machinery	7,200·00	
	————		Premises	4,000·00	
		11,250·00		————	
					12,600·00
		————			————
		19,250·00			19,250·00

(*a*) What is the capital owned by the proprietor?
(*b*) What is the capital employed in the business?
(*c*) What is the working capital?
(*d*) Express the profit as a percentage of the capital invested by the proprietor.

(East Anglian Examination Board—Adapted)

No. 2. Castle and Cary are in partnership as retail traders, and the following is their Balance Sheet:

BALANCE SHEET
(as at December 31st, 19..)

LIABILITIES		ASSETS	
Capital:		Premises	7,500·00
Castle	2,500·00	Transport Vehicles, *less*	
Cary	2,000·00	Depreciation	1,200·00
Current Account: Castle	750·00	Fixtures and Fittings, *less*	
Loan, secured by mortgage		Depreciation	850·00
of Premises	4,000·00	Stock	1,400·00
Sundry Creditors	2,850·50	Sundry Debtors	150·50
Expenses Due, but not yet		Bank Balance on Current	
paid	100·00	Account	875·00
		Current Account: Cary	
		(overdrawn)	225·00
	12,200·50		12,200·50

You are required to state:

(*a*) The amount of the capital owned by the partnership.
(*b*) The total capital employed in the business.
(*c*) Whether the business has sufficient working capital.

For (*a*) and (*b*) the basis of your calculations should be stated; for (*c*) your reasons should be given; both very briefly.

(R.S.A.—Adapted)

No. 3. (*a*) From the following details find D. Jones's capital and show his Balance Sheet at March 31st, 19..:

Debtors 4,374·00; Stock 3,586·00; Creditors 2,472·00; Loan from K. Hind 3,000·00; Accrued expenses 74·00; Motor vans 1,340·00; Furniture and fittings 1,500·00; Premises 8,000·00; Payments in advance 124·00; Bank overdraft 2,000·00; Cash in hand 48·00.

(*b*) In relation to your completed Balance Sheet answer the following questions:

(i) What is the total of fixed assets?
(ii) How would you find the working capital, and what is its amount?
(iii) Was Jones solvent or insolvent? Give your reasons.

(R.S.A.—Adapted)

No. 4. The following Trial Balance was extracted from the partnership books of Grouse and Moor after the Trading and Profit and Loss Account for the year had been prepared.

TRIAL BALANCE

(as at December 31st, 19. .)

Profit and Loss Account (net profit)		2,010·00
Cash in Hand	15·25	
Balance at Bank	830·75	
Trade Debtors and Creditors	933·00	516·50
Provision for Bad Debts		78·00
Insurance Prepaid	24·25	
Rent Owing		40·75
Furniture, Fittings, and Equipment (cost 1,200·00)	880·00	
Stock-in-Trade	2,640·00	
Motor Van	480·00	
Loan (Grouse)		600·00
Capital Accounts (January 1st):		
Grouse		2,378·00
Moor		1,410·00
Drawings Accounts:		
Grouse	710·00	
Moor	520·00	
	7,033·25	7,033·25

NOTES: (1) The motor van had been purchased for 600·00 on January 1st, 19...

(2) Grouse's loan—made for the purchase of the van—bears interest at 5 per cent per annum, and this has not been provided for.

(3) Moor is entitled to be credited with a partnership salary of 500·00.

(4) The partners share profits and losses in the proportions: Grouse, three-quarters; Moor, one-quarter.

(*a*) From the above information, prepare the Profit and Loss Appropriation Account and the Balance Sheet of the partnership.

(*b*) State the amount of:

(i) The current assets.
(ii) The fixed assets.
(iii) The liquid assets.
(iv) The current liabilities.
(v) The working capital.

(*R.S.A.—Adapted*)

No. 5. From the following balances prepare the Balance Sheet of B. Hopeful as at December 31st, 19..:

Trade Debtors	1,200·00
Insurance Paid in Advance	40·00
Stock at December 31st, 19..	4,625·00
Wages Outstanding	85·00
Trade Creditors	3,720·00

Profit and Loss Account to December 31st, 19..	Dr.	240·00
Bank Overdraft		1,250·00
Motor Van at Cost *less* Depreciation		800·00
Premises at Cost		2.500·00
B. Hopeful's Capital	Cr.	5,000·00

Drawings Account	650·00

Comment briefly on the financial position disclosed by the Balance Sheet.

(R.S.A.—Adapted)

No. 6. Given below in abridged form is the Balance Sheet of C. Cantone:

C. CANTONE

BALANCE SHEET

(as at March 1st, 19..)

Creditors	1,890·00	Cash	20·00
Capital Account	2,355·00	Debtors	625·00
		Stock	2,100·00
		Machinery	1,500·00
	4,245·00		4,245·00

The following transactions took place on March 2nd, 19..:

(*a*) Cantone receives a loan of 500·00 which he used to pay 200·00 to a creditor and 300·00 for the purchase of new machinery.

(*b*) A debtor pays 120·00 on account.

(*c*) Cantone purchases on credit goods for resale (stock) costing 75·00.

(*d*) Old machinery is sold for 100·00 in cash; the book value was 250·00.

(*e*) It is decided to correct the valuation of stock on March 1st, 19.., reducing it by 320·00.

(*f*) Goods were sold on credit for 190·00 (cost price 145·00).

Show Cantone's Balance Sheet as it would appear on March 2nd, 19.., after the transactions, as noted, had been recorded.

(R.S.A.—Adapted)

No. 7. The following is the Balance Sheet of Dee and Jaye, who share profits and losses equally:

DEE AND JAYE

BALANCE SHEET

(as at March 31st, 19. .)

Capital:		Freehold Premises	2,500·00
Dee	2,000·00	Machinery	1,200·00
Jaye	1,500·00	Stock-in-Trade	1,500·00
Loan on Mortgage	1,800·00	Debtors	900·00
Trade Creditors	1,300·00	Cash at Bank and In Hand	500·00
	6,600·00		6,600·00

(*a*) From the above you are asked to state, showing your calculations, the amount of (i) the current assets, and (ii) the working capital of the partnership.

(*b*) Suppose that the value of the stock at March 31st, 19. ., had been 1,200·00 and the freehold premises had been written up, as the result of a revaluation, to 3,000·00, state the effect on the amount of working capital and on the Capital Accounts of Dee and Jaye respectively.

(R.S.A.—Adapted)

No. 8. State what you understand by the term 'working capital' and say how you would ascertain the working capital of A. Bunn (a sole trader) from his Balance Sheet.

Giving your reasons, indicate whether or not the following transactions would tend to increase or decrease Bunn's working capital:

(*a*) Bunn receives a loan for business purposes repayable at the end of five years.

(*b*) A delivery truck, no longer required, is sold.

(*c*) 150·00 is paid for goods purchased for resale.

(*d*) 30·00 is received from a trade debtor.

(*e*) An old machine is replaced by an up-to-date model at a cost of 300·00.

(R.S.A.—Adapted)

No. 9.

(*a*) The following statement, which is incomplete, sets out information regarding the position, at a particular date, of five different businesses identified in the statement as A, B, C, D and E. Copy it and insert the missing amount in each case.

	Liabilities	Capital	Assets	Deficiency
A	231·00		420·00	
B		7,310·00	12,830·00	
C	1,942·00	5,617·00		
D	9,715·00			1,234·00
E			8,162·00	418·00

(*b*) What book-keeping terms are used to indicate the following?

(i) Assets held not for resale but merely to increase the profit-earning capacity of the business.

(ii) Loans to the business of a semi-permanent nature.

(iii) Debts falling due to be settled by the business in the immediate future.

(iv) Assets which fluctuate in the ordinary course of trading.

Which of the above items would you use in determining the amount of the working capital?

(R.S.A.—Adapted)

No. 10. Each of the following transactions of a sole trader affects either the Balance Sheet only, or the Trading and Profit and Loss Account only, or, in some cases, both:

(*a*) The trader settles an account for 100·00 due to a creditor, by sending the creditor a cheque for 97·10, the balance being allowed as discount.

(*b*) The trader withdraws 60·00 from his Business Account at the bank for his personal expenses.

(*c*) A debtor's account for 25·00 is irrecoverable and written off as a bad debt.

(*d*) A second-hand motor van, costing 425·00 and standing in the books at that figure, is sold on credit for exactly that sum.

(*e*) A debtor, who owes 50·00 settles his indebtedness in full, by cheque.

(*f*) At the close of the trading year an entry is passed for Bank Charges, 9·75.

(*g*) The trader moves into new premises, which he rents. In consequence, his old premises, which he owned freehold and which stand in the books at 6,500·00, are sold for 7,000·00, which is paid into bank.

You are required to write down the words 'Balance Sheet' or 'Profit and Loss Account', as may be appropriate, against each of the items (*a*) to (*g*). If in your judgement the correct answer should be 'both', write 'both'.

No. 11. Give the effect of each of the following transactions on the capital of a business, stating exactly by how much the capital would be increased or decreased. If you think there would be no change write 'none'.

(*a*) A sale of goods on credit for 200·00, their purchase price having been 165·00.

(*b*) The cash purchase of a motor vehicle for 750·00.

(*c*) The payment of an insurance premium, 35·00.

(*d*) The increase of a Provision for Bad Debts from 200·00 to 250·00.

(*e*) The receipt of 95·00 from a debtor.

No. 12. From a trader's Final Accounts for the year his Net Profit was 3,750·00, but he had made the following errors:

(*a*) Fixtures and fittings had been over-depreciated by 100·00.

(*b*) Of the amount charged to his Profit and Loss Account for insurance, 50·00 represented a prepayment for the following year.

(*c*) 25·00 interest allowed on his Bank Deposit Account had been left out of his calculations.

(*d*) Bank Charges, 10·00, had similarly been omitted.

(*e*) 50·00, the debit balance of a hopelessly insolvent customer, had been left out of his Bad Debts Account.

(*f*) Final stock had been over-valued by 150·00.

(*g*) 250·00 rent for the final quarter, had been neither paid nor allowed for in his Profit and Loss Account.

Considering each of the above items entirely separately from the others, write down against (*a*) to (*g*) the corrected amount of the Net Profit as altered from the original 3,750·00.

CHAPTER TWENTY-SEVEN

DEPARTMENTAL ACCOUNTS

(1) Introduction

Where a business has several departments, the proprietor, as explained in Chapter Twelve, may prefer to take out Departmental Trading and Profit and Loss Accounts, which throw up the profitability of each department as well as the profitability of the whole business. Even a firm with only two departments, which is making profits as a whole, might find that one department was running at a loss while the other department was making all the profit. If a firm has ten or more departments the chance is increased that one of them is not contributing to the profits. It is a basic principle of modern accounts that every section or department must contribute in a reasonable way to the profits of the enterprise, or be closed down.

(2) Departmental Accounts—The Basic Figures

In order to prepare departmental accounts we must have the basic figures that we need in departmental form. This will involve having Departmental Purchases Day Books and Sales Day Books, Departmental Returns Books and Departmental Expense Accounts.

This might seem a big reorganization of the book-keeping arrangements, but if a system is decided upon and then strictly adhered to it will cost very little more in the way of new rulings of paper, etc., and the figures available will give the proprietor a much clearer view of his business.

Consider some of the basic figures for the Final Accounts in a firm which has two Departments, A and B. The Stock Account will be recording the opening stock at the start of the year and the closing stock at the end of the year. To provide the necessary figures all we need do at stock-taking is to calculate the stocks for each department and then record them in a Stock Account that has extra columns ruled on it, as shown in Fig. 184.

STOCK ACCOUNT L. 137

19..		Dept. A	Dept. B	Total
Jan. 1	To Opening Stock	1,762·50	1,665·75	3,428·25

Fig. 184. A Departmental Stock Account

345

Fig. 185. Departmental Trading and Profit and Loss Accounts
(for year ending December 31st, 19..)

Particulars	Dept. A	Dept. B	Total	Particulars	Dept. A	Dept. B	Total
19.. Dec. 31 To Opening Stock	4,360·00	2,240·00	6,600·00	19.. Dec. 31 By Sales	29,206·50	27,384·25	56,590·75
" Purchases	14,162·00	13,236·00	27,398·00	*Less* Returns	42·50	284·25	326·75
Add Carriage In	48·50	24·25	72·75		29,164·00	27,100·00	56,264·00
	14,210·50	13,260·25	27,470·75				
Less Returns Out	10·50	160·25	170·75				
	14,200·00	13,100·00	27,300·00				
Total Stock Available	18,560·00	15,340·00	33,900·00				
Less Closing Stock	2,560·00	1,340·00	3,900·00				
	16,000·00	14,000·00	30,000·00				
To Wages	2,000·00	7,000·00	9,000·00				
Cost of Sales	18,000·00	21,000·00	39,000·00				
To Gross Profit	11,164·00	6,100·00	17,264·00				
	29,164·00	27,100·00	56,264·00				

Particulars	Dept. A	Dept. B	Total	Particulars	Dept. A	Dept. B	Total
19.. Dec. 31 To Light and Heat	140·00	120·00	260·00	19.. Dec. 31 By Gross Profit	11,164·00	6,100·00	17,264·00
" Salaries	980·00	740·00	1,720·00	" Commission Received	24·50	11·50	36·00
" Office Stationery	115·00	85·00	200·00				
" Sundry Expenses	79·50	70·50	150·00				
	1,314·50	1,015·50	2,330·00				
" Net Profit	9,874·00	5,096·00	14,970·00				
	11,188·50	6,111·50	17,300·00		11,188·50	6,111·50	17,300·00

Similarly the Purchases Account and the Sales Account will be ruled up to show both the departmental and total Purchases and Sales.

Expenses of the business would need to be allocated either directly to the departments or in some fair way. For instance, with wages we can allocate the wages of the workers in Department A to be charged against that department, and similarly for the wages of workers in Department B. Where the expense is not directly separable into two parts in this way, we must adopt some agreed policy. For instance, rates are often apportioned according to the floor space occupied by each department, and advertising costs might be allocated in proportion to their turnover.

(3) A Set of Departmental Final Accounts

Once the basic figures are available, a set of Departmental Accounts is exactly the same as ordinary Final Accounts. In Fig. 185 the student will see that the layout has not changed except that extra columns are used and the proprietor can now see clearly how much of the profit is being contributed by each department.

EXERCISES SET XLIX

(4) Departmental Accounts

No. 1. Prepare a Departmental Trading Account from the following, so that the Gross Profit is discovered on each department and on the business as a whole:

	Dept. A	Dept. B
Opening Stocks	2,760·50	3,820·50
Purchases	14,250·75	26,380·50
Sales	29,204·25	42,000·50
Carriage In	106·50	102·70
Returns In	260·25	360·75
Returns Out	420·50	240·75
Closing Stock	1,800·50	1,500·75
Wages	2,000·00	3,000·00

No. 2. Prepare a Departmental Trading Account and a Departmental Profit and Loss Account from the following information:

	Dept. A	Dept. B
Opening Stocks	2,400·50	3,400·65
Purchases	14,260·75	17,000·75
Sales	29,890·75	43,050·80
Returns Out	240·50	380·10
Returns In	160·25	220·95
Closing Stocks	2,800·20	2,160·75
Salaries	400·65	650·45
Wages	2,400·75	2,900·25
Light and Heat for Office	40·45	60·65
Sundry Expenses	240·80	640·35

No. 3. (*a*) W. Wellesley manufactures two products, 'Junior' and 'Senior'. From the following information prepare a Departmental Trading Account for the year ending December 31st, 19..:

	Junior	Senior
Stocks of Raw Materials at December 31st	1,100·00	795·00
Stocks of Raw Materials at January 1st	1,000·00	900·00
Purchases of Raw Materials	3,500·00	2,700·00
Carriage Inwards	120·00	95·00
Wages	2,800·00	3,100·00
Allowances Received in Respect of Defective Raw Materials	20·00	50·00

Wellesley's sales during the period were: 4,200 'Juniors' at 2·00 each, and 1,120 'Seniors' at 5·00 each.

(*b*) What advice would you give Wellesley on the future conduct of his business?

(*R.S.A.—Adapted*)

No. 4. A. New and J. Castle are in partnership in a retail business dealing in groceries and fruit, and the balances on the books of the firm at December 31st, 19.., are:

	Dr.	Cr.
Capital Account:		
New		8,000·00
Castle		4,000·00
Drawings Account:		
New	1,200·00	
Castle	800·00	
Fixtures and Fittings	714·00	
Bank Balance	3,740·75	
Sales:		
Groceries		32,496·75
Fruit		9,738·75
Light, Heat, and General Expenses	2,608·25	
Purchases:		
Groceries	24,284·50	
Fruit	3,876·50	
Carriage Inwards: Groceries only	237·50	
Discounts Received		188·50
Wages (Dealt with in Profit and Loss Account)	7,870·50	
Rent	1,000·75	
Debtors:		
Groceries	4,523·00	
Fruit	820·00	
Creditors:		
Groceries		2,600·00
Fruit		1,010·00
Stocks at January 1st, 19..:		
Groceries	5,224·00	
Fruit	374·00	
Bad Debts	50·25	
Carriage Outwards	310·00	
Rates	400·00	
	58,034·00	58,034·00

Prepare Departmental Trading Accounts and the General Profit and Loss Account for the year ending December 31st, 19.., and Balance Sheet at that date, taking into consideration the following:

(*a*) The values of the stocks at December 31st, 19.., were: groceries 5,678·00, fruit 510·00.

(*b*) A provision of 45·00 for further bad debts is required.

(*c*) Fixtures and fittings are to be depreciated at the rate of 12½ per cent per annum on the cost 816·00.

(*d*) An account for the supply of electricity to December 31st, 19.., amounting to 26·00 was received after the completion of the Trial Balance.

(*e*) The partnership agreement provides for interest on the partners' Capital Accounts (which are fixed) but not on drawings, at the rate of 5 per cent per annum, and for the balance of profit to be divided equally between New and Castle.

No. 5. A business is to be carried on in two departments, A and B. From the Trial Balance given below prepare Trading and Profit and Loss Accounts in departmental form so as to bring out clearly the profit on each department as well as on the business as a whole. Where not specifically given, expenses are to be allocated to the departments in the same ratio as their sales.

TRIAL BALANCE
(as at December 31st, 19..)

	Dr.	Cr.
Cash at Bank	1,034·50	
Capital		10,000·00
Goodwill	2,500·00	
Debtors	6,715·50	
Creditors		4,851·50
Stock:		
Department A	4,400·00	
Department B	3,000·00	
Purchases:		
Department A	5,260·00	
Department B	4,800·00	
Salaries	1,250·00	
Sales:		
Department A		9,600·00
Department B		6,400·00
Rents, Rates, and Insurance	465·00	
Water and Electricity	106·00	
Discounts	86·50	
Stationery	159·00	
Carriage In	35·50	
Carriage Out	850·00	
Telephone Expenses	49·00	
Telephone Receipts		8·50
General Expenses	149·00	
	30,860·00	30,860·00

Value of Closing Stock December 31st, Department A: 3,850·50; Department B: 3,975·50.

CHAPTER TWENTY-EIGHT

MANUFACTURING ACCOUNTS

(1) Introduction

A manufacturer does not buy goods to sell again, but buys raw materials which he processes to yield some more sophisticated product. He then sells the finished goods at such a price as to yield him a profit on the total enterprise. Such manufacturing processes may be very long and complicated, requiring skilled scientists and engineers to control them, and the accounts recording the expenditure and apportioning costs are fairly complex too.

In *Book-keeping Made Simple* we cannot go over the entire field of Manufacturing Accounts and Costing Accounts, but we can take a first look at them. First we must consider some of the important terms used in this type of accounting.

(2) The Vocabulary of Manufacturing Accounts

(a) *Stocks and Work in Progress.* Since a manufacturer buys raw materials and makes them up into finished goods, he must, at any stock-taking time, have stocks of both raw materials and finished goods in hand. In addition he is bound to have a stock of items which are neither in the raw material state, nor the finished goods state. Such partly-finished goods are called **Work in Progress**. The book-keeper must therefore expect to have three classes of Opening Stock and three classes of Closing Stock:

   (i) Stock of raw materials.
   (ii) Stock of work in progress or partly finished goods.
   (iii) Stock of finished goods.

Naturally, like all Closing Stocks, these three classes of stock will appear on the Balance Sheet as assets of the business. Like all stocks it is essential to value them as fairly as possible. This is straightforward with stocks of raw materials and stocks of finished goods. With stocks of partly finished goods it is a little more difficult. Some firms value them at Prime Cost, but the more usual method is to value them at Factory Cost. Some explanation of these terms is given below in section (d). For a factory cost valuation you add in a share of the overhead costs to the prime costs already expended on the Work in Progress.

(b) *Variable (or Direct) Expenses.* In Manufacturing Accounts there is an important distinction of expenses into two groups. The first group is called **Variable Expenses**, or **Direct Expenses**. Both these words are applied to the type of expense that alters in relation to the volume of output of the factory. To take a particular example—a furniture factory. The raw materials are wood, cloth, plastic, or latex foam and an assortment of metal fixing materials, nuts, bolts, etc.

Suppose we double the output of furniture; would we expect to use double the wood, double the cloth, double the number of bolts? Clearly, we *would* expect to do so; the amount used of these materials would vary with output, and 'raw materials' is therefore a Variable Expense. 'Direct Expense' refers to expenses which are attributable to a particular product, rather than to the business as a whole. Raw materials are direct expenses, rent and rates are not.

Another Variable Expense is the wages of the operators. If we double our output, would we expect to pay more wages? We certainly would if the workers were on 'piece work', and even if they were paid by the hour we would need to pay overtime or take on more workers to get a larger volume of production through the factory.

The commonest Variable Expenses, or Direct Expenses, are therefore:

(i) Raw materials.
(ii) Labour costs—wages.

There are a number of doubtful cases, for instance Depreciation on Machines. Is it Variable, or is it an Overhead expense? It is up to the accountant to lay down how he will treat it for his own system of book-keeping.

(c) *Overhead (Invariable, or Indirect) Expenses.* Overhead Expenses are expenses that do not necessarily vary with output. If we double the output of our factory we shall not have to pay double the rent, or double the rates. We shall not need to redecorate twice as often, or to employ two General Managers. Such expenses are **fixed**, at least in the short run. The phrase 'overhead costs' refers to this type of expense precisely because these costs have to be borne, irrespective of the actual output of the factory. Even if the factory shuts down production altogether it will still be necessary to pay the rent, and the salaries of top executives. These are not involved directly with the product, but form the overhead framework of the enterprise, which must be established before production can begin.

The chief overhead costs are:

   (i) Rent, rates, and insurance.
   (ii) Salaries of administrative staff.
   (iii) Repairs and depreciation of machines, etc.
   (iv) Office expenses of all kinds, connected with the manufacturing side of the business.

(d) *Prime Costs and Overhead Costs.* In preparing a Manufacturing Account we usually prepare it in two sections, a **Prime Cost Section** and a **Cost of Manufactured Goods Section**. 'Prime Cost' means first cost, and refers to the Variable, or Direct, Expenses. The phrase 'Cost of Manufactured Goods' refers in addition to the second set of costs, the Overhead, or Invariable, or Indirect, or Fixed Costs. Four names for the same costs—all the terms are widely used.

(3) The Preparation of Manufacturing Accounts

When preparing the final accounts of a manufacturing business, the accountant would need to produce the following accounts:

(*a*) A Manufacturing Account in two parts, the Prime Cost Section and the Cost of Manufactured Goods Section.
(*b*) A Trading Account.
(*c*) A Profit and Loss Account.
(*d*) In the case of partnerships or limited companies an Appropriation Section of the Profit and Loss Account.
(*e*) A Final Balance Sheet.

This makes a lengthy piece of work, most of which the student can do already. It is not necessary to take a whole Trial Balance, but only the matter that is needed for the Manufacturing and Trading Accounts. The Profit and Loss Account, etc., are no different from usual.

There are two ways of preparing these accounts:

(*a*) Disregarding the profit on manufacture, the profits all appearing in the Trading Account as Gross Profits.
(*b*) So as to bring out a profit on manufacture.

The example given below is dealt with under method (*a*) and later is treated under method (*b*) to show how the Manufacturing Profit can be obtained if desired.

Example 1. T. Jones is a manufacturer. Prepare his Manufacturing Account and Trading Account for year ending December 31st, 19... He does *not* extract a Manufacturing Profit but leaves all profits to accumulate as Gross Profit in the Trading Account.

Stocks at January 1st, 19..:	
Raw Materials	2,400·50
Work in Progress (valued at Factory Cost)	3,800·75
Finished Goods	7,200·25
Purchases of Raw Materials	28,750·00
Sales	66,300·00
Returns In	300·50
Factory:	
Wages (variable)	7,800·50
Power (fixed)	600·50
Salaries (fixed)	2,800·00
Rent and Rates (fixed)	300·00
Factory:	
Lighting (fixed)	400·75
Repairs (fixed)	1,600·25
Depreciation (fixed)	2,300·00
Warehouse:	
Wages	3,600·50
Rates	600·00
Stocks at December 31st, 19..:	
Raw Materials	2,800·50
Work in Progress (valued at Factory Cost)	6,000·25
Finished Goods	3,000·50

Method (a). The Manufacturing Account is prepared first, as shown in Figs. 186 and 187, with its two sections: the Prime Cost section and the Cost of Manufactured Goods section. Points worth noting are:

(i) *Raw Materials.* This is similar to the opening of a normal Trading Account, with the Opening Stock, Purchases less Returns and Closing Stock. If there is any Carriage In or Duty on Imported Purchases they would go in the usual place, added to the purchases figure before deducting returns.

(ii) *Labour and other Prime Costs.* These are now added to the cost of materials used, to give us the total Prime Costs of the goods produced.

(iii) *Cost of Manufactured Goods Section.* In this section we add the Overheads to the Prime Costs and also adjust for the Work in Progress. We thus get the total Cost of Manufactured Goods. This is carried to the Trading Account.

(iv) *Work in Progress.* This simply consists of an Opening Stock, which has all been pushed through the manufacturing process at the start of the year, and a Closing Stock which has not gone through, but is in suspense until the next year begins. The effect can be either a positive or negative one. If the opening figure is greater than the closing figure it means that more Work in Progress was pushed through the manufacturing process at the start of the year than has been held back at the end of the year. This results is an increased cost of materials used.

In this example the closing figure was larger than the opening figure, so that the extra balance, 2,199·50, has to be deducted from the factory costs, since this amount of extra partly finished goods is being held back and will not now become finished goods until next year.

(v) *The Trading Account.* This is exactly the same as the ordinary Trading Account except that there are no purchases, since the manufacturer does not purchase any goods to sell, he manufactures them. Instead of a purchases figure we have the Cost of Manufactured Goods figure, coming from the Manufacturing Account. The Gross Profit is then calculated in the usual way.

T. JONES

MANUFACTURING ACCOUNT

(for year ending December 31st, 19. .)

PRIME COST SECTION

RAW MATERIALS			By Prime Costs (carried to	
To Stock at Start		2,400·50	Cost of Manufactured	
To Purchases	28,750·00		Goods Section)	36,150·50
Less Returns	—			
		28,750·00		
		31,150·50		
Less Closing Stock		2,800·50		
Cost of Raw Materials used		28,350·00		
LABOUR				
Wages		7,800·50		
		36,150·50		36,150·50

COST OF MANUFACTURED GOODS SECTION

To Prime Costs		36,150·50	By Cost of Manufactured	
OVERHEADS			Goods (transferred to	
To Power	600·50		Trading Account)	41,952·50
„ Salaries	2,800·00			
„ Rent and Rates	300·00			
„ Lighting	400·75			
„ Repairs	1,600·25			
„ Depreciation	2,300·00			
		8,001·50		
		44,152·00		
WORK IN PROGRESS				
To Stock at Start	3,800·75			
Less Closing Stock	6,000·25			
		−2,199·50		
		41,952·50		41,952·50

Fig. 186. A Manufacturing Account

TRADING ACCOUNT

(for year ending December 31st, 19. .)

To Opening Stock of Finished Goods	7,200·25	By Sales		66,300·00
		Less Returns In		300·50
To Cost of Manufactured Goods	41,952·50	Net Turnover		65,999·50
	49,152·75			
Less Closing Stock	3,000·50			
Cost of Stock Sold	46,152·25			
To Warehouse Wages	3,600·50			
„ Warehouse Rates	600·00			
	4,200·50			
Cost of Sales	50,352·75			
Gross Profit	15,646·75			
	65,999·50			65,999·50

PROFIT AND LOSS ACCOUNT

(for year ending December 31st, 19. .)

By Gross Profit	15,646·75

Fig. 187. A Manufacturer's Trading Account, etc.

(4) Taking Manufacturing Profit into Account

The type of Manufacturing Account shown in the last section has one disadvantage. It does not reveal how profitable the factory was, compared with other factories. For instance, the Cost of Manufactured Goods was 41,952·50. Suppose we made 20,000 articles for this money, and that these articles could have been purchased from another manufacturer for 50,000·00? Was it worth while running the factory? Yes, because we made the goods for 8,047·50 less than the price for which we could have bought them.

On the other hand, supposing we could have bought them from someone else for 35,000·00? In that case we might as well close down the factory, and leave the manufacturing to our more efficient competitor. We are losing 6,952·50 by trying to make them in our own inefficient way.

How can we bring out the extent of the Manufacturing Profit, or Loss? It is very simple. All we need do is to transfer the goods manufactured not at cost price to the Trading Account but at **Current Market Price**. Suppose the Current Market Price is 50,000·00, as suggested above? The second half of our Manufacturing Account, and

the Trading Account and the Profit and Loss Account will now read
as follows:

COST OF MANUFACTURED GOODS SECTION

To Prime Costs	36,150·50	By Market Value of	
OVERHEADS		Manufactured Goods	50,000·00
To Power	600·50		
„ Salaries	2,800·00		
„ Rent and Rates	300·00		
„ Lighting	400·75		
„ Repairs	1,600·25		
„ Depreciation	2,300·00		
	8,001·50		
	44,152·00		
WORK IN PROGRESS			
To Stock at Start	3,800·75		
Less Closing Stock	6,000·25		
	− 2,199·50		
To Cost of Manufactured			
Goods	41,952·50		
„ Manufacturing Profit	8,047·50		
	50,000·00		50,000·00

TRADING ACCOUNT

(for year ended December 31st, 19. .)

To Opening Stock of		By Sales	66,300·00
Finished Goods	7,200·25	*Less* Returns In	300·50
To Market Value of			
Manufactured Goods	50,000·00	Net Turnover	65,999·50
	57,200·25		
Less Closing Stock	3,000·50		
Cost of Goods sold	54,199·75		
To Warehouse			
Wages	3,600·50		
„ Warehouse			
Rates	600·00		
	4,200·50		
	58,400·25		
Gross Profit	7,599·25		
	65,999·50		65,999·50

PROFIT AND LOSS ACCOUNT

(for year ending December 31st, 19. .)

	By Manufacturing Profit	8,047·50
	„ Gross Profit	7,599·25

Fig. 188. Bringing out the Manufacturing Profit

Notice that the profit still comes to 15,646·75, but it has now been divided into the two components: the profit on manufacture and the profit on trading.

Where should Work in Progress appear?

If Work in Progress is valued at prime cost only it should appear as an adjustment in the Prime Cost section of the Manufacturing Account. If it is valued at factory cost it should appear, as in Fig. 186, as an adjustment to the Cost of Manufactured Goods section of the Manufacturing Account.

EXERCISES SET L

(5) Manufacturing Accounts

No. 1. F. Wayman is a manufacturer. From the following information prepare his Manufacturing Account and Trading Account, and open his Profit and Loss Account for the year ended December 31st, 19..:

Sales	34,690·00
Stocks at January 1st, 19..:	
Raw Materials	510·00
Work in Progress (valued at Factory Cost)	810·00
Finished Goods	3,120·00
Purchases of Raw Materials	5,298·50
Stocks at December 31st, 19..:	
Raw Materials	490·50
Work in Progress (valued at Factory Cost)	670·75
Finished Goods	2,980·25
Factory:	
Wages Paid	14,340·50
Wages Due at December 31st, 19..	150·00
Factory and Machinery Maintenance	520·00
Depreciation on Plant and Machinery	1,140·00
Factory Power (not a Prime Cost)	490·75
Factory Salaries	1,830·00
Factory Expenses:	
Rent, Rates, and Insurance	570·50
Lighting and Heating	72·25

(University of London 'O' Level—Adapted)

No. 2. **T.** Jones is a manufacturer. Prepare his Manufacturing Account and Trading Account. He does *not* extract a manufacturing profit but leaves all profits to accumulate as Gross Profits in the Trading Account. Carry down the gross profit to open the Profit and Loss Account.

Stocks at January 1st, 19..:

Raw Materials	1,850·50
Work in Progress (at Factory Cost)	3,250·50
Finished Goods	6,800·75
Purchases of Raw Materials	27,500·45

Sales	66,295·75
Returns In	255·75
Factory:	
Wages (variable)	7,860·00
Power (fixed)	660·00

Salaries (fixed)	2,899·00
Rent and Rates (fixed)	300·00
Factory:	
Lighting (fixed)	350·75
Repairs (fixed)	1,550·50
Depreciation (fixed)	2,225·50

Warehouse:	
Wages	3,660·00
Rates	660·00

Stocks at December 31st:

Raw Materials	2,550·00
Work in Progress (at Factory Cost)	5,500·75
Finished Goods	2,326·55

No. 3. L. Langton is a manufacturer of children's toys. It is his custom to work out a Manufacturing Account which tells him (*a*) the Prime Cost, and (*b*) the Cost of Manufactured Goods. He then transfers these goods to the Trading Account not at the cost price, but at the price it would cost him to buy them on the market. This price gives him a Manufacturing Profit before he works out a Gross Profit on the Trading Account. Prepare his Manufacturing and Trading Account for the year ended December 31st, 19.., and carry the respective profits to the Profit and Loss Account.

Stocks at Start:	
Raw materials	2,040·00
Work in Progress (at Factory Cost)	3,240·50
Finished Goods	12,480·50
Purchases of Raw materials	21,192·75
Sales of Finished Goods	138,760·50
Stocks at Close of Year:	
Raw Materials	1,960·00
Work in Progress (at Factory Cost)	2,680·50
Finished Goods	11,920·50
Factory:	
Wages Paid	57,360·75
Wages Due at End of Year	600·25
Factory and Machine Repairs	2,000·00
Depreciation of Plant and Machinery	4,640·00
Power for Machines	1,960·50
Factory:	
Salaries	7,320·75
Rent, Rates, and Insurance	2,280·50
Light and Heat	288·50
Warehouse Wages and other costs	4,720·50

The value of the manufactured goods on the market is considered to be 110,000·00.

No. 4. R. Lawson is a manufacturer of household utensils. It is usual for him to work out a Manufacturing Account in the usual two sections, Prime Cost section and Cost of Manufactured Goods section. He then 'sells' the articles made at current market value to the Trading Account, thus taking a separate Manufacturing Profit. Prepare his Manufacturing Account and Trading Account for 19.. and open his Profit and Loss Account, given these figures:

Stocks at January 1st:	
Raw Materials	2,800·65
Work in Progress	3,600·55
Finished Goods	13,000·35
Purchases of Raw Materials	22,000·50
Sales of Finished Goods	148,200·50
Stocks at December 31st:	
Raw Materials	2,300·35
Work in Progress	3,100·55
Finished Goods	12,000·65
Factory Wages Paid	54,000·50
Repairs to Machines	1,800·00
Depreciation on Machines	3,600·00
Power for Factory	1,400·00
Depreciation of Patent Rights	250·00
Factory Salaries	6,000·00
Warehouse Rates	800·50
Factory Rates	2,200·50
Warehouse Wages	3,500·50
Warehouse Salaries	1,000·50

The value of the manufactured goods on the open market at trade price was 128,500·00.

No. 5. M. Leman is a manufacturer. Every year he does the usual type of Manufacturing Account and Trading Account but he charges the Trading Account with the costs of the manufactured goods at *market price*. Prepare his Manufacturing Account, Trading Account, and begin his Profit and Loss Account.

Stocks at January 1st, 19..:	
Raw Materials	2,000·00
Work in Progress (at Factory Cost)	5,000·00
Finished Goods	3,000·00

Stocks at December 31st, 19..:	
Raw Materials	1,650·50
Work in Progress (at Factory Cost)	2,500·50
Finished Goods	2,800·50
Purchases	18,000·75
Sales	42,000·50
Returns In	2,000·50

Factory:	
Wages	7,000·25
Power	600·75
Depreciation	2,300·00
Salaries	2,000·00
Rent and Rates	1,800·00

Warehouse Wages	3,000·75

Market price of manufactured goods estimated at 33,500·00.

No. 6. From the following figures prepare a Manufacturing Account and Trading Account in such a way as to show (*a*) the cost of raw materials used, (*b*) the prime cost, (*c*) the total cost of manufacture and the manufacturing profit, (*d*) the cost of goods sold, and (*e*) the cost of sales and Gross Profit. Carry both profits to the Profit and Loss Account.

Stocks at January 1st, 19..:	
Raw Materials	11,600·00
Work in Progress (at Factory Cost)	3,850·50
Finished Goods	5,250·50
Stocks at December 31st, 19..:	
Raw Materials	8,800·75
Work in Progress (at Factory Cost)	4,250·25
Finished Goods	4,600·50
Purchases of Raw Materials	32,500·75
Factory:	
Wages (Prime)	12,800·75
Wages (Indirect)	2,560·25
Carriage In on Raw Materials	225·25
Power	3,000·00
Rent and Rates of Factory	1,300·00
Depreciation of Machinery	600·00
Warehouse:	
Expenses	1,400·50
Wages	2,300·50
Factory Expenses	1,650·50
Sales during Year	82,650·75

The trade price of manufactured goods charged to Trading Account was estimated at 65,000·50.

CHAPTER TWENTY-NINE

THE ACCOUNTS OF LIMITED COMPANIES

(1) Introduction—What is a Limited Company?

A Limited Liability Company is a type of business organization authorized by Act of Parliament, whose capital is contributed by members who are accorded the privilege of Limited Liability. This means that they are liable for the debts of the company to the extent of the shareholding that they have contributed, or have agreed to contribute. Beyond that sum they are not liable for the company's debts.

The Limited Company is the only practicable way of collecting the vast sums of capital required for the complex industrial projects of the modern world, at a time when taxation is high. High taxation is a feature of most national finances these days, because the services supplied by governments are so far-reaching and expensive. If you tax people heavily it is natural to tax the rich more than the poor; and if you tax the rich heavily you cannot collect capital from them for industrial purposes. Even if there were no taxation at all it seems likely that no single rich family could afford to run the giant enterprises that we need today to take full advantage of mass-production methods. We have to rely instead on collecting small sums from a multitude of shareholders. These shareholders can have little voice in the conduct of the company's affairs, and it would be unfair to hold them liable for the actions of directors whom they are unable to control. In the early years of the industrialization of Great Britain such shareholders were considered partners in the firm, and were held fully liable for the firm's debts. The bankruptcies of some of the early railway companies resulted in many poor persons being arrested for debt, and their homes and property being sold to pay the debts of the firms concerned. This was obviously unfair, and the Limited Liability Company solved the problem by limiting the shareholders' losses to the amount of money they had actually contributed, or promised to contribute.

The result of this is that persons who deal with a Limited Liability Company on credit, supplying it with goods or services, run a certain risk; they may never be paid. Every person who engages in trade with a company ought to know he is running such a risk, and for this reason the word Limited must appear as the last word of the name of the firm. It is a warning to all: this firm has Limited Liability. Many people think a Limited Company is safer and more reliable to deal with than a Sole Trader or Partnership, but this is not necessarily so. A few basic points about the accounts of Limited Companies are dealt with in the next section.

(2) Special Features of Company Accounts

There are many features of company accounts which the advanced student needs to know, particularly as the requirements of the law become more onerous each year. For British students the requirements of the Companies Act, 1948, as amended by the Acts of 1967 and 1976, are important. Other students should discover their own law on the matter. It is not within the scope of *Book-keeping Made Simple* to make a full study of these accounting requirements, but students who wish to consider them in detail should consult published copies of the Acts themselves, especially the second schedule of the 1967 Act. However, the following points are important and give a basic introduction to the subject.

(a) *The Capital of a Limited Company.* The capital that a public company may invite the public to subscribe is authorized by the Registrar. It is a requirement of Schedule 2 of the Company Act of 1967 that the amount so authorized must be stated on the Balance Sheet even though it has not yet been collected from the members. The capital is subscribed by investors who become shareholders. They may be private persons or institutional investors. These are organizations which collect funds from small savers for a variety of reasons, and invest it in industrial and commercial firms. The commonest examples are banks, insurance companies, unit trusts and trade unions.

The shares which shareholders hold may be of about a dozen different types of which the most common are **Ordinary Shares** and **Preference Shares**. Ordinary Shares are often called **Equity Shares** because they divide up the available profits equally among the shareholders, according to the size of their shareholding. They are also called **Risk Shares**, since they suffer the losses of the company equally fairly. Preference Shares, as their name implies, have a preferential right to some reasonable level of profit. At the time of writing this is about 7 per cent, but it varies with the supply of, and demand for, available funds. When the Preference Shareholders have had their 7 per cent profit the Ordinary Shareholders divide up the rest of the profits equally. Preference Shareholders usually have a prior right to the refund of their capital should the company get into difficulties, but this is not always so. Where it is so, it is clear that the Preference Shares are less risky than Equities.

(b) *Loans to a Company.* Where a company borrows money from people other than the shareholders who are actually taking an active interest in its affairs by becoming members, it does so by means of a bond called a **Debenture**. A Debenture is a loan to a company secured on the assets of the firm. There are two main kinds, **Fixed Debentures** and **Floating Debentures**. Fixed Debentures are secured on the fixed assets, and if the interest is not paid regularly, the Debenture holders may seize the fixed assets and sell them to regain their money. This naturally winds up the company. A Floating Debenture is secured on the circulating assets of the company, chiefly the stock, which can be seized if the interest is not paid.

(c) *Investing in a Company—Who Buys What?* Consider the case of a timid, elderly lady with a few pounds to invest. Should she buy Ordinary Shares, Preference Shares, or Debentures? If she buys Ordinary Shares she runs the chance of losing her money, but she may get very good profits when the dividend is announced. If she buys Preference Shares she will earn a fixed rate, say 7 per cent interest, but she runs less risk of losing her money. If she buys Debentures she will be absolutely sure she will not lose her money, but she will earn a smaller rate of interest, say 6 per cent. She will probably choose the debentures.

(d) *The Final Accounts of a Limited Company*. Under the 1976 Companies Act every company must specify to the Registrar of Companies on a special form a date called an **accounting reference date**. This date will be the date at which an **accounting reference period** comes to an end. Final accounts for the period will then be prepared and submitted to the Registrar, and of course to the members. Accounts for public companies must be published. These published accounts differ from the accounts used for internal accounting so that the accountant must modify his ordinary accounts to comply with the regulations. A Manufacturing Account (for manufacturing companies), a Trading Account, a Profit and Loss Account, an Appropriation Account, and a Balance Sheet will be required in a full set of Final Accounts. At this stage students should observe the following points about the Appropriation Account and Balance Sheet.

(3) The Appropriation Account of a Limited Company

A company is in some ways like a very large partnership, except that the shareholders have limited liability. Each shareholder hopes to receive an appropriation of profit, but the directors will decide this, and not even the Preference Shareholders can insist on being paid a dividend. The directors have the right to keep profits in reserve for a variety of purposes, and to be niggardly with their dividends—provided they are prepared to risk being dismissed at the Annual General Meeting of the shareholders.

One way in which the Appropriation Account of a company differs from the Appropriation Account of a partnership is that the shareholders cannot be given every last penny of the profits. If you have 27,213 shareholders and you make 10,000·00 profit, it is impossible to give away the last penny. You cannot divide the profit equally. There must always be a balance left over and carried down to next year. An

Appropriation Account for a company therefore usually starts with an opening balance on the credit side. Then the Net Profit is transferred from the Profit and Loss Account to the credit side, under the balance.

Here is a typical Appropriation Account for a Limited Company:

THE X CO. LTD.

APPROPRIATION ACCOUNT

(for year ended December 31st, 19..)

19..			19..			
Dec. 31	To Goodwill	500·00	Jan. 1	By Balance B/d		427·50
	„ Plant and Machinery Reserve	1,000·00	Dec. 31	„ Net Profit		17,256·75
	„ General Reserve	3,000·00				17,684·25
	„ Preference Dividend	2,000·00				
	„ Ordinary Dividend	8,000·00				
	„ Balance c/d	3,184·25				
		17,684·25				17,684·25
			19..			
			Jan. 1	By Balance B/d		3,184·25

Fig. 189. A Company's Appropriation Account

The Appropriation of the Profit

The directors here have followed a middle-of-the-road policy. They have put a good deal of the profit away as reserves, and have given a generous share of it as profits to the shareholder. Without knowing how many shareholders there are we cannot say how generous they have been.

First they have reduced the value of goodwill by 500·00. Goodwill was fully explained in Chapter Twenty-two and this is the same cautious reduction of an intangible asset whose value is not certain. Secondly, they have put away in Reserve 1,000·00 for plant and machinery, and 3,000·00 in the **General Reserve**. Remember that this only retains the profit in the business, but it may not be in cash form. If they want money to be available from a source outside the business they should use the Sinking Fund Method referred to in Chapter Fourteen, page 185.

The General Reserve is a reserve set aside for any purpose the directors may decide, but the chief one is the equalization of the dividend, as between good and bad years. It is a fact that shareholders who are paid fluctuating dividends get restless, because their expectations are disappointed in a bad year. A group of shareholders who are paid a 40 per cent dividend one year and a 2 per cent dividend the next year will be much more restive and unsettled than if they had been paid 20 per cent each year. In fact they have done better by the first method, but their natural feeling of disappointment the second year overrides a sensible appraisal of the results. If the directors create a General

Reserve from which the above-average profits of good years can be recouped to help the less-than-average profits of bad years, the shareholders will be spared this feeling of frustration.

Each of these debit entries in the Appropriation Account will be credited to the account named. The credit in the Goodwill Account reduces the value of this asset. The credit in each of the Reserve Accounts means that this is outstanding profit, which has been put away for the reasons stated, and may not be enjoyed by the shareholders this year. In many ways it is just like a Provision for Bad Debts. The distinction between *provisions* and *reserves* is explained carefully below. Finally the dividends will be credited in the Preference Share Dividend Account and the Ordinary Share Dividend Account. The Preference Dividend will have been paid on the last day of the year but the Ordinary Dividend will become a current liability to the shareholders. As the shareholders' **Dividend Warrants** are paid, the cash credited in the Cash Book will be debited to the Dividend Account.

The Difference between Provisions and Reserves

Both Provisions and Reserves are sums taken from the profits and put away where the owners or shareholders of a business cannot have them. They are both credit items, since they are like extra capital retained in the business and belonging to the proprietor.

A Provision is *a charge against the profits*, to provide for some anticipated loss the amount of which cannot be accurately determined. Provisions for Bad Debts and Provisions for Discounts are the two best known. Reserves are not a charge against the profits but an appropriation of profit. They may be **Reserves for Corporation Tax, Specific Reserves** like **Plant Replacement Reserve,** or **General Reserves** to equalize dividends from year to year or expand the enterprise. Apart from Tax Reserves these are voluntary decisions by the members to reduce dividends temporarily.

(4) The Balance Sheet of a Limited Company

Schedule 2 of the Companies Act 1967 lays down Parliament's rules for British companies with regard to the published Balance Sheet. The legislature rightly held that since companies appeal to the public for funds the published Balance Sheet should reveal as much information as possible to potential investors. The aim of a good book-keeper should be to produce a Balance Sheet giving as clear a picture of the affairs of the company as is possible, and many progressive firms go beyond the requirements of Schedule 2 of the Act. All the ideas outlined in this section have been suggested because they help present a really accurate picture of the position of any firm. The more important requirements of this section will be made clear in the following example, which is typical of the type of examination question set about Limited Company Accounts at the elementary level. (The one feature that is usually completely disregarded at this level is the requirement to show last year's figures as well, for comparison purposes.)

Example. After taking out the Trading and Profit and Loss Accounts at December 31st, 19.., the revised Trial Balance of Enterprise Ltd. is as follows:

	Dr.	Cr.
Cash	1,750·25	
Bank	19,250·00	
Stock at End of Year	27,500·00	
Balance from January 1st on Appropriation Account		894·50
Preliminary Expenses	1,000·00	
Net Profit for Year		26,106·50
Furniture and Fittings (cost 4,000·00)	2,500·00	
Patent Rights Owned (cost 2,000·00)	1,000·00	
Premium on Preference Shares		1,000·00
Ordinary Capital (authorized 100,000 shares of 1·00)		60,000·00
6% Preference Share Capital (authorized 40,000·00)		20,000·00
5½% Debentures of 100·00 each		10,000·00
General Reserve		20,000·00
Land and Buildings (at cost)	18,000·00	
Plant and Machinery (cost 20,000·00)	8,000·00	
Quoted Investments held (market value 34,750·00)	33,000·00	
Unquoted Trade Investments (valued by directors at 12,050·00)	12,000·00	
Motor Vehicles and Spares (cost 14,500·00)	12,999·00	
Debtors and Creditors	4,700·75	3,699·00
	141,700·00	141,700·00

You are to show the Appropriation Account and Balance Sheet after taking into account the following decisions of the Directors:

(*a*) A dividend of 6 per cent on the Preference Shares is to be paid.

(*b*) A dividend of 10 per cent is recommended on the Ordinary Shares.

(*c*) 4,000·00 is to be put to General Reserve Account.

(*d*) 250·00 to be written off Preliminary Expenses.

(*e*) 10,000·00 is to be appropriated as a Taxation Reserve.

A solution to this question is given in Fig. 190 and incorporates the main requirements of Schedule 2.

ENTERPRISE LTD.

APPROPRIATION ACCOUNT

(for year ending December 31st, 19..)

To Taxation Reserve	10,000·00	By Balance	894·50
„ Preliminary Expenses	250·00	„ Net Profit	26,106·50
„ Transfer to General Reserve	4,000·00		
„ Preference Dividend	1,200·00		
„ Ordinary Dividend	6,000·00		
„ Balance	5,551·00		
	27,001·00		27,001·00
		By Balance	4,351·00

BALANCE SHEET
(as at December 31st, 19. .)

ORDINARY SHAREHOLDERS' INTEREST IN THE CO.				FIXED ASSETS		
	Authorized	Issued				
Ordinary Shares of 1·00 fully paid	100,000·00	60,000·00		Land and Buildings (at cost)		18,000·00
				Plant and Machinery (at cost)	20,000·00	
RESERVES				*Less* Depreciation	12,000·00	
Capital Reserves						
Share Premium Account		1,000·00				8,000·00
Revenue Reserves				Furniture and Fittings (at cost)	4,000·00	
General Reserves (at start)	20,000·00			*Less* Depreciation	1,500·00	
Add New Appropriation	4,000·00					2,500·00
	24,000·00			Patent Rights Owned (at cost)	2,000·00	
Balance on Approp. Account	5,551·00			*Less* Depreciation	1,000·00	
		29,551·00				1,000·00
		90,551·00		Motor Vehicles (at cost)	14,500·00	
Less Fictitious Asset				*Less* Depreciation	1,501·00	
Prelim. Expenses (1,000·00— 250·00)		750·00				12,999·00
						42,499·00
Ordinary Shareholders' Equity		89,801·00				
				TRADE INVESTMENTS (valued by Directors at 12,050·00)		12,000·00
				CURRENT ASSETS		
				Other Investments (Market value 34,750·00)	33,000·00	
PREFERENCE SHAREHOLDERS' INTEREST IN THE COMPANY				Stock (at cost)	27,500·00	
	Authorized			Debtors	4,700·75	
Preference Shares of 1·00 fully paid	40,000·00	20,000·00		Bank (19,250·00— 1,200)	18,050·00	
				Cash in Hand	1,750·25	
DEBENTURES						85,001·00
5½% Debentures of 100·00 each		10,000·00		*Less*		
Reserve for Future Taxation		10,000·00		CURRENT LIABILITIES		
				Ordinary Dividend	6,000·00	
				Creditors	3,699·00	
					9,699·00	
				Net Working Capital		75,302·00
		129,801·00		Net Value of Assets		129,801·00

Fig. 190. The Appropriation Account and Balance Sheet of a Limited Company

In Fig. 191 (see page 372) the same Balance Sheet is reproduced in vertical style, so that this method of presentation may be followed.

The Accounting Requirements of the Companies Acts, 1948–76
(*Notes on the Balance Sheet of Enterprise Ltd.*)

The preparation of a full set of company final accounts is inappropriate for *Book-keeping Made Simple*. The following points will explain why the Balance Sheet of Enterprise Ltd. has been displayed in the ways shown on page 369 and page 372, either in accordance with Schedule 2 of the 1967 Act, or as an improvement upon those requirements. The very best companies are always ahead of Parliament in the efficient presentation of their affairs to shareholders.

Assets Side. Schedule 2 requires that Fixed Assets, Current Assets and assets that are neither fixed nor current shall be distinguished from one another. The value of any Fixed Asset shall be its cost, less the total depreciation to date. This is made easier if the method of accumulating depreciation in a separate account, as described in Chapter Fourteen, page 184, is adopted. In this example the assets have been listed in the order of permanence, less the depreciation to date. The chief advantage of the vertical-style balance sheet, shown in Fig. 191, is the improved presentation of the depreciation.

Patent Rights Owned is an asset which is less common than most. Where a firm buys Patent Rights it buys the right to use an invention for a number of years. It is a Fixed Asset whose benefit to the business lasts for the length that the Patent Right has to run, and it will therefore be depreciated rather like a lease.

Trade Investments are a special type of asset, required to be shown separately under Schedule 2. Their position is intermediate between Fixed Assets and Current Assets and is justified by their dual nature. Trade Investments are investments held by a company for the sake of controlling, or attempting to achieve control of, a subsidiary firm in the same line of business. For a variety of reasons firms may wish to gain control of other firms in the same line of business as themselves; to reduce competition, or to ensure supplies of vital components, or to market their goods in a particular area. Control of 51 per cent of the voting shares gives effective control of such subsidiaries. Rules about such holding companies are complex, but it is enough to realize that these investments can be sold like any other investment, so that they are, in a way, Current Assets. On the other hand, if sold, the parent company will lose control of the subsidiary, so that the assets are Fixed Assets. The position shown on the Balance Sheet reflects this dual feature of Trade Investments; they are assets which are neither fixed nor current. The phrase 'valued by the directors at 12,050·00' implies that these are unquoted investments. They cannot be dealt with on the Stock Exchange, probably because the subsidiary is a Private Limited Company, not a Public Limited Company. It is therefore impossible to say what the market value is. Schedule 2 requires that **Quoted Invest-**

ments be stated separately from **Unquoted Investments,** and that the market price, or directors' valuation, be shown either in the Balance Sheet or by way of a note.

The Current Assets are listed in the order of permanence, but the style of presentation here is in advance of the present legal requirements. The Current Liabilities have been brought over to the assets side of the Balance Sheet, and have been deducted from the Current Assets figure. The student who understands Working Capital will realize that this style enables us to find the Net Working Capital and actually state the amount of this Net Current Assets figure. This is a very good method of presentation, enabling the investor to see at a glance the Working Capital position.

One asset which is not shown on the assets side at all in this presentation is the **Fictitious Asset, Preliminary Expenses** which is taken over to the liabilities side and deducted from the Ordinary Shareholders' Interest in the company. Preliminary Expenses are expenses involved in setting up a Limited Company.

Liabilities Side

The Ordinary Shareholders' Interest in the Company. Here the presentation is in advance of the requirements of the Companies Acts, and conforms to the very best ideas of accountants. The important feature here is the clear distinction between the Ordinary Shareholders' Interest in the Company as distinct from the Preference Shareholders' Interest. So often on Company Balance Sheets the Ordinary and Preference Capitals are added together, and Capital and Revenue Reserves are shown below. This is not at all helpful, because it does not make clear who owns what. The presentation shown here is being adopted by most progressive companies. It makes absolutely clear that the Capital Reserves and Revenue Reserves belong to the Ordinary Shareholders and form part of their interest in the Company. Capital Reserves are profits made in an unusual way, for example in this Balance Sheet the Share Premium Account is a sum of capital contributed by the Preference Shareholders as a premium on entry to the company. By paying more than the face value of the shares the Preference Shareholders are compensating the Ordinary Shareholders for their efforts in building up the company. A Debenture Premium Account is similar. These Capital Reserves therefore belong to Ordinary Shareholders, not to the people who actually contributed the money. However such profits may not be withdrawn by the Ordinary Shareholders, they must be left in the business as permanent capital: sometimes they are issued as bonus shares to the Ordinary Shareholders. Other Capital Reserves are Profits Prior to Incorporation and Written-up appreciations on fixed assets like Revaluation of Premises Account.

Revenue Reserves are reserves set aside out of profits, like the General

ENTERPRISE LIMITED

BALANCE SHEET IN VERTICAL STYLE
(as at December 31st, 19..)

ORDINARY SHAREHOLDERS' INTEREST IN THE COMPANY

	Authorized	Issued
Ordinary Shares of 1·00 each, fully paid	100,000·00	60,000·00

RESERVES
Capital Reserves
  Share Premium Account   1,000·00
Revenue Reserves
  General Reserves (at start)   20,000·00
  Add New Appropriation   4,000·00

                                 24,000·00
  Balance on Appropriation Account   5,551·00
                                         29,551·00
                                                   30,551·00

                                                 90,551·00

Less Fictitious Asset
  Preliminary Expenses 1,000·00 — 250·00   750·00

    Ordinary Shareholders' Equity   89,801·00
PREFERENCE SHAREHOLDERS' INTEREST IN THE COMPANY

	Authorized	
6% Preference Shares of 1·00 each, fully paid	40,000·00	20,000·00

DEBENTURES
5½% Debentures of 100·00 each   10,000·00
Reserve for Future Taxation   10,000·00

                                           129,801·00

REPRESENTED BY

FIXED ASSETS	COST	*Less* DEPRECIATION TO DATE	VALUATION
Land and Buildings	18,000·00	—	18,000·00
Plant and Machinery	20,000·00	12,000·00	8,000·00
Furniture and Fittings	4,000·00	1,500·00	2,500·00
Patent Rights Owned	2,000·00	1,000·00	1,000·00
Motor Vehicles	14,500·00	1,501·00	12,999·00
			42,499·00
TRADE INVESTMENTS (valued by Directors at 12,050·00)			12,000·00

CURRENT ASSETS

Other Investments (Market Value 34,750·00)		33,000·00	
Stock	27,500·00	27,500·00	
Debtors		4,700·75	
Cash at Bank (19,250 — 1,200·00)		18,050·00	
Cash in Hand		1,750·25	
		85,001·00	

Less
CURRENT LIABILITIES

Ordinary dividend	6,000·00		
Creditors	3,699·00		
		9,699·00	

                      Net Working Capital   75,302·00

                      Net Value of Assets   129,801·00

Fig. 191. A Vertical Style Balance Sheet

Reserve used for equalizing dividend over good and bad years. Such reserves may be taken out and distributed to the Ordinary Shareholders. Why do such reserves still belong to the Ordinary Shareholders only? Because the Preference Shareholders never leave any profits in the firm but always take their full fixed dividend out and enjoy it. It follows that the Ordinary Shareholders' interest in the Company includes all the reserves.

Fictitious Assets. We can now see that the 60,000 Ordinary Shares in Enterprise Ltd. are worth 90,551·00. But there is one point further to consider. One of the assets is a Fictitious Asset—Preliminary Expenses. These are the legal expenses incurred in floating a company. We spent money on them but what we got for the money was just permission to go ahead and trade. It is no sort of real asset at all, and the best way to show it is to deduct it from the Ordinary Shareholders' Interest. This leaves the value of the 60,000 shares at 89,801·00.

The Vertical Style of Balance Sheet. The Balance Sheet of Enterprise Ltd. can be rearranged in vertical style. The advantage of this method is that it is easy to print, it gives plenty of room to print the depreciation, etc., and it at last does away with the mistakes Simon Stevin left us with over the reversal of the sides of the Balance Sheet. We now have a top and a bottom, but no sides at all. Many firms are adopting this style, and the student should compare it with the more traditional style in Fig. 190.

Contingent Liabilities. Another requirement of Schedule 2 is that Contingent Liabilities should be stated as notes on the Balance Sheet. These are liabilities that may arise in certain contingencies. The commonest one is where **Bills of Exchange** are dishonoured by our debtors. In such cases we may become liable for them. Lawsuits pending also give rise to a possibility that the Court will find against us. A note on the bottom of the Balance Sheet stating the directors' valuation of likely Contingent Liabilities ensures that investors are aware of such possibilities, but we do not need to specify the matter because this would tell the Court we expected to lose the case.

EXERCISES SET LI

(5) Limited Company Accounts

No. 1. A limited liability company has an Authorized Capital of 100,000·00 divided into 20,000 6 per cent Preference Shares of 1·00 each and 80,000 Ordinary Shares of 1·00 each. All the Preference Shares and 60,000 of the Ordinary Shares are issued and fully paid. On December 31st, 19.., it was ascertained that the company had made a Net Profit of 13,050·00. There was a balance of 1,350·00 brought forward from the previous year. The directors decided to transfer 2,500·00 to General Reserve and to pay one year's dividend on the Preference Shares. They proposed a dividend of 15 per cent on the Ordinary Shares.

Show how the above information would appear on the Appropriation Account and draw up the liabilities side only of the Balance Sheet as at December 31st, 19 .. Ignore Corporation Tax.

(*University of London 'O' Level—Adapted*)

No. 2. A limited liability company has an Authorized Capital of 200,000·00 divided into 20,000 6 per cent Preference Shares of 1·00 each and 180,000 Ordinary Shares of 1·00 each. All the Preference Shares are issued and fully paid: 100,000 Ordinary Shares were issued with 0·75 per share paid on each share.

On December 31st, 19..., the company's Revenue Reserves were 30,000·00, Current Liabilities 7,500·00, Current Assets 62,750·00, Fixed Assets (at cost) 90,000·00, and Provisions for Depreciation on Fixed Assets 20,250·00.

Make a summarized Balance Sheet as at December 31st, 19..., to display this information. Set out the Balance Sheet in such a way as to show clearly the Net Value of Current Assets.

(*University of London 'O' Level—Adapted*)

No. 3. A limited company has authorized capital of 200,000·00 Ordinary Shares of which 100,000·00 shares of 1·00 are issued, and 50,000·00 Preference Shares of 1·00 of which 30,000·00 are issued. On March 31st, 19..., it was found that the Net Profit was 27,050·00 for the year. There was also a balance on the Appropriation Account of 1,150·00 from the previous year.

The directors resolved:

(*a*) To put 5,000·00 to General Reserve and 2,000·00 to Plant Replacement Reserve.

(*b*) To reserve 4,500·00 for Corporation Tax.

(*c*) To pay the 5 per cent Preference Dividend.

(*d*) To recommend a 10 per cent dividend on the Ordinary Shares.

Show the Appropriation Account and the liabilities side of the Balance Sheet. There are no current liabilities other than any resulting from the appropriation.

No. 4. From the following data and information you are asked to prepare a Balance Sheet for Brown and Jones, Ltd., which brings out the separate classes of shareholders' funds and the Net Working Capital.

BROWN AND JONES LTD.

BALANCE SHEET

(as at December 31st, 19..)

Share Capital (0·75 paid)	30,000·00	Stocks:	
Creditors and Bank Overdraft	6,212·00	Raw Materials	2,500·00
7% Debentures Fully Paid	4,000·00	Finished Goods	5,100·00
Proposed Dividend	1,000·00	Work in Progress	400·00
Balance on Appropriation		Preliminary Expenses	1,000·00
Account	2,658·00	Land and Buildings	12,000·00
General Reserve	4,500·00	Plant	10,520·00
Plant Replacement Reserve	2,500·00	Motor Vehicles	1,480·00
Premium on Debentures		Cash	5,500·00
Account	1,000·00	Debtors	4,500·00
Bad Debts Provision	250·00	Trade Investments	6,000·00
Expenses Accrued	280·00	Other Investments	3,400·00
	52,400·00		52,400·00

NOTES: (*a*) The Authorized Capital is 40,000 shares of 1·00 each.

(*b*) The Bank Overdraft is 2,500·00.

(*c*) The Debentures are secured on the Plant and Machinery.

(*d*) The Preliminary Expenses are not to appear on the assets side of the Balance Sheet.

(*e*) The original costs of the following assets are:

Land and Buildings (at cost)	12,000·00
Plant (at cost)	15,000·00
Motor Vehicles	1,600·00

(*f*) The present value of the Trade Investments according to the directors' estimates is 5,900·00.

The other investments are all quoted shares, Current Market Value 2,800·00.

(*g*) Contingent Liabilities exist on Bills of Exchange 485·00.

No. 5. Draw up the Appropriation Account and Balance Sheet of Trihard Ltd., whose Authorized Capital is 100,000·00 made up of 80,000 1·00 Ordinary Shares and 20,000 1·00 7 per cent Preference Shares. Details are:

Balance on Appropriation Account, January 1st, 19..	725·00
Profits for Year	11,206·00
Ordinary Share Capital Fully Paid	60,000·00
Preference Share Capital Fully Paid	20,000·00
Profits prior to Incorporation	8,260·00
Revenue Reserves—General Reserve	10,000·00
5% Debentures 600 at 10·00 each, secured on Land and Buildings of company.	
Land and Buildings (at cost)	32,000·00
Plant and Machinery (at cost)	24,000·00
Provision for Depreciation on Plant and Machinery	6,000·00
Provision for Bad Debts	2,000·00
Motor Vehicles	2,300·00
Stock	17,561·00
Investments (at Market Value)	6,390·00
Cash at Bank	7,250·00
Debtors	18,500·00
Creditors	1,860·00
Cash in Hand	50·00
Trade Investments (valued by Directors at 19,500·00)	18,000·00

The directors decide:

(*a*) To pay the Preference Dividend for the year.

(*b*) To put 5,000·00 into the General Reserve.

(*c*) To recommend a dividend of 8 per cent on the Ordinary Shares.

No. 6. The following Trial Balance was extracted from the books of Strangford, Ltd., at December 31st, 19..:

TRIAL BALANCE

(as at December 31st, 19..)

Share Capital: Authorized and Issued 30,000 shares of 1·00 each		30,000·00
Carriage In	100·00	
Provision for Bad Debts, January 1st		200·00
Stock-in-Trade, January 1st	7,350·00	
Purchases	81,400·00	
Sales		102,540·00
Trade Debtors	9,500·00	
Trade Creditors		3,800·00
Freehold Property at Cost	16,000·00	
General Expenses	7,240·00	
Wages and Salaries	6,130·00	
Rates	250·00	
Directors' Fees (Profit and Loss Account)	1,000·00	
Furniture and Fittings at Cost	4,000·00	
Provision for Depreciation of Furniture and Fittings, January 1st		600·00
Bad Debts Written Off	630·00	
Profit and Loss Account Balance, January 1st		2,050·00
Balance at Bank	5,590·00	
	139,190·00	139,190·00

The following matters are to be taken into account:

(*a*) Wages and salaries outstanding at December 31st 240·00.

(*b*) The Provision for Bad Debts required at December 31st is 370·00.

(*c*) Rates paid in advance at December 31st amounted to 60·00.

(*d*) Stock-in-Trade December 31st was valued at 5,480·00.

(*e*) Provide for depreciation of furniture and fittings at the rate of 5 per cent of cost.

(*f*) The directors propose to pay a dividend of 10 per cent for 19.. on the issued capital as at December 31st, 19...

You are required to prepare a Trading and Profit and Loss Account for 19.. and a Balance Sheet as at December 31st, 19...

(R.S.A.—Adapted)

No. 7. The following Trial Balance was extracted from the books of Pembroke, Ltd., as on December 31st, 19..:

TRIAL BALANCE

Share Capital, Authorized and Issued, 100,000 Ordinary Shares of 1·00 each		100,000·00
5% Debentures		25,000·00
Purchases	150,430·00	
Sales		188,590·00
Stock-in-Trade at January 1st	15,325·00	
Provision for Bad Debts		225·00
Freehold Properties (at cost)	115,000·00	
Furniture and Equipment (at cost)	13,400·00	
Provision for Depreciation of Furniture and Equipment		5,360·00
Debenture Interest to June 30th, 19..	625·00	
Bank Overdraft		140·00
Trade Debtors	16,440·00	
Trade Creditors		9,870·00
Preliminary Expenses	1,800·00	
Wages and Salaries	19,200·00	
Rent and Rates	1,850·00	
General Expenses	3,950·00	
Bad Debts	1,360·00	
Profit and Loss Account: Balance at January 1st, 19..		10,195·00
	339,380·00	339,380·00

You are given the following information:

(*a*) Stock-in-Trade at December 31st, 19.., 18,220·00.

(*b*) The Provision for Bad Debts is to be increased to 295·00.

(*c*) Rates paid in advance at December 31st were 90·00.

(*d*) Provision is to be made for depreciation of furniture and equipment at the rate of 10 per cent per annum (on cost).

(*e*) One-quarter of the balance on the Preliminary Expenses Account is to be written off.

(*f*) The directors have decided to recommend a dividend of 7 per cent. (Ignore taxation.)

You are required to prepare a Trading and Profit and Loss Account, a Profit and Loss Appropriation Account for the year 19.., and a Balance Sheet as on December 31st, 19...

(*R.S.A.—Adapted*)

CHAPTER THIRTY

CONTROL ACCOUNTS—TAKING THE TRIAL OUT OF A TRIAL BALANCE

(1) Introduction

With very large firms, handling thousands of accounts, the work involved in a Trial Balance used to be very laborious. These days we have almost magical aids in the form of computerized systems or automatic machines which pick up, read off, and print out, the balances on Ledger Accounts automatically. This chapter explains how we can take some of the trial out of a Trial Balance even if we are not provided with a mechanized or computerized system. The student who hopes eventually to work with advanced accounting systems will learn here the fundamental ideas behind their control activities.

(2) The Subdivision of the Ledger

The diagram Fig. 192 illustrates how the Ledger has been subdivided over the years as businesses have increased in size. We have to progress from the idea of a bound Ledger to one where at least the personal accounts are kept in a loose-leaf system, and probably a filing cabinet card-index system. Such systems are operated by junior typists, each of whom cannot take care of more than about 500 accounts. Suppose we have 20,000 debtors; we shall need forty girls to look after them.

If we make a rule that no one may go home until the Trial Balance is correct, our forty young ladies will become more and more depressed as the hours go by. Pity the luckless girl who has made the mistake when they all catch the last bus home.

What is needed to avoid such trouble is a system of **Control Accounts** which enable a section of the work to be balanced off by itself, and the clerk who has prepared it will know whether she is correct or not. Those members of staff whose section balances will go off to catch their trains and keep their evening appointments. Those less fortunate, or less efficient, stay behind and look for the mistake with the help of the supervisor. Some offices call this work **Sectional Balancing.**

(3) Control Accounts—The Basic Idea

Consider a typical section of the Debtors' Ledger—say the A–E section. Fig. 193 depicts it in its filing cabinet tray. At the back one more account, the Control Account, has been added. This account is

(1) The Cash Account and Bank Account were removed into the Three Column Cash Book.

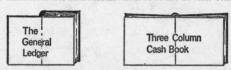

(2) The Capital Account, Current Account and Drawings Account were removed into the Private Ledger.

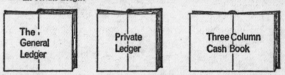

(3) The Debtors' Accounts and Creditors' Accounts were removed into the Debtors' and Creditors' Ledgers, leaving the Real Accounts and the Nominal Accounts in the General Ledger.

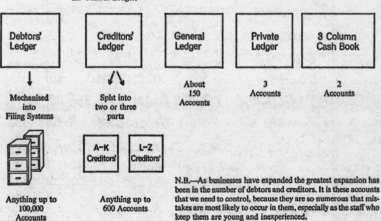

N.B.—As businesses have expanded the greatest expansion has been in the number of debtors and creditors. It is these accounts that we need to control, because they are so numerous that mistakes are most likely to occur in them, especially as the staff who keep them are young and inexperienced.

Fig. 192. How the Ledger has been subdivided

only a **Memorandum Account**, that is to say an account which is not a part of the double entry system, but simply a useful 'memo' or note. This book is kept by Miss Wright, one of our best posting clerks. How can we help Miss Wright to prove that she has done her work correctly, and deserves to go home at the normal time?

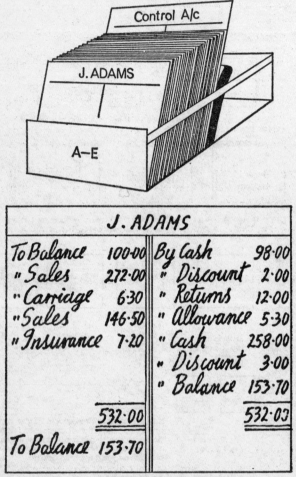

Fig. 193. A Section of the Ledger

A careful consideration of Miss Wright's tray of accounts shows the following matters:

(*a*) Nearly all these accounts have opening debit balances (after all— these people are debtors).

(*b*) Just the odd one or two have opening credit balances, usually because they have returned goods after paying for them. They are therefore debtors who are, just for a week or so, creditors instead.

(*c*) Nearly every account has a debit item 'To Sales', because goods were bought during the month.

(*d*) Some of them have debit items, 'To Carriage', 'To Insurance', etc., for small items we have charged up to the accounts.

(*e*) Nearly all the accounts have credit items 'By Cash', 'By Discount', because goods purchased last month have been paid for this month.

(*f*) Some people's accounts will have 'By Returns', 'By Allowance', etc., entered on the credit side, because they have returned goods or been given allowances this month.

If we now record on the Control Account the total opening balances, the total sales, the total returns, the total cash, and the total discounts, etc., we shall be able to see whether the book agrees with the **total figures.** If it does, then Miss Wright's section of the work is correct and she may go home. Her section has balanced.

This simple type of Control Account is all that we need to consider for Book-keeping Made Simple, but more advanced systems that are fully integrated with the double entry system are also used.

(4) Where Do We Get the Total Figures for the Control Accounts?

The ideal thing is to get the total figures for the Sales, the Returns, the Cash and Discount, and the remaining items from a source separate from the source of Miss Wright's information. This involves a little extra organization.

First we must institute departmental systems (see Chapter Twenty-seven) into all the major books of original entry, so that the Sales, the Purchases, the Sales Returns, and the Purchases Returns can be analysed into the various sections we need. Miss Wright keeps the A–E Sales Ledger so that the Sales Day Book will need analysis columns, as shown in Chapter Twelve, for A–E, F–K, L–S, and T–Z, or whatever the sections are called. From this analysis column we can collect the total sales figure for Miss Wright's Ledger without any difficulty whenever we want it—usually on the last day of the month. The Sales Returns Book will need similar analysis columns to give the total returns figure for the A–E book. The Three-column Cash Book will need a similar set of analysis columns to give us the total cash and discount figures for the A–E book.

The Journal Proper cannot have analysis columns in it, but the entries are so few that we can easily analyse them off when required. We simply open the Journal Proper at the beginning of the month we want and run our eye down it for any items concerning debtors whose names begin with A–E. We find one—a bad debt—and make a note of it.

Are there any more? None on the next three pages, but on the last page there are two more, another bad debt and a dishonoured cheque. We make a note of the details and put them in the Control Account.

(5) A Simple Control Account

A typical control account is shown below. It is the type of Memorandum Control Account which is not part of the double entry system.

SALES LEDGER A–E CONTROL ACCOUNT   L. 175

19..				19..			
Jan. 1	To Balances	2,762·50		Jan. 1	By Balances	25·50	
31	„ Total Sales	9,578·75		31	„ Cash	4,726·75	
31	„ Interest Charged	5·65		31	„ Discounts	175·55	
31	„ Carriage Charged	97·65		31	„ Returns	476·50	
31	„ Dishonoured			31	„ Bad Debts		
	Cheques	14·60			Written Off	46·60	
31	„ Balances	17·20		31	„ Balances	7,025·45	
		12,476·35				12,476·35	
19..				19..			
Feb. 1	To Balances	7,025·45		Feb. 1	By Balances	17·20	

Fig. 194. A simple Control Account

The account shown in Fig. 194 is exactly like that of any ordinary debtor, except that it has balances on both sides. A debtor cannot be both a debtor and a creditor on the first day of the month, but as our Control Account, or Total Account, gives us the total figures for the whole of the A–E Ledger there may be some debtors who are creditors for a short while. Apart from this, the usual transactions are recorded. These are:

(*a*) Many of the debtors have bought goods during the month, and the total sales are debited in the Control Account.

(*b*) Many of the debtors have paid cash, and have been allowed discount. These total payments and discounts have been credited on the Control Account.

(*c*) Many of the debtors have returned goods, and the total returns have been credited to the Control Account.

(*d*) Finally a number of other items have been analysed out from the Journal Proper: interest charged, dishonoured cheques and bad debts.

Miss Wright can now compare the Control Account with her own ledger tray. She will balance off each of the accounts in her tray (or they may already be kept on a 'running balance' method—see p. 157). She will then list the balances, and should find that the total debit balances agree with the Control Account above; and that the total credit balances of those debtors who are temporarily creditors also agree with the credit items shown above. If the tray fails to agree with the Control Account she must look for an error in her month's work.

(6) The Manager Who is Wrong

A manager may prefer to keep the Control Account in the General Ledger where Miss Wright cannot see it. He prepares it himself. She must come to the manager and tell him what her book totals. 'I'm sorry,' he says, 'You've made a slip somewhere. Will you check it please?' She must go back and look for a mistake.

Supposing Miss Wright's tray does not balance? Is it necessarily her fault? Could the manager be wrong? Well of course he could, because if he prepares the Control Account incorrectly the tray will not agree. The manager must make absolutely sure he gets the Control Account right, because if he keeps Miss Wright in until late in the evening looking for the mistake and she then discovers it is his fault, she will take great pleasure in letting the whole office know. The aim for a good manager should be (a) to get his Control Account right, and (b) to approach the problem of correcting Miss Wright's work in a sympathetic and co-operative way. If it turns out to be his fault he can then apologize gracefully and save face. He can never know until the tray is correct whose fault it is that it won't agree with the control.

Exercises Set LII

(7) Simple Control Accounts

No. 1. Thomas is in business in only a small way, but he works out each month a Sales Ledger Control Account which is kept at the back of the Sales Ledger. Prepare it for the month of July given these figures:

19..	July 1	Opening Balances	260·00
	31	Sales for Month	842·00
	31	Cash Received	255·75
	31	Discount Allowed	14·25
	31	Bad Debt	5·00
	31	Returns	4·75
	31	Allowance for Damaged Goods	10·00

Bring down the balance.

No. 2. B. Irving keeps a Control Account as a control on his Creditors' Ledger. It is kept in the back of the Creditors' Ledger. Prepare it from these figures:

19..	Jan. 1	Amounts owed to Creditors	2,806·50
	31	Purchases for Month	2,602·75
	31	Payments to Creditors	3,175·50
	31	Discount Received	156·20
	31	Returns to Creditors	140·65
	31	Interest Charged by a Creditor	5·65
	31	Carriage Charged by a Creditor	4·75
	31	Outstanding Balance Owed by a Creditor to Irving	27·35

No. 3. Why do we draw up a Sales Ledger Control Account? Set out the following items in an account of this kind appearing in the back of the Sales Ledger A–C tray.

Credit Sales for January	42,756·45
Cash Received from Debtors during Month	41,100·95
Discount Allowed to Debtors during Month	1,786·65
Opening Balances on January 1st	33,728·60
Dishonoured Cheques	147·25
Bad Debts Written Off	49·80
Sales Returns for the Month	1,346·20

No. 4. Prepare a Sales Ledger Control Account from the following information which relates to the month of October, 19..:

Balances on Debtors' Accounts at October 1st	4,175·50
Receipts from Debtors	4,596·65
Sales on Credit	5,255·50
Sales Returns	64·60
Discounts Allowed	124·40

This account is in the back of the Sales Ledger, but on taking out a balance of the book it proves not to be correct. What possible explanations are there?

(8) Contra Entries in Control Accounts

We usually connect Contra Entries with the Three-column Cash Book—that type of entry which is done when we take cash out of the bank for office use, or take cash out of the till to put it in the bank. A quite different kind of Contra Entry occurs with Control Accounts. These entries arise in the following way:

We usually have one Ledger Account for each person with whom we deal, but this becomes very awkward in a sophisticated book-keeping system where we have split the Ledger up into several pieces as shown in Fig. 192. If we have a single person with whom we deal in two capacities, as a debtor and as a creditor, it will be impossible to have all our transactions with him recorded on one page in the Ledger, because the debtors are split away from the creditors. Our debtors' accounts will perhaps be in a mechanized ledger-card system, while our creditors' accounts may be hundreds of yards away in another office, or on different floors perhaps.

The solution is for our client to have two accounts, one in the Debtors' Ledger and one in the Creditors' Ledger, and as these accounts are opposite in character we call them Contra Accounts.

Consider the case of M. Grenfell, a trader with whom we deal in both capacities. He is a wholesale druggist who buys considerable quantities of drugs from our firm, which manufactures pharmaceutical products. He also allows us to purchase, on behalf of staff, any chemist's sundries they wish to buy, at specially favourable terms. In any given month Grenfell buys from us about 5,000·00 of pharmaceutical goods, while we buy for our staff about 200·00 of chemist's sundries from Grenfell. On our books Grenfell has two Contra Accounts, a debtor's account for his large purchases from us, and a creditor's account for the small purchases we make from him.

Here are these two accounts:

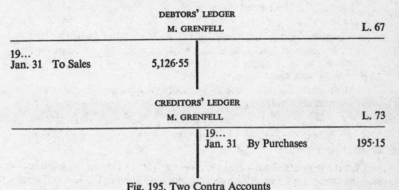

DEBTORS' LEDGER

M. GRENFELL   L. 67

19... Jan. 31 To Sales	5,126·55	

CREDITORS' LEDGER

M. GRENFELL   L. 73

	19... Jan. 31 By Purchases	195·15

Fig. 195. Two Contra Accounts

What shall we do about these accounts at the end of the month? Is there any point in sending Grenfell a cheque for the 195·15 we owe him when he owes us 5,126·55? Clearly there is not. The sensible thing is to contra the small item off against the big item, and let M. Grenfell pay us the outstanding balance, i.e. 4,931·40. A simple Journal Entry will settle the matter. Here it is:

19..
Jan. 31
	M. Grenfell (Creditors' Ledger) Dr.
	    To M. Grenfell (Debtors' Ledger)
	    Being contra entry against out-
	        standing debtor's balance
		L. 73
		L. 67
			195·15	195·15

Fig. 196. Journalizing a Contra Entry

When posted into the Ledger Accounts this will clear off the Creditors' Ledger Account completely, and leave the Debtors' Ledger Account at a lower figure. This lower figure represents what Grenfell owes us for pharmaceutical goods supplied. He has paid for some of them by giving us the goods for our staff who use this opportunity to purchase cheap goods.

How does this affect the Control Accounts? The Journal Entry, Fig. 196, is one of the Journal Entries we shall pick up when we analyse the Journal for Control Account items. It is going to affect two Control Accounts, the Debtors' Ledger Control Account and the Creditors'

Ledger Control Account. In each case it affects the Control Account just like cash paid, the entry 'To Contra' or 'By Contra' will come in, just like cash paid, to reduce both the debtors' debts to us and our debts to our creditors.

EXERCISES SET LIII

(9) More Difficult Control Accounts

No. 1.

(a) What accounts would you expect to find in a Sales Ledger?

(b) R. Blenkinsop checks his Sales Ledger monthly by means of a Control Account. Name the sources from which he is likely to ascertain the figures to prepare this Control Account.

(c) What should the balance of the Control Account represent and with what amount should it agree?

No. 2. A firm keeps a Purchases Ledger which is checked by a Control Account. For the month of May the following figures are available for the Control Account:

Credit Balance at May 1st, 19..	4,609·00
(agreeing with total balances in Purchases Ledger)	
Purchases for Month	5,402·00
Purchases Returns for Month	110·00
Cash Paid	4,875·00
Discount Received	257·00
Transfers of Debit Balances in Sales Ledger to Purchases Ledger (Contra Entries)	80·00

(a) Construct the Control Account for May 19...

(b) State the source from which each of the above figures would be ascertained.

(c) State what the balance of the Control Account represents.

(London University 'O' Level—Adapted)

No. 3. Goldbourn Ltd. keep a separate Sales Ledger and Purchases Ledger, with special Memorandum Control Accounts, kept in the back of these two Ledgers.

You are asked to draw up the Sales Ledger Control Account and the Purchases Ledger Control Account.

Jan.	1	Balances on Debit Side of Sales Ledger Accounts	27,206·00
	1	Balances on Credit Side of Sales Ledger Accounts	46·00
	1	Balances on Credit Side of Purchases Ledger Accounts	5,946·50
	1	Balances on Debit Side of Purchases Ledger Accounts	24·50
	31	Cash Received from Customers	48,612·00
	31	Sales to Customers	96,216·50
	31	Cash Paid to Creditors	4,960·00
	31	Goods Purchased	19,206,00
	31	Returns Inwards	450·75
	31	Returns Outwards	670·25

31	Amounts Charged to Customers for Carriage	48·00
31	Bad Debts Written Off	75·50
31	Sales Ledger Debits Written Off to Creditors Accounts	185·00
31	Interest Charged to A. Debtor (overdue account)	5·00

(London University 'O' Level—Adapted)

No. 4. From the following particulars prepare the Sales Ledger Control Account of T. Thompson:

Amounts Owing by Customers on January 1st	5,000·00
Amounts Due to Customers on January 1st	48·00
Sales in January	49,200·00
Bought Ledger Contras (Credits on the Bought Ledger transferred)	502·00
Goods taken by Landlord in Lieu of Cash for Rent Due	50·00
Discounts Allowed	700·00
Bad Debts	800·00

On January 10th A. Brown, who owed 130·00 since the previous August, paid in full. Thompson had already reduced this Account to 70·00 as a doubtful debt.

Cash Received (excluding A. Brown above)   45,000·00

An Invoice of 480·00 had been issued in duplicate and charged twice to A. Debtor's Account. This had been corrected by a Journal entry.

You are now told that the total balances on Thompson's Sales Ledger are 6,550·00 and that there is an error of 10·00 in the Trial Balance. What conclusion do you draw?

No. 5. Prepare the Bought Ledger Control Account and Sold Ledger Control Account from the information given below.

Debtors on Sold Ledger at January 1st, 19..	18,932·54
Creditors on Bought Ledger at January 1st, 19..	14,365·15
Goods Purchased on Credit during Month	73,691·17
Goods Sold on Credit during Month	92,461·45

Sundry Credit Balances on Sold Ledger, January 31st	93·28
Cash Payments by Debtors during Month	85,471·85
Bills Receivable Received during Month	927·55
Bills Payable Issued during Month	930·71

Cheques Paid to Creditors during Month	60,149·88
Discounts Received	761·22
Discounts Allowed	837·49
Bad Debts	1,043·31

Goods Returned Outwards during Month	836·25
Interest Charged on Overdue Sales Ledger Accounts	79·18

CHAPTER THIRTY-ONE

THE AMALGAMATION OF BUSINESSES

(1) Introduction

When two sole traders amalgamate their businesses a variety of arrangements are possible, but it usually means some adjustment to the existing firms. For instance, they may not need both sets of premises, or both sets of plant and machinery, or both sets of motor vehicles. The terms of the agreement drawn up will set out what assets and liabilities each partner is bringing in. It may also be agreed that either or both partners shall open a Goodwill Account to value the goodwill of the businesses being merged. This will be included as one of the assets of the new business. Any adjustment in this way to the Balance Sheets of the old businesses alters the Capital Account of the trader concerned, which will form his capital in the new partnership being established.

(2) Drawing Up the Statements of Affairs on Amalgamation

Consider the following example:

T. Younger and R. Elder are in business separately as sole traders. They decide to set up a partnership from January 1st, 19..., using Younger's premises and fixtures and fittings. Elder is to sell his premises and fittings privately, but is to bring in 3,000·00 as capital in addition to his existing bank balance. Younger's motor vehicles consist of one new and one old vehicle. The latter is valued at 300·00 on his books, and as it is surplus to the needs of the new business he will sell it privately. Younger will be allowed to open a Goodwill Account for 1,000·00 to compensate him for the hard work done in the past, since Elder will now share the benefits of this. Their existing Balance Sheets are shown below. Carry out the amalgamation and show the Balance Sheet of the new business after the books have been opened.

T. YOUNGER

BALANCE SHEET

(as at December 31st, 19..)

LIABILITIES		ASSETS	
Creditors	2,300·00	Cash	200·00
Capital	14,000·00	Cash at Bank	3,800·00
		Stock	4,700·00
		Motor Vehicles	1,800·00
		Furniture and Fittings	800·00
		Land and Buildings	5,000·00
	16,300·00		16,300·00

R. ELDER
BALANCE SHEET
(as at December 31st, 19..)

LIABILITIES		ASSETS	
Creditors	1,900·00	Bank Balance	400·00
Capital	11,500·00	Debtors	2,600·00
		Stock	3,000·00
		Motor Vehicles	1,800·00
		Furniture and Fittings	1,600·00
		Land and Buildings	4,000·00
	13,400·00		13,400·00

The first thing to do is to reconstruct these Balance Sheets in the light of the information given, so that the new Statements of Affairs leave out any items not being brought into the new business. The result will be the following Statements of Affairs:

T. YOUNGER
STATEMENT OF AFFAIRS
(on amalgamation with R. Elder on January 1st, 19..)

CURRENT LIABILITIES		CURRENT ASSETS		
Creditors	2,300·00	Cash	200·00	
		Cash at Bank	3,800·00	
		Stock	4,700·00	
				8,700·00
CAPITAL		FIXED ASSETS		
At Start	14,700·00	Motor Vehicles	1,500·00	
		Furniture and		
		Fittings	800·00	
		Land and Buildings	5,000·00	
		Goodwill	1,000·00	
				8,300·00
	17,000·00			17,000·00

R. ELDER
STATEMENT OF AFFAIRS
(on amalgamation with T. Younger on January 1st, 19..)

CURRENT LIABILITIES		CURRENT ASSETS		
Creditors	1,900·00	Balance at Bank	3,400·00	
		Debtors	2,600·00	
		Stock	3,000·00	
				9,000·00
CAPITAL		FIXED ASSETS		
At Start	8,900·00	Motor Vehicles		1,800·00
	10,800·00			10,800·00

(3) Amalgamating the Two Businesses

All that is now required on amalgamation is to put these two statements together into one Opening Journal Entry, post it to the Ledger Accounts and the Cash Book, and extract a Balance Sheet. The Opening Journal Entry will be as follows:

19.. Jan. 1				
	Cash in Hand	Dr.	C.B. 1	200·00	
	„ at Bank	„	„	7,200·00	
	Stock	„	L. 1	7,700·00	
	Debtors	„	L. 2	2,600·00	
	Motor Vehicles	„	L. 3	3,300·00	
	Furniture and Fittings	„	L. 4	800·00	
	Land and Buildings	„	L. 5	5,000·00	
	Goodwill	„	L. 6	1,000·00	
	To Creditors		L. 7 etc.		4,200·00
	„ Capital Y		L. 99		14,700·00
	„ „ E		L. 100		8,900·00
				27,800·00	27,800·00
	Being assets and liabilities at this date				

Fig. 197. Opening the books of the New Business

and the amalgamated Balance Sheet will read:

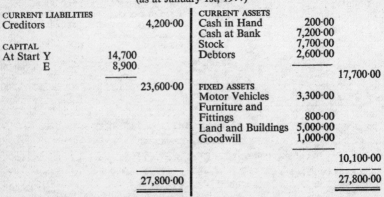

T. YOUNGER AND R. ELDER

BALANCE SHEET

(as at January 1st, 19..)

CURRENT LIABILITIES			CURRENT ASSETS		
Creditors		4,200·00	Cash in Hand	200·00	
			Cash at Bank	7,200·00	
CAPITAL			Stock	7,700·00	
At Start Y	14,700		Debtors	2,600·00	
E	8,900				17,700·00
		23,600·00	FIXED ASSETS		
			Motor Vehicles	3,300·00	
			Furniture and Fittings	800·00	
			Land and Buildings	5,000·00	
			Goodwill	1,000·00	
					10,100·00
		27,800·00			27,800·00

Fig. 198. An Amalgamation Completed

EXERCISES SET LIV

(4) Amalgamations

No. 1. Flower agreed to take Rose into partnership as from July 1st, 19... On that day the following balances were extracted from their books:

	FLOWER	ROSE
Freehold Premises	6,000·00	4,600·00
Machinery and Tools	2,700·00	1,400·00
Stock of Materials	850·00	450·00
Cash at Bank	600·00	—
Stock of Finished Goods	1,450·00	950·00
Bank Overdraft		765·00
Cash in Hand	30·00	20·00
Sundry Creditors	2,540·00	1,270·00
Rates and Insurance Prepaid	50·00	40·00
Sundry Debtors	1,630·00	970·00
Provision for Bad Debts	130·00	—
Current Accounts—Credit Balances	40·00	195·00

Rose was to pay off the amount of his bank overdraft out of his private funds and to make a Provision for Bad Debts of 165·00.

The terms of the partnership were:

(*a*) Interest on capital to be allowed at 5 per cent per annum.

(*b*) Rose was to act as manager of the business and receive a bonus of 15 per cent of profits after charging interest on capital. The remainder of the profits was to be divided equally between Flower and Rose.

(i) Draft the opening Balance Sheet of the new firm as at July 1st, 19...

(ii) On December 31st, 19.., the Net Trading Profit for the half-year, before charging interest on capital and Rose's bonus, was 4,830·00. Draft the Profit and Loss Appropriation Account for the half year.

(*University of London 'O' Level—Adapted*)

No. 2. Miss P. Whitehead agrees to enter into partnership with Miss D. Poole as from January 1st, 19... On that day their records showed the following situation:

	P. WHITEHEAD	D. POOLE
Land and Buildings	7,000·00	3,000·00
Machinery	2,800·00	4,000·00
Furniture and Fittings	600·00	400·00
Stocks:		
Raw Materials	550·00	450·00
Work in Progress	1,350·00	1,250·00
Finished Goods	2,000·00	1,800·00
Cash	80·00	475·00
Bank	2,500·00	2,156·00
Creditors	154·00	334·00
Rent Due	50·00	60·00
Debtors	1,800·00	1,350·00
Bad Debts Provisions	150·00	120·00
Current Accounts	420·00 (Cr.)	350·00 (Dr.)

Miss Whitehead will not bring in her machinery and Miss Poole will not bring in her Land and Buildings or her Furniture and Fittings.

Draw up the Amalgamated Balance Sheet.

No. 3. R. Brown and B. Jones are in business separately as sole traders. They decide to set up a partnership business with effect from January 1st, 19... Brown's premises, furniture and fittings, and motor vehicles are to be sold separately by Brown and not brought into the partnership business. He will bring in, instead, a further 5,000·00 cash, as well as all his stock-in-trade and book debts. Jones brought in all his assets and liabilities. Here are their two business Balance Sheets. Draw up the Amalgamated Balance Sheet as at January 1st, 19...

Balance Sheet details at 31st December

ASSETS	R. Brown	B. Jones
Cash	200·00	500·00
Debtors	3,000·00	3,000·00
Stock	4,500·00	5,000·00
Motor Vehicles	1,800·00	2,800·00
Furniture and Fittings	600·00	1,200·00
Land and Buildings	3,500·00	5,000·00
LIABILITIES		
Creditors	1,600·00	1,500·00
Capital	12,000·00	16,000·00

No. 4. A. and B. are independent traders in the same line of business, their respective Balance Sheets on December 31st, 19.., being as follows:

Balance Sheet details at 31st December

ASSETS	A.	B.
Goodwill	5,000·00	—
Property and Land	4,400·00	—
Fixtures and Fittings	590·00	400·00
Motor Vehicles	—	1,100·00
Stock	9,860·00	4,000·00
Debtors	8,590·00	3,000·00
Cash at Bank	1,070·00	—
LIABILITIES		
Capital	27,400·00	5,870·00
Creditors	2,097·00	2,398·00
Bank overdraft	—	232·00
Wages due	13·00	—

They decide to amalgamate on the following terms:

(*a*) All assets and liabilities to be taken over at their agreed values except B.'s fixtures and fittings which he will dispose of privately, and stocks, which will each be reduced by 10 per cent.

(*b*) B.'s goodwill to be valued at 2,000·00.

(*c*) B.'s overdraft to be cleared privately, and A. to pay the wages due out of his own pocket.

Draw up the Opening Entry for the new business and the Opening Balance Sheet as at January 1st, 19...

CHAPTER THIRTY-TWO

THE PURCHASE OF A BUSINESS

(1) Introduction

When one person purchases a business from another the buyer agrees to pay a sum, called the purchase price, to the seller—usually called the **vendor**. The purchase price nearly always includes a payment for goodwill over and above the value of the actual assets taken over. The signing of the agreement is the moment when the contract takes effect, unless a specific moment of time is embodied in the agreement. At that time the purchaser will open his books with the necessary opening Journal Entries, and will assume control of the business.

(2) The Purchase Price and the Goodwill Figure

Consider the following example:

Example. On January 1st, 19.., T. Brown's Balance Sheet is as follows:

T. BROWN

BALANCE SHEET

(as at January 1st, 19..)

LIABILITIES		ASSETS	
Capital	5,000·00	Shop premises	3,200·00
Trade Creditors	1,500·00	Furniture and Fittings	800·00
		Motor Vehicle	500·00
		Stock	1,750·00
		Cash at Bank	250·00
	6,500·00		6,500·00

At this date Brown agrees to sell his business to R. Gray for 7,200·00. Gray will take over all the assets except the bank balance and will also pay the trade creditors. Gray decides to value the shop premises at 4,000·00, the furniture and fittings at 500·00, the motor vehicle at 350·00, and the stock at 1,500·00. Show the records for the purchase of the business in Gray's books, his capital contribution being 8,000·00 in cash.

The important point to remember in recording these matters is that the valuations of the purchaser, Gray, are the important ones in the calculations. The purchase price is agreed at 7,200·00. What does Gray expect for his money? The list of assets reads:

Assets taken over:		
Premises	4,000·00	
Furniture and Fittings	500·00	
Motor Vehicle	350·00	
Stock	1,500·00	
	6,350·00	
The liability to the trade creditors must be deducted from this:	1,500·00	
Net Value of Assets	4,850·00	

Gray is receiving assets valued at the net figure of 4,850·00, yet he is prepared to pay 7,200·00. This extra sum must be Gray's valuation of the goodwill, i.e. 2,350·00.

When listing the assets in the Opening Entries we shall include goodwill, 2,350·00.

(3) Opening the Accounts of the New Business

The stages of this series of entries are most easily understood if we number them in the correct order of events.

(*a*) At the moment of purchase Gray agrees to pay the vendor the purchase price. The vendor therefore becomes a creditor, and to enable us to credit him at once we open up a special account called the Purchase of Business Account which can be debited. The Journal Entry reads:

19..
Jan. 1
	Purchase of Business Account Dr.
	    To T. Brown
	Being agreed price of business taken
	    over
		L. 1
		L. 2
			7,200·00	7,200·00

Fig. 199. The Vendor becomes a Creditor

and the accounts read as follows:

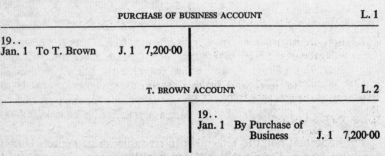

PURCHASE OF BUSINESS ACCOUNT   L. 1

19.. Jan. 1 To T. Brown	J. 1	7,200·00	

T. BROWN ACCOUNT   L. 2

	19.. Jan. 1 By Purchase of Business	J. 1	7,200·00

Fig. 200. The accounts are opened

(*b*) The next thing Gray needs to do is to take on the assets, including goodwill, at his own valuations. The Journal Entry will look like this:

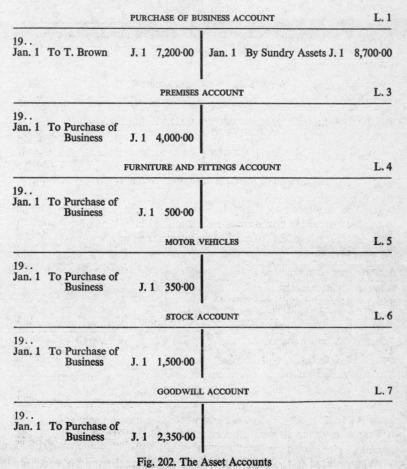

19..					
Jan. 1	Premises Account	Dr.	L. 3	4,000·00	
	Furniture and Fittings Account	,,	L. 4	500·00	
	Motor Vehicle Account	,,	L. 5	350·00	
	Stock Account	,,	L. 6	1,500·00	
	Goodwill Account	,,	L. 7	2,350·00	
	To Purchase of Business Account		L. 1		8,700·00
	Being assets taken over				

Fig. 201. Opening the Asset Accounts

and the accounts now look like this:

PURCHASE OF BUSINESS ACCOUNT L. 1

19..				19..			
Jan. 1	To T. Brown	J. 1	7,200·00	Jan. 1	By Sundry Assets	J. 1	8,700·00

PREMISES ACCOUNT L. 3

19..			
Jan. 1	To Purchase of Business	J. 1	4,000·00

FURNITURE AND FITTINGS ACCOUNT L. 4

19..			
Jan. 1	To Purchase of Business	J. 1	500·00

MOTOR VEHICLES L. 5

19..			
Jan. 1	To Purchase of Business	J. 1	350·00

STOCK ACCOUNT L. 6

19..			
Jan. 1	To Purchase of Business	J. 1	1,500·00

GOODWILL ACCOUNT L. 7

19..			
Jan. 1	To Purchase of Business	J. 1	2,350·00

Fig. 202. The Asset Accounts

(*c*) Gray now has to take on the liability. The effect of this will be to clear the Purchase of Business Account, which has served its purposes and is closed off. The Journal Entry will be:

19.. Jan. 1	Purchase of Business　　　　　　　Dr. To Trade Creditors	L. 1 L. 8, etc.	1,500·00	1,500·00
	Being liabilities taken over on purchase			

Fig. 203. Taking over the Creditors

In fact this is not a very sensible Journal Entry because each creditor would have an account opened in his name and a large number of accounts would really be credited with sums of money which in total would come to 1,500·00. The Purchase of Business Account would now read:

PURCHASE OF BUSINESS ACCOUNT　　　　　　　　　　　L. 1

19.. Jan. 1 1	To T. Brown " Creditors	J. 1 J. 1	7,200·00 1,500·00	19.. Jan. 1	By Sundry Assets J. 1	8,700·00
			8,700·00			8,700·00

Fig. 204. The Purchase of Business Account cleared

(*d*) The last thing for Gray to do is to pay the vendor, Brown, his purchase price. He contributes his capital 8,000·00, paying Brown by cheque. The relevant Journal Entries are as follows:

19.. Jan. 1	Bank Account　　　　　　　　　　Dr. To Capital Account	C.B. 1 L. 100	8,000·00	8,000·00
	Being Capital contributed by R. Gray at this date			
19.. Jan. 1	T. Brown Account　　　　　　　　Dr. By Bank	L. 2 C.B. 1	7,200·00	7,200·00
	Being cheque in settlement			

Fig. 205. Paying the Vendor

N.B. It is not strictly necessary to Journalize cash entries, but on occasions like this a full record of the day to day events is desirable.

When posted to the Cash Book and the Ledger the vendor's account is cleared and the Opening Balance Sheet of the new business is as follows:

R. GRAY

BALANCE SHEET

(as at January 1st, 19. .)

CAPITAL		FIXED ASSETS		
At Start	8,000·00	Goodwill	2,350·00	
		Premises	4,000·00	
		Furniture and Fittings	500·00	
CURRENT LIABILITIES		Motor Vehicles	350·00	
Creditors	1,500·00			
				7,200·00
		CURRENT ASSETS		
		Stock	1,500·00	
		Cash at Bank	800·00	
				2,300·00
	9,500·00			9,500·00

Fig. 206. The Balance Sheet of the new Business

EXERCISES SET LV

(4) Purchase of a Business

No. 1. On December 31st, 19. ., A. Brownjohn purchased for 22,000·00 all the assets of A. Rowntree, a trader, with the exception of the debtors. At that date the assets shown in A. Rowntree's Balance Sheet were:

Freehold Property	10,000·00
Furniture and Fittings	2,500·00
Stock-in-Trade	5,700·00

It was agreed that these figures represented fair valuations. Brownjohn contributed 24,000·00 as capital and Rowntree was paid by cheque.

Show the Journal Entries in Brownjohn's books for the purchase of this business—including the Cash Book entries, and the new firm's Balance Sheet.

No. 2. The following is the Balance Sheet of J. Whitty on April 30th, 19. .:

Capital	4,842·00	Fixtures and Fittings		750·00
Creditors	1,261·00	Motor Van	800·00	
		Less Owing on Hire		
		Purchase	250·00	
				550·00
		Stock		2,579·00
		Debtors		2,224·00
	6,103·00			6,103·00

On this date A. Walsall purchased the business, taking over all the assets and liabilities at the values shown, and the purchase price was 6,842·00.

Draft the entries in the Journal of the purchaser to open his books, and the Balance Sheet of the new business.

(*R.S.A.—Adapted*)

No. 3. On October 31st, 19.., A. Coughlan arranged to take over the business carried on by J. Frost.

The assets were taken over at the following valuations: Goodwill 5,000·00; Fixtures and fittings 2,250·00; Stock 7,750·00. Trade creditors amounted to 562·00 and it was found that:

(*a*) Rent was owing for one month at the rate of 600·00 per annum.

(*b*) Rates amounting to 120·00 had been paid for the half-year to March 31st, next.

(*c*) The Telephone Account owing amounted to 13·00.

(*d*) The Electricity Account owing amounted to 25·00, against which the suppliers held a deposit for 50·00 which was taken over by the purchasers.

(*e*) On October 15th, 19.., A. Coughlan had paid a deposit of 1,500·00.

Prepare a statement showing the amount due to the vendor at the completion of the transaction.

(*R.S.A.—Adapted*)

No. 4. On January 1st, 19.., A-B purchased for 23,000·00 the business of Smith, a trader. At that date the assets appearing in the books of Smith were:

Buildings	6,500·00
Plant	4,700·00
Motor Vans	1,800·00
Stock-in-Trade	4,300·00

There were liabilities to trade creditors of 475·00. These valuations were accepted as fair by A-B and the assets and liability were entered in his books at those figures. The purchase price was paid by cheque after A-B had contributed capital of 25,000·00.

Show the Journal Entries in the books of the new business and its Balance Sheet.

CHAPTER THIRTY-THREE

HOW BOOK-KEEPING RECORDS ARE COMPUTERISED

(1) The Computer Revolution

In the last quarter of a century the development of computers has revolutionised office practices. A program of instructions is fed into the computer which enables it to process any data supplied. Thus the entire debtors' ledger can be stored on a fast computer medium such as disc or magnetic tape, each debtor being given a unique code number which identifies him in the system. The average computer works at a speed of a million operations per second. Tedious manual preparation of invoices, credit notes and payments can be performed at electronic speeds, and the accounting entries done simultaneously. Although preparatory work must still be performed, for example, when an order is received, all the operations which follow from that order—e.g. invoicing, accounting records, statements, etc.—can be carried out automatically.

(2) Computer Hardware

Whilst a detailed knowledge of computer hardware is not necessary, it is useful to be familiar with the names of the units and the parts they play in meeting the firm's accounting requirements. Fig. 207 shows a typical commercial computer configuration.

The three essential elements in computerisation are **inputs, processing** and **outputs**. We must be able to put data into the computer, which will then process the data and put out the results so that they can be understood. These three elements are provided for in the following ways.

(*a*) *Input Devices.* Some typical input devices are punched-card readers, paper-tape readers, key-edit devices and the console communicator, which is like an electric typewriter. All these devices are relatively slow in the preparation and checking stage. At the time of input the card reader operates at about 160,000 characters per minute—much slower than the computer's million operations per second. The key-edit device is faster, since information is fed onto magnetic tape, rather than cards or paper tape. The term 'edit' refers to the ability of the device to detect when an operator miskeys and feeds an error into the system. When a collection of documents, such as purchases invoices, is to be put into the computer, the documents are 'batched up', coded with any necessary codes and passed to the punch or key

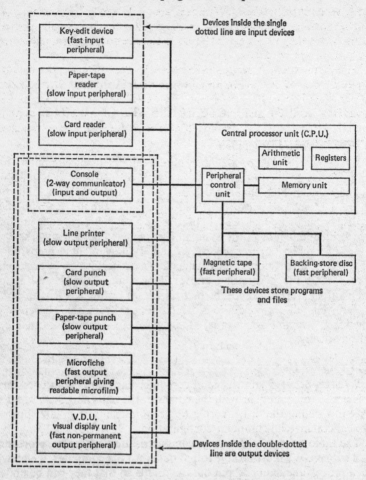

Fig. 207. A Commercial Computer Configuration

operator. The resulting punched cards, paper tape or magnetic tape can then be used to pass data into the computer. This is called **data transfer.** The data can now be processed according to the programs already stored in the computer.

(*b*) *The Central Processor Unit.* The C.P.U. is the main section of the computer and contained within it are the **memory unit,** the **peripheral control unit or units,** the **arithmetic unit** and the **registers.**

The memory unit of the C.P.U. determines the power of the computer, since it is here that the actual processing of data according to programmed instructions takes place.

The arithmetic unit is located in the C.P.U., and here the calculations such as multiplication and division are performed. The answers, and partial answers, to the calculations are stored in the registers temporarily, from where they may be transferred to the memory unit for subsequent output to tape or disc storage.

Peripheral control units are designed to deal with all the ancillary equipment used for input and output of information. Outside components are known as peripherals. The word 'periphery' means 'outside boundary' and the peripherals may be regarded as surrounding the C.P.U. Note that in some instances the peripheral control units are themselves peripheral to the C.P.U.

(c) *Output Devices.* The chief method of output in the final stage is the line printer. This prints out the result of the processed data. It is the computer's most convenient method of communication since it can be read by the human user. Speeds vary with the type of device but an output of 1,300 lines per minute, each line having a maximum of 132 characters, is representative. Other output devices such as punched cards or paper tape are less easily understood by the human user. As can be imagined, the production of output information is governed by the printer speed, which is low. To overcome this difficulty matter for printing is 'queued' on a fast medium, such as tape or disc, and then printed by a specialist program divorced from the original program. This is known as 'off-line' printing. Another method which avoids vast collections of paper computer print-out is the development of microfiche output, which can be produced direct from a magnetic tape file, so that no printing is required. The computer output consists of a succession of microfilm exposures photographed from a cathode ray tube which can be read in a microfilm reader.

(3) How Computers have changed Book-keeping

On pages 32–3 a chart shows how the double entry book-keeping system works. If we wish to see how computers have modified book-keeping it is useful to redraw this chart, in computerised form, and this is done in Fig. 208 (see pages 402–3). The chart is largely self-explanatory.

It is not usual for computers to prepare final accounts, although they can be programmed to do so. The point here is that the cost of a program to make decisions at the final accounts level is greater than the cost of the work saved. Generally speaking the preparation of final accounts from the print-outs of the ledgers supplied by the computer is a straightforward task easily carried out manually. The reader should now study the chart on pages 402–3.

(1) Every transaction has an original document
(but now most of these documents will be produced by the computer automatically instead of manually)

Petty Cash vouchers

Other Firms' Statements

Our Statements

Letters about Errors

Invoices for Assets Bought

Bankruptcy Notices

Second Copies of our Credit Notes, sales returned to us

Credit Notes from other firms, our purchases returned

Second Copies of our own invoices, our Sales to other firms

Invoices from other firms, all different shapes and sizes, our Purchases

And our cheques

Recd. with thanks

And cheques from the Debtors

(2) Documents are no longer entered into Books of Original Entry. Instead groups of similar documents are coded with the necessary computer codes and 'batched-up' for preparation by the punched card operators or the key-edit operators. The resulting input media can then be fed in for processing by the computer. The sales procedure has been represented in diagrammatic form below. Other procedures have been indicated by brief notes

Other documents such as debit notes, credit notes, journal documents for journal entries are treated similarly according to their own requirements and lead to inputs, data processing and updating of all ledger accounts. The computer will thus hold the entire ledger system on its files, or as much of the system as the management decides

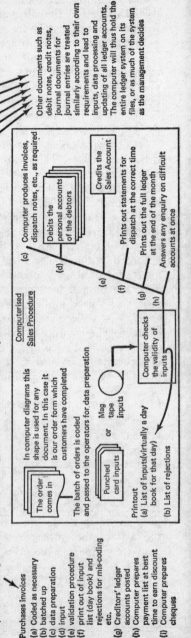

Computerised Sales Procedure

In computer diagrams this shape is used for any document. In this case it is our order form which customers have completed

The order comes in

The batch of orders is coded and passed to the operators for data preparation

Punched card inputs   or   Mag tape inputs

Computer checks the validity of inputs

Printout
(a) List of inputs(virtually a day book for that day)
(b) List of rejections

(c) Computer produces invoices, dispatch notes, etc., as required

(d) Debits the personal accounts of the debtors

Credits the Sales Account

(e) Prints out statements for dispatch at the correct time

(f) Prints out the full ledger at the end of the month

(g) Answers any enquiry on difficult accounts at once

(h)

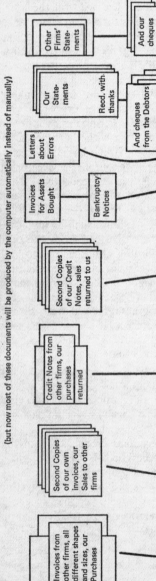

Purchases Invoices
(a) Coded as necessary
(b) batched up
(c) data preparation
(d) input
(e) validation procedure
(f) print out of input list (day book) and rejections for mis-coding etc.
(g) Creditors' ledger accounts posted
(h) Computer prepares payment list at best time to earn discount
(I) Computer prepares cheques

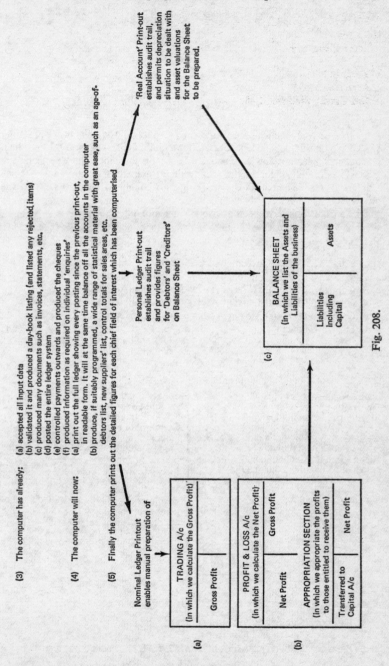

(3) The computer has already:

(a) accepted all input data
(b) validated it and produced a day-book listing [and listed any rejected items]
(c) produced many documents such as invoices, statements, etc.
(d) posted the entire ledger system
(e) controlled payments outwards and produced the cheques
(f) produced information as required on individual 'enquiries'

(4) The computer will now:

(a) print out the full ledger showing every posting since the previous print-out, in readable form. It will at the same time balance off all the accounts in the computer
(b) produce, if suitably programmed, a wide range of statistical material with great ease, such as an age-of-debtors list, new suppliers' list, control totals for sales areas, etc.

(5) Finally the computer prints out the detailed figures for each chief field of interest which has been computerised

Nominal Ledger Printout enables manual preparation of

'Real Account' Print-out establishes audit trail, and permits depreciation situation to be dealt with and asset valuations for the Balance Sheet to be prepared.

Personal Ledger Print-out establishes audit trail and provides figures for 'Debtors' and 'Creditors' on Balance Sheet

(a)
TRADING A/c
(In which we calculate the Gross Profit)

	Gross Profit

(b)
PROFIT & LOSS A/c
(In which we calculate the Net Profit)

Net Profit	Gross Profit

APPROPRIATION SECTION
(In which we appropriate the profits to those entitled to receive them)

Transferred to Capital A/c	Net Profit

(c)
BALANCE SHEET
(In which we list the Assets and Liabilities of the business)

Liabilities Including Capital	Assets

Fig. 208.

ANSWER SECTION

In this answer section one question in most of the sets has been fully worked to enable the student to see what a complete answer should look like.

The first question has not usually been chosen, since the questions are graded in difficulty. One of the more difficult questions in each main set has therefore been selected, as the working most likely to be of benefit to the student.

Other questions have been answered in abbreviated form.

CHAPTER 1, EXERCISES SET I, p. 9

1. Total 37,500·00; Current Assets 23,000·00; Fixed Assets 14,500·00.
2. Totals 33,250·00; Current Assets 17, 750·00; Fixed Assets 15,500·00.
3. Capital 18,101·00; Current Assets 5,561·00; Fixed Assets 12,540·00.
4. Capital 11,566·00; Current Assets 6,006·00; Fixed Assets 5,560·00.
5. Capital 5,000·00; Current Assets 3,284·00; Fixed Assets 6,363·50.
6. Shown below:

PETER CLEMENS

BALANCE SHEET

(as at January 1st, 19..)

CURRENT LIABILITIES			CURRENT ASSETS		
Wages Due	49·50		Prepaid Expenses	17·25	
Creditors	1,052·00		Cash in Hand	32·50	
			Cash at Bank	726·50	
		1,101·50	Stock	1,520·00	
LONG-TERM LIABILITIES			Trade Debtors	1,584·25	
Bank Loan	1,000·00				
Mortgage	3,000·00				3,880·50
		4,000·00	FIXED ASSETS		
CAPITAL			Motor Vehicles	1,655·50	
At Start		12,000·00	Furniture	325·50	
			Plant and Machinery	7,240·00	
			Land and Buildings	4,000·00	
					13,221·00
		17,101·50			17,101·50

CHAPTER 2, EXERCISES SET II, SIMPLE DEBTORS' ACCOUNTS, p. 18

1. Balance 255·53 Dr.; Account totals 447·16.
2. Balance 116·11 Dr.; Account totals 372·01.
3. Balance 253·07 Dr.; Account totals 296·51.

4. Shown below:

19..			19..		
Jan. 1	To Balance	247·16	Jan. 3	By Cheque	240·00
2	„ Sales	55·00	3	„ Discount	7·16
14	„ „	48·00	19	„ Returns	14·00
14	„ Carriage	2·50	31	„ Balance	136·75
29	„ Sales	45·25			
		397·91			397·91
Feb. 1	To Balance	136·75			

R. THOMAS — D.L. 37

CHAPTER 2, EXERCISES SET III, SIMPLE CREDITORS' ACCOUNTS, p. 20

1. Balance 366·07 Cr.; Account totals 618·92.
2. Balance 1,413·01 Cr.; Account totals 1,785·13.
3. Balance 225·27 Cr.; Account totals 481·46.
4. Shown below:

G. M. WHITEHEAD — C.L. 59

Dr. — Cr.

19..			19..		
Oct. 2	To Cheque	705·00	Oct. 1	By Balance	720·40
2	„ Discount	15·40	11	„ Purchases	426·50
14	„ Returns	26·50	19	„ „	224·50
27	„ Motor		20	„ Carriage	25·10
	Lorry	750·00	31	„ Balance	100·40
		1,496·90			1,496·90
19..					
Nov. 1	To Balance	100·40			

Written Answers to No. 4

(*a*) On October 27th our firm sold Whitehead a motor lorry. This is unusual, but it does happen that excess assets will be disposed of in this way.

(*b*) It upsets the balance of this account so that Whitehead owes 100·40 to us.

(*c*) The missing word is 'debtor'—our creditor has temporarily become a person who owes us money.

CHAPTER 2, EXERCISES SET IV, p. 25

1. Shown below:

No. 1.				CASH ACCOUNT			G.L. 27
Dr.							Cr.
19.. Dec. 1	To Balance	B/d	17·10	19.. Dec. 1	By Wages	G.L. 5	12·60
1	„ Cash	G.L. 26	20·00	1	„ Postage	G.L. 14	1·15
3	„ R. Jones	L. 1	2·10	2	„ Sundries	G.L. 15	0·30
3	„ P. Brown	L. 2	3·80	2	„ Stationery	G.L. 16	3·10
4	„ Cash Sales	L. 3	24·10	2	„ Stationery	G.L. 16	2·25
				3	„ R. Lewis	G.L. 27	1·15
				4	„ Sundries	G.L. 15	2·25
				4	„ Gratuities	G.L. 19	0·20
				4	„ Balance	c/d	44·10
			67·10				67·10
19.. Dec. 5	To Balance	c/d	44·10				

2. Balance 64·42; Totals 119·02.
3. Balance 58·91; Totals 101·61.
4. Balance 39·72; Totals 67·50.

CHAPTER 2, EXERCISES SET V, p. 27

1. Balance 415·25; Totals 681·85.
2. Balance 52·01; Totals 114·01.
3. Balance 1,017·93; Totals 1,183·78.
4. Balance 229·65; Totals 281·30.

CHAPTER 4, EXERCISES SET VI, p. 45

1. Total of Purchases Day Book = 100·30.
2. Total of Purchases Day Book = 412·65.
3. Total of Purchases Journal = 38·50.
4. Total of Purchases Journal = 54·50.

5. Shown below:

PURCHASES DAY BOOK

19..				
Jan. 1	O. Spinoza			
	3 Letra typewriters at 56·00 each		168·00	
	Less 25% Trade discount		42·00	
		C.L. 1		126·00
12	R. Ingram			
	12 Bruch teletypers at 340·00 each		4,080·00	
	6 long carriage Bruch manual typers at 40·00		240·00	
	24 portables at 30·00		720·00	
			5,040·00	
	Less 33⅓% Discount		1,680·00	
		C.L. 2		3,360·00
23	W. Owndell			
	200 reams white duplicating paper at 0·55 ream		110·00	
	Less 10% Trade Discount		11·00	
		C.L. 3		99·00
31	M. Tobler			
	300 dozen scribbling pads at 0·05 each		180·00	
	50 dozen at 0·03 each		18·00	
			198·00	
	Less 33⅓% Trade Discount		66·00	
		C.L. 4		132·00
				3,717·00
				G.L. 27

6. Total of Purchases Journal = 142·20.

CHAPTER 4, EXERCISES SET VII, THE SALES DAY BOOK, p. 52
Total of Sales Day Book as follows:

1. 84·65	2. 40·60	3. 748·00
4. 146·95	5. 1,070·16	6. 237·60

CHAPTER 4, EXERCISES SET VIII, THE PURCHASES RETURNS BOOK, p. 59
Totals of Purchases Returns Books as follows:

1. 9·85	2. 80·90	3. 31·50
4. 6·40	5. 58·10	6. 17·26

CHAPTER 4, EXERCISES SET IX, THE SALES RETURNS BOOK, p. 64
Totals of Sales Returns Books are as follows:

1. 63·10	2. 68·20	3. 30·00
4. 28·40	5. 14·85	6. 43·45

CHAPTER 5, EXERCISES SET X, THE THREE-COLUMN CASH BOOK, p. 84

1. Cash Balance 30·50; Bank Balance 653·97; Discount Totals — Discount Allowed = 0·53; Discount Received 1·25.

2. Cash Balance 11·19; Bank Balance 237·61; Discount Allowed 2·65; Discount Received 18·59.

3. Cash Balance 29·79; Bank Balance 356·80; Discount Allowed total 4·77; Discount Received total 6·80.

4. Cash Balance 51·04; Bank Balance 1,387·12; Discount Allowed total 6·24; Discount Received total 2·60.

5. Cash Balance 76·33; Bank Balance 1,521·19; Discount Allowed total 0·74; Discount Received total 2·90.

6. Cash Balance 22·97; Bank Balance 1,322·37; Discount Allowed 1·43; Discount Received ——.

7. Cash Balance 34·91; Bank Balance 152·57; Discount Allowed 1·44; Discount Received 2·90.

8. Shown opposite (page 407).

9. Cash Balance 42·69; Bank Balance 339·45; Discount Allowed, nil; Discount Received 5·20.

10. Cash Balance 17·85; Bank Balance 610·75; Discount Allowed 1·00; Discount Received, nil.

CHAPTER 6, EXERCISES SET XI, OPENING JOURNAL ENTRIES, p. 94

1. Capital = 160·00
2. Capital = 3,410·00
3. Capital = 6,945·00
4. Capital = 1,807·60
5. Capital = 53,363·16
6. Capital = 5,912·00
7. Capital = 28,794·19
8. Capital = 12,305·28
9. Capital = 7,400·50 each
10. See below.

19..					
Aug. 1	Cash in Hand	Dr.	C.B. 1	60·00	
	Cash at Bank	„	C.B. 1	580·00	
	Stock	„	L. 1	500·00	
	M. Larkin	„	L. 2	50·00	
	P. Holm	„	L. 3	80·00	
	Furniture	„	L. 4	400·00	
	To R. Romer		L. 5		140·00
	„ F. Cruncher		L. 6		140·00
	„ Capital		L. 7		1,390·00
				1,670·00	1,670·00
	Being assets and liabilities at this date				

CHAPTER 6, EXERCISES SET XII, PURCHASES OF ASSETS, p. 98

1. Debit Typewriters 75·00; Credit Cash 75·00.

2. Debit Machinery 165·00; Credit Bank 165·00.

3. Debit L. & B. Account 2,800·00; Credit Loamshire Property Ltd. 2,800·00.

JOHN BROWN'S CASH BOOK

Dr.

Date	Particulars	F.	Discount	Cash	Bank
19.. May 1	To Balance	B/d		27·50	
3	,, R. Wich	L.9	2·90	5·00	
4	,, Cash Sales	L.10		87·70	
4	,, Cash	C			50·00
6	,, R. Libbey	L.11			97·10
7	,, Balance	c/d			220·30
			2·90	120·20	367·40
			L.12		
19.. May 8	To Balance	B/d		40·78	

Cr.

Date	Particulars	F.	Discount	Cash	Bank
19.. May 1	By Overdraft	B/d			270·65
2	,, Postage	L.1		2·60	
2	,, Repairs	L.2		1·47	27·10
2	,, R. Jones	L.3	1·90		
3	,, Travelling Expenses	L.4		0·35	
4	,, Bank	C		50·00	
5	,, Cash Purchases	L.5			17·50
5	,, Rent	L.6		10·00	29·50
5	,, Wages	L.7			
7	,, Rates	L.6		15·00	22·65
7	,, Drawings	L.8		40·78	
7	,, Balance	c/d			
			1·90	120·20	367·40
			L.13		
19.. May 8	By Balance	B/d			220·30

4. Yachts Account Debit 280·00; Credit Seaway Ltd. 280·00.

5. Sports Equipment Account Dr. 220·50; Credit Tuff Hessian Ltd. 220·50.

6. Showcase Account Debit 60·00; Credit Shopfitters Ltd. 60·00.

7. Debit Weighing Machines 40·00; Furniture and Fittings 25·00; Purchases 220·00; Motor Vehicles 120·00; Credit Cash 405·00.

8. Shown below:

19.. Aug. 1	Furniture and Fittings Dr. Office Machinery ,, To Business Supplies Ltd. Being purchase of new equipment at this date	L.1 L.2 L.3	68·10 161·75	229·85

9. Debit Pipelayer 1,000·00; Trench Cutter 1,850·00; Water Carrier 1,450·00; General Equipment 1,700·00; Credit Bank Account 6,000·00.

10. Debit Plant and Machinery 2,200·00; Motor Vehicles 450·00; Furniture and Fittings 280·00; Purchases Account 800·00; Credit Bank 3,730·00.

CHAPTER 6, EXERCISES SET XIII, DEPRECIATION OF ASSETS, p. 100

1. Debit depreciation 200·00; Credit Motor Vehicles 200·00.

2. Dr. Depreciation 148·00; Credit Furniture and Fittings 148·00.

3. Depreciation 190·00.

4. Final Value 24,000·00.

5. Total Depreciation 1,494·00.

6. Total Depreciation 4,600·00.

CHAPTER 6, EXERCISES SET XIV, THE SALE OF WORN-OUT ASSETS, p. 103
The numerical answers here are obvious.

CHAPTER 6, EXERCISES SET XV, SIMPLE BAD DEBTS, p. 107

1, 2 and 3. The numerical answers are obvious.

4. Cash 12·00; Bad Debt 228·00.

5. Cash 280·00; Bad Debt 120·00.

6. Cash 71·50; Bad Debt 58·50.

7–11. The numerical answers are obvious.

CHAPTER 6, EXERCISES SET XVI, THE CORRECTION OF ERRORS, p. 111
Numerical answers are obvious.

CHAPTER 6, EXERCISES SET XVII, DISHONOURED CHEQUES, p. 114
Numerical answers are obvious.

CHAPTER 6, EXERCISES SET XVIII, BANK LOANS, INTEREST, AND CHARGES, p. 117
Numerical answers are obvious.

CHAPTER 7, EXERCISES SET XIX, THE PETTY CASH BOOK, p. 123

1. Total Column 13·48; Balance 16·52.

2. Total Column 6·44; Balance 3·56.

3. Total Column 12·07; Balance 7·93.

4. Total Column 31·31; Balance in Hand 19·14.

5. Shown here:

| Dr. | | THE PETTY CASH BOOK | | | | | | | | | | Cr. |

THE PETTY CASH BOOK

Dr.	19..		P.C.V.	Total	Postage	Trav. Exp.	Sundry Exp.	Wages		Folio	Ledger A./cs.
25·00	Jan. 1	To Imprest	C.B. 1								
	1	By Postage	1	2·50	2·50						
	2	,, Repairs	2	2·45			2·45				
	2	,, Sundries	3	0·10			0·10				
	2	,, Postage	4	4·25	4·25						
	2	,, R. Morgan	5	1·75						L. 5	1·75
	3	,, Sundry Expenses	6	0·62			0·62				
	3	,, Cleaner's Wages	7	2·50				2·50			
	4	,, Postage	8	0·36	0·36						
	4	,, Travelling Expenses	9	0·25		0·25					
	5	,, Sundry Expenses	10	0·55			0·55				
	5	,, Stamps	11	1·45	1·45						
	6	,, Postage	12	1·43	1·43						
	6	,, Wages	13	3·65				3·65			
				21·86	9·99	0·25	3·72	6·15			1·75
		,, Balance	c/d	3·14	L. 1	L. 2	L. 3	L. 4			
25·00				25·00							
3·14		To Balance	B/d								
21·86		,, Restored Imprest	C.B. 9								

6. Total Spent 7·36; Debit side total 13·07; Balance 5·71.
7. Total Column 10·94; Balance in Hand 9·06.
9. Total Column 5·72; Balance in Hand 4·28.
10. Total Column 14·98; Balance in Hand 6·70; Total of Dr. side 21·68.
11. Total Column 8·83; Balance in Hand 1·17.
12. (*a*) 47·17.

(*b*) Carriage Inwards 18·10; General Expenses 2·15; Postage and Tele-phone 2·10; Stationery 0·15; Travelling Expenses 21·13; Carriage Outwards 3·54.

(*c*) Carriage Outwards Account.

CHAPTER 8, EXERCISES SET XX, BOOK-KEEPING TO THE TRIAL BALANCE, p. 142

1. Opening Capital 3,726·00; Cash Book Balances Cash 145·25; Bank 691·25; Trial Balance totals 4,881·55.
2. Opening Capital 2,530·00; Cash Book Balances Cash 94·05; Bank 717·00; Trial Balance totals 3,670·15.
3. Opening Capital 2,521·87; Cash Book Balances Cash 41·88; Bank 778·50; Trial Balance totals 2,891·04.
4. Opening Capital 3,500·00; Cash Book Balances Cash 131·15; Bank 2,956·00; Trial Balance totals 4,075·05.
5. Opening Capital 2,678·00; Cash Book Balances Cash 35·50; Bank 510·10; Trial Balance totals 3,803·00.
6. Opening Capital 7,859·85; Cash Book Balances Cash 54·64; Bank 886·50; Trial Balance totals 10,685·19.

CHAPTER 9, EXERCISES SET XXI, TRIAL BALANCES AND SUSPENSE ACCOUNTS, p. 152

8. (*b*) Suspense Account Debited with 18·54.

CHAPTER 10, EXERCISES SET XXII, CONTINUOUS BALANCE ACCOUNTS, p. 161

1. Balance 48·50; Bird is a debtor, owing us the balance.
2. Balance 79·80 Credit. Balance should go on credit side of Trial Balance. George & Co. to pay.
3. Balance = 153·00 Debit balance.
4. Balance 33·10—a credit balance.
Source of information: 4th Purchases Day Book; 7th Purchases Returns Book; 11th Cash Book; 30th Journal Proper.
5. Balance 72·00 Owed by Hurst to Billings.
6. Balance 49·48.
Double Entry would be in Fixtures and Fittings Account.

CHAPTER 11, EXERCISES SET XXIII, BANK RECONCILIATION STATEMENTS, p. 167

1. New Cash Book Balance = 357·65.
2. New Cash Book Balance = 347·00.
3. New Cash Book Balance = 45·01.
4. New Cash Book Balance = 259·93.
5. ——.
6. New Cash Book Balance = 610·00.
7. New Cash Book Balance = 200·94.

8. ——.   9. ——.
10. New Cash Book Balance = 456·03.
11. New Cash Book Balance = 908·82.
12. New Cash Book Balance = 184·34.

CHAPTER 12, EXERCISES SET XXIV, ANALYSIS DAY BOOKS, p. 173

3. Total 611·50; Gramophones 186·00; Wireless Sets 51·00; Miscellaneous Instruments 374·50.
4. Total 261·90; Seeds 153·25; Bulbs 10·40; Flowers 82·25; Plants 16·00.
5. Total 49·66; Stationery 11·30; Confectionery 20·46; Chemists' Sundries 7·10; Toys 10·80.

CHAPTER 13, EXERCISES SET XXV, THE BANK CASH BOOK, p. 177

1. Balance at Bank 1,007·65; Totals of Bank Columns = 1,080·27; Discount Allowed 3·03.
2. Balance at Bank 861·77; Totals of Bank Columns = 1,028·27.
3. Balance at Bank 612·98; Totals of Bank Columns = 1,200·58; Discount Allowed 2·50; Discount Received 5·00.
4. Balance as per Cash Book 1,583·47; Totals of Bank Columns = 1,842·00; Discount Allowed 19·45; Discount Received 7·55.

CHAPTER 14, EXERCISES SET XXVI, DEPRECIATION, p. 186

1. Depreciation = 160·00 per year.
2. Depreciation 1st year 150·00, 2nd year 285·00, 3rd year 256·50; Final Balance 2,308·50.
3. 1st year depreciation 320·00, 2nd year depreciation 256·00, but car sold for 450·00 was valued on books as 384·00 so we recoup 66·00 appreciation on it.
4. Depreciation 55·00 per year.
5. Depreciation 2,475·00.
6. Depreciation 202·00.
7. Depreciation 800·00, 720·00, 648·00.
8. Depreciation year 1 = 480·00; year 2 = 720·00; year 3 = Depreciation = 780 − 30 = 750·00. Balance of Motor Lorry A/c 3,900·00. Balance of Provision for Depreciation A/c = 1,500·00.

CHAPTER 15, EXERCISES SET XXVII, WAGES BOOKS, p. 194

1. Net pay 16·95, 15·80, 14·65; Total 47·40.
2. Net Pay 10·77, 12·48, 11·53, 12·81; Total 47·59.
3. Net Pay 17·59, 16·76, 28·78, 18·06; Total 81·19.
4. Net Pay 18·74, 13·62, 12·92, 13·82; Total 59·10.

CHAPTER 16, EXERCISES SET XXVIII, THE TRIAL BALANCE, p. 200

1. Totals of Trial Balance = 95,275·00.
2. Totals of Trial Balance = 27,534·00.
3. Totals of Trial Balance = 188,910·00.
4. Totals of Trial Balance = 54,659·90.
5. Totals of Trial Balance = 676,800·00.

6. (1) Dr. Column—Asset; (2) Cr. Column—Liability; (3) Cr. Column—Liability; (4) Dr. Column—Loss; (5) Cr. Column—Profit; (6) Dr. Column—Capital withdrawn.

7. Trial Balance totals = 17,625·00.

8. Totals of Trial Balance = 46,400·00.

9. Totals of Trial Balance = 8,610·00.

10. Totals of Trial Balance = 55,232·25.

CHAPTER 17, EXERCISES SET XXIX, TRADING ACCOUNTS, p. 213

1. Gross Profit 11,888·90.
2. Gross Profit 26,689·35.
3. Gross Profit 4,569·55.
4. Gross Profit 3,293·30.
5. Shown below:

E. RANDALL

TRADING ACCOUNT

(for year ended December 31st, 19. .)

To Opening Stock		2,785·00	By Sales	7,642·00
„ Purchases	6,908·00		*Less* Returns In	262·00
„ Import Charges	126·00			
			Net Sales	7,380·00
	7,034·00			
Less Returns	195·00			
Net Purchases		6,839·00		
Total Stock Available		9,624·00		
Less Closing Stock		4,440·00		
Cost of Stock Sold		5,184·00		
To Wages	700·00			
„ Wages Due	20·00			
		720·00		
Cost of Sales		5,904·00		
To Gross Profit		1,476·00		
		7,380·00		7,380·00

6. Gross Profit 3,262·00.

7. Gross Profit 3,000·00; (*b*) it would have been 2,160·00.

8. ——.

CHAPTER 18, EXERCISES SET XXX, PROFIT AND LOSS ACCOUNTS, p. 220

1. Net Profit 1,028·70.
2. Net Profit 3,243·00.
3. Net Profit 3,950·80.
4. Gross Profit 3,786·49; Net Profit 2,466·41.
5. Gross Profit 9,955·00; Net Profit 2,490·00.
6. Gross Profit 39,300·00; Net Profit 33,600·00.

CHAPTER 19, EXERCISES SET XXXI, SIMPLE FINAL ACCOUNTS, p. 226

1. Gross Profit 5,130·00; Net Profit 1,670·00; Balance Sheet 17,460·00.
2. Gross Profit 4,310·00; Net Profit 1,179·90; Balance Sheet totals 34,201·20.
3. Gross Profit 1,757·90; Net Profit 641·65; Balance Sheet totals 5,852·40.
4. Gross Profit 5,172·00; Net Profit 2,595·25; Balance Sheet totals 10,710·75.
5. Gross Profit 7,799·00; Net Profit 944·00; Balance Sheet totals 17,844·00.
6. Gross Profit 8,149·50; Net Profit 6,231·50; Balance Sheet totals 16,284·75.
7. Gross Profit 18,728·00; Net Profit 7,356·00; Balance Sheet totals 47,348·00.
8. Shown below:

TRADING ACCOUNT

(for year ending December 31st, 19..)

To Opening Stock		4,256·00	By Sales	28,680·50
„ Purchases	15,340·75		*Less* Returns	756·50
+Carriage Inwards	115·50			
			Net Sales	27,924·00
	15,456·25			
—Returns Outwards	126·25			
Net Purchases		15,330·00		
Total Stock Available		19,586·00		
—Closing Stock		4,000·00		
Cost of Stock Sold		15,586·00		
To Wages	2,340·00			
„ Power, Light, and Heat	2,300·00			
		4,640·00		
Cost of Sales		20,226·00		
To Gross Profit		7,698·00		
		27,924·00		27,924·00

PROFIT AND LOSS ACCOUNT

(for year ending December 31st, 19..)

To Discount Allowed		730·75	By Gross Profit	7,698·00
„ Rent and Rates		1,250·00	„ Discount Received	228·25
„ Miscellaneous Expenses		521·50	„ Interest Received	100·50
„ Salaries		730·00		
„ Office Expenses		630·00		8,026·75
„ Depreciation				
Lease	200·00			
Freehold	200·00			
		400·00		
		4,262·25		
„ Net Profit		3,764·50		
		8,026·75		8,026·75

BALANCE SHEET

(for year ending December 31st, 19. .)

CAPITAL			FIXED ASSETS		
At Start		8,960·00	Freehold Premises	1,300·00	
Add Profit	3,764·50		Leasehold Premises	2,300·00	
Less Drawings	2,100·00		Fixtures and Fittings	1,760·00	
		1,664·50			5,360·00
		10,624·50	CURRENT ASSETS		
LONG-TERM LIABILITIES		0·00	Debtors	6,300·50	
			Stock	4,000·00	
CURRENT LIABILITIES			Cash at Bank	3,210·00	
Creditors		10,500·50	Cash in Hand	2,254·50	
					15,765·00
		21,125·00			21,125·00

CHAPTER 20, EXERCISES SET XXXII, CAPITAL AND REVENUE EXPENDITURE, p. 237

1. Telephone expenses and office salaries would be revenue expenses. New weighing machines and new counters are capital expenses. Wages of men fitting counters are a revenue expense that has to be capitalized so they count as a capital expense.

2. The Gorilla and the Monkey House are capital expenses and go in the Balance Sheet. The hire of equipment and repairs are revenue expenses and go in the Profit and Loss Account. Keepers' wages are a revenue expense and go in the Trading Account, or some people might put them in the Profit and Loss Account.

3. The crockery loss is taken in as a reduction of stock.

4. Debit Plant and Machinery with 2,510·00, Credit Carriage Account 85·00, Wages Account 75·00, and Wormco Eng. Ltd. 2,350·00.

5. Motor van and typewriter are capital expenses. Postage, goods for resale, repairs, and teas for staff are Revenue Expenses. The motor vehicle and typewriter will still be on his books—also possibly some of the goods for resale.

6. The painting machine, the new canteen, and the wages of the building workers are capital items which appear in the Balance Sheet, the wages of the lino workers, and the pitch are revenue items appearing in the Trading Account, and the paper and string is a revenue item appearing in the Profit and Loss Account.

7. These losses appear as reduced stock.

8. Wages as attendants are a revenue expense appearing in the Trading Account, wages as repairers are a revenue expense appearing in the Profit and Loss Account, wages paid erecting the sideshow are a capital expense, appear as Sideshows in Balance Sheet.

9. (*a*) See text; (*b*) Cooker and alterations to premises—capital expense. Hire charges and redecorations revenue expenses—but some of the redecorations might be capitalized.

10. See Text.

11. This loss appears as reduced stock.

12. (*a*) See text; (*b*) Adding listing machine and two typewriters for office use are capital expenditure—other items revenue expenditure; (*c*) Premises increase by 250·00, profits increase by 250·00.

13. (*a*) See text; (*b*) Premises are debited with 5,500·00, altogether, Repairs Account with 80·00, painting and decorating 170·00, and Bank Account is credited with a total of 5,750·00.

14. (*a*) See text; (*b*) ——; (*c*) Debit Premises Account with 400·00 and Decorations in Suspense Account 200·00, credit Wages Account 300·00, and Purchases Account 300·00.

CHAPTER 21, EXERCISES SET XXXIII, STOCK VALUATION, p. 246

1. 3,945·00.
2. 3,000 units valued at 2,366·00.
3. 3,360·00
4. Gross Profit 1,262·20.
5. Gross Profit 2,956·00.
6. Gross Profit 1,235·00.
7. Closing Stock = 5,000·00.
8. Closing Stock = 5,570·00.
9. Closing Stock = 2,696·00.
10. Closing Stock = 3,877·00.
11. Closing Stock = 5,200·00.
12. Stock lost in fire = 3,210·00.

CHAPTER 22, EXERCISES SET XXXIV, PAYMENTS IN ADVANCE, p. 253

1. Debit Balance of 100·00; Transfer to Profit and Loss Account 400·00.
2. Debit Balance 49·00; Transfer to Profit and Loss Account 137·50.
3. Credit Balance of 255·00; Transfer to Income and Expenditure Account is 6,225·00.
4. Credit Balance 525·00; Transfer to Profit and Loss Account 5,586·50.

CHAPTER 22, EXERCISES SET XXXV, ACCRUED EXPENSES AND ACCRUED RECEIPTS, p. 257

1. Debit Balance 39·00; Profit carried to Profit and Loss Account = 156·00.
2. Credit Balance 82·50; Loss carried to Manufacturing Account 151·10, and to Profit and Loss Account 75·55.
3. Credit Balance of 20·00; Balance Sheet entry, Rent due 20·00.
4. Debit Balance 1,020·45; Amount transferred to Profit and Loss Account 10,171·05; Balance Sheet entry, Repairs unpaid—asset side 1,020·45.

CHAPTER 22, EXERCISES SET XXXVI, FINAL ACCOUNTS EXERCISES WITH PAYMENTS IN ADVANCE AND ACCRUED EXPENSES, p. 258

1. (*a*) Salaries Credit Balance 28·00; Rates Debit Balance 185·00; (*b*) The profits would have been 157·00 less.

2. Amount chargeable to Profit and Loss Account 230·35; Credit Balance 22·10 or can be shown as Debit Balance 27·90, and Credit Balance 50·00.

3. Amount charged to Profit and Loss Account = 567·50; Balances Debit side 42·50; Credit side 100·00.

4. Gross Profit 5,320·25; Net Profit 4,599·50; Balance Sheet totals 10,442·50.

5. Gross Profit 10,017·00; Net Profit 9,653·25; Balance Sheet totals 18,782·50.

6. Gross Profit 16,268·25; Net Profit 15,039·25; Balance Sheet totals 23,346·75.

7. Gross Profit 591·25; Net Loss 153·25; Balance Sheet totals 4,572·50.

CHAPTER 22, EXERCISES SET XXXVII, BAD DEBTS AND PROVISIONS FOR BAD DEBTS, p. 266.

1. (*a*) Net Amounts provided 1st year 126·00, 2nd year 77·00; (*b*) Debtors 5,130·00

2. (*a*) Total charge to Profit and Loss Account 540·00; Final Value of Debtors after deducting Provision = 6,300·00.

3. Charge to Profit and Loss Account 100·37.

4. Charge to Profit and Loss Account 143·00; Final Value of Debtors after deducting Provision 2,337·00.

5. Charge to Profit and Loss Account 47·00; Final Provision 72·00.

6. Charge to Profit and Loss Account 87·00; Final Provision 47·00.

7. Charge to Profit and Loss Account for Provision 41·00, for Legal Charges 8·40; Profit taken to Profit and Loss Account 3·00.

8. Gross Profit 9,944·00; Net Profit 3,052·00; Balance Sheet totals 11,753·00.

9. Gross Profit 4,354·65; Net Profit 2,670·50; Balance Sheet totals 15,140·00.

10. Gross Profit 1,155·00; Net Profit 525·65; Balance Sheet totals 3,933·75.

CHAPTER 22, EXERCISES SET XXXVIII, FINAL ACCOUNTS WITH ALL TYPES OF ADJUSTMENTS. p. 273

1. Net Profit 1,050·00; Balance Sheet totals 9,483·00.

2. Net Profit 2,480·50; Balance Sheet totals 6,541·25.

3. Gross Profit 3,300·00; Net Loss 331·00; Balance Sheet totals 13,319·50.

4. Gross Profit 8,803·00; Net Profit 5,481·00; Balance Sheet totals 16,718·00.

CHAPTER 23, EXERCISES SET XXXIX, THE APPROPRIATION ACCOUNT, p. 282

1. Share of Residue for each 1,775·00.

2. Share of Residue: 300·00 to Arthur; 200·00 to Brian.

3. Share of Residue: 1,500·00 to Sybrandt; 750·00 to Cornelis.

4. Share of Residue: Nelson 1,200·00; Blake 1,800·00; Hardy 1,800·00.

5.

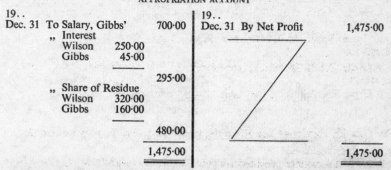

G. WILSON AND W. GIBBS

APPROPRIATION ACCOUNT

19..			19..		
Dec. 31	To Salary, Gibbs'	700·00	Dec. 31	By Net Profit	1,475·00
	„ Interest				
	Wilson 250·00				
	Gibbs 45·00				
		295·00			
	„ Share of Residue				
	Wilson 320·00				
	Gibbs 160·00				
		480·00			
		1,475·00			1,475·00

CHAPTER 23, EXERCISES SET XL, CURRENT ACCOUNTS OF PARTNERS, p. 286

1. Balance on Current Accounts: Wilson 1,370·00 Credit; Brown 1,000·00 Credit.

2. Balance on Current Account 478·00 Credit.

3. Capital Accounts are unchanged at Hemp 12,000·00; Wool 10,000·00; Cotton 8,000·00.
Current Accounts: Hemp 1,770·00 Credit; Cotton 1,900·00 Credit; Wool 730·00 Credit.

4. Current Account balance 75·00 Credit.

5. Appropriation Account totals 1,281·00.
Current Account balances: David 79·60 Credit; Peter 346·40 Credit.

CHAPTER 23, EXERCISES SET XLI, THE FINAL ACCOUNTS OF PARTNERSHIPS, p. 288

1. Net Profit = 2,198·00.
Appropriation Account Residue: Arthur 658·80; Brian 439·20.
Current Account balances: Arthur 135·30; Brian 253·45.
Balance Sheet totals 14,740·25.

2. Current Account balances: Bath 965·00 Credit; Wells 55·00 Debit; Balance Sheet totals 4,575·00.

3. Current Account balances: Peele 1,800·00 Credit; Melles 1,380·00 Credit; Balance Sheet totals 9,301·00.

4. Gross Profit 3,299·00; Net Loss 250·00; Current Account balances (both debits): Haig 1,050·00; Grant 800·00; Balance Sheet totals 15,850·00.

5. Gross Profit 6,099·75; Net Profit 2,339·00; Current Account balances: King 108·00; Snagsby 731·00; Balance Sheet totals 7,266·00.

6. Gross Profit 6,821·50; Net Profit 2,201·50; Current Accounts balances: Forsyth 212·65 Credit; Gordon 301·50 Credit; Balance Sheet totals 14,000·50.

7. Gross Profit 6,322·50; Net Profit 3,752·00; Current Accounts balances: Tree 789·00; Branch 763·00; Balance Sheet totals 20,972·75.

CHAPTER 24, EXERCISES SET XLII, RECEIPTS AND PAYMENTS ACCOUNTS, p. 300

1. Cash Balance 153·35.
2. No answer needed.
3. Cash Balance 293·40.
4. Cash Balance 482·95.

CHAPTER 24, EXERCISES SET XLIII, CLUB FINAL ACCOUNTS, p. 306

1. Income and Expenditure Account totals 451·00; Surplus 161·00; Balance Sheet totals 246·50.
2. Income and Expenditure Account totals 343·00; Surplus 40·00; Balance Sheet totals read 163·00; Accumulated Fund total 163·00.
3. Income and Expenditure Account totals 640·00; Surplus 223·50; Balance Sheet totals 340·00.
4. Income and Expenditure Account totals 381·00; Surplus 37·95.
5. Income and Expenditure Account totals 510·25; Surplus 320·85; Balance Sheet totals 944·15.
6. Income and Expenditure Account totals 4,536·00; Surplus 581·50; Balance Sheet totals 8,105·50.
7. Profit on Refreshments 61·50; Income and Expenditure Account totals 629·00; Surplus 53·00; Balance Sheet totals 2,701·00.
8. Amount of Subscription income 350·00.
9. Balance on Life Members' Subscription Account 11·00 Credit; Balance on Ordinary Members' Subscription Account 3·00 Debit.
10. Cash Balance 67·00; Income and Expenditure Account totals 324·00; Surplus 43·00; Balance Sheet totals 1,173·00.
11. Receipts and Payments Account totals 2,982·00; Balance in Hand = 104·00; Income and Expenditure Account totals 1,304·00; Surplus for year 19·00.
12. Bar Profits 996·50; Dances and Socials profits 51·50; Income and Expenditure Account totals 1,538·00; Surplus 449·00; Balance Sheet totals 1,489·00.

CHAPTER 25, EXERCISES SET XLIV, FINDING PROFITS BY THE INCREASED NET WORTH METHOD, p. 317

1. Profits for the year = 2,762·00.
2. Profits for the year = 1,798·50.
3. Profits for the quarter-year = 499·00.
4. Profits for the half-year = 580·00.
Singleton cannot tell the turnover of his business, the gross profit he is making, or the expenses of the business under any particular heading.
5. Profit for the year = 1,000·00.
6. Profit for the year = 400·00.

CHAPTER 26, EXERCISES SET XLV, GROSS PROFIT PERCENTAGE, p. 325

1. Gross Profit = 500·00, which is $33\frac{1}{3}$ per cent.
2. No numerical answer required.

3. No numerical answer required.

4. (*a*) Gross Profit 20,000·00; Trading Account totals 120,000·00; (*b*) 20·8 per cent; (*c*) 120,000·00; (*d*) 16⅔ per cent.

CHAPTER 26, EXERCISES SET XLVI, GROSS AND NET PROFIT PERCENTAGES, p. 329

1. Gross Profit percentages: year 1 = 24·46, year 2 = 23·41.
Net Profit percentages: year 1 = 5·84, year 2 = 12·8.

2. Stock valuation 2,000·00: Revenue Expenditure must be limited to 1,500·00.

3. Gross Profit 2,291·00; Sales 9,164·00; Purchases 7,373·00.

4. Estimated Results 3,350·00.

5. Sales figure 16,500·00; Purchases figure 14,700·00.

6. (*a*) (i) Cost Price of goods sold 50,000·00; (ii) Turnover 80,000·00; (iii) Gross Profit on Cost = 60 per cent; (iv) Gross Profit on Turnover = 37½ per cent; (v) Net Profit on Turnover = 12½ per cent.

(*b*) Net Profit for following year = 15,900·00.

7. Sheffield Gross Profit percentage: 1st year = 25, 2nd year = 25; Sheffield Net Profit percentage: 1st year = 16⅔, 2nd year = 16⅔.

Manchester Gross Profit percentage: 1st year = 33⅓, 2nd year = 40; Manchester Net Profit percentage: 1st year = 14·68, 2nd year = 21.

8. Gross Profit percentage: 1st year = 33, 2nd year = 30. Net Profit percentage: 1st year = 12, 2nd year = 12½.

9. No numerical answer required.

10. No numerical answer required.

CHAPTER 26, EXERCISES SET XLVII, RATE OF STOCK TURNOVER, p. 333

1. Gross Profit 2,500·00.

2. Net Profit 2,200·00.

3. Net Profit 2,500·00.

4. Net Profit 1,000·00.

5. (*a*) (i) Net Profit 1,600·00; (*b*) (ii) Net Profit 4,000·00.

6. Gross Profit 5,400·00; Net Profit 2,592·00; Expenses 2,808·00. Estimated Sales 28,728·00; Estimated Gross Profit 6,048·00; Estimated Expenses 3,160·00; Estimated Net Profit 2,888·00.

7. Gross Profit 8,400·00; Net Profit 5,250·00; Expenses 3,150·00. Estimated Sales 63,000·00; Estimated Gross Profit 7,000·00; Estimated Expenses 3,150·00; Estimated Net Profit 3,850·00.

8. Turnover = 33,604·00
Cost of Goods sold = 25,536·00
Purchases = 22,344·00
Rate of Turnover of Stock = 16 times
Gross Profit percentage = 24

CHAPTER 26, EXERCISES SET XLVIII, BALANCE SHEET INTERPRETATION, p. 338

1. Capital owned 11,250·00; Capital employed 17,400·00; Working Capital = 3,650·00; Profit = 18·75 per cent of Capital invested.

2. Capital owned 5,025·00; Capital employed 12,050·00; Deficiency of Working Capital = 525·00.

3. Fixed Assets = 10,840·00; Working Capital = 3,586·00.

4. Balance Sheet totals 5,725·25; Current Account balances: Grouse 430·00, Moor 350·00; Current Assets 4,365·25; Fixed Assets 1,360·00; Liquid Assets 1,701·00; Current Liabilities 557·25; Working Capital 3,808·00.

5. Balance Sheet totals 9,165·00.

6. Balance Sheet totals 4,195·00.

7. Current Assets 2,900·00; Working Capital 1,600·00; Effect on Working Capital—reduced by 300·00; Effect on Capital of Dee and Jaye—each increased by 100·00.

8. Numerical answers not required.

9. (a) Capital 189·00; Deficiency 0·00.

(b) Liabilities 5,520·00; Deficiency 0·00.

(c) Assets 7,559·00; Deficiency 0·00.

(d) Capital 0·00; Assets 8,481·00.

(e) Capital 0·00; Liabilities 8,580·00.

10. Numerical answers not required.

11. (a) Increase of Capital by 35·00.

(b) None.

(c) Decrease of Capital by 35·00.

(d) Decrease of Capital by 50·00.

(e) None.

12. (a) 3,850·00 (e) 3,700·00
(b) 3,800·00 (f) 3,600·00
(c) 3,775·00 (g) 3,500·00
(d) 3,740·00

CHAPTER 27, EXERCISES SET XLIX, DEPARTMENTAL ACCOUNTS, p. 347

1. Gross Profits: Dept. A 12,047·25; Dept. B 10,077·55; Total 22,124·80.

2. Gross Profits: Dept. A 13,709·20; Dept. B 22,069·05; Total 35,778·25. Net Profits: Dept. A 13,027·30; Dept. B 20,717·60; Total 33,744·90.

3. Gross Profits: Junior 2,100·00; Senior: Loss of 350·00; Total 1,750·00.

4. Gross Profits: Groceries 8,428·75; Fruit 5,998·25; Total 14,427·00. Net Profit 2,202·75. Balance Sheet totals 15,838·75.

5. Gross Profit: Dept. A 3,769·20; Dept. B 2,561·30; Total 6,330·50. Net Profit: Dept. A 1,905·60; Dept. B 1,318·90; Total 3,224·50. Balance Sheet totals 18,076·00.

CHAPTER 28, EXERCISES SET L, MANUFACTURING ACCOUNTS, p. 357

1. Prime Cost 19,808·50; Cost of Manufactured Goods 24,571·25; Gross Profits 9,979·00.

2. Prime Cost 34,660·95; Cost of Manufactured Goods 40,396·45; Gross Profit 16,849·35.

3. Prime Costs 79,233·75; Manufacturing Profit 11,716·00; Gross Profit 23,480·00.

4. Prime Costs 76,501·30; Manufacturing Profit 36,248·20; Gross Profit 13,399·30.

5. Prime Costs 25,350·50; Manufacturing Loss 1,050·75; Gross Profit 3,299·75.

6. Prime Costs 48,326·00; Manufacturing Profit 7,963·50; Gross Profit 13,299·25.

CHAPTER 29, EXERCISES SET LI, LIMITED COMPANY ACCOUNTS, p. 373

1. Balance on Appropriation Account 1,700·00; Balance Sheet total 94,400·00; Ordinary Shareholders' Interest in the Company 64,200·00.

2. Ordinary Shareholders' Interest 105,000·00; Net Value of Current Assets 55,250·00; Balance Sheet totals 125,000·00.

3. Balance on Appropriation Account 5,200·00; Ordinary Shareholders' Interest 112,200·00; Balance Sheet total 158,200·00.

4. Ordinary Shareholders' Interest 39,658·00; Balance Sheet totals 43,658·00.

5. Balance on Appropriation Account 731·00; Ordinary Shareholders' Interest in the Company 83,991·00; Balance Sheet totals 109,991·00.

6. Gross Profit 19,170·00; Net Profit 3,370·00; Balance Sheet totals 32,420·00.

7. Gross Profit 41,055·00; Net Profit 12,125·00; Balance on Appropriation Account 14,870·00; Balance Sheet totals 138,520·00; Ordinary Shareholders' Interest 113,520·00

CHAPTER 30, EXERCISES SET LII, SIMPLE CONTROL ACCOUNTS, p. 383

1. Balance on Control Account 812·25.

2. Balance on Control Account 1,974·65.

3. Balance on Control Account 32,348·70.

4. Balance on Control Account 4,645·35.

CHAPTER 30, EXERCISES SET LIII, MORE DIFFICULT CONTROL ACCOUNTS, p. 386.

1. No numerical answer required.

2. Balance on Control Account 4,689·00. This represents the total owed to Sundry Creditors at this date.

3. Balance on Sales Control Account 74,106·25. Balance on Purchases Control Account 19,312·75.

4. Balance on Control Account = 6,550·00. Therefore we conclude that no matter where the error on the Trial Balance may be it certainly is NOT in the Sales Ledger.

5. Balance on Bought Ledger Control Account = 25,378·26. Balances on Sales Ledger Control Account = 23,286·25 Debit, 93·28 Credit.

CHAPTER 31, EXERCISES SET LIV, AMALGAMATIONS, p. 390

1. Capital: Flower 10,600·00, Rose 6,800·00; Balance Sheet totals of new business 21,445·00.

2. Capital: Whitehead 15,106·00, Poole 11,317·00; Balance Sheet totals of new business 27,441·00.

3. Capitals: Brown 11,100·00, Jones 16,000·00; Balance Sheet totals of new business 30,200·00.

4. Capitals: A. 26,427·00, B. 7,302·00; Balance Sheet totals of new business 38,224·00.

CHAPTER 32, EXERCISES SET LV, PURCHASE OF A BUSINESS, p. 398

1. Goodwill 3,800·00; Balance Sheet totals 24,000·00.

2. Goodwill 2,000·00; Balance Sheet totals 8,103·00.

3. Amount due to vendor 13,000·00.

4. Goodwill 6,175·00; Balance Sheet totals 25,475·00.

V.A.T. ACCOUNTS

(1) What is Value Added Tax?

Value Added Tax is a tax which is added whenever goods or services are supplied by one person to another. At present (January 1977) the standard rate of tax is 8 per cent, and the higher rate (on petrol and luxury goods) is $12\frac{1}{2}$ per cent. Since it is added at every stage of production, everyone who buys goods for resale, or for use in his business, pays tax on the goods he buys. This is called **Input Tax.** Later, when he sells the goods, or charges people for his services, he also charges the appropriate rate of tax to the customer. The businessman thus collects tax from his customers every time he supplies an output of goods or services, and this is called **Output Tax.** Of course this Output Tax has to be paid over to the collecting authority, which is H.M. Customs and Excise Department (V.A.T.), but before doing so the businessman is allowed to deduct the amount of Input Tax which he paid when he bought the goods, raw materials, etc. He therefore only pays over the *extra* tax which he has collected from his customers, since the Output Tax will usually be bigger than the Input Tax. The formula is:

OUTPUT TAX — INPUT TAX = Tax payable to H.M. Customs

A few classes of goods, notably food and children's clothes, are not taxed, and are said to be zero-rated. It follows that a grocer does not charge his customers V.A.T. on the food they buy from him, but he will pay V.A.T. on many things he buys for use in his shop, like cash registers, paper bags, etc. For such a trader the Input Tax he pays will always be greater than the Output Tax, which is zero. He will therefore be entitled to a refund of Tax from H.M. Customs and Excise.

Tax due to H.M. Customs is paid every three months. Refunds to zero-rated traders are paid back every month, to avoid hardship to retailers paying V.A.T. which they cannot collect back from their customers.

(2) The V.A.T. Account

V.A.T. fits very easily into the double-entry system; it is just one more account that we have to deal with. In the case of an ordinary trader the Customs and Excise Department is a creditor to whom the trader owes money. In the case of the zero-rated trader the Customs and Excise Department is a debtor, who owes the trader money. The two examples given below illustrate the two types of account. The standard rate account is cleared up every three months by paying the tax due to H.M. Customs. The zero rate account is cleared up each month by a refund from H.M. Customs. In the Trial Balance at the end of any particular month the V.A.T. Account will appear either as a creditor (standard-rate trader owing money to H.M. Customs) or as a debtor (H.M. Customs owing money to the zero-rated trader).

Dr.	H.M. Customs and Excise Department (V.A.T.)						C.L. 163 Cr.
19.. Mar. 31	To V.A.T. on Purchases	PDB33	295·20	19.. Mar. 31	By V.A.T. on Sales	SDB9	498·70
Apr. 17	To Capital Item	J72	36·80	Apr. 30	By V.A.T. on Sales	SDB13	786·50
Apr. 30	To V.A.T. on Purchases	PDB42	387·50	May 31	By V.A.T. on Sales	SDB17	1,295·27
May 19	To Capital Item	J74	47·20				
May 31	To V.A.T. on Purchases	PDB47	462·65				
May 31	To Balance	c/d	1,351·12				
			2,580·47				2 580·47
Jun. 8	Bank	CB57	1,351·12	Jun. 1	Balance	B/d	1,351·12

Fig. 207. A Standard-Rated V.A.T. Account

Dr.	H.M. Customs and Excise Department (V.A.T.)						D.L. 77 Cr.
19.. Mar. 1	To Balance	B/d	167·25	19.. Mar. 14	By Refund from H.M. Customs	CB8	167·25
18	„ Capital Item	J53	47·16	31	By Balance	c/d	155·91
19	„ Capital Item	J54	23·45				
31	„ Services	J62	48·20				
31	„ M.V. Expenses	N63	37·10				
			323·16				323·16
May 1	Balance	B/d	155·91				

Fig. 208. A V.A.T. Account in a zero-rated trade

(3) Special Retailers' Schemes

Because many retail traders do not issue invoices when they supply goods, V.A.T. for small retailers is arranged under special schemes. These are described in Notice No. 727, *Special Schemes for Retailers*, which are available free from local V.A.T. offices of H.M. Customs and Excise Department. These are very interesting to read, but are not usually recorded in ordinary book-keeping records. Students who are interested should look at such books as the Simplex VAT book—to be found at stationers or obtainable by post from George Vyner Ltd., Holmfirth, Huddersfield.

EXERCISES SET LVI

(4) V.A.T. Accounts

No. 1. M. Lawrence is a wholesale furniture dealer. In the three-month period commencing on March 1st, 19.. his V.A.T. records were as follows:

Input tax on invoices from suppliers of goods:

March   19,726·25   April   27,328·40   May   45,726·65

Input tax on other items:

March   3,506·25   April   4,712·35   May   5,816·42

Output tax charged to customers:

March   33,726·54   April   35,297·62   May   47,263·52

Draw up the V.A.T. Account for the quarter in date order, and balance it off on May 31st, 19... This balance is paid by cheque to H.M. Customs on June 27th, 19...

No. 2. R. Hardy is a wholesale hardware merchant. In the three-month period commencing on October 1st, 19.. his V.A.T. records were as follows:

Input tax on invoices from suppliers of goods:

October   14,976·54   November   15,812·63   December   12,724·95

Input tax on other items:

October   256·25   November   817·14   December   245·32

Output tax charged to customers:

October   19,726·30   November   23,954·74   December   17,654·36

Draw up the V.A.T. Account for the quarter in date order and balance it off on December 31st, 19... This balance is paid by cheque to H.M. Customs January 7th, 19...

No. 3. R. Dovey is a wholesale fashion merchant. In the three-month period commencing on April 1st his V.A.T. records were as follows:

Input tax on invoices from suppliers of goods:

April   37,256·50   May   45,328·75   June   38,296·25

Input tax on other items:

April   4,175·30   May   3,895·60   June   7,212·45

Output tax charged to customers:

April   60,275·45   May   65,385·75   June   72,726·30

Draw up the V.A.T. Account for the quarter in date order and balance it off on June 30th. This balance is paid by cheque to H.M. Customs on July 29th, 19...

No. 4. R. Kemp is a wholesale grocer, dealing in zero-rated items only His input tax records show the following for the month of April 19..

(*a*) Input tax on capital items   47·56
(*b*) Input tax on consumable items   75·65
(*c*) Input tax on services   48·50

His output tax was, of course, zero. The balance owing by H.M. Customs to Kemp on April 1st was 138·50, and this sum was duly received on April 17th. Show the V.A.T. Account for the month of April, and bring down the balance due from H.M. Customs on April 30th.

No. 5. P. Burns is a wholesale fishmonger dealing in zero-rated items only. His input tax records show the following for the month of July:

(*a*) Input tax on capital items   147·36
(*b*) Input tax on consumable items   38·48
(*c*) Input tax on services   15·75

His output tax was, of course, zero. The balance owing by H.M. Customs to Burns on July 1st was 236·25, and this sum was duly received on July 14th. Show the V.A.T. Account for the month of July and bring down the balance due from H.M. Customs on July 31st.

Answers to V.A.T. Exercises

1. Totals 116,287·68 Due to Customs 9,471·36
2. Totals 61,335·40 Due to Customs 16,502·57
3. Totals 198,387·50 Due to Customs 62,222·65
4. Totals 310·21 Due from Customs 171·71
5. Totals 437·84 Due from Customs 201·59

INDEX

Accounting
  Machines, 156, 158, 159
  Reference date, 365
  Reference period, 365
Accounts, 2
  Asset, 23
  Cash and Bank, 24, 25, 27
  Columnar, 172
  Continuous Balance, 156–63
  Nominal, 12, 14, 15, 28, 29
  Personal, 12, 14, 15, 16, 19
  Real, 12, 14, 15, 21, 22
  Rules for Keeping, 14, 15
  Tidying Up, 131
Accruals
  Expenses, 254
  Receipts, 254
Accumulated Fund, 302
Acid Test Ratio, 337
Adjustments, 250–76
  Accrued Expenses, 254
  Accrued Receipts, 256
  Bad Debts, 261
  Depreciation, 272
  Goodwill, 272
  Increased Net Worth, 317
  List of, 250
  Payments in Advance, 250–3
  Provision for Bad Debts, 262
  Provision for Discounts, 271
  Purpose of, 250
  Receipts Accrued, 256
  Receipts in Advance, 252
  Why Necessary? 250
Allowances, 55
Amalgamations, 388–92
Analytical Day Books, 171–4, 381
Appraisal of Balance Sheet, 334
Appreciation of Land and Buildings, 371
Appropriation Account
  Limited Company, of, 365
  Partnership, of, 279
Assets, 3, 11, 23

Assets, *contd.*
  Circulating, 3
  Classification of, 3
  Contribution of by Proprietor, 2
  Current, 3, 335
  Depreciation of (*see* Depreciation)
  Fictitious, 37
  Fixed, 3, 335
  Intangible, 272
  Purchase of, 96–9
  Replacement of, 185
  Retained on Books at Cost Price, 184
  Sale of Worn-out, 101–4
  True and Fair View, 180

Bad Debts, 104–8
  Adjustments, 261
  Provision, 272
  Recovered, 106
Balance Sheet, 5, 34
  Complete, in Good Style, 8
  Final Accounts (Sole Trader), 223–31
  Historical muddle, and, 224
  Limited Company, 367
  Order of Liquidity, 225
  Order of Permanence, 225
  Partnership, 288
  Vertical Style, 372–3
Bank:
  Accounts, 24, 27
  Cash Book, 175–9
  Charges, 116–17
  Interest, 115–16
  Loans, 115
  Overdrafts, 82–3
  Reconciliation Statements, 164–70
  Statements, 159
Bills of Exchange, 373
Bonds, Fidelity, 69
Bonus, 324
Books of Original Entry, 31
Borrowing Money, 8, 115–17